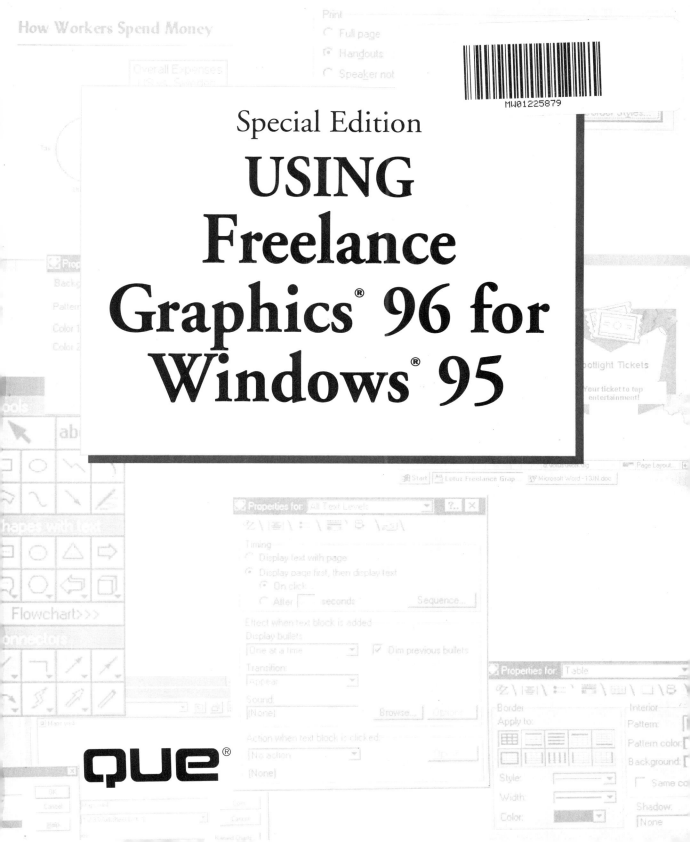

Special Edition
USING
Freelance
Graphics® 96 for
Windows® 95

que®

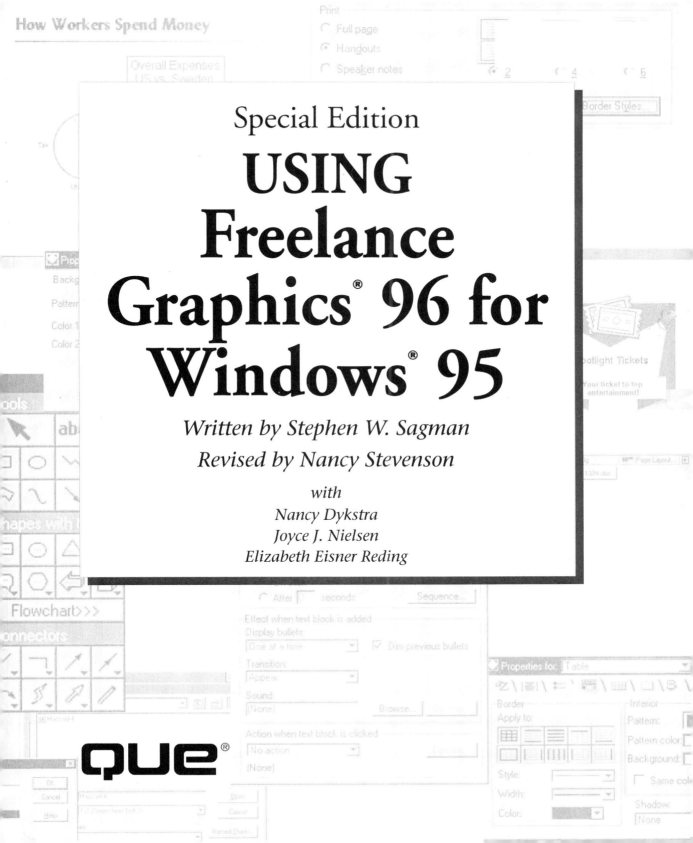

Special Edition

USING
Freelance
Graphics® 96 for
Windows® 95

Written by Stephen W. Sagman

Revised by Nancy Stevenson

with

Nancy Dykstra

Joyce J. Nielsen

Elizabeth Eisner Reding

Special Edition Using Freelance Graphics® 96 for Windows® 95

Library of Congress Catalog No.: 95-71760

ISBN: 0-7897-0671-7

98 97 96   6 5 4 3 2 1

Interpretation of the printing code: the rightmost double-digit number is the year of the book's printing; the rightmost single-digit number, the number of the book's printing. For example, a printing code of 96-1 shows that the first printing of the book occurred in 1996.

All terms mentioned in this book that are known to be trademarks or service marks have been appropriately capitalized. Que cannot attest to the accuracy of this information. Use of a term in this book should not be regarded as affecting the validity of any trademark or service mark.

Screen reproductions in this book were created using Collage Plus from Inner Media, Inc., Hollis, NH.

Composed in *Stone Serif* and *MCPdigital* by Que Corporation.

Credits

President
Roland Elgey

Vice President and Publisher
Marie Butler-Knight

Associate Publisher
Don Roche Jr.

Editorial Services Director
Elizabeth Keaffaber

Managing Editor
Michael Cunningham

Director of Marketing
Lynn E. Zingraf

Senior Series Editor
Chris Nelson

Publishing Manager
Brad Koch

Acquisitions Editor
Elizabeth A. South

Product Director
Lisa W. Wagner

Production Editor
Lisa M. Gebken

Editors
Charles K. Bowles II
Lori A. Lyons
Theresa Mathias
Rebecca Mounts
Paige Widder

Assistant Product Marketing Manager
Kim Margolius

Technical Editors
Bob Reselman
Tony Schafer

Technical Specialist
Nadeem Muhammed

Acquisitions Coordinator
Tracy M. Williams

Operations Coordinator
Patty Brooks

Editorial Assistant
Carmen Krikorian

Book Designer
Ruth Harvey

Cover Designer
Dan Armstrong

Production Team
Steve Adams
Claudia Bell
Chad Dressler
Amy Gornik
Jason Hand
Michelle Lee
Bobbi Satterfield
Suzanne Whitmer
Paul Wilson
Karen York

Indexers
Craig Small and Ginny Bess

To Susan, Bill, Ted, and Joan: my own West Coast support group!

And, as always, to G.

About the Authors

Stephen W. Sagman is the president of a New York City-based company that provides training, courseware, documentation, and user interface consulting. He writes about personal computing in *PC/Computing, PC Week, Computer Shopper,* and *PC Magazine* and gives classes and seminars on desktop publishing, graphics, and multimedia. He is also the author of *Using Harvard Graphics 3.0, Using Windows Draw,* and *1-2-3 Graphics Techniques* from Que, the author of *Getting Your Start in Hollywood,* and a contributor to *Mastering CorelDraw 3.* He can be reached via CompuServe (**72456,3325**) or at CCM, Inc., 140 Charles St., New York, NY 10014.

Nancy Stevenson is a freelance writer, teacher, and consultant. Her most recently completed book, *Using Word for Windows,* was published by Que in the spring of 1995. Stevenson teaches technical writing at Purdue University in Indianapolis. Prior to becoming a freelancer, she was a publishing manager at Que, and before that worked as a trainer, consultant, and product manager at Symantec Corporation in California.

Nancy Dykstra is a consultant with UserTech and is currently acting as an online help architect for the Ceridian Project. Previously, she worked for Aeronomics, where she developed training, documentation, and online help for Delta Airline's revenue management system. She has also worked as a technical writer for Lotus and IBM, and has won several STC awards. She has a B.A. from Western Illinois University and is currently working on her master's in Technical Communications Management at Mercer University. She can be reached at **ndykstra@mindspring.com**.

Joyce J. Nielsen is a freelance writer for Que Corporation, where she focuses on the development of spreadsheet, database, and word processing books. Before joining Que five years ago, Nielsen worked as a research analyst for a shopping mall developer, where she began using 1-2-3 in 1984 to develop and document 1-2-3 business applications used nationwide. She is the author of *1-2-3 Release 4 for Windows Quick Reference, 1-2-3 Release 2.4 Quick Reference, 1-2-3 Release 3.4 Quick Reference*; and contributing author to many other Que titles, such as *Using 1-2-3 Release 5 for Windows,* Special Edition. Nielsen received a B.S. in Quantitative Business Analysis from Indiana University.

Although a native of the east coast, **Elizabeth Eisner Reding** lives in the beautiful splendor of northwest New Mexico. She writes computer books, consults, trains individuals and corporate clients, and teaches at the Gallup branch of the University of New Mexico. To date, Reding has written computer boks on Microsoft Excel, Microsoft PowerPoint, Novell Quattro Pro, and Lotus 1-2-3. She has provided technical edits on many other subjects for Que including Internet topics such as Netscape and HTML. In her copious spare time, she rides her mountain bike, renovates her house, and makes sure her cats have enough to eat.

Acknowledgments

It was my pleasure to act as lead author on this revision of *Special Edition Using Freelance Graphics 96 for Windows 95* for several reasons.

First, Steve Sagman wrote an excellent book to begin with, which made the job of revision a lot easier.

Second, the team of authors who worked on the book—Joyce Nielson, Nancy Dykstra, and Liz Reding—are all highly professional writers who lent their individual expertise to their chapters. Each added a great deal to make this the most extensive and in-depth version of this book to date.

Thanks to the gang at Que, who make these books possible. Thanks to Elizabeth South, who as our very supportive acquisitions editor, assembled the team and helped all the authors get their jobs done. Thanks to Lisa Wagner and Lisa Gebken for lending their editorial expertise and keen eyes to the flow and details of the text itself. Last, but not least, with the substantial revisions made to the latest Freelance product, the contribution of the technical editors, Bob Reselman and Tony Schafer, was vital to ensure the most accurate book possible.

Finally, thanks to Lotus for bringing out a greatly enhanced and impressive product in Freelance Graphics 96 for Windows 95.

We'd Like to Hear from You!

As part of our continuing effort to produce books of the highest possible quality, Que would like to hear your comments. To stay competitive, we *really* want you, as a computer book reader and user, to let us know what you like or dislike most about this book or other Que products.

You can mail comments, ideas, or suggestions for improving future editions to the address below, or send us a fax at (317) 581-4663. For the online in-clined, Macmillan Computer Publishing has a forum on CompuServe (type **GO MACMILLAN** at any prompt) through which our staff and authors are available for questions and comments. The address of our Internet site, the Macmillan Information SuperLibrary, is **http://www.mcp.com** (World Wide Web). Our Web site has received critical acclaim from many reviewers—be sure to check it out.

In addition to exploring our forums, please feel free to contact me personally to discuss your opinions of this book:

CompuServe:	**74404,3307**
America Online:	**ldw indy**
Internet:	**lwagner@que.mcp.com**

Thanks in advance—your comments will help us to continue publishing the best books available on computer topics in today's market.

Lisa D. Wagner
Product Director
Que Corporation
201 W. 103rd Street
Indianapolis, Indiana 46290
USA

Contents at a Glance

Getting Started

Using SmartMaster Sets

Adding Charts to Pages

Adding Text and Graphics

Presentations

Customizing Freelance

Appendixes

Contents

6 Formatting a Data Chart   103

12 Editing Objects   225

13 Adding Clip Art Symbols and Bitmaps   249

14 Importing and Exporting Drawings and Charts   267

V Working with Presentations   279

15 Managing Presentations   281

16 Using the Outliner to Organize a Presentation   297

Index of Common Problems   491

Index   497

Introduction

You have a presentation to make, and you haven't got much time. You need something polished and professional, but you can't learn complex, new software in just a few hours. So where do you turn? To Freelance Graphics 96 for Windows 95, and this book, of course.

Freelance Graphics 96 for Windows 95 is designed for presentation makers who need to create top-of-the-line slides, overheads, and handouts quickly and easily, and with enough flexibility to make their presentations both communicative and memorable.

Freelance manages to satisfy all of these needs. Creating basic "dog and pony" shows is shockingly simple, but the automatic presentations that come out of Freelance are hardly bare-boned. Instead, they are fully realized, tastefully designed, and attractively coordinated sequences of slides, pages, or animated screens. And if you are willing to get under the hood and modify a few easily controlled options, you can customize a chart, table, or drawing so that it expresses virtually any message.

The ease of using Freelance comes from several key features. Freelance offers dozens of presentation designs called *SmartMasters*, each of which includes a complete set of page layouts. Simply select an overall design and a page layout and then fill in the blanks with your text or numeric data. Freelance creates the presentation pages, attending to such details as their background design, the text styles used, and the formatting of charts and tables.

Whenever you must make a design decision, such as the type of chart to create, Freelance provides a centralized operations center called the Properties InfoBox. From here you can make dozens of changes to various pieces of the object you're working on. And when it comes time for you to decide among alternatives, Freelance displays them on-screen as you work. You see the colors that you can use in pie slices, for example, or the typefaces that you can select for text. Freelance is so easy to use that you will be up and running, creating basic presentations in no time.

Who Should Read This Book?

Using Freelance Graphics 96 for Windows 95 is written and organized both for new users of Freelance Graphics and for experienced veterans of other presentation graphics programs who are upgrading to Freelance Graphics. Much of the information will be relevant to users of Freelance Graphics Release 2.0 for Windows also.

To make your earliest experiences with Freelance positive, the first two chapters of this book take you on a brief tour of the program and then teach the few concepts and procedures you must know in order to create presentations. With these skills under your belt, you will be able to create presentations that will inform and impress your audience.

Later in the book, you will learn to embellish basic Freelance presentations with special charts and tables, symbols, drawings, and imported graphics files. You'll learn about exciting new features in this version of Freelance, such as the capability to publish Freelance presentations to the Internet, and several new team tools for workgroup computing. Before you finish, you will learn to create printed or slide output, create screen shows, and customize Freelance so that it will work the way you like best.

The Organization of This Book

By browsing the pages of this book, you can get a good sense of its organization. The topics are presented in the order in which you are likely to need them when both learning and using Freelance Graphics 96 for Windows 95.

Part I: Getting Started

Chapter 1, "Understanding the Freelance Window," takes you on a tour of the parts of the Freelance window, including the buttons, controls, and tools it contains. This chapter introduces the look and feel of the three Freelance views where you'll get your work done.

Chapter 2, "Getting Started," gives you a hands-on opportunity to explore the basic features used to create a presentation. Here's where you get your first look at an actual presentation screen show and learn to save your Freelance presentation files. You'll see how easy using Freelance really is.

Part II: Using SmartMaster Sets

Chapter 3, "Making Basic Changes to the Presentation," teaches you how to quickly accomplish the most elemental changes to the presentation. Once you complete Chapter 3, you'll be able to create sophisticated, polished presentations.

Chapter 4, "Using Page Sorter View," describes in more detail the three views you can use to examine and edit your work in Freelance. This chapter concentrates on the capabilities of Page Sorter view to quickly organize and structure the flow of your presentation.

Part III: Adding Charts to Pages

Chapter 5, "Adding a Data Chart," describes how to create charts and graphs that can depict numbers visually. You learn to distinguish among data chart types, start a data chart, and enter the numbers that Freelance needs so that it can construct the chart for you.

Chapter 6, "Formatting a Data Chart," shows you how to make changes to the appearance of the data charts that Freelance creates.

Chapter 7, "Importing the Data for a Data Chart," describes how to pull in the data for a chart from another program or from a file on disk so that you don't have to retype the numbers into Freelance again.

Chapter 8, "Creating Organizational Charts," tells you everything you need to know about creating charts that depict the structure of an organization, including the new diagramming feature that provides dozens of ready-made process diagrams.

Chapter 9, "Creating Table Charts," teaches you to create tables that can contain text or numbers and to format the appearance of those tables in various ways.

Part IV: Adding Text and Graphics to Pages

Chapter 10, "Adding and Formatting Text Blocks," shows you how to add additional text to text blocks on pages and how to format those text blocks to customize their appearance.

Chapter 11, "Drawing Objects," teaches you to use the drawing tools of Freelance to embellish presentation pages with graphic shapes.

Chapter 12, "Editing Objects," shows you how to edit individual drawing objects that you have created and how to arrange groups of drawing objects.

Chapter 13, "Adding Clip Art Symbols and Bitmaps," describes how to incorporate pictures or symbols in your presentation, that come with Freelance in the extensive symbol library. This chapter also shows you how to incorporate images that have been created with painting programs or scanning software.

Chapter 14, "Importing and Exporting Drawings and Charts," shows you how to use drawings from other programs in your presentations and how to export a presentation for use in other Windows applications.

Part V: Working with Presentations

Chapter 15, "Managing Presentations," shows you how to use the features of Freelance that give you overall control of a presentation. For example, you learn to spell-check a presentation, change to a different color palette, and copy pages from one presentation to another.

Chapter 16, "Using the Outliner to Organize a Presentation," teaches you to use the Outliner view of Freelance, which displays the text content of your presentation. This view lets you focus on content organization; here you can enter, edit, and reorganize the topics of the presentation without being distracted by the presentation design.

Chapter 17, "Creating Screen Shows," gives you the knowledge you need to design presentations that can include slides that build their points on-screen one at a time, as well as transition effects between slides. This chapter also explores the exciting multimedia capabilities of Freelance, including movies, sound clips and animations to give your presentations punch.

Chapter 18, "Creating Output," shows you how to generate several different forms of printed output that Freelance offers and how to create 35mm slides.

Chapter 19, "Publishing Freelance Graphics Presentations to the Internet," tells you how to place your Freelance presentation on the Information Superhighway and let others view it online.

Part VI: Customizing Freelance Graphics

Chapter 20, "Editing SmartMaster Sets," describes how to customize the presentation designs that come with Freelance and how to create your own presentation design templates.

Chapter 21, "Using and Editing Color Palettes," teaches you to select and modify the color palettes that control the colors of all objects in the presentation.

Chapter 22, "Modifying the Default Settings," shows you the controls, commands, and settings that let you alter, to your liking, the way Freelance works.

Part VII: Appendixes

Appendix A, "Freelance Graphics Gallery of Figures," shows you some of the things you can do with different combinations of objects and designs, and each example refers you to the corresponding chapter in the book that helps you create similar effects yourself.

Appendix B, "SmartMaster Sets," identifies the SmartMaster sets stored in Freelance. You can scan the pages of this appendix rather than preview the SmartMaster sets on-screen one by one.

Appendix C, "The Symbol Library," identifies the symbols you can select from the symbol library. As with the SmartMaster sets, you can scan this appendix to see all the symbols instead of combing tediously through the many categories of symbols in the online symbol library within Freelance.

Conventions Used in This Book

A number of conventions appear in *Using Freelance Graphics 96 for Windows 95* to help you learn the program. This section includes examples of these conventions to help you distinguish among the different elements in this book.

Special typefaces in this book include the following:

Typeface	Meaning
italic	New terms or phrases when initially defined or terms that require special emphasis
boldface	Information you are asked to type; menu and dialog box options that appear underlined on-screen, called hotkeys
monospace	Direct quotations of words that appear on-screen or in a figure

SmartIcons, such as the New Presentation icon beside this paragraph, appear in the margin to indicate that the procedure described in the text includes instructions for using the appropriate SmartIcons or toolbox buttons in Freelance Graphics 96 for Windows 95. SmartIcon sets have become context-specific in this version of Freelance. That means that if you are working on a chart, chart buttons will automatically be available to you; if you're working on text, additional text buttons will appear, and so on.

In most cases, keys are represented as they appear on the keyboard. The arrow keys are usually represented by name (for example, the up-arrow key). All key names will be spelled out in this book, such as Page Up, Page Down, and Delete keys, but they may be abbreviated on your keyboard (such as PgUp, PgDn, and Del). The only exception to this practice are the Alt and Ctrl keys, which will be abbreviated throughout the book.

When two keys appear together with a plus sign, such as Shift+F9, you are to press and hold down the first key and then press the second key.

The function keys F1 through F10 are used for special situations in Freelance. You also can use the Alt, Ctrl, and Shift keys with certain function keys as shortcut keys to perform commands or tasks in Freelance.

Note

This paragraph format indicates additional information that may help you avoid problems or that should be considered in using the described features.

Tip

This item suggests easier or alternative methods of executing a procedure, or discusses advanced techniques related to the topic described in the text.

Caution

This paragraph format warns the reader of hazardous procedures (for example, activities that delete files).

Troubleshooting

What's going on when you see this feature?

Troubleshooting is a question-and-answer format that anticipates common trouble spots that people encounter when learning Freelance.

▶ See "Starting a New Presentation and Choosing Its Look," p. 23

A For Related Information cross-reference like the one beside this paragraph directs you to related information in other parts of the book. Right-facing triangles indicate later chapters, and left-facing triangles point you back to information earlier in the book.

Finally, although the full name of the product covered in this book is *Freelance Graphics 96 for Windows 95*, the short form of *Freelance* or *Freelance Graphics* is used throughout the chapters. ❖

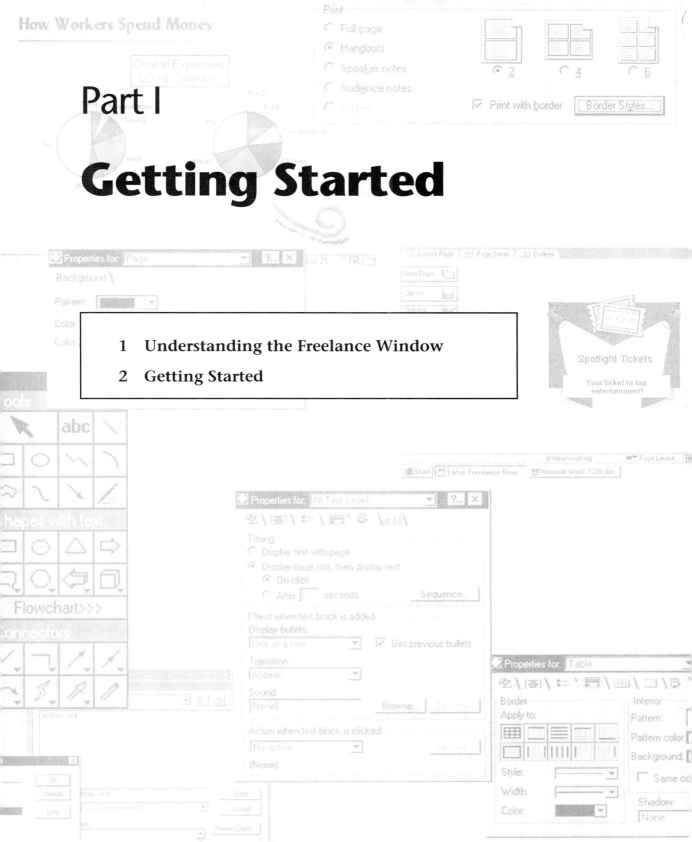

Part I

Getting Started

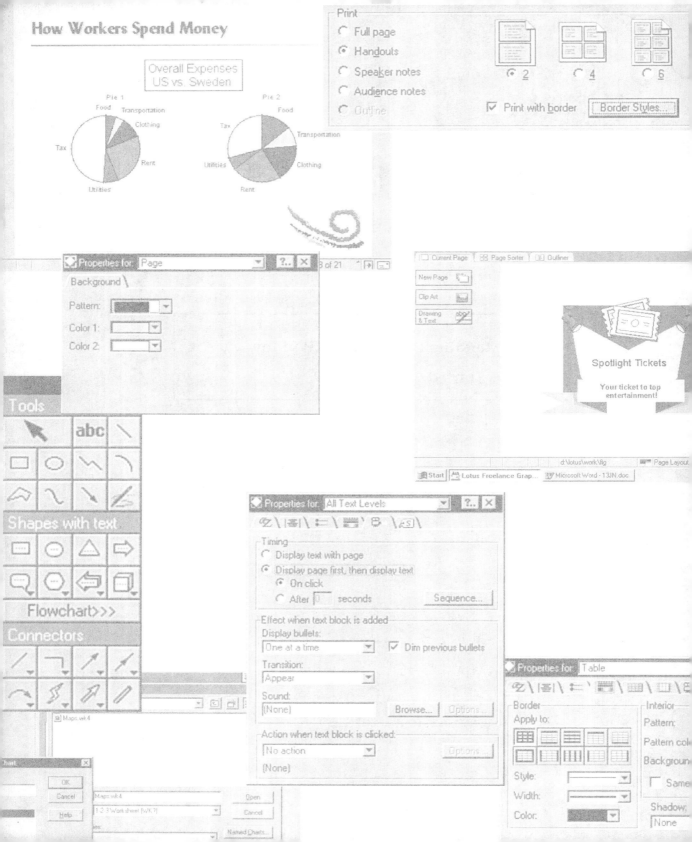

CHAPTER 1

Understanding the Freelance Window

by Nancy Stevenson

Freelance Graphics 96 for Windows 95 is the happy union of the latest Windows environment and the newest version of Freelance, which has a better graphical interface than ever before. Your first glimpse of Freelance will be one filled with tools, tabs, and menus that can take you where you want to go with no more effort than the click of a button. Some of these belong to Windows, and some to Freelance Graphics itself. Learning your way around all these elements is the first step to becoming comfortable with Freelance Graphics.

In this chapter, you'll get your first look at the Freelance Graphics window, and begin all of the following:

- Exploring the title and menu bars
- Using SmartIcons to get work done
- Seeing your presentation from different perspectives using the view tabs
- Learning what's on the status bar
- Organizing your page with rulers and grids

Freelance's New Look

Whether you're new to Freelance Graphics or you've used previous versions of the software, you'll be pleased by new graphical features like easy-to-use view tabs and shortcut buttons for adding a new page or clip art.

This version of Freelance Graphics also boasts a *task sensitive interface (TSI)*. TSI means that Freelance displays only the tools that are useful for what you're doing at the moment, keeping on-screen clutter to a minimum, and offering the new user an intuitive, task-oriented environment.

In addition, if you installed Freelance Graphics as part of Lotus SmartSuite, you'll enjoy the capability to move easily among the products in the suite and link data from one type of file to another. Plus, many of the features you discover in this chapter are common to other parts of SmartSuite, so you can get up to speed on all the products quickly.

But whether you own the entire SmartSuite or purchased Freelance Graphics by itself, the first step to learning your way around is to get comfortable with the main Freelance window.

Looking at the Title Bar, Windows Taskbar, and Menu Bar

Freelance's clear and logical on-screen controls are a key ingredient to the program's power and ease of use. When you first open Freelance, you'll see the title bar across the top, and the menu bar right beneath it, as shown in figure 1.1. The Windows 95 taskbar runs along the bottom of the screen. The taskbar can be set to Autohide mode, if you prefer, so it might not appear at all times.

The title bar and Windows taskbar are elements of Windows 95, which appear on the screens of all Windows software. Although the menu bar is an element found in all Windows programs, the menu items are specific to the functions of Freelance Graphics.

Fig. 1.1
The Freelance Graphics screen offers functionality at the click of a SmartIcon.

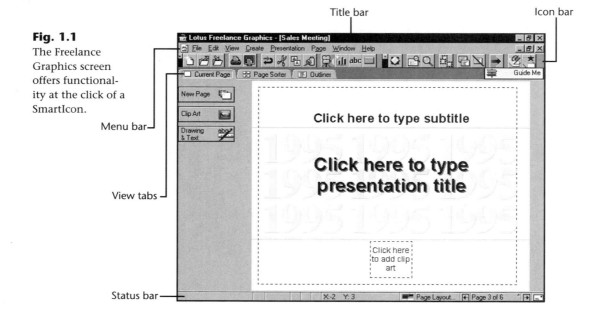

The Title Bar and Windows Taskbar

The *title bar* appears at the top of the Freelance window (refer to fig. 1.1). It states that you are indeed working in Freelance Graphics and identifies the file name of the current presentation. If you have not yet named the presentation, [Untitled1] appears. When you open a Freelance Graphics dialog box to perform an action, the Windows title bar turns gray, and the title bar of the dialog box itself becomes active. When you close the dialog box, the Windows title bar becomes active again.

There are three control buttons on the right-hand side of the title bar. Clicking the Minimize button (the button with a single line at the bottom) minimizes the entire Freelance window so that it is a button on the Windows taskbar. Clicking the Freelance button on this taskbar maximizes the program window again.

The middle button on the far right of the title bar can have two looks. When it contains a double-window image, it functions as a *resizing button*, reducing your Freelance window so that it floats on-screen instead of filling it. Once you've clicked on this button, however, the picture on the button changes to a single, large window. Clicking it this time maximizes the Freelance window to fill the screen. In Resizing mode, you can shrink the window to not fill the screen; this means that you can change the size (height and width) of the screen. However, you can do this only if the window is not originally sized to be screen size.

The Close button on the far right of the title bar is used to quickly close down Freelance Graphics. If an open presentation has not been saved when you press this button, you are asked whether to save it before closing the Freelance window.

There is also a centralized menu for performing these functions. Clicking the Control icon at the left end of the title bar summons the Control menu, which displays menu items that enable you to minimize, maximize, restore, and close the Freelance window. (Double-clicking the Control icon also closes the Freelance window.)

The Menu Bar

When you're in the Current Page view, the menu bar might look familiar. It offers names common to many Windows applications' menus, such as File and Edit, so you'll find it easy to make the transition to Freelance's environment. Freelance Graphics menus include the menu options File, Edit, View, Create, Presentation, Page, Window, and Help. You select a menu by clicking it.

> **Note**
>
> The underlined letter in each menu name is called the *hot key*. You can use that key in combination with the Alt key to pull down the menu.

When you select any of these menu names, a menu drops down (see fig. 1.2) and stays on-screen until you either make a selection or click anywhere outside of it. You can make your selection by either clicking the choice, or typing the underlined hotkey letter. To retract a drop-down menu, just press Esc.

Fig. 1.2
The Presentation menu offers a variety of options for your final Freelance presentation.

> **Tip**
>
> To see a description of each menu command, click the menu name, then place your cursor on the menu item. A brief description of its function appears in the status bar.

 Clicking the Control icon at the left end of the menu bar pulls down a menu of commands that you can use to control the presentation window within the Freelance window:

- *Minimize.* Converts the currently selected presentation window into an icon.
- *Restore.* Converts the presentation window to a window that you can move and resize within the Freelance window. (The Restore button at the right end of the menu bar also performs this function.)
- *Maximize.* Fills the Freelance window with the selected presentation window.
- *Close.* Closes the currently selected presentation window.

> **Note**
>
> Depending on which view you are using, the menu names and choices may vary slightly, based on what you are likely to want to do from that view. Specific changes are discussed in chapters dealing with those views.

Exploring SmartIcons and Drawing Tools

Many functions can be performed in Freelance with a single click of a button. Some of these buttons reside on toolbars, which may appear or disappear depending on what task you're performing. Some choices appear in special drop-down menus, and a few—those used for the most common functionality—appear on the Freelance desktop in all views.

SmartIcons

The Universal toolbar, shown in figure 1.3, is the basic set of SmartIcons that is available by default. It appears just under the menu bar. Each SmartIcon offers a shortcut alternative to one or more menu selections. There are several other toolbars that will appear, depending on what function you are performing at the time. By default, this is determined by Freelance Graphic's new TSI. However, you can customize when these toolbars will appear according to your own preferences.

▶ See "Using SmartIcons," p. 392

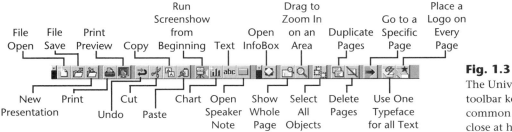

Fig. 1.3
The Universal toolbar keeps common functions close at hand.

The Drawing Toolbox

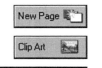

There are four buttons that always appear on the desktop of Freelance when you're in Current Page view, because their use is so common. The first three are on the left of your presentation in the Current Page and Outliner views. These are the New Page button, the Clip Art button, and the Drawing & Text button. The last one is a new Help feature, called Guide Me, which is available in all three views. This button is to the far right of the view tabs and provides context-sensitive help.

▶ See "Adding a Second Page," p. 28

When you click the Drawing & Text button, the Drawing toolbox appears, as in figure 1.4. This holds icons that represent the tools you use to create and edit objects such as flowcharts, graphic shapes, and shapes with text.

The toolbox is a *floating toolbox*; that is, it can be dragged anywhere on-screen. When you're done with it, you can close it by either clicking the Drawing & Text button, or double-clicking the Close button in the upper-right-hand corner of the toolbox.

Fig. 1.4
The Drawing & Text toolbox brings many common drawing and text functions together in one place.

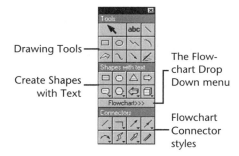

Drawing Tools

Create Shapes with Text

The Flow-chart Drop Down menu

Flowchart Connector styles

> **Tip**
>
> The bottom row of tools in the Shapes with Text section have little downward-pointing arrows in them. These indicate additional drop-down palettes that you access by clicking the arrow.

The bottom two sections of this toolbox offer a multitude of shape choices for flowcharts and connectors that allow you to build organizational and flowcharts. The top set of tools is used to draw objects. These tools have the following uses, as shown in table 1.1.

Table 1.1	Drawing Tools	
Icon	**Tool**	**Description**
	Selector tool	Produces an on-screen arrow that you use to select menu commands, SmartIcons, and other tools from the toolbox. You also use the Selector tool to select objects to modify.
	Text tool	Adds a free-form text block anywhere on a page, or selects for editing the text you've already added.
	Polygon tool	Draws a closed object with three or more sides.
	Rectangle tool	Draws a rectangle or square.
	Line tool	Draws a straight line.
	Arrow tool	Offers a selection of lines that can be drawn with an arrowhead at one or both ends.
	Curve tool	Draws a curving line.
	Polyline tool	Draws a line with more than one segment.
	Circle tool	Draws a circle or ellipse.
	Arc tool	Draws an arc.
	Freehand tool	Enables you to draw a Freehand shape.

Getting Around with the View Tabs

The main desktop of Freelance Graphics presents you with three tabs for selecting which view of the presentation you see (see fig. 1.5). One of the three tabs is always selected.

Fig. 1.5
The view tabs are new in Freelance Graphics 96, and offer easy access to the three views.

Fig. 1.5
The view tabs are new in Freelance Graphics 96, and offer easy access to the three views.

The following list describes what selecting each of the view tabs will show you:

- *Current Page tab.* Causes Freelance to show the current presentation page. Use this view to do the detailed work on individual pages of your presentation.

- *Page Sorter tab.* Switches to Page Sorter view. Text editing tools disappear from the status bar. Use this view to arrange all the slides in an order that works for the overall flow of your presentation.

- *Outliner tab.* Switches to Outliner view, and changes the Page menu to a Text menu. Use this view to work with the text of your presentation and organize its content.

As you begin to use Freelance Graphics, you'll notice that various elements of the screen may change depending on which view tab you've chosen. For example, when you select the Outliner View tab, an Outliner toolbar is displayed. Also, when in Outliner view, the Page menu changes to a menu called Text. In addition, selections in the status bar near the bottom of the page may change. These changes are task-sensitive: for example, when you're in Page Sorter view, the buttons to add text effects like bold and underline disappear from the status bar, because you're sorting pages, not editing text.

The Status Bar

The *status bar*, shown in figure 1.6, is a narrow band at the bottom of the screen. The controls that appear in the status bar give you access to a variety of functions, and are likely to change depending on what task you're trying to accomplish.

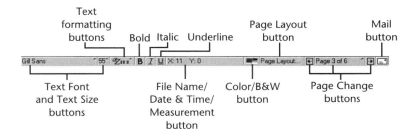

Fig. 1.6
The status bar can change, but here are most of the common elements.

The following list describes the buttons in the status bar:

- *Page Change buttons*. Enable you to change pages in the presentation. Click the right- or left-arrow symbol to turn a page forward or back, respectively. Click the button that displays the current page number to see a list of page names from which you can choose.

- *Page Layout button*. Opens the Choose Page Layout dialog box, from which you can select a different page layout for the current page.

- *Color/B&W button*. Enables you to switch instantly from a color palette to the corresponding black-and-white palette, and back again if you like. (This back and forth functionality is called *toggling*; toggle buttons take you to one function when clicked, then to the next when clicked again.) After you create a color presentation for color slides, you can click this button to switch to the matching black-and-white palette for printing handouts on a black-and-white printer.

- *Text Font/Size buttons*. Display the text font and size for a selected text block.

- *Bold*, *Italic*, and *Underline*. Appear in the status bar when you select text.

- *File Name/Date & Time/Measurement button*. Toggles among three functions as you click it: click once and it shows the name of the file you're working on, click again to see the time and date, or click for the position of your cursor on the page in whatever unit of measurement you have designated.

Tip

You can change the units of measurement that appear on the Status Line button by selecting View, Set Units & Grids and designating a new unit.

■ *Mail button.* Shortcut to retrieving any electronic mail messages from Lotus cc:Mail.

Organizing the Page with Rulers and Grids

To help you place objects on your slides, Freelance Graphics provides the ruler and the grid. The *ruler* shows you a vertical and horizontal measurement of the output page size. The *grid* helps you pinpoint a specific place on the page where the X and Y axes of the vertical and horizontal rulers intersect on your slide.

The Drawing Ruler

By clicking Show Ruler in the View menu, you turn on or off a set of rulers running across the top and down the left edges of the page display (see fig. 1.7). When you select an object, a blue line appears in the ruler which reflects the position of the object. Also, a yellow line appears, reflecting the position of the mouse cursor within the selected object. As you move the object, the yellow cursor line moves. Once the object is re-placed, the existing blue line repositions itself to the new position of its object, which coincidentally happens to be the same location as the yellow mouse cursor line.

Fig. 1.7
Rulers and the grid are both displayed here.

Horizontal ruler

Vertical ruler

Grid dots

▶ See "Changing the Drawing Environment," p. 220

The measurement units of the drawing rulers can be changed. To change the Units & Grids settings, select View, Set Units & Grids. Then from Millimeters, Centimeters, Inches, Points, or Picas, select the unit of measurement you would like to use.

The Grid

The grid appears as a pattern of dots across the on-screen presentation page (refer to fig. 1.7). You can use these dots to align objects visually, or you can cause objects to be pulled to the nearest dot as they are being drawn. To turn the grid on or off, choose View, Set Units & Grids. Then choose Display Grid to change the setting on or off, and Snap to Grid to turn on or off the pulling effect of the grid dots. Note that you can leave on the Snap to Grid function, even if you aren't displaying the grid itself on-screen.

> **Tip**
>
> You can also use the keystroke combination, Shift+F7, to turn on and off the Snap to Grid function.

You use the Horizontal Space and Vertical Space text boxes to enter a new number for the spacing of the dots in the grid. The number's unit of measurement is determined by the Units setting in the same dialog box. To display grid dots one inch apart, for example, enter **1.0** for both Horizontal Space and Vertical Space and then select Inches as the Units of measurement.

When you've made your selections, click OK to return to the current page, where a small gray pattern of dots measures the grid you've set. ❖

▶ See "Using a Grid," p. 221

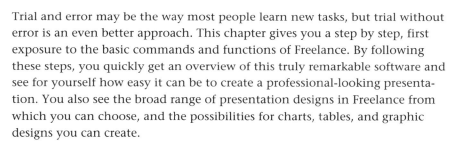

CHAPTER 2

Getting Started

by Nancy Stevenson

Trial and error may be the way most people learn new tasks, but trial without error is an even better approach. This chapter gives you a step by step, first exposure to the basic commands and functions of Freelance. By following these steps, you quickly get an overview of this truly remarkable software and see for yourself how easy it can be to create a professional-looking presentation. You also see the broad range of presentation designs in Freelance from which you can choose, and the possibilities for charts, tables, and graphic designs you can create.

In this chapter you learn how to do the following:

- Take advantage of Freelance Graphics help
- Start a new presentation
- Select a page layout
- Add text and objects to your presentation page
- Add new pages to your presentation
- Work with Page Sorter and Outliner views
- View and save a presentation

Getting Help When You Need It

When you begin working with a new software product, the first thing to know is how to get help if you get stuck. This version of Freelance Graphics has a greatly enhanced help system to assist the new user in becoming comfortable with its various features. Whenever possible, Freelance guides you with visual or textual clues on-screen. For example, when you begin a new presentation, you are provided with Click Here blocks for text and objects. These placeholders contain text that tells you what to do to add specific content to build your presentation.

There's even a context-sensitive Guide Me feature that guesses what you might want to do, and shows you how to do it. So, for example, if you're in Outliner view and choose Guide Me, you're offered help with topics related to outlining. You can get to this feature anytime by clicking the Guide Me button. However, if you seem to be fumbling with a particular function, Guide Me senses that you're not making any progress, and just might display a message asking if you need help with what you're doing.

> **Tip**
>
> If you don't want Guide Me to appear without you summoning it, deselect the check box in the bottom-left-hand corner of the Guide Me screen the next time it appears.

Later, when you're on your own and are unsure of how to use a command or control, you can look for a button on-screen that you click to get to the Help Index. There's always one in dialog boxes, and the button always summons Help information about the options that are currently on-screen.

> **Tip**
>
> If you can't find a Help button, press F1 or select the <u>H</u>elp menu.

Creating a Presentation

Imagine that you plan to give an important presentation. You'll need to include text and maybe a chart or two, and, of course, a little design pizazz. You'll want to add as many slides as you need to get your message across, and make some modifications to their content and organization. And you'll certainly want to save your presentation for future use. You'll be glad to know that the steps involved in creating and saving this kind of basic presentation aren't difficult at all.

▶ See "Displaying a Presentation as a Screen Show," p. 311

▶ See "Printing the Pages," p. 342

> **Note**
>
> Fortunately, Freelance does not require that you decide before you begin the presentation whether you're going to create an on-screen presentation called a *screen show*, generate 35mm slides, or create black-and-white printed output. You can create all three kinds of output from the same presentation.

Starting a New Presentation and Choosing Its Look

To begin creating a new presentation, start Freelance Graphics 96 for Windows 95 by selecting it from the Programs section of the Start menu in the Windows Desktop. After the Freelance Graphics window opens, the Welcome to Lotus Freelance Graphics dialog box appears. This box contains two tabs: Open an Existing Presentation (see fig. 2.1) and Create a New Presentation Using a SmartMaster.

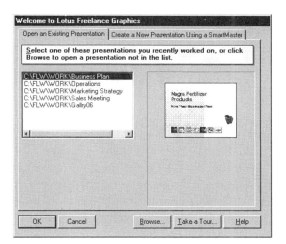

Fig. 2.1
The welcoming Freelance dialog box offers the opportunity to open an existing presentation.

The first page allows you to open a presentation you previously created and saved, and it displays the title slide from a selected presentation in a preview box on the right of the screen like the one shown in figure 2.1.

> **Tip**
>
> Both tabs also offer you the option to Take a Tour. This is a brief demo of the features of Freelance Graphics that might be useful if you're new to the product.

Click the second property page of the Welcome to Freelance Graphics property sheet dialog box, shown in figure 2.2, to create a brand new presentation. On-screen options in this sheet are to Select a Content Topic related to the purpose of your presentation, or to Select a Look for your presentation by selecting a SmartMaster look. *SmartMaster looks* hold background designs for presentations, as well as the formatting and placement of text, charts, tables, and symbols on pages. After you select a SmartMaster set, you'll get an opportunity to enter the data for the presentation (the text and numbers) and get a finished and polished presentation in almost no time.

Fig. 2.2
SmartMaster looks give your presentation a design headstart.

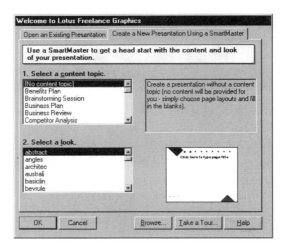

Both options for creating a new presentation provide a SmartMaster look to give you a basic look for your slides. It's really up to you. If you feel more comfortable telling Freelance what type of presentation you're creating and letting the program select a SmartMaster look, then select a content topic. But if you'd rather browse through the SmartMaster looks yourself and choose a design that appeals to you, you can do that instead.

Caution

The idea is to choose *one* of these approaches—they don't work together. So, if you select a look carefully and then select a content topic, Freelance gets rid of the look you chose and replaces it with the content topic's own associated SmartMaster look.

Click several of the SmartMaster looks using these two options and examine their previews. You also can press the down-arrow key on the keyboard to scroll down the list, highlighting and previewing each SmartMaster look sequentially.

Tip

You don't want Freelance to provide a look for you? Go to the Select a Look list box and choose [No Look—Blank Background].

Make sure that the look you prefer is highlighted and appears in the preview, and then click OK or press Enter to proceed.

> **Tip**
>
> If you know the name of the SmartMaster look you want, you can use the keyboard for a shortcut. Press the first letter in the name of the SmartMaster look to jump to the first SmartMaster look on the list that begins with that letter, and scroll down from there to select the exact SmartMaster look you want.

Selecting a Page Layout

The next property sheet to appear, the New Page dialog box, asks you to define your page layout. A *page layout* places placeholders for things like bulleted lists, charts and title text on your page, so you can create these elements instantly by clicking on what are called the page layout Click Here objects. Freelance provides 12 predefined page layouts.

The New page dialog box (shown in fig. 2.3) lists your page layout choices, which are named by elements that will be included on your slides. The page layout called Bulleted List, for example, creates a page with a page title and a list of bulleted text points below the title. The page layouts also set the text attributes, such as the point size and typeface, of the text elements on the pages.

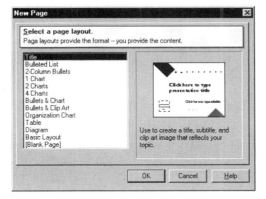

Fig. 2.3
Standard layouts incorporate typical presentation elements such as titles and charts.

Although there are only 12 standard page layouts, you are likely to find one that's appropriate for just about any presentation need. If you need a special page design, you can always arrange the elements on the page manually or create a new, custom page layout.

▶ See "Changing Page Layouts," p. 47

Most presentations start with a title page, so choose the Title page layout and then click OK. The Title page layout appears full-screen. Although your choices of look and layout may be different than those shown here, you can see a typical title slide in figure 2.4.

Fig. 2.4
Title, subtitle, and clip art placeholders are already in place on this title slide.

Filling in Your Presentation Contents

When you begin a new presentation, unless you've chosen the blank presentation option in the opening sheet, there are a few elements in place: design elements and Click Here blocks. You begin the process of building a presentation by simply entering information in the Click Here blocks on the first page, then creating new pages and repeating the process until you've added all the points you want to make.

Using Click Here Blocks

A *page layout* is an arrangement of named placeholders that you can click to create presentation elements. These are called *Click Here blocks* because each asks you to "Click Here" to create a presentation element such as a page title or subtitle, chart, or table. The Title page layout has three Click Here blocks— two that create text titles and one that enables you to select a symbol from the clip art symbol library.

To type the presentation title, click the Click Here to Type Presentation Title text block. A box appears surrounding the text block that offers some simple tools (shown in fig. 2.5). This is where you can type the title.

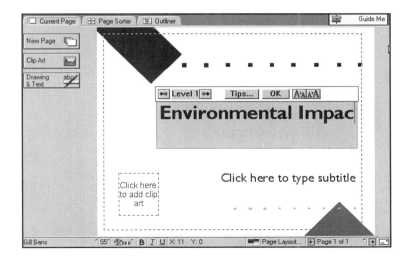

Fig. 2.5
A box appears
around a Click
Here block when
you click it.

Getting Started

There are five preset levels for text, one relating to each outline level that you move text to. A *level* applies a set of properties to text, including font, color, size, and indentation. Clicking the arrows on either side of this element moves you up or down, one level at a time. Clicking the Tips button offers advice for formatting the text you're creating. You can also enlarge or reduce the typeface size in preset increments using these two buttons.

Type a title, and click OK. To enter the subtitle, click the Click Here to Type Subtitle text block, type a subtitle, and click OK. When you do, the Click Here block now appears with eight small handles around it, as shown in figure 2.6. You see these whenever you click this block. They can be used to resize the block.

For now, the Click Here to Add Clip Art block will be left alone.

The first presentation page is now complete. It's time to begin building additional pages to include the presentation content.

▶ See "Changing
the Size and
Font of Text
Blocks," p. 54

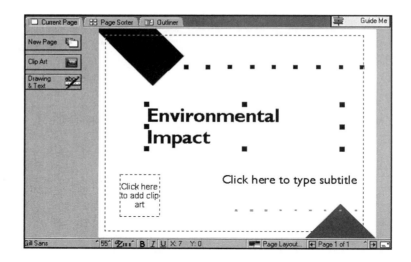

Troubleshooting

I don't want clip art on my title page, but I can't seem to get rid of the corresponding Click Here block. How do I delete it?

You can't, and in fact, you don't have to. The box and the prompt text inside the box appear only while you are working on the presentation. When you show the presentation as a screen show or print the presentation, any unused Click Here blocks do not appear, so just leave them alone. If they bother you as you're working, you might consider using a page layout without that element.

Adding a Second Page

It's simple to create a new page by clicking the New Page button to the left of your page. The New Page dialog box opens, as shown earlier in figure 2.3.

Click the Standard Page Layouts page, and choose the Bulleted List layout. The preview shows a page title at the top of the page and the first of a series of bulleted text points. To use the Bulleted List page layout, click OK or press Enter. The Bulleted List page layout appears with its own Click Here blocks, as shown in figure 2.7.

The Bulleted List page layout contains only two Click Here text blocks—one for the page title and one for the list of bulleted text points.

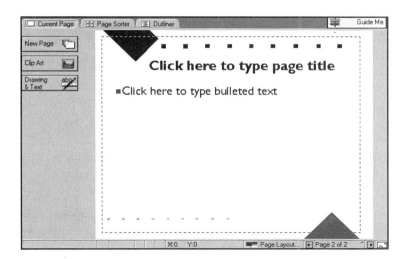

Fig. 2.7
Notice that the design elements on the bulleted list page are different from those on the title page.

Click Click Here to Type Page Title and enter a title. Then press the down-arrow key to move to the next Click Here block. The typing cursor appears next to the first bullet.

Type a first bullet point and press Enter. A second bullet appears, and your cursor has moved to the second bullet line. Type several more bullet points, pressing Enter after each, until your list resembles the one in figure 2.8.

Tip

If you don't want a bullet symbol, you can modify the bullet style to no bullet. Select the bulleted list, then choose Text, Bullets & Numbers. Change the style to none.

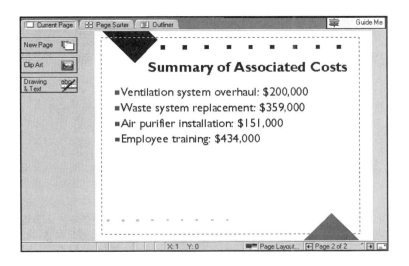

Fig. 2.8
A bulleted list gives your audience the facts clearly and succinctly.

> **Tip**
>
> A good rule of thumb to keep bullet points easy to read is to keep them short—six or seven words each—and to use no more than about six bullets per page.

Working with Charts

▶ See "Selecting a Chart Type and Style," p. 77

Data charts can show information in your presentation in an easy-to-read way that your audience can quickly comprehend. Charts come in a variety of styles, such as bar, line, and pie, and you can format them in many ways. Freelance Graphics provides a built-in charting feature that makes creating charts quick and easy.

Adding the Chart Page

Add a new page to your presentation by clicking the New Page button at the left of the Freelance window. Choose any standard layout from the New Page dialog box, which includes one or more charts.

The new page layout offers one or more Click Here Data Chart blocks that you can click to begin the process of creating a chart. The Click Here Data Chart block also indicates the positioning of the chart you will create. Figure 2.9 shows the 1 Chart page layout as it appears in the Freelance window.

Fig. 2.9
The 1 chart page layout offers a title block and chart block.

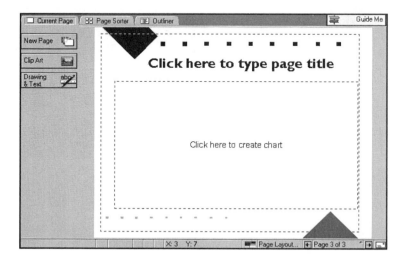

Click the Click Here to Create Chart block. The Create Chart dialog box opens, as shown in figure 2.10.

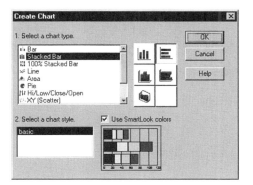

Fig. 2.10
Several options for chart style appear in the Create Chart dialog box.

Notice that the dialog box displays two numbered steps. Whenever possible, Freelance numbers the steps you should follow to respond to a dialog box. Complete the first step by choosing one of the chart types from the first list. Notice that the display of chart styles on the right changes to show different chart styles available. Choose a chart type by clicking it in the list. Basic is the default style, but you can create your own styles as well. Then click OK.

▶ See "Selecting a Chart Type and Style," p. 77

Entering Chart Data

The next step is to enter the numbers to chart. Freelance opens the Edit Data dialog box shown in figure 2.11 and displays a spreadsheet-like grid into which you can enter the data for the data chart. Text and an arrow in the window point to the first column as the destination for Axis Labels. More text and another arrow points to the first two rows as the destination for Legend entries. The sequences of numbers that you must supply to create a chart are arranged in columns below each Legend entry.

Use the arrow keys to move the highlight from cell to cell in the Edit Data dialog box. You also can click a cell with the mouse pointer to "jump" the highlight directly to a cell.

▶ See "Entering the Data," p. 87

Note

Notice the Import Data button on the right. If you keep your data in another software program on your system (for example, Lotus 1-2-3), you can import the data rather than retype it in Freelance.

Getting Started

Fig. 2.11

A simple spreadsheet interface allows you to enter data for your chart.

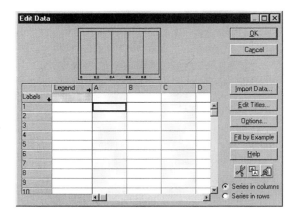

To enter data, move the highlight around the Edit Data dialog box and type entries into each cell until you have completed the data, as in the Edit Data sheet shown in figure 2.11.

To create a chart title, click the Edit Titles button and the Edit Titles dialog box shown in figure 2.12 appears. In the Chart Title text box, type a chart title.

Fig. 2.12

You can add a title, note, or label for each axis in the Edit Titles dialog box.

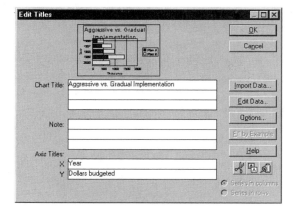

Click OK to return to the Edit Data dialog box, then OK again to have Freelance create a chart based on the data you have entered. Figure 2.13 shows a typical bar chart.

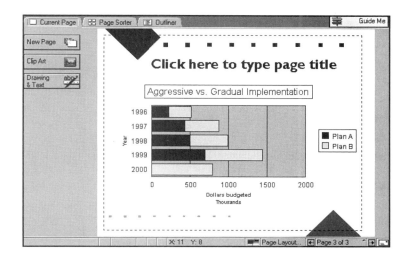

Fig. 2.13
A simple bar chart
compares two
options visually.

Changing an Object's Attributes

Every object that you create—whether it is a text block, chart, table, or drawn
object—has a set of attributes that controls its appearance. To change the
attributes, right-click the object in question. A pop-up menu like the one in
figure 2.14 appears with options that are specific to the object you have
selected.

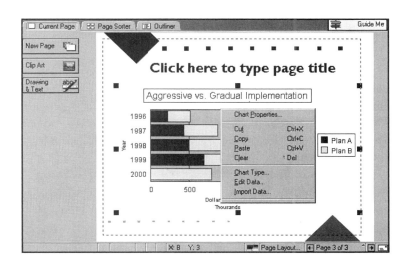

Fig. 2.14
Shortcut menus
appear when you
right-click an
object.

Choose Chart Properties, and a dialog box appears with special settings that change the appearance of the object (see fig. 2.15). This is actually the Lotus InfoBox, a new feature in Freelance Graphics 96 for Windows 95. The *InfoBox* is a centralized location where you can make changes to all the elements associated with the object you have selected. The InfoBox has multiple tabs (the number differs depending on what kind of object you're working with) and a drop-down list in the title bar to change the aspect of the object you'd like to make changes to.

Fig. 2.15
The Lotus InfoBox offers one-stop formatting of various objects.

> **Note**
>
> As usual, Freelance offers several other ways to accomplish the same thing. You can access the same sheet by selecting the Chart, Text, or Group menu, depending on whether you're working on a chart, text, or clip art symbol, and choosing the item that includes the word Properties... after you select an object.
>
> The appearance of these menu items are dependent upon the object that is selected at a given time. For example, if the user selects a Click Here text block, the menu entry will be Text.

For example, if you click the chart you've created, then click the right mouse button and choose Chart Properties, an InfoBox appears like the one in figure 2.15. You can use it to change the color and width of the lines in the chart, and to make many other changes to the appearance of the chart. Try using its various settings. Notice that as you change options, you can see the results of the new attribute setting reflected on the on-screen chart. The InfoBox can be moved around the screen to allow you to see these changes more clearly.

When you're happy with the look of your chart, click the Close button in the top-right-hand corner to close the sheet and implement the changes.

Modifying the Presentation in Page Sorter View

Now that you have completed the first few pages of your presentation, you can turn back and forth among the pages by pressing the Page Up and Page Down keys or by clicking the Page Change arrow buttons on the status line at the bottom of the Freelance window. You also can click the current page number displayed on this button and choose a different page from the pop-up list.

Examining presentation pages like this, however, enables you to see only one page at a time. To see multiple pages, use the Page Sorter view. You can get there by clicking the Page Sorter tab. It's waiting, along with the Outliner view, right behind the Current Page tab on the main Freelance window.

Page Sorter view shows tiny pages displayed next to each other, as shown in figure 2.16.

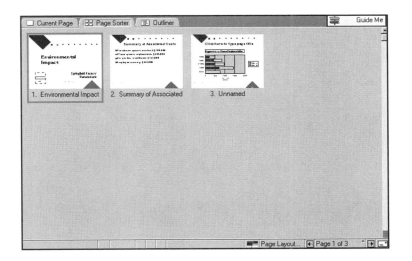

Fig. 2.16
Get the impact of the overall presentation in Page Sorter view.

In Page Sorter view, you can see the consistency of design that the SmartMaster look imposes on the presentation. The title page has one design, and the other pages have a second design that is related to the title page. You also see the page titles and their number in sequence below each page.

In Page Sorter view, you can also change the SmartMaster look attached to a presentation, rearrange the order of pages, and duplicate pages that have contents you want to copy. You can even arrange two presentations that are in Page Sorter view in side-by-side windows and then copy the contents of a page from one presentation to another.

▶ See "Understanding the Three Presentation Views," p. 63

For now, try rearranging the order of the pages by clicking the first page on the left to select it and then dragging it to the far right, or end of the presentation. When you release the mouse button, the page appears in the new position.

 Duplicating a page is also simple. For example, you might like to repeat your title slide at the end of a presentation as a closing slide. Select the title page and click the Duplicate Pages SmartIcon on the Universal toolbar. You can also select the Page menu, then choose Duplicate. You then have two identical pages next to each other. You can move the duplicate to the end of the presentation by simply clicking it and dragging it to the far-right, as shown in figure 2.17.

Fig. 2.17
Duplicating any slide to repeat it elsewhere in the presentation is a simple process.

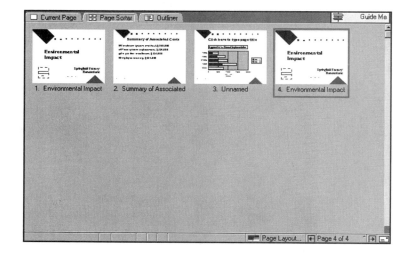

> **Tip**
>
> You can also duplicate a slide in Page Sorter view by selecting it and pressing Alt+F7.

 Deleting pages in your presentation is also quick and easy in Page Sorter view. With a page selected, click the Delete Pages SmartIcon, or press the Delete key on the keyboard. The page disappears. If you have deleted the wrong page, you can immediately choose Undo Delete Page(s) from the Edit menu.

Working with the Presentation in the Outliner

The Outliner in Freelance offers a third view of a presentation. This view shows both the text and page layout at the same time. This helps you concentrate on the organization of the content of the presentation rather than the design of the pages. To switch to Outliner view, click the Outliner tab. Figure 2.18 shows a presentation in Outliner view.

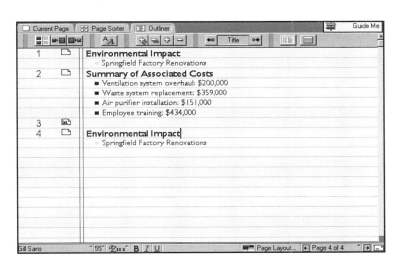

Fig. 2.18
The Outliner view helps you see how well your content is organized.

Notice that the text of the presentation appears on what looks like a yellow legal pad. Next to each page is a page number and icon. The page icon for the third page shows a data chart to indicate the contents of the page.

In Outliner view, you can edit the text contents of pages by editing the text on the Outliner legal pad. You can also rearrange the order of pages and of bulleted text points on Bulleted List pages. Just as in Page Sorter view, you can duplicate pages and delete extraneous pages, too.

▶ See "Adding and Editing Presentation Text," p. 300

Reorganizing Pages in Outliner View

To rearrange the pages in Outliner view, click the page icon—a small box symbol to the left of a page. A border appears around the page. Drag the page icon up the page while holding down the mouse button. A dark horizontal bar appears where the page will drop if you release the mouse button. Release the mouse button when the bar appears to place it in another location. The page will now be automatically renumbered. If you switch to Page Sorter view, you see the data chart page in its new position.

Editing Text in Outliner View

Sometimes it's easier to type in text or edit it in the text-oriented Outliner view rather than in the Current Page view. In fact, you can type the entire content of your presentation here, then switch to the Current Page view to deal with design issues or format the text:

■ To edit text in Outliner view, click and hold down the left mouse button, then move the mouse pointer across the words you want to change to select them. Then press Delete to delete the text, and type the new text.

■ To insert new text in a line, click where you'd like to insert the text in an existing line, and then type the text. Remove any extra spaces in the line, if necessary.

■ To create new bullet points in Outliner view, place your cursor at the end of the line you'd like it to follow, and press Enter. A new bullet appears, and you can simply type your text. A Click Me bullet must exist on the page being edited, and the level that is being edited in Outline view must be associated with that Click Me.

■ To start a new page, place your cursor at the end of the line you'd like to precede it and press Shift+Tab. A new page icon appears. Be careful, though. If you use Shift+Tab from a first-level preceding line, this will not work. You must use it from at least one sub-level.

Modifying the Outline Structure

The Outliner also enables you to work at varying levels of detail. This capability to view and modify the organization of the information in your presentation is, in fact, one of the great strengths of Outliner view. For example, to see only the title of a page, click the page icon and then click the light-gray minus icon at the top of the Outliner screen. A plus sign to the left of the page icon indicates that the contents of the page are collapsed under the page title.

To see only the page titles of all pages, click the dark-gray triple-minus icon at the top of the Outliner screen. This action does not delete the entries under the page titles. It just hides them so that you can consider the flow of the main topics of the presentation.

To see the detail points again, click the single-plus button to expand a single page's content. Or, click the triple-plus button to expand all the details of all pages at once.

Displaying Pages and Text in Outliner View

Finally, if you're both a visual and a word person, you might like to see your pages alongside of your outline text. To do that, click the Show/Hide Slide button. The individual pages appear where the page icon had previously been, as shown in figure 2.19.

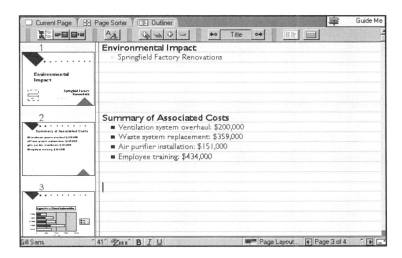

Fig. 2.19
Get an idea of how your changes will look without ever leaving Outliner view.

To return to page icons and hide the pages themselves, simply click again on the Show/Hide Pages button.

Viewing the Presentation as a Screen Show

You've had the chance to view miniatures of the pages in Page Sorter view and the text content of the pages in Outliner view. Fortunately, Freelance offers yet another way to view a presentation. You can have the pages appear one after another, with fancy transition effects between pages such as having the new slide appear from the side, top, or gradually in a checkboard pattern, in an on-screen production called a *screen show*.

▶ See "Displaying a Presentation as a Screen Show," p. 311

To create a screen show, click the Run Screen Show From Beginning button, or choose <u>P</u>resentation, <u>R</u>un Screen Show. You can also press Alt+F10 to start the show. After a moment, the first page of the show appears full-screen. To advance to the next page, press Enter or click the left mouse button. Continue advancing through the screen show until you have seen all the pages. To move back through the presentation, click the right mouse button.

The default screen show uses a simple transition effect to change from one page to the next. The new page simply replaces the preceding page. This is only one of the many transition effects you can use to change from page to page. In fact, you can assign a different transition effect for each page. You can also have the pages advance automatically or have the show run continuously if it will be running as part of a display in a store window, company lobby, or trade show booth.

To leave the screen show mode from any slide, press Esc. A dialog box appears that gives you the option of quitting the screen show. If you're on the last slide, you can also press Enter or double-click to return to the main Freelance screen.

Saving the Presentation

To make a permanent record of the presentation you have just completed, choose File, Save. The dialog box in figure 2.20 lets you designate the location to where you'd like to save your file, and allows you to give it a unique name. To move to different locations for saving your file, use the Save In drop-down list, or click the Up One Level button. You can even create a new folder to store your presentation from this sheet with the Create New Folder button.

Fig. 2.20
Don't forget to save your presentation with a name that you can locate later on!

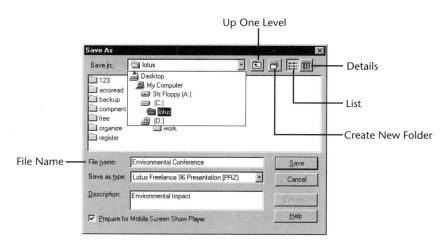

When you're satisfied with your settings, click Save.

Congratulations! You have successfully created and saved your first presentation. Even though you have used the essential commands and techniques of presentation making, however, you have seen only a sampling of the many powers of Freelance. ❖

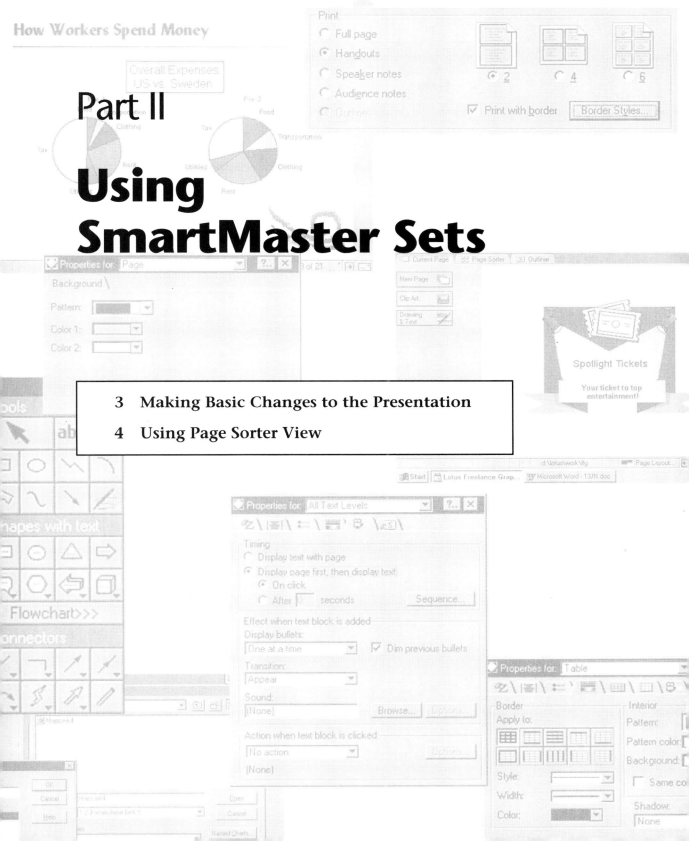

Part II

Using SmartMaster Sets

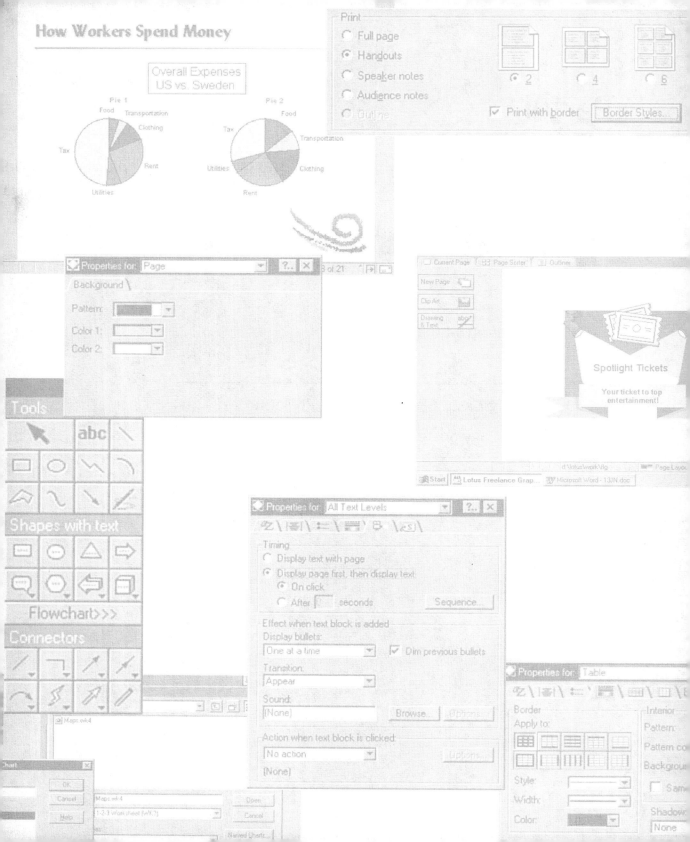

CHAPTER 3

Making Basic Changes to the Presentation

by Nancy Stevenson

After you've worked through the basic steps of selecting a SmartMaster look, choosing page layouts, and using the Click Here blocks, the presentation you obtain is likely to meet the needs of a simple presentation. No presentation is perfect after the first go-around, however. You probably will notice corrections that should be made, pages that could benefit from page subtitles, and charts and bulleted lists that would look a little better if they were repositioned on the pages. You may even decide that a different SmartMaster look would give the presentation a more desirable look.

In this chapter, you'll learn about the minor revisions, adjustments, and formatting changes your presentation may need, including:

- Naming pages
- Changing SmartMaster looks
- Changing page layouts
- Editing text
- Moving and resizing objects
- Changing the attributes of objects

Naming the Pages

Especially in a large presentation, keeping track of pages by number can get tricky. It's sometimes useful to assign to the different slides in your presentation, page names that reflect their content. That way, rather than looking for page 32, you can zero in quickly and easily on the 1994 Sales Figures page by name.

When you click the Page Number button at the lower-right corner of the Freelance window, a list of page names appears, as in figure 3.1. Freelance gets these names from the page titles in the page layout unless you enter a specific name for a page. If you have not yet entered a page name or a page title, the page is labeled Unnamed.

Fig. 3.1
This pop-up list gives the name of all pages in your presentation.

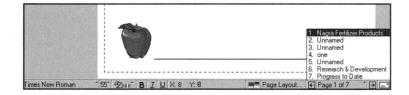

You can enter your own page name, which will override the title. First, make sure none of the objects on the page is selected. Click on the Open InfoBox SmartIcon, or choose Page, Page Properties. The InfoBox in figure 3.2 appears. Simply type a page name into the Page Name text box and close the box. The new page name now appears in the pop-up list of page names in the status bar.

Fig. 3.2
The Page Properties InfoBox allows you to name your own pages.

Caution

If you have used the InfoBox to apply a name to a page, it will override the feature that takes the page name from the text in the title block. Changing the title text going forward will not change the page name back. You must use the InfoBox again to make any future changes to the name.

Changing SmartMaster Looks

After you create a presentation, you may decide that a different SmartMaster look would give it a better look. A slightly more conservative design might fit a particular presentation, or the SmartMaster look created for a new client could be applied to an old presentation to make it look custom-tailored.

Changing the SmartMaster look for a presentation gives the overall presentation a new look. It accomplishes this task in two ways:

- The SmartMaster look provides the presentation with a different background design, which can include a background color, graphic shapes, a drawing, and even a company logo. A variation of the background is used for the title page.

- The Click Here blocks in the page layouts of the new SmartMaster look have different designs for the text and charts you have created on the page. The corresponding page layouts in the new SmartMaster look take over; the new Click Here blocks change the fonts, colors, and chart designs on the pages.

In addition to applying different designs to the objects you have created from Click Here blocks, the new page layouts try to reposition any objects you may have moved (see figs. 3.3 and 3.4).

Fig. 3.3
The original SmartMaster look is called Festive.

Fig. 3.4
Changing the SmartMaster look to Food after you've entered text moves things around.

> **Caution**
>
> If you have already moved objects created from Click Here blocks when you attempt to switch SmartMaster looks, Freelance displays a warning message. This message tells you that switching SmartMaster looks will reposition these objects according to the new settings. Unfortunately, you cannot both change SmartMaster looks and preserve your custom page arrangements. You would have to reposition everything manually on the page if you wanted them back in the same place.

Changing the SmartMaster look for a presentation is easy. Simply follow these steps:

1. Choose Presentation, Choose a Different SmartMaster Look.

2. Choose a SmartMaster look from within the Choose a Look for Your Presentation sheet, shown in figure 3.5. Click a SmartMaster look name to preview it. By default, SmartMasters are stored in a directory called Masters. If you have moved some or created new ones in another directory, get to them by clicking Browse.

Tip

To quickly scan the various SmartMasters available, click the Scan button in this dialog box. The Scan button changes to a Stop Scan button, and the different looks appear one after another until you click Stop Scan.

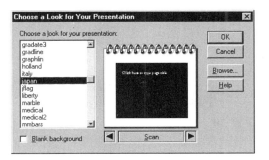

Fig. 3.5
Choose a SmartMaster look from the Choose a Look for Your Presentation page.

When you've made your selection, click OK. After a moment, the presentation is reformatted according to the design of the new SmartMaster look. Compare the way a new SmartMaster rearranges the elements of an existing presentation in figures 3.3 and 3.4. The text fonts, the colors, and the placement of objects on the pages change, but all your text and objects are still present.

▶ See "Changing SmartMaster Looks and Page Layouts in Page Sorter View," p. 69

Changing Page Layouts

In addition to changing the overall design of the presentation pages by changing SmartMaster looks, you can change the types of objects included on a presentation page by choosing another page layout for it. The new page layout contains a different combination of Click Here blocks.

◀ See "Using Click Here Blocks," p. 26

A page can have the Bulleted List page layout, for example, but only two Click Here blocks (see fig. 3.6). To change the design so that the page contains both a bulleted list and a chart, you can change the page layout to Bullets & Chart. The new Click Here to Type Bulleted Text block is now positioned on the left-half of the page, leaving room for the Click Here to Create Chart block on the right (see fig. 3.7).

II

Using SmartMaster Sets

Fig. 3.6
The Bulleted List
page layout has
title and bullet list
Click Here boxes.

Fig. 3.7
The Bullets &
Chart page layout
shifts the bullets
to the left.

To change the layout of a page, click the Page Layout button at the bottom of the Freelance window. Choose a different page layout from the Choose Page Layout dialog box shown in figure 3.8. Click OK to apply the new layout.

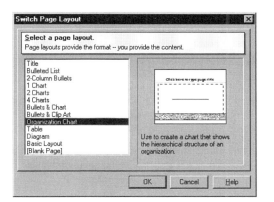

Fig. 3.8
You can preview
different layouts
from this dialog
box.

Tip

You can also change the page layout by choosing Page, Switch Page Layout.

If the new page layout doesn't contain a Click Here block for a block of text, or a chart already on the page, the text or chart remains in its current position with its current formatting. If you've created a bullet chart with the Bulleted List page layout and you want to change the chart to the Organization Chart page layout, for example, the new page will still display the bulleted points in their original position but also will include a Click Here to Create Organization Chart block. You may need to manually resize the organization chart so that it doesn't overlay the bulleted points.

Customizing Page Layouts

Page layouts come with a preset number and arrangement of Click Here blocks, but sometimes you may need extra elements to complete a page. You might want to place your company logo on every bulleted list page, for example.

You can actually go in and modify a chosen layout to add new elements. Then, any page in that presentation that uses the layout you've modified will have the new elements already in place. Modify a page layout by performing the following steps:

1. Choose Presentation, Edit Page Layouts. The dialog box in figure 3.9 appears.

II

Using SmartMaster Sets

Fig. 3.9
The Redesign Page
Layout dialog box
lets you select a
layout to edit.

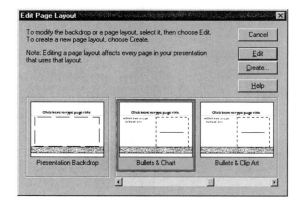

2. Select a page layout by browsing through the images using the horizontal scroll bar at the bottom of the dialog box. Click a layout to select it.

3. Click Edit. The screen in figure 3.10 appears.

Fig. 3.10
A full-screen view
appears to allow
you to edit a
layout easily.

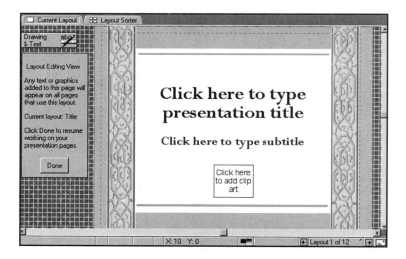

You can now use the Drawing & Text button to add lines or shapes to your layout. You can also use the Create menu to add a clip art symbol or chart to your layout. When you click Done, every page that has that layout in your presentation will now also have the element or elements.

Tip

If you want to make a permanent change to the standard page layout, so that you are actually changing the SmartMaster look, save the file as a SmartMaster look file type (one of the file types offered in the Save As dialog box).

Troubleshooting

I selected the Organization Chart layout to change, and went in to edit it, then I realized I should really edit the Bullets & Chart layout. Do I have to back out and begin the procedure again?

If you decide you'd like to change a different layout, or an additional layout, you can use the second tab in the Layout Editing view to do so. Choose the Layout Sorter tab, and the screen in figure 3.11 appears. Use the tow arrows at the bottom-right corner of the page to scroll through all the possible layouts. Click one of the pages you see, and when you return to the Current Layout tab, it will be displayed, ready for editing.

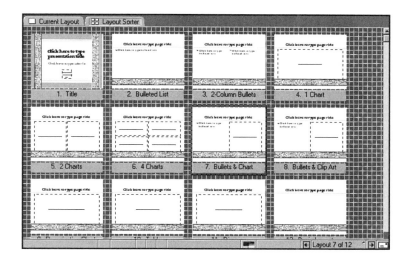

Fig. 3.11
The Layout Sorter lets you change your mind about which layout to edit.

II

Using SmartMaster Sets

Editing Text

You can edit any text on a presentation page—correcting or deleting text that is already entered or adding new text to existing blocks. To edit text in a Click Here block, follow these steps:

1. Click anywhere on the text.

2. If you have not entered text, the Click Here message disappears, and your cursor appears at the beginning of the blank line, ready for you to enter text.

3. If you have already entered text in the Click Here block, click to place your cursor wherever you like in the text, ready to begin editing.

To edit text that was created outside of a Click Here block, things work a little differently:

1. You must double-click this type of text block to select the text for editing. (A single click would select the text block so you can resize it or move it around the page.)

2. After you double-click the text, a box appears around the text block, as in figure 3.12.

Fig. 3.12
Here is a text block ready for editing.

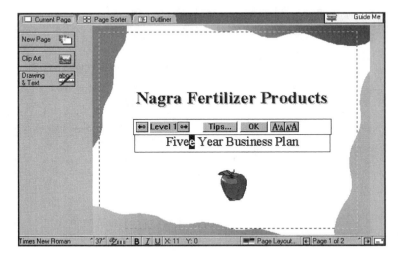

3. Click the text block again to place the cursor.

> **Note**
>
> You also can click a text block once and then press the F2 key to edit the text in the text block. Yet another approach is to right-click a text block and then choose <u>E</u>dit from the pop-up commands menu.

When the typing cursor is placed in the text block, you can do several things:

- Enter new text, starting at the position of the cursor.
- Delete text to the right of the cursor by pressing the Delete key.
- Delete text to the left of the cursor by pressing the Backspace key.
- Toggle Freelance from Insert mode to Overtype mode so that typed text replaces existing text, rather than push the existing text to the right. Do this by pressing the Insert key.
- Add new text to the end of the text block by moving the cursor to the end of the last line of the text and beginning to type.

> **Tip**
>
> You can press the End key to quickly "jump" the cursor to the end of a line. To jump the cursor to the beginning of a line, press the Home key.

Table 3.1 lists the text-editing keys you can use after you have placed a typing cursor in a text block.

Table 3.1   Text-Editing Keys

Key(s)	Action
Delete	Deletes a character to the right of the cursor
Backspace	Deletes a character to the left of the cursor
$\rightarrow$	Moves the cursor one position to the right
$\leftarrow$	Moves the cursor one position to the left
Ctrl+$\rightarrow$	Moves the cursor one word to the right
Ctrl+$\leftarrow$	Moves the cursor one word to the left
Home	Moves the cursor to the beginning of the line
End	Moves the cursor to the end of the line
Insert	Toggles between Insert and Overtype modes

II

Using SmartMaster Sets

You can also highlight text by holding down the mouse button and dragging across it. Then simply begin typing to delete the old text and enter new.

> **Tip**
>
> There's another way to select a block of text. When you press the Shift key and press the right- or left-arrow key, the text that the cursor passes across is highlighted.

You can also use the same steps to edit the text in tables, organization charts, and graph charts.

Changing the Size and Font of Text Blocks

Although SmartMaster looks include formatting for text font and size, you may want to get creative and change the formatting. Freelance offers several methods to change the size and font of text in text blocks. You can use the Text Font and Text Size buttons, or you can access the Font InfoBox.

Using the Text Font and Text Size Buttons

The easiest way to change the entire text block is to select it and then use the Text Font and Size buttons in the status bar at the bottom of the Freelance window.

To make changes with these buttons, do the following:

1. Click a Click Here text block, or double-click any other text block and select the text you want to edit.

2. Click either the Text Font button or the Text Size button.

3. From the pop-up list of options, select the text font or text size you want.

When you select a text block, the name of the current font of the selected text appears on the Text Font button. The Text Size button displays the current point size of the text. When you click the Text Font button, you see a list of alternative fonts for the selected block. If you have installed more fonts in Windows than can fit in the pop-up menu, you must use the scroll bar on the pop-up menu to view all the available fonts.

When you select text, the current point size of the selected text appears in the Font Size button. When you click this button, if the point size that you want does not appear on the list, click Custom Size to display the Text Size Other dialog box. In this dialog box, you can enter any point size you want.

You can use the same buttons to change the font or size of only part of the text in a text block. Simply highlight the specific text that you want to change before you click the Text Font or Text Size button. To highlight the text, drag the mouse cursor across it, or hold down the Shift key while using the keyboard to move the cursor across the text.

Using the Font Dialog Box

A second way to choose a different font and point size for text is to use the Lotus InfoBox. To get there, click on the text, then click the Open InfoBox SmartIcon, or choose <u>T</u>ext, <u>T</u>ext Properties. The InfoBox appears (see fig. 3.13).

Fig. 3.13
Change a multitude of text properties from this centralized InfoBox.

This dialog box gives you more options than you have by simply using the Text Font and Text Size buttons. From here, you can select a font from a scrollable list of typefaces and a point size from a second scrollable list. There's also a box under the size list that enlarges or reduces text by preset increments.

The Font InfoBox also allows you to change the color and attributes of the selected text, or to add a shadow of a different color. For a very interesting effect, click Curved Text in this dialog box to bend the line of text in various shapes, as shown in figure 3.14.

▶ See "Creating Curved Text," p. 198

Another way to get to this dialog box is to select the text that you want to modify and then right-click. A small pop-up menu displaying the commands you use most frequently with text then appears. Among those commands is Text Block Properties, which leads to the same InfoBox.

II

Using SmartMaster Sets

Fig. 3.14
Add visual appeal
to a heading by
curving the text.

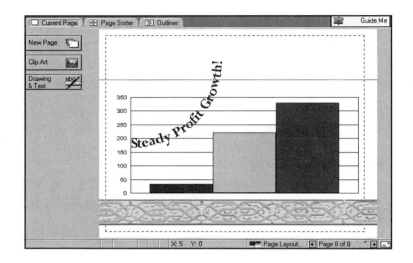

Note

If the Change Font SmartIcon has been added to the SmartIcon palette, you can click that icon after you select text. The Font dialog box then appears.

▶ See "Using
SmartIcons,"
p. 392

Changing the font and size of text overrides the text font and size that is determined by the SmartMaster look. The changes are preserved even when you apply a different SmartMaster look to the presentation.

Changing the Character Attributes of Text

To give text special emphasis, you may want to apply character formatting to it—making it bold, underlined, or italicized. As usual, Freelance offers several ways to accomplish this. The easiest way to apply such formats is to select the text and use the Bold, Italic, and Underline buttons in the status bar.

Another way to add effects to text is to highlight the text to be formatted and then use one of the character-attributes accelerator keys. Table 3.2 lists these keys.

Table 3.2 Character-Attributes Accelerator Keys	
Key(s)	**Description**
Ctrl+B	Bold text
Ctrl+I	Italic text
Ctrl+U	Underlined text
Ctrl+N	Normal text (the absence of any special character formatting, no bold, italic, underlined, and so on)

Remember that you must first select a text block or text within a block and then use the accelerator keys. To remove all the character attributes you've applied to text, use Ctrl+N (Normal).

Don't forget, you can also change all these attributes in the InfoBox shown in figure 3.13.

> **Note**
>
> The character attributes that you apply to text will be preserved even if you change SmartMaster looks. You can italicize a word in a page title, for example, and the word remains italicized after you choose a different SmartMaster look.

One final effect you may add to text is color. There's a Text Color button on the status bar—between the Font Size button and the effects buttons—that provides a pop-up palette to make changes to selected text.

Justifying Text

Another easy change that you can make in a presentation is to change the justification of a text block. Most page titles are left-aligned, for example, but you can easily center or right-align a title to change the look of a page.

The fastest way to change justification is to select the text block. When you do, additional text buttons appear on the toolbar at the top of the screen. Use the four alignment buttons to align left, center, right, or justify.

If you prefer, you can select text and then press Ctrl+L to left-align the block, Ctrl+R to right-align the block, or Ctrl+E to center the block. All text within the text block will be affected. You can even select more than one block and use these accelerator keys to affect all the selected blocks simultaneously.

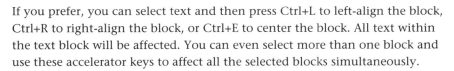

Caution

Text justification settings, unlike character attribute settings, override only the current SmartMaster look. If you change SmartMaster looks, the new SmartMaster look has jurisdiction over the justification of all text blocks. Any justification changes you have made are lost.

Moving and Resizing Objects

You may want to reposition and resize the objects you've created from Click Here blocks. In Freelance, it's simply a matter of selecting which object to move or resize and then using the object's handles to do the operation.

Handles are the eight small squares that appear in a rectangle around objects when its selected. Four handles appear at the corners of the rectangle and four appear at the sides. Figure 3.15 shows the handles that appear around a selected text block.

Fig. 3.15
Handles allow you to resize and move objects.

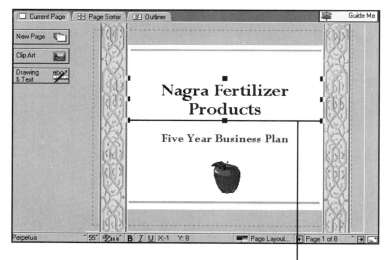

Handles indicating a selected object

To move an object, follow these steps:

1. Click the object once to select it. Handles appear around the object.

2. Place the cursor anywhere within the rectangle formed by the handles.

3. Click and hold down the left mouse button and then drag the mouse.

4. Release the mouse button when the object is at the new position.

While you're dragging the block, the mouse turns into a small fist, and a dashed box moves on the page to indicate where the block will drop when you release the mouse button, as in figure 3.16.

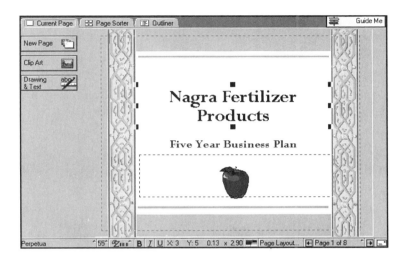

Fig. 3.16
Notice that the
mouse cursor
changed and a
dashed-line
rectangle appeared
to indicate the
move.

To resize an object, follow these steps:

1. Click the object once to select it. Handles appear around the object.

2. Place the point of the cursor on one of the handles.

3. Click and hold down the left mouse button and then drag the mouse.

4. Release the mouse button when the object is correctly resized.

To stretch an object horizontally, use a handle at the right or left side of the object. To stretch an object vertically, use a handle at the top or bottom of the object. To stretch the corner of an object diagonally, use a handle at a corner of the object.

Tip

To resize an object but keep its shape in proportion, press and hold down the Shift key while dragging a corner handle.

II

Using SmartMaster Sets

Changing the Attributes of Objects

The text, tables, and charts that you create for presentation pages are a combination of their contents and the attributes that govern their appearance (the *content* is what's in them, and the *attributes* are how they look). When you first create an object, you have the opportunity to supply its content, but the appearance attributes are contributed by the SmartMaster look. You can change the attributes that determine an object's appearance, however, and override the attributes selected by the SmartMaster look.

In the same way that the Text Properties InfoBox gives you a centralized place for changing all kinds of text formatting, there are InfoBoxes for objects, such as clip art symbols, tables, and charts.

 If you select a clip art symbol object, a Group menu becomes available on the menu bar. Click on the Open InfoBox SmartIcon, or choose Group, Group Properties to see the InfoBox in figure 3.17.

Fig. 3.17
Change attributes of clip art symbols here.

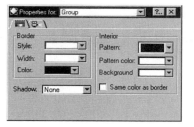

▶ See "Editing Clip Art in Click Here Blocks," p. 254

In a similar way, you can modify charts and tables. With a chart selected, for example, a Chart menu is available. Choose Chart, Chart Properties. The InfoBox in figure 3.18 gives you several tabs of options for modifying charts.

Fig. 3.18
The Chart Properties InfoBox offers multiple formatting options through its four tabs.

Whenever you want to make such modifications to an object, just click the Open InfoBox SmartIcon, or look for its properties InfoBox in a comparable menu. Or, you can select the properties item from the shortcut menu that appears when you select the object and then right-click. Later chapters in this book give more in-depth information about exactly how to use all the tools available to modify objects. ❖

II

Using SmartMaster Sets

CHAPTER 4

Using Page Sorter View

by Nancy Stevenson

Viewing pages one at a time gives you the detailed perspective necessary to hone a presentation to perfection. But it doesn't give you a sense of the over-all flow of a presentation. That's why Freelance includes Page Sorter view, which displays all the pages of your presentation on the screen as miniatures.

Page Sorter view displays as many miniature pages as can fit in the Freelance window. Each page looks just as it does when examined in Current Page view, complete with text, graphics, and the background provided by the SmartMaster set.

In this chapter, you learn how to

- View the sequence of pages in a presentation
- Rearrange the order of pages
- Apply a new SmartMaster set
- Change page layouts
- Duplicate pages that are especially useful, or remove pages that are no longer necessary.

Understanding the Three Presentation Views

Page Sorter view is only one of three views of the content of a presentation:

- *Current Page view.* Displays a single page in the Freelance window. To see the next page, press the Page Down key. This view lets you work in detail on a single page. Figure 4.1 displays a page in Current Page view.

Fig. 4.1
Current Page view
is the place to
handle details for
each page.

■ *Page Sorter view.* Displays as many miniature pages of the presentation as
   will fit in the Freelance window. This view enables you to see all or
   most of the pages at once, rearrange the order of pages, duplicate pages,
   and remove pages you no longer need. You cannot work with the objects on pages, though. Figure 4.2 displays a presentation in Page Sorter
   view.

Fig. 4.2
Page Sorter view is
where you
organize the
overflow of your
presentation.

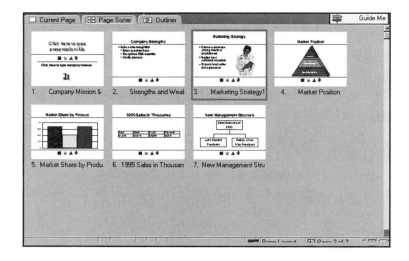

■ *Outliner view.* Displays the text of the presentation in outline form. You
   can easily create and organize the text content of the presentation,
   checking and correcting the flow of ideas. Figure 4.3 displays the same
   presentation in Outliner view.

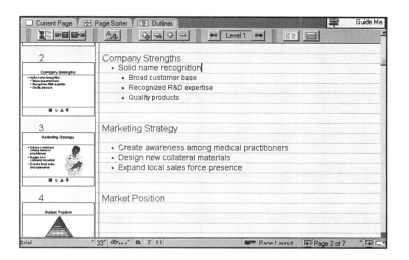

Fig. 4.3
The text from each
page appears all
together, in an
organized format
in Outliner view.

Switching from one view to another gives different perspectives on the presentation and allows you to perform different actions.

▶ See "Switching
to Outliner
View," p. 298

Tip

Arranging the Page Sorter views of two presentations side by side is an excellent way to copy pages from one presentation to another.

▶ See "Copying
Work Between
Presentations,"
p. 286

Switching to Page Sorter View

You can change to Page Sorter view any time by clicking the Page sorter tab in the Freelance window. An alternative path to Page Sorter view is to choose View, Page Sorter.

In Page Sorter view (refer to fig. 4.2), Freelance draws the entire presentation in miniature pages. If you cannot see all the pages in the current presentation, use the scroll bar at the right to scroll down to the next set of pages.

Tip

If you want to fit more pages on one screen, try choosing View, Zoom Out. To see the images a little larger again, choose View, Zoom In.

Rearranging the Order of Pages

Because Page Sorter view helps you see the overall flow of your presentation, one common use for this view is to rearrange the order of pages. You may decide to cover a topic earlier or later in a presentation, and Page Sorter view provides an easy way to move the corresponding page.

To move a page, follow these steps:

1. Place the mouse pointer on the page to move.

2. Click and drag the page to the desired position in the presentation.

3. Release the mouse button.

As you move the page, a dotted outline of the page appears, and a vertical bar next to one of the miniatures indicates where the page will go if you release the mouse button. Figure 4.4 shows the page being moved. Notice the vertical bar at the chosen destination for the page (between pages 2 and 3).

Fig. 4.4
Move pages quickly by dragging them to a new position

Fisted mouse cursor —

Dashed line shows as you drag the page

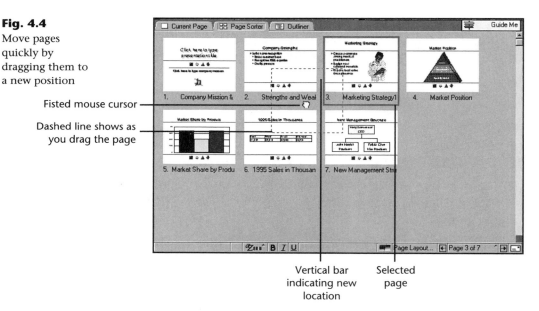

Vertical bar indicating new location

Selected page

You can move more than one page by selecting multiple pages before dragging them to a new position in the presentation. To select multiple pages, use either of the following procedures:

■ Press and hold down the Shift key as you click each page. With Shift still pressed, you can click a page again to deselect it. Using this method, you can select noncontiguous pages to move.

■ Use the pointer to draw a box that entirely encloses the pages you want in the group. To draw the box, move the cursor to the corner of an imaginary rectangle that would surround the group, hold down the left mouse button, and then move the cursor diagonally to the far corner of the rectangle. A dashed line surrounds the selected pages, as shown in figure 4.5. When you release the mouse button, all pages entirely within the rectangle you created are selected.

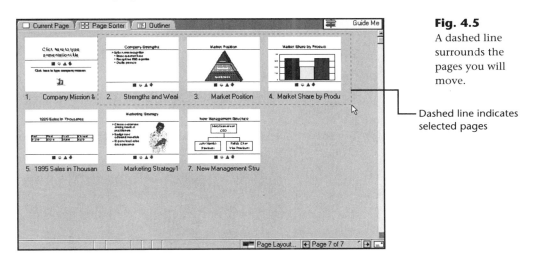

Fig. 4.5
A dashed line surrounds the pages you will move.

Dashed line indicates selected pages

To add more pages to the group, hold down the Shift key and click each page one by one. After you've selected multiple pages, place the cursor on any page, hold down the left mouse button, and move the cursor to the new position for the pages in the presentation.

Duplicating a Page

Another easy task to accomplish in Page Sorter view is to duplicate a page. Suppose that you need a series of pie charts, all alike except for one of the slices. Or perhaps you want to repeat your presentation title page at the start of each new section of the presentation. After you have created a model page in Current Page view, switch to Page Sorter view, copy the page, and then paste it back into the presentation as many times as necessary.

To duplicate a page in Page Sorter view, follow these steps:

1. Select a page or pages by clicking each.

2. Click the Duplicate Pages button on the Universal toolbar.

3. A duplication of the page appears to the right of the original. Now simply click this duplicate and drag it to wherever you'd like it to appear in the presentation.

Tip

You can also press Ctrl+C or select Edit, Copy to copy the page. Press Ctrl+V or Shift+Insert to paste the duplicate(s) into the presentation following the selected page.

Deleting Pages

When you're using Page Sorter view to get an overview of your presentation, you sometimes see a page that doesn't belong. Or, you might wish to modify an existing presentation to use for another occasion, and some of the pages may not fit. Deleting pages in Page Sorter view is very similar to duplicating them.

1. From Page Sorter view, click the page you want to delete.

2. Click the Delete Pages button on the Universal toolbar. You can also choose Edit, Cut.

If you want to delete several pages at a time, click one, then, while holding down the shift key, click the others you'd like to delete. Once all the pages you want to delete are selected (they will have a thick gray border around them), use the method just described to finish deleting them.

Troubleshooting

I deleted a page, then did a few other things before I realized I shouldn't have deleted it. Undo only undoes my last action, right? How do I get my page back?

Actually, the Undo button undoes up to the last 10 things that you did. If you deleted your page, say, three steps ago, just click the Undo button three times to get it back. Of course, you'll have to redo the other two things you did after the page deletion, but if getting a complete page back is more trouble than redoing those other steps, undo would be the way to go.

Changing SmartMaster Sets and Page Layouts in Page Sorter View

SmartMaster looks give a definite feel to the presentation through a particular set of color and backgrounds. Page Sorter view is useful for seeing the effects of different SmartMaster sets on a presentation. While in Page Sorter view, you can choose Presentation, Choose a Different SmartMaster Look to select a different SmartMaster set. You'll see the new SmartMaster set revise every page in the presentation (compare fig. 4.5 with fig. 4.6), and you can easily spot particular pages that need special attention without having to peruse the presentation a page at a time.

◀ See "Changing SmartMaster Sets and Page Layouts in Page Sorter View," p. 65

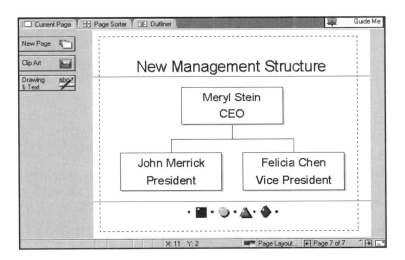

Fig. 4.6
Notice that the new SmartMaster has moved around some elements of the page, such as titles or charts.

You can even change the page layout for a page by selecting the page and then clicking the Page Layout button, located on the status bar at the bottom of the Freelance window. For example, you may decide to add a second chart to a page by clicking the page, clicking the Page Layout button, and then choosing the 2 Charts layout from the Choose Page Layout dialog box.

Changing Typeface Globally and Adding a Logo in Page Sorter View

Two other functions new to Freelance allow you to make changes to your presentation, which you can see take effect globally across your pages in Page Sorter view.

II

Using SmartMaster Sets

You can change the typeface used in the entire presentation with one command. However, be aware that once changed, there's no way to undo the change to reinstate the SmartMaster typefaces. Here's how to do it:

1. From the Current Page view, click the Use One Typeface for All text button on the Universal toolbar, or from any view choose Presentation, Change the Typeface Globally.

2. Make your typeface selection from the Change Typeface Globally dialog box in figure 4.7. The new typeface is previewed in a box in the middle of the dialog box.

3. If you want to change the typeface in special elements such as tables or charts, use the check boxes at the bottom of this dialog box to do so.

Fig. 4.7
Choose from any
available typefaces
in this dialog box.

When you click OK, you get a warning that you can't undo this change. Be aware that if you've used more than one typeface in your presentation, all of them will be overwritten with the global typeface style. When you click OK again, the new typeface is reflected on all the pages.

The second global change you can make is to add a company logo or other image to each page in your presentation:

1. Click the Place a Logo on Every Page button on the main toolbar, or choose Presentation, Add a Logo to Every Page.

2. The screen changes to a full-page view, with the Drawing & Text button available, and instructions for adding a logo on the left side of the page (see fig. 4.8).

3. Draw a logo, type text, or insert a clip art symbol. A dashed box will surround the image. Whatever you've created appears on each page wherever you have placed it on this screen.

Click Done, and the new image appears on every page of your presentation.

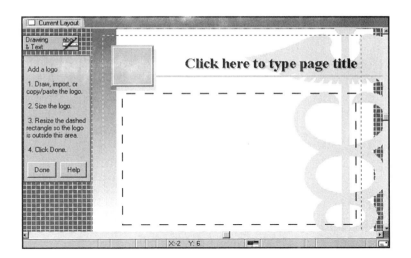

Fig. 4.8
Instructions for adding a logo appear on the left of this screen.

Returning to Current Page View

When you work in Freelance, the odds are that you'll want to move among the views often to get different perspectives. To return from Page Sorter view to Current Page view and examine one page closely, you can use any of these methods:

- Double-click the page
- Click the page and then click the Current Page tab
- Use the arrow keys to move the dark border to the page, and then press Enter

The page will then appear in Current Page view. ❖

II

Using SmartMaster Sets

Part III

Adding Charts to Pages

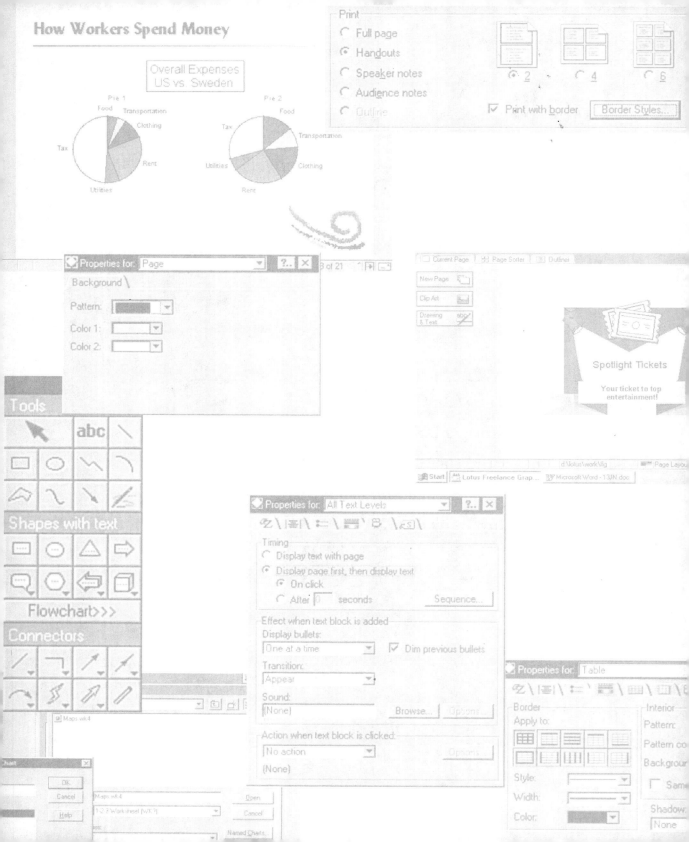

CHAPTER 5

Adding a Data Chart

by Nancy Stevenson

Whenever the information that you need to present is numeric, you may want to show it graphically in a data chart. A data chart can make clear a short-term change, a long-term trend, a comparison, a breakdown of a total, or even a simple, aberrant result in a way that a table of numbers simply cannot.

Freelance makes it easy to create a data chart from a set of numbers. In this chapter, you learn how to

- Add a chart page
- Add a chart to any page layout
- Select a chart type and style
- Enter data for a chart
- Preview a chart
- Add titles and labels to a chart

Adding a Chart

Freelance includes a charting program called Lotus Chart. This is one of several applications shared among the various Lotus SmartSuite products. Using Lotus Chart, charts can be created in two ways. The easiest way to create a page containing a data chart is to select a page layout that includes a chart Click Here block. Then click the Click Here to Create Chart block. The second method allows you to add a chart to any page layout using a command in the Create menu.

Using a Chart Page Layout

To add a page containing a chart Click Here block to a presentation, simply create a new page with a chart layout:

1. Click the New Page button. The New Page dialog box appears.

2. From the New Page dialog box, click the Standard Page Layouts tab.

3. Choose the 1 Chart, 2 Charts, 4 Charts, or Bullets & Chart page layout. Notice that Freelance shows you a preview of these various page layouts within the New Page dialog box (see fig. 5.1).

Fig. 5.1

The New Page dialog box offers several standard page layouts that include charts.

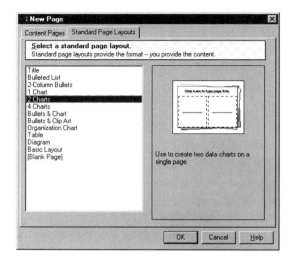

4. Click OK. A page containing the layout you chose appears on-screen.

5. Click the Click Here to Create Chart block. The Create Chart dialog box appears (see fig. 5.2).

Adding a Chart to Any Page

Freelance allows you to add data charts to any page in a presentation, even a page that does not include a Click Here to Create Chart block. To create a chart on a page, first turn to the page where you want to add the chart, then follow either of these methods:

■ Click the Chart icon on the toolbar.

■ Choose Create, Chart.

Either method accesses the Create Chart dialog box, as shown in figure 5.2. You can select a chart type and chart style from the choices in this dialog box, or you can select the default chart design.

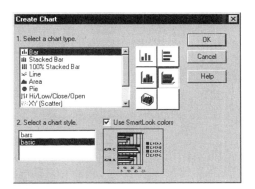

Fig. 5.2
Choose a chart
type and style
from the Create
Chart dialog box

Selecting a Chart Type and Style

As in nearly all Freelance dialog boxes, the selections available in the Create Chart dialog box are both numbered and clearly described. The first selection, Choose a Chart Type, asks you to scroll through and choose one of the eleven items in the list on the left side of the dialog box. This selection determines the chart's category.

The second selection, Choose a Chart Style, asks you to choose a style. A style is a saved set of all the attributes for your chart, excluding the chart type and the specific data that you enter for each chart. The basic style is the default, but you can also create new styles. Using a single style for all charts in a presentation gives it a cohesive look.

Note

To create a new chart style simply make changes to an individual chart's attributes, then select Chart, Chart Style, Create. In the dialog box that follows, save the style with a name, or make it the default style for future charts.

Finally, select one of the available buttons showing chart designs. These buttons change to show variations of the chart type you select. A preview feature shows you a sample of how the style and type of chart will look. After you choose a chart type and style, click OK.

The Edit Data dialog box opens (see fig. 5.3). You can type the contents of the chart—its text labels and numbers—directly into this dialog box, or you can import the contents from another file. After you enter the chart's data, Freelance takes care of the appearance of the chart, representing the data in the exact format of the chart type and style you selected.

▶ See "Importing
Data From a
Lotus 1-2-3 or
Microsoft Excel
File," p. 127

III

Adding Charts to Pages

Fig. 5.3
Enter data for your
chart in this
spreadsheet-like
form.

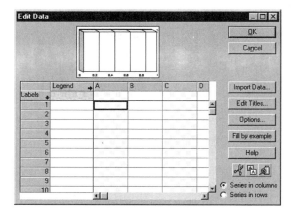

Choosing an Appropriate Chart Type

Choosing the best chart type for your particular needs may be the hardest part of creating a presentation with Freelance. The appropriate chart can enhance the meaning of a set of numbers, increasing the persuasiveness of your presentation. The wrong chart, or even the right chart designed poorly, can send the wrong message entirely.

The first step in creating crystal-clear charts, therefore, is to select a suitable chart for the job. To make the correct selection, you first must understand the job. Ask yourself what message you want to convey. Then try to match that message with the message delivered best by each different chart type.

The following sections may help you determine which chart type best matches the message you want to convey.

Bar

A *bar chart* compares numbers by using side-by-side bars. Bar charts are best used for comparisons of numbers at specific moments in time. Figure 5.4 shows a bar chart.

Stacked Bar

A *stacked bar chart* stacks bars on top of one another. This type of chart displays the grand total of each set of bars and the breakdowns of these totals. The colors or patterns of the stacked bars enable you to distinguish among them. Figure 5.5 shows a stacked bar chart.

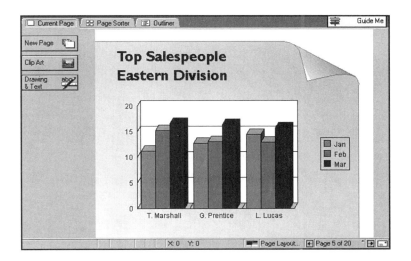

Fig. 5.4
A bar chart makes side-by-side comparisons easy.

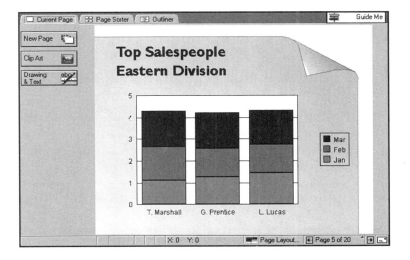

Fig. 5.5
You can stack the segments of your data in separate bars.

Horizontal Bar

A *horizontal bar chart* is just like a standard bar chart except that this chart type switches the positions of the horizontal and vertical axes, and all the bars run horizontally rather than vertically. A horizontal bar chart suggests progress toward a goal, accomplishment, or distance traveled. This chart also is useful if axis labels are unusually long.

Horizontal Stacked Bar

A *horizontal stacked bar chart* is similar to a stacked bar chart except that this chart type stacks its bars horizontally. This type of chart best demonstrates cumulative progress or movement across a distance. Figure 5.6 shows a horizontal stacked bar chart.

Fig. 5.6
Stacked bar charts can be either horizontal or vertical.

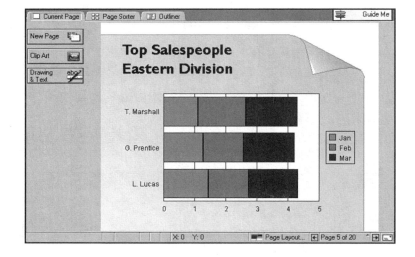

Line

A *line chart* represents a series of numbers by using a line that runs from data point to data point. Line charts emphasize continuous change or a trend over time rather than values at discrete intervals. A line chart is appropriate for census data, for example, to represent a continuously increasing population. Figure 5.7 shows a line chart.

Fig. 5.7
Note general trends, such as market share, with a line chart.

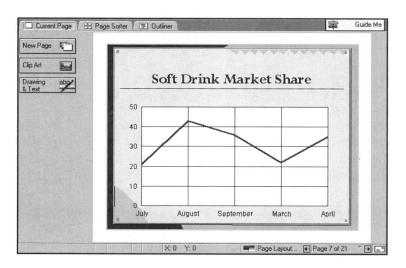

Single Pie

A *single pie chart* portrays the breakdown of a total. The size of each pie slice represents the percentage of each component. Use this type of chart only if you can add all the numbers in a data set to create a meaningful total. Figure 5.8 shows a single pie chart.

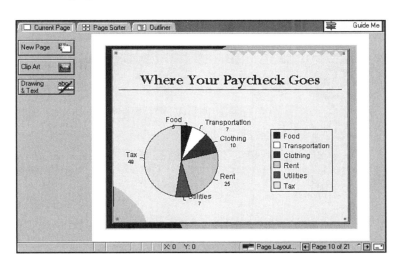

Fig. 5.8
Quickly see where most of your money goes using a pie chart.

Multiple Pies

A *multiple pies chart* draws more than one pie on a page so that you can compare two breakdowns or see how a breakdown changes over time. Figure 5.9 shows a multiple pies chart drawn with two pies. You can have up to four pies in a multiple pies chart.

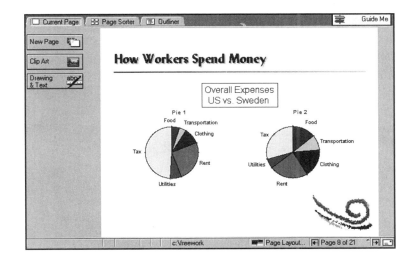

Fig. 5.9
Break down details of one pie with a second pie if you like.

Mixed

A *mixed chart* displays both bars and lines in the same chart (see fig. 5.10). You can show one or two sets of data in both bar and line format. Data sets A and B are shown as bars. Data sets C and D are shown as lines. Bar-line charts are useful for emphasizing certain data sets or depicting two different types of data in the same chart. You may show sales volume with bars, for example, and selling price with a line.

Fig. 5.10

Chart the price of materials and how often they're used in housing on the same mixed chart.

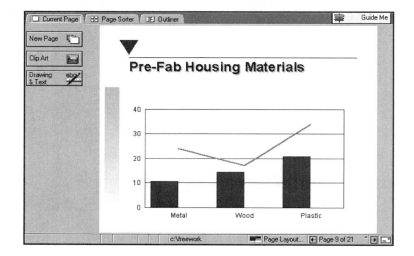

High-Low-Close-Open

A *high-low-close-open (HLCO) chart* is most often used to track the performance of stocks, but this type of chart also can be used for any measurement that fluctuates during intervals. Other data that are well-suited for this chart include daily high, low, and average temperatures or work production. Each vertical line portrays the extents of the values measured during the interval. A tick mark at the left side of the line shows the opening value. A tick mark at the right side shows the closing value. HLCO charts also can include a set of bars to represent the volume of transactions during the day. Figure 5.11 shows a high-low-close-open chart.

Area

An *area chart* displays a data set as a line with the area underneath filled in by a color or pattern. The data sets are stacked. Like a line chart, an area chart demonstrates change over time. The filled areas below the lines emphasize volume (such as sales volume). Figure 5.12 shows an area chart.

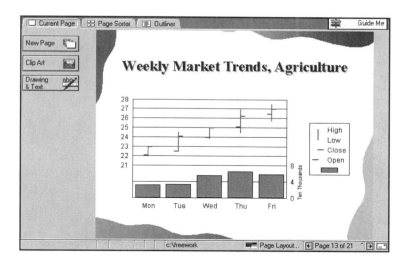

Fig. 5.11
Chart several sets of data with a high-low-close-open chart.

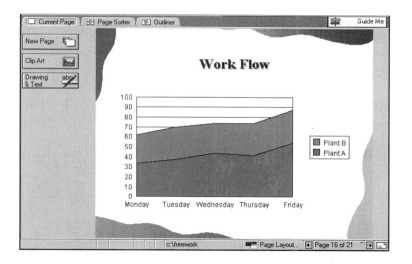

Fig. 5.12
An area chart compares workflow at two plants.

XY (Scatter)

An *XY (scatter) chart* displays the correlation between two data sets. Data values are plotted on the chart as points. Both the x-axis and y-axis are numeric. The more the points clump together in a line, the more closely are the two sets of data correlated. An XY (scatter) chart may show the correlation between home sales and mortgage interest rates, for example. Figure 5.13 shows an XY (scatter) chart.

III

Adding Charts to Pages

Fig. 5.13
Compare sets of
data with a scatter
chart.

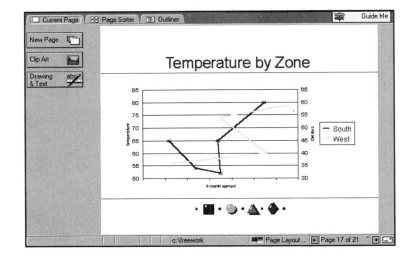

Radar

A *radar chart* depicts different measurements relating to a subject on different axes that radiate from a center point. A line connects the data set values on the axes. This type of chart is applicable if each number in a data set measures a different aspect of a subject. A single radar chart can display more than one data set. A single radar chart, for example, can show the following measurements for several health clubs (with each measurement on a different axis extending from the center): number of visitors, number of instructors, number of hours open each day, and average weight lifted by all muscle builders. Figure 5.14 shows a radar chart.

Fig. 5.14
Get a picture of
several types of
data on one chart
with a radar chart.

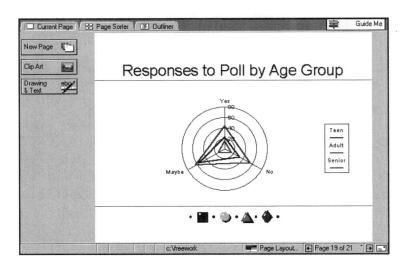

Number Grid

A *number grid chart* is basically a number table. This type of chart is useful if you want to show actual numbers rather than a graphic representation of the numbers. A number grid chart is applicable if the message is clear from the numbers alone; interpreting the numbers with data is not necessary.

Troubleshooting

How do I know when to use a table and when to use a number grid chart?

Tables offer you more formatting flexibility than the number grid chart. With a table, you have the option of changing such things as text alignment within cells, adding bullets to data, and adjusting the column and row sizing and spacing. A number grid chart won't allow you to format individual cells, although you can use a title and note feature to add explanatory text for the overall message of the chart.

3D Bar

A *3D bar chart* is essentially the same as a bar chart, but the bars are shown with depth for visual interest.

3D Stacked Bar

A *3D stacked bar chart* serves the same purpose as a stacked bar chart, but the bars are shown with depth. Figure 5.15 shows a 3D stacked bar chart.

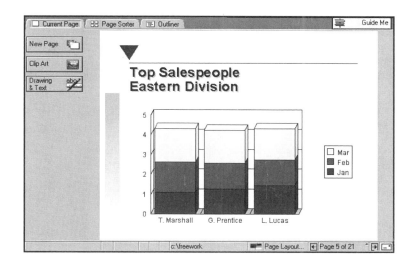

Fig. 5.15
The 3D effect can make your page more visually appealing.

III

Adding Charts to Pages

3D Bar (XYZ)

A *3D bar (XYZ) chart* serves the same purpose as a bar chart, but the three-dimensional bars are arranged behind one another rather than next to one another. The depth of the chart makes interpreting individual values difficult, however. This type of chart is most useful for depicting trends.

3D Pie

A *3D pie chart* is the same as a pie chart, but its slices have thickness for visual interest. Figure 5.16 shows a 3D pie chart.

Fig. 5.16
Looking more like a true pie, the 3D pie chart adds depth to the slices.

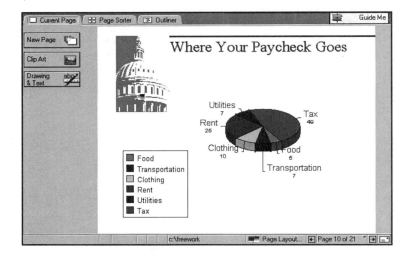

3D Area/Line

A *3D area/line chart* displays data as 3D areas or 3D lines. You can determine whether individual data sets are displayed as areas or lines. This type of chart serves the same purpose as area and line charts, but with more visual interest. Figure 5.17 shows a 3D area/line chart.

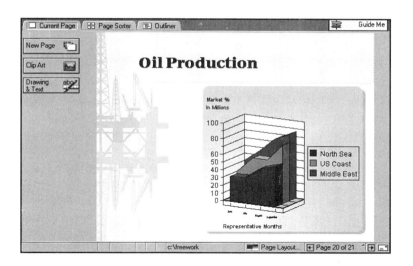

Fig. 5.17
Compare sets of
data in 3D areas
with a 3D area
chart.

Entering the Data

After you select a chart type and style, the Edit Data dialog box opens within
the Freelance window. The appearance of the Edit Data dialog box, which
provides space for you to type the chart's data and text labels, depends on the
chart type you select. Figure 5.18 shows the Edit Data dialog box for a bar
chart.

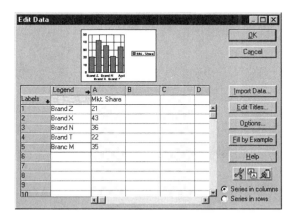

Fig. 5.18
Type in data in a
spreadsheet-like
interface and
preview your chart
here.

III

Adding Charts to Pages

In the upper part of the window, a preview displays a sample of the chart
type you selected. Other buttons along the right edge of this dialog box enable you to create titles, import numbers, and fill in number trends by example. You learn about creating titles in the section "Supplying Titles" later

▶ See "Importing
Data from a
Lotus 1-2-3 or
Microsoft Excel
File," p. 127

in this chapter, and you learn about previewing charts in the section "Editing Data." The rest of this dialog box is occupied by the grid into which you enter the data for the chart; three SmartIcons used to cut, copy, and paste your data; and two radio buttons for displaying series in either columns or rows.

The grid, arranged in lettered columns and numbered rows of cells looks much like a spreadsheet grid. Its function is to hold, but not calculate, data. Each lettered column holds one data set—a related sequence of numbers, such as the month-by-month sales total for a particular product. The far-left column is reserved for entering the labels that appear along an axis of the chart (usually the x-axis). The first row is reserved for the descriptive labels to appear in the chart's legend. If the column is to hold the sales figures for different products, for example, you enter the label Product Sales at the top of the column.

To enter the contents of a chart, you move the highlight from cell to cell and enter labels and data for the chart into the highlighted cells. To move the highlight, click the destination cell for the highlight or use the arrow keys to move cell by cell. You also can press the Tab key to move the highlight to the right. To move your view of the grid one window's length in any direction, use the scrollbars, or hold down the Ctrl key while you press an arrow key. To move the highlight to the bottom of the window, use the scrollbar on the right, or press the Page Down key. Press Home to return the highlight to cell A1.

Pressing the End key and then an arrow key moves the highlight to the last cell in a group filled with data, in the direction of the arrow key you press. Pressing End and the down-arrow key, for example, moves the highlight to the last cell in the column that is filled with data. If there is no more data in the row or column, pressing End and then an arrow key moves the highlight to the end of the row or bottom of the column. Press Home to return to the top-left corner of the data area.

Tip

To see more data at one time, you can resize the Edit Data dialog box by clicking the Maximize button in the top-right corner.

Entering the Data for a Line, Bar, or Area Chart

After you select any line, bar, or area chart type and style, the Edit Data dialog box displays as many columns as can fit in the current window size. The total number of columns is 26, labeled A through Z, and the total number of rows is 4,000—so you can enter 4,000 values in each of 26 data sets. You actually use only a tiny portion of those available cells, however, because you are likely to have only a small amount of data to chart.

Tip

Don't try to include too much data—especially too many data sets. It can make a chart cluttered and incomprehensible, not to mention difficult for an audience to read.

The Axis Labels column is blank but ready to hold the labels that are to appear along the x-axis of the chart. These labels often mark the passage of time, listing successive days, weeks, months, or years, but you can type any text into the Axis Labels column. To chart the popularity of three television game shows, for example, you can enter their names in the Axis Labels column. Make sure that you keep the axis labels as short as you can so that the labels fit easily along the axis.

Tip

Freelance provides a method called Fill by Example to enter a series of successive numbers automatically. You learn about this method in the section "Entering Axis Labels Automatically," later in this chapter.

The best approach to entering data into the Edit Data dialog box is to provide the axis labels and legend entries first, setting up the structure of the data, and then to enter the columns of numbers in the data area.

To type an entry, move the highlight to the cell for the entry and begin typing the text. Use the Backspace key to delete errors. After you finish typing, follow any of these actions:

- Press Enter, which moves your cursor to the next cell.
- Press an arrow key or tab to move the highlight to the next cell.
- Click a different cell.

Figure 5.19 shows a completed set of data in the Edit Data dialog box. The data plots the sales of three salespeople over six months. Figure 5.20 shows the resulting chart.

III

Adding Charts to Pages

Fig. 5.19
Complete data for
three salespeople
over three months
is shown in this
chart.

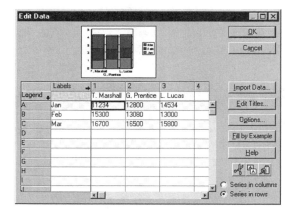

Fig. 5.20
This chart shows
the results from
the data in the
previous figure.

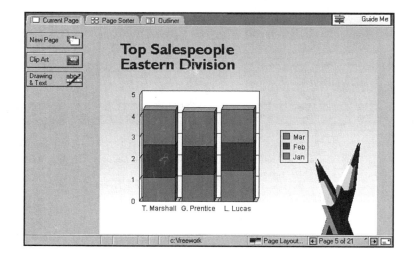

Tip

An easily understood bar, area, or line chart should include no more than six data
sets.

Editing, Copying, and Moving the Data

To edit a text label or number, move the highlight to the cell containing the
label or number and then type a new label or number into that cell. The new
entry replaces the current entry. You also can move the highlight to a cell
and press F2 (Edit). This deletes any contents and places your cursor at the
left edge of the cell, ready to enter text.

To move a data set to a different column, click the column letter button at the top of that data set's column to highlight the entire column. Click the Cut SmartIcon on the right side of the dialog box. Click the column letter button at the destination column, and then use the Paste SmartIcon to paste the column of data. To move only some of the numbers in the column, highlight those numbers by dragging across them with the mouse pointer. (You also can use the arrow keys to move the highlight to the first number, hold down the Shift key, and then move the highlight to the last number.) Then click the Cut SmartIcon, move the highlight to the destination for the first of the numbers, and click the Paste SmartIcon.

Moving data sets enables you to rearrange the order of lines, bars, or areas in a chart. To copy a data set, highlight the set and click the Copy SmartIcon.

> **Note**
>
> To give the chart additional meaning, you can order the bars or areas from largest to smallest or from smallest to largest by organizing the data cells accordingly. Figures 5.21 and 5.22 show two charts, one before and one after ordering the data.

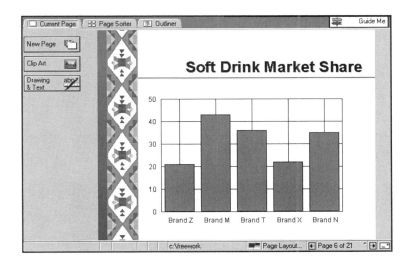

Fig. 5.21
Before ordering the data in a chart the bars look haphazard.

If you make a change to the data in the Edit Data dialog box but then decide to revert to the original data, choose Edit, Undo Setting Change, or press Ctrl+Z. The Undo Setting Change command, however, remembers only the *last* change you made to the data.

III

Adding Charts to Pages

Fig. 5.22
Organizing data makes a more attractive and meaningful chart.

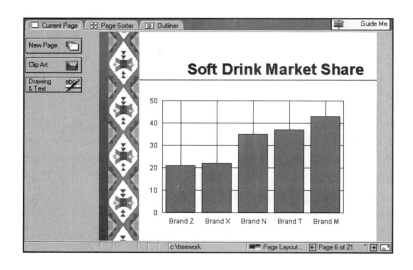

Entering the Data for Different Chart Types

Each type of chart has slight variations in how you enter text so that the chart reflects your data correctly. Particularly with charts that show multiple data sets, understanding how the columns and rows of the Edit data dialog box relate to the chart itself is vital.

Entering Data for a Pie Chart

If you select Single Pie as your chart type, the Edit Data dialog box holds only one data set column, labeled A. This data set holds the values represented by the various pie slices. Figure 5.23 shows the Edit Data dialog box for a single pie chart.

Fig. 5.23
Only two columns of data need be filled in to create a single pie chart.

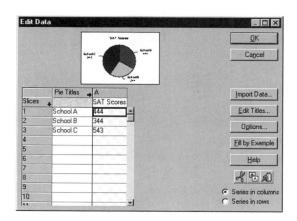

You enter slice labels, which identify the pie slices, in the Pie Titles column of the chart. If you want a title for the chart, you can enter a Pie Title for the pie chart in the first space of the A column. The row number buttons to the left portray each pie slice and show the colors of these slices.

You enter the actual numbers that each slice represents in the A column. Do not enter percentages. Freelance calculates percentages from the data you enter and displays the slices sized accordingly.

Figure 5.24 shows the single pie chart that results from the data displayed in figure 5.23.

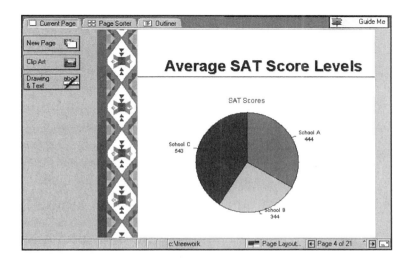

Fig. 5.24
A simple pie chart shows relative information for three schools.

Note

Use six or fewer slices in a pie chart. More than six slices can make a pie chart hard to interpret. If you have more than six components in a total, give the five largest components their own slices and add the remaining components together to represent the total of these components as a sixth slice labeled All Others. You can show the breakdown of the All Others slice in a second pie if necessary.

If you need to compare two or more breakdowns or depict how a breakdown changes over time, you can create more than one pie on a page by selecting Multiple Pies as the chart type. Freelance then provides enough columns to enter up to four data sets in the Edit Data dialog box—one data set for each pie. Instead of labeling each slice in each pie, Freelance creates a legend that identifies the slices in all four charts. Figure 5.25 shows the Edit Data dialog box for two pies. Figure 5.26 shows the resulting pies and the legend that applies to all pies.

Fig. 5.25

You can enter data for up to four pie charts if you choose a multiple chart type.

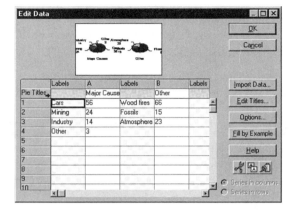

Fig. 5.26

Two to four pies can display at once.

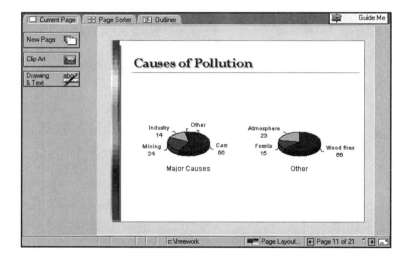

Sometimes multiple pies have the same elements, and sometimes, as in the pie in figure 5.26, the information represented by the slices is different. Instead of showing a single legend for both pies, you can show individual labels for the slices instead. You must change the options setting for the current pie chart.

To change the options setting, follow these steps:

1. Make sure that the chart is selected, then click the Open InfoBox SmartIcon.

2. From the Properties For drop-down list, choose Pie. The resulting dialog box is shown in figure 5.27.

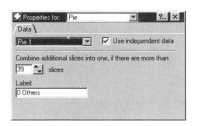

Fig. 5.27
Choose to use different data for each pie in the InfoBox.

3. Click the Use Independent Data check box.
4. Click OK.

> **Tip**
>
> You can also get to the Pie Properties InfoBox by choosing Chart, Pie.

If you are displaying a legend, you see that the legend disappears, and the slice labels in Pie 2, 3, and 4 become generic (Slice 1, Slice 2, and so on). To supply slice labels for the other pies, return to the Edit Data dialog box. After you select Use Independent Data in the Pie dialog box, the Edit Data dialog box displays a Labels column to the left of each Pie data column.

> **Tip**
>
> Giving more than two pies their own labels can make your screen very cluttered and difficult to read. Consider creating two separate pages for this data if this is the case.

Entering the Data for a High-Low-Close-Open Chart

High-low-close-open (HLCO) charts track the performance of stocks and other financial instruments that have high, low, closing, and opening prices during set periods. HLCO charts also can be used to track other measurements that have minimums and maximums during successive time intervals, such as barometric pressure, temperature, or even the mood swings of a boss.

After you select an HLCO chart type and a chart style from the Create Chart dialog box, the Edit Data dialog box opens. The first four data columns already have legend entries (High, Low, Close, and Open). The fifth column is not labeled, but if you type numbers into this column (to represent stock volume, for example), these numbers appear as bars in the resulting chart. The sixth series of numbers entered in the window is plotted as a line in the chart. (You may want to use this line to plot the average selling price, for example.)

Figure 5.28 shows a typical collection of data for an HLCO chart. Notice that the Axis Labels indicate the time intervals during which activity is depicted by the vertical lines. Notice also that the stock prices must be entered in decimal form. The number 24 $\frac{7}{8}$, for example, must be entered as **24.875**, because the Edit Data dialog box does not accept fractions. The day-to-day volume figures for the stock have been entered in Column E. Figure 5.29 shows the chart that results from the data shown in figure 5.28.

Fig. 5.28
Several columns of data must be completed for a HLCO Chart.

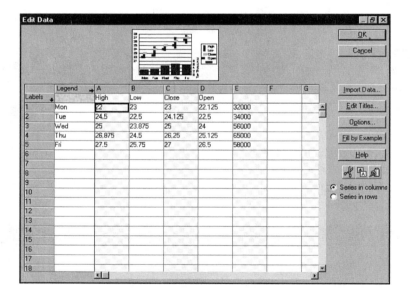

Entering the Data for a Radar Chart

Each row of data in the Edit Data dialog box for a radar chart is another axis that extends from the center of the chart. You enter Axis Titles in the far left cell of each row.

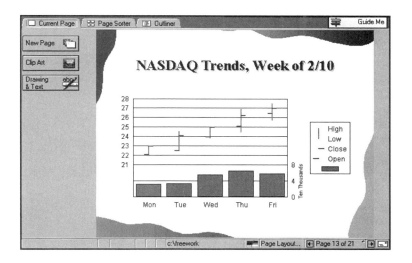

Fig. 5.29
Follow trends
using the HLCO
chart.

Each column of numbers is represented by a line that extends from axis to axis in a rough circle around the center. Each column letter button at the top of the window displays the color and line type of that line.

Figure 5.30 shows a sample set of data entered in the Edit Data dialog box for a radar chart. Figure 5.31 shows the chart that results from the data shown in figure 5.30.

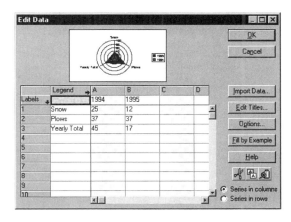

Fig. 5.30
Preview the radar
chart within the
Edit Data dialog
box.

Fig. 5.31
Compare trends
by comparing axis
in a radar chart.

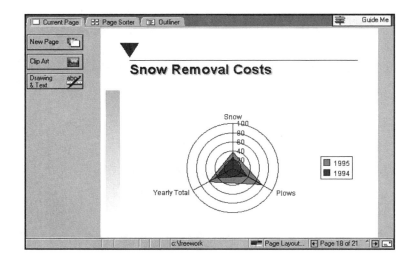

Editing Data

After you finish entering the data for any chart in the Edit Data dialog box,
you can view the chart that Freelance draws in the preview shown at the top
of the dialog box. You can inspect the chart for any irregularities. If you have
inadvertently entered too many zeros for one number, for example, the error
should be obvious as you preview the chart.

Tip

If it's hard to make out the preview, maximize the dialog box window by clicking the
middle icon in the top-right corner of the title bar for the dialog box.

If the preview seems fine, you can leave the Edit Data dialog box by clicking
OK. You can always return to the chart's data to make changes by following
any of these methods:

- Select the chart. Click the Show/Edit Chart Data SmartIcon.
- Click the chart with the right mouse button and then choose Edit Data
  from the pop-up commands menu.
- Select the chart and then choose Chart, Edit Data.

Supplying Titles

After you enter the content of the chart, you may want to add text for the chart's titles. You can specify up to three lines of text (headings) for the top of the chart, three lines of small text notes at the bottom, and axis titles. Figure 5.32 identifies these titles on a sample chart.

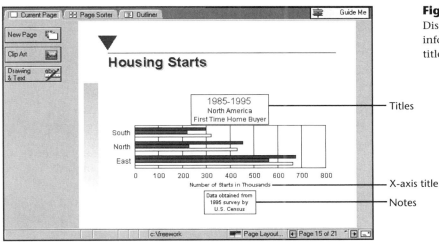

Fig. 5.32
Display additional information using titles and notes.

To enter the titles for a chart, open the chart's Edit Data dialog box and click the Edit Titles button. Text boxes appear in which you can enter the text for each title. Press the Tab key to move from one entry to the next; press Shift+Tab to move back to the preceding entry. Figure 5.33 shows the completed Edit Data dialog box for the chart shown in figure 5.32.

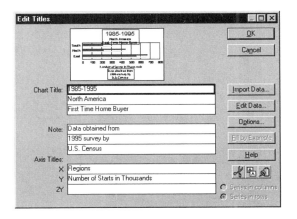

Fig. 5.33
Enter all your title information in one place from the Edit Titles dialog box.

III

Adding Charts to Pages

To return to the view of the Edit Data dialog box that shows the data for the chart, click the Edit Data button.

To add titles to a completed chart or to edit the existing titles, you must select Chart, Edit Data to access the Edit Data dialog box. Then, click the Edit Titles button. Another way to edit the titles of a chart is to select Titles, Notes or either axis in the Properties For drop-down list in the Chart Properties InfoBox. Once the appropriate InfoBox appears, click the Titles tab to enter title information, or to select whether you wish to show the titles or not.

The titles you enter appear on the chart in preset fonts and colors. You can edit both the content and appearance of the titles just as you can any other text in a presentation.

Entering Axis Labels Automatically

 If a chart requires a sequence of dates or numbers along the x-axis or in the legend, you can take advantage of Freelance's Fill by Example command, which automatically enters the completion of a series of numbers in a column or row of the Edit Data dialog box. To use Fill by Example, you must open the Edit Data dialog box by clicking the Show/Edit Chart Data SmartIcon and then follow these steps:

1. Move the highlight to the cell in the Labels column or the Legend row where you want the sequence of numbers to begin.

2. Drag across the numbers in sequence that have already been entered, then across the remaining cells you'd like to fill based on that example. For example, if you entered 10, 15, 20, and 25, you could use Fill by Example to enter the next three cells, 30, 35, and 40.

3. Click the Fill by Example button.

▶ See "Formatting Axis Titles and Labels," p. 109

The rest of the series is filled in. This works for any logical sequence of numbers, whether whole or fractions or numbers, as well as dates.

Changing the Chart Type

After you create a chart, you may decide that another chart type better represents the data. You can easily switch chart types even after you complete a chart. As usual, Freelance offers several ways to do this.

 First, you can select the chart, and click the Set Chart Type SmartIcon. The Chart Properties InfoBox opens, and the Chart Type tab is displayed on top.

You can get to this same InfoBox by clicking the Open InfoBox SmartIcon. Using this method, you may have to click the Chart Type tab to bring it forward. ❖

Note

To supply two perspectives in the presentation of a set of data, you may want to duplicate the page containing a chart in Page Sorter view and then change the chart type on one of the pages. One page can show the data as a bar chart, for example, to emphasize comparisons at discrete intervals. Another page can show the same data as a line chart to emphasize how the data changes over time.

◀ See "Duplicating a Page," p. 67

III

Adding Charts to Pages

CHAPTER 6
Formatting a Data Chart

by Nancy Stevenson

Using the default chart formatting settings in Freelance, you can create attractive, professionally designed data charts. With Freelance, however, you can also easily change the formatting of any chart to fit a particular presentation need or to correspond with your own aesthetic sense.

In this chapter, you learn to

- Change chart styles and color sets
- Format axes, including titles and labels
- Set a chart frame
- Change chart grids and backgrounds
- Format headings and notes
- Set formatting as the default for the presentation
- Ungroup a chart to work with pieces of a data chart as drawing objects

Formatting Bar, Line, Area, and XY Charts

Bar, line, area, and XY charts share most features, so the steps to follow in formatting them are very similar. As with all charts and most objects in Freelance, you select the portion of the chart to format, and you then double-click it, bringing up a Properties InfoBox with settings tailored for that chart portion.

You can double-click the labels along the y-axis of a bar chart, for example, to open a Properties InfoBox. This InfoBox displays properties for the selected chart with pages that format various elements.

Making Changes to the Entire Chart

You can make changes to some global chart settings, for example, by applying new SmartMaster color sets to the chart, changing the spacing between the pieces, adding a border, or manipulating the way the chart is used when you run a presentation. Do this by double-clicking a background area of a chart (a spot where no single element of the chart appears). The Chart Properties InfoBox offers several pages for the above settings. You can even quickly change the type of chart you're using (see fig. 6.1).

Fig. 6.1
Select a new chart style or modify the overall chart properties here.

Changing the Color of a Data Set

The colors of the bars, lines, or areas in a chart are set by the presentation's color palette to fit well with the design of the presentation background, but you can override these settings.

To change the color of a data set (one set of bars, one line, or one area), click any bar in the data set or click the line or area. Handles appear around the chart; a second set of handles appears along or within the selected bar, line, or area for that entire data set. Double-click at the same spot. A Properties InfoBox opens. Click the Color tab to see the page shown in figure 6.2. This InfoBox is the same one that appears when you select the bar, and click the Open InfoBox SmartIcon in the toolbox.

Fig. 6.2
A Series Properties InfoBox has several pages to choose from.

You can change the fill color (the color of the interior of the chart element). You can add a pattern and make the pattern—say a vertical stripe—a different color. In the bottom half of this dialog box you can use the drop-down Width and Style lists and the Color palette to make changes to the line surrounding the fill color, making the line a different color, width, or style. After you make changes to these settings, you can move the InfoBox to one side to preview the changes on-screen. You can make more changes, or click the Close button to accept the changes you already made.

Tip
If you are using a black-and-white palette, it has shades of gray rather than colors.

Changing the 3D Effect of a Bar Chart

When you choose a 3D bar chart from the chart gallery as you begin a data chart, Freelance automatically turns on a 3D effect for the bars. You can change to a 3D effect in any bar chart, whether it's 3D initially or not. Click the Open InfoBox SmartIcon. Select the Type tab, then click one of the sample charts that show a 3D effect. When you turn on 3D effects, then select Plot in the Properties for list, a 3D tab becomes available (see fig. 6.3).

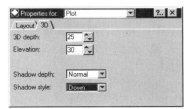

Fig. 6.3
You can adjust the way you view a 3D chart in the 3D page by adjusting the plot properties.

To change the depth and angle of the 3D effect, use the Rotation and Elevation boxes. Increasing these settings increases the depth of the effect. The Rotation setting, for example, enables you to change the angle at which the 3D effect extends from the bar. Zero degrees is equivalent to the 3 o'clock position; 135 degrees extends the 3D effect diagonally to the left, so its starting point moves up and to the left by 35 degrees, as shown in figure 6.4.

In a 3D view, you can choose to have a platform of varying heights appear under the data elements, as shown at the base of the chart in figure 6.4. You can also shift the lighting effect so the lighter side of the 3D object is either on the right or left, as though light were shining on it from that direction. Use the Platform and Lighting drop-down lists to control these effects. If you have a 3D pie chart, the choices here are no longer Platform and Lighting, but Shadow.

Fig. 6.4
Rotating a 3D bar chart shifts the angle of the chart.

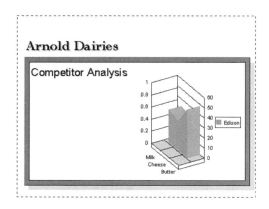

Hiding Data Sets

Occasionally, you might need to hide one or more data sets in a chart—and not necessarily because a data set displays poor results. For example, you might have 12 groups of data in the Chart Data & Titles dialog box of a chart but you wisely plan to compare only three or four data sets in each chart to prevent clutter.

To hide a data set, click one element of the set (for example, one of a series of bars in a bar chart), then click the Open InfoBox SmartIcon to open the Properties InfoBox for the chart. Make sure the correct data set is selected from the Properties for list (for example, the y-axis properties or x-axis properties) and then deselect the Show Series check box. Freelance will not display the data set in the chart or in the legend.

Setting Up a Second Y-Axis

When you create a vertical or horizontal bar chart, you can plot certain data sets against a second y-axis. The second y-axis, which appears on the opposite side of the chart from the first y-axis, can have different formatting and different scaling.

Using a second y-axis is helpful when you want to compare two data sets that have different units of measure or vastly different high and low ranges. You can plot the rising and falling value of two foreign currencies in one chart by setting up a second y-axis, for example. Against the first y-axis, you plot the rising and falling value of the U.S. dollar. The first y-axis is formatted in dollars. Against the second y-axis, you plot the value of the Japanese yen. The second y-axis is formatted in yen. Figure 6.5 illustrates this example.

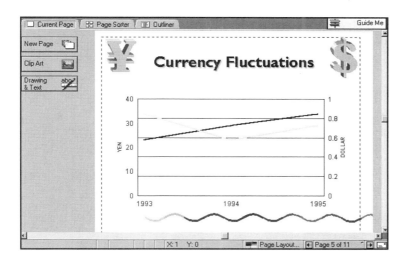

Fig. 6.5
Plot two different
trends using a
second y-axis.

To add a second y-axis to a chart, select the chart and choose Chart, Axes & Grids, 2nd Y Axis & Grids. Click the Show Scale Labels Every X Ticks check box, and adjust the number of ticks as you want. You can change the selection in the Properties For box to show the Properties InfoBox for either the y-axis or the second y-axis, select the Format tab, then change the format type of the data to currency, then the current format to Japanese yen or U.S. dollars. Figure 6.6 shows a portion of the available list of currencies.

Fig. 6.6
Determine the
format of numbers
in your chart in
the axis InfoBox,
including a world
of currency
choices.

When you change the format of the axis labels, you can choose whether to format the x-axis labels, the y-axis labels, or the second y-axis labels. In addition, you can set different scales for the y-axis and the second y-axis. You learn about scaling axes and formatting axis labels in the next section.

III

Adding Charts to Pages

Formatting the Axes

With all charts that have axes (pie charts are a notable exception), you can change the appearance of the axes by selecting the chart, and clicking the Open InfoBox SmartIcon. In the Properties For drop-down list, which is at the top of every InfoBox, select the axis you want to format. That Properties InfoBox appears. Then choose the Scale tab to open the Scale page (see fig. 6.7).

Fig. 6.7
The Scale tab allows you to set measurements for tick marks on an axis.

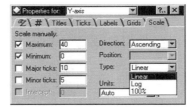

To use this InfoBox, use the controls on the left to change the formatting of the axis.

Minimum and Maximum change the minimum and maximum values at the beginning and end of the axis. Major Ticks and Minor Ticks set the intervals along the axis at which tick marks appear. *Tick marks* are small lines, like the marks on a ruler, that register intervals along the axis. Axis labels appear at major ticks. Minor ticks are evenly spaced between major ticks. Figure 6.8 shows one group of settings for Minimum, Maximum, Major Ticks, and Minor Ticks.

Tip

Always set the Minimum of a bar chart to 0 because you cannot gauge the relative heights of bars unless you can see their entire lengths. A bar chart with the Minimum set to anything other than 0 is inaccurate and deceptive.

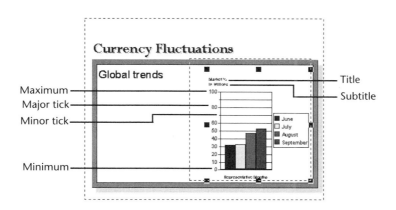

Fig. 6.8
This chart
illustrates the
settings in the
Scale page shown
in figure 6.7.

To use a logarithmic rather than linear scale, open the Type drop-down list on the Scale tab. Each successive value along the selected axis will be ten times the previous value. Use logarithmic axis scaling only if the variation in the data is very large. When you choose logarithmic axis scaling, you can choose the position of the logarithmic grid lines by using the Position drop-down list.

If you are using only one y-axis, you can use the Position drop-down list to determine whether the axis should appear along the left or right side of the chart, or both.

Formatting Axis Titles and Labels

If you entered axis titles at the same time you entered the data for the chart, you can make some minor changes to the appearance of the titles. (If you have not entered axis titles, you can do so by selecting the chart and choosing Chart, Edit Data.)

Freelance offers two methods for changing the appearance of a title or the labels that appear along an axis. You can double-click the title or the labels themselves, or you can click the Open InfoBox SmartIcon and use the Properties For drop-down list to select either axis, then click the Title tab.

Changing the Appearance of Axis Titles

The Titles tab of the Properties InfoBox is shown in figure 6.9.

Note
Select the Show Title check box to turn off the display of the selected axis title. Turning off titles when the descriptions of the axes are obvious leaves more space for the graphic part of the chart.

Fig. 6.9
You can have both a title and subtitle for your chart, and place it in various locations on your page.

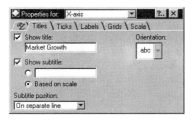

To add or edit existing title text, click in the Show Title text box and type a title.

To place a second text line underneath the Axis Scale Settings title, select the Show Subtitle check box. Type a subtitle in the box and choose a position for it from the Subtitle Position drop-down list.

> **Tip**
>
> If you want the subtitle to simply reflect the measurement labels, click Based On Scale. That way, if the labels of your access read, say, 1,000, 2,000, 3,000, and so on, the subtitle will automatically read "Thousands."

To change the appearance of title text, click the Text tab (see fig. 6.10). Here is where you control the Font Name setting. You can choose from among the available typefaces installed in your copy of Windows. With the Size setting, you can choose from among preset type sizes, or use the adjustment arrows to create a custom size. You can also adjust the style and color of text here.

Fig. 6.10
You can modify the font, size, style, and color of the text that appears on chart axes from the Text tab.

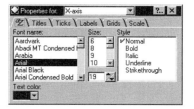

Formatting Axis Labels

To work with axis labels, click the Labels tab, shown in figure 6.11.

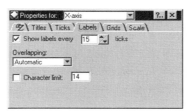

Fig. 6.11
You can determine at what intervals to show labels, and how any overlapping labels should be treated on the Labels tab.

Select the Show Labels Every check box to display labels, and use the up and down arrows to adjust how frequently the labels will show, based on the number of grid *ticks*. Deselect the Show Labels Every check box to turn off the display of axis labels in the chart. Use this control when you want to convey the general growth or decline of data shown by a set of bars or lines without attempting to depict the actual values.

You can set a character limit for the labels, and determine how overlapping labels should be treated using the Overlapping drop-down list. This option is available only when you format x-axis labels. The setting enables you to change the appearance of the x-axis labels when they are crowded along the axis. Slant sets the labels at an angle along the axis. Stagger alternates labels on two rows under the axis. Vertical displays the labels side by side with a vertical orientation.

To change the way label numbers appear, select the y-axis in the Properties For list, then click the Format Number tab, shown in figure 6.12. Notice that the x-axis in figure 6.11 doesn't offer the number format tab. The y-axis, which typically contains number series as shown in figure 6.12, does offer this. This is where you choose a format, such as date, time, currency, general, and so on, and determine the number of decimal places to which numbers display. You can choose any number from 0 to 5 decimal places.

Fig. 6.12
Whether you need Swedish Krona or numbers with a comma, like 2,000, the format is available on the number format tab.

III

Adding Charts to Pages

The Format Number settings, available only when you select a y-axis to format, determines the format used to display the numbers. Some of the common settings are:

- *General.* Displays the numbers with as many decimal places as entered. No separator appears between the thousands and hundreds digits.

- *Fixed.* Displays the numbers with the chosen number of decimal places.

- *Scientific.* Displays the numbers in scientific notation. Scientific notation is always used when the number is greater than or equal to 1×10^{11} or smaller than 1×10^{-4}.

- *Currency.* Displays a currency sign before the numbers and a separator between thousands and hundreds. The currency sign used depends on the Current Format chosen.

- *Comma.* Places a comma between the thousands and hundreds digits in the numbers and encloses negative numbers in parentheses.

- *Percent.* Shows the numbers as percentages with percent signs. The number entered is multiplied by 100. For example, 0.12 becomes 12%.

- *Date.* Offers a variety of date formats, such as 02/10/94 or February 10, 1994.

Figure 6.13 shows a data chart with staggered x-axis labels and y-axis labels displayed with General formatting. Figure 6.14 shows a chart with slanted x-axis labels and with y-axis labels displayed as Currency.

Fig. 6.13
Here the labels appear staggered.

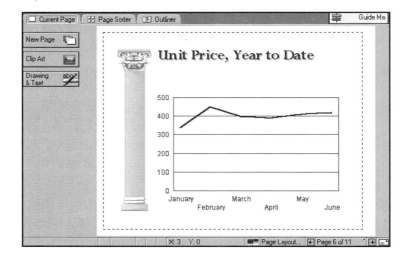

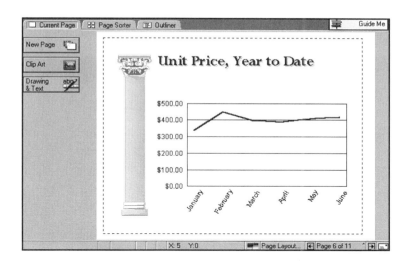

Fig. 6.14
To fit longer chart labels, try using a slanted format.

Changing the Chart Frame

The plot for a chart is the area defined by the axes, as shown in figure 6.15. This is where the data you enter is plotted. You can make changes to the frame, or the four outside lines that surround the plot area, as well as changing the color or pattern that fill the plot area itself for all chart types except number grid.

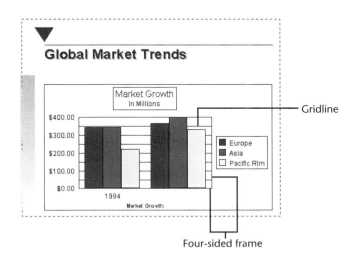

Fig. 6.15
A full frame defines the edges of the plotted data area.

III

Adding Charts to Pages

Click anywhere around the outer edge of the chart to select it (a box will appear around it, as shown in fig. 6.15), then double-click to open the Chart Properties InfoBox (or click the Open InfoBox SmartIcon). In the Properties For list, select Plot. There are three tabs available here (see fig. 6.16). You can select the color, width, and style of the line from the Format tab in this dialog box. To change the plot position and size, click the Options tab.

Fig. 6.16
The Plot InfoBox offers choices for modifying the plot frame.

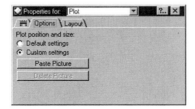

Changing the Chart Grid

Gridlines are the horizontal and vertical lines that run across and down the background of a data chart (refer to fig. 6.15). Gridlines help visually align bars, lines, and areas with the x- and y-axes. To change the appearance of the grid lines and tick marks along the axes, you must adjust the grid setting for the x-, y-, and second y-axis (if any) separately. The x-axis offers only a check box to show or not show major gridlines. These lines run up and down on the chart, and are used less frequently. You can set the y-axis and second y-axis for major and minor grid lines running across the chart from left to right. To set the y-axis grid, select the chart, then choose Chart, Axes & Grids. Select the y-axis from the side menu. The Y-axis Properties InfoBox appears; click the Grids tab (see fig. 6.17).

Fig. 6.17
Gridlines on a chart help the reader see information more clearly. Set them in the Axes InfoBoxes.

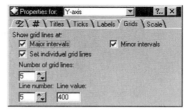

The Major Intervals and Minor Intervals options refer to the gridlines that appear at the intervals you specified when you set the scale of the axis. Major ticks have axis labels beside them. Major grid lines extend from the ticks to the other side of the chart. Minor grid lines and ticks appear evenly spaced between major grid lines and ticks.

You can choose whether to display the grid for the y-axis by selecting the Major Intervals or Minor Intervals check box. If you want to set grid lines individually, set the Number of Grid Lines, Line Number, and Line Value options. Figure 6.18 shows a chart with both x- and y-axis gridlines, with both major and minor gridlines for the y-axis.

> **Tip**
>
> If you want tick marks to extend beyond the chart frame at gridline intervals, use the Ticks tab and check Show Tick Marks at Major Intervals.

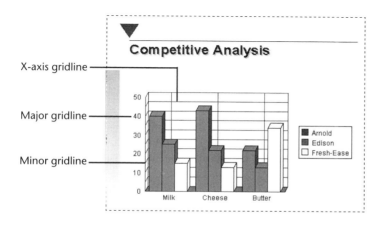

Fig. 6.18
Both horizontal and vertical gridlines provide reference points for reading chart data.

Changing the Chart Border and Background

By default, the background of a chart—a rectangle on which the chart sits—usually does not display. But you can use the background to visually frame the chart, or to set it off from other elements on the page (see fig. 6.19).

To display the background or place a border around it, select the chart and click the Open InfoBox SmartIcon to open the Chart InfoBox. Open the Border & Fill tab (see fig. 6.20). You can place a border line around the background by using the Style, Width, and Color drop-down lists in the Border section. By selecting the Shadow check box, you can also display a subtle shadow behind the background to give it a raised appearance. Making a selection from the Rounding drop-down list gently rounds the corner of the rectangle for a nice design effect. To fill the background rectangle with a color, use the drop-down lists in the Fill section. You must have a Pattern selected if you're going to use a fill color. For a solid color, simply choose the solid black pattern. There are also several gradient styles, like the one used in figure 6.19, that give a shaded effect, from darker to lighter.

Fig. 6.19
This chart has a gradient background, rounded corners, and a shadow.

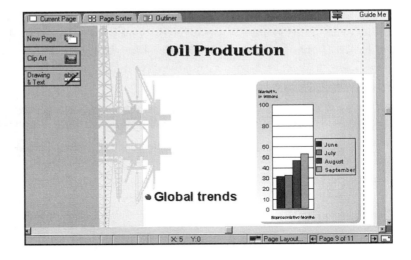

Fig. 6.20
Add a border and fill the background with a pattern from this tab.

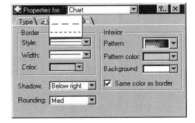

Creating and Formatting the Legend

Most charts you create display a legend automatically. The legend helps you distinguish among the data sets in the chart. Choose Chart, Legend to open the Legend Properties InfoBox (see fig. 6.21). You can show the legend outside or inside the plot area.

Fig. 6.21
Use the Position buttons to place the legend where you want it on your page.

If you choose Show Legend (the default setting), use the font settings on the Font tab to change the appearance of the text in the legend. You can use the Lines & Colors tab to change the appearance of the box surrounding the legend.

With the position radio buttons displayed around the preview on this tab, you can determine the position for the legend on the chart. Choose Left, Right, Top, or Bottom, and choose whether the legend will be Inside or Outside the chart.

If you want to use a number grid instead of a legend, deselect the Show Legend check box. Then close the Legend Properties InfoBox, select the chart and choose Chart, Table. A Table InfoBox appears. Click Show Data Table. When you close this InfoBox, Freelance places a number grid under the chart to display the numbers represented by bars, lines, or areas, and to identify the data sets as a legend does. Figure 6.22 shows a chart with a standard legend. Figure 6.23 shows the same chart with a number grid table.

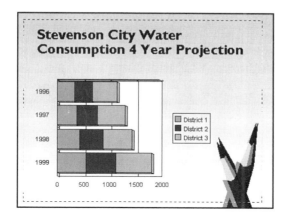

Fig. 6.22
The legend is next to the chart in the position you selected.

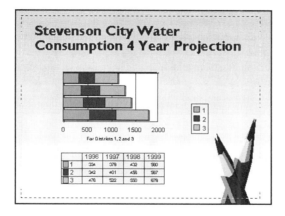

Fig. 6.23
To show the data in detail, place a number grid table under the chart.

Formatting a Number Grid

You can format the number grid using the Table Properties InfoBox shown in figure 6.24. You open this InfoBox by selecting the chart and then choosing Chart, Table. If you already turned on the number grid, you can double-click the number grid to get to this InfoBox.

Fig. 6.24

Change the color, pattern, and line for number grid tables on the Format tab.

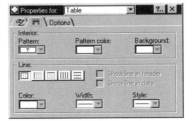

The choices on the Lines & Colors and Font tabs allow you to set the appearance of different aspects of the number grid. The Lines & Colors tab is where you can modify the background and border for the number grid. Select the line you want to modify, then adjust its color, width, or style with the drop-down lists at the bottom of this InfoBox. Add a pattern to the background of the box if you want using the Fill settings.

> **Tip**
>
> If you don't want to see certain gridlines in a table, simply select the button for that line displayed in the line area (shown in fig. 6.24) and deselect Show Line in Header (just the first row of the chart) or Show Line in Data (all rows following) to hide it.

Formatting the Title and Notes

You can add a title, as well as notes, to your chart to help explain the content. You can also place these elements at various points around the chart. Entering a title and a note is a virtually identical process. After you create the text for either one, you can edit the title or note of a chart as you would any other text in a presentation (by clicking once to place the cursor and then using the standard text-editing keystrokes). However, you cannot format the text as you can most other text. The text for titles and notes is an integral part of a chart. Therefore, you must format this text with the same techniques you use to format any other chart element. Double-click a title or note or select the chart, and then choose Chart, Title or Chart, Note to open a properties InfoBox with format settings. Figure 6.25 shows the Title Properties InfoBox and its corresponding text selected on the chart.

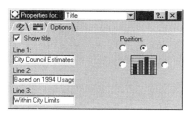

Fig. 6.25
Use the three lines
of the title to add a
heading and
subheadings to
your chart.

Select the Show Title check box to display the title on your chart. Then, enter up to three lines of text in the appropriate text boxes. Use the Position buttons to position the title on the page.

You can use the settings on the Font tab to change the appearance of the text. Opening the Lines & Colors tab allows you to design a frame that will appear around all the titles.

Figure 6.26 shows a chart with both a title and note.

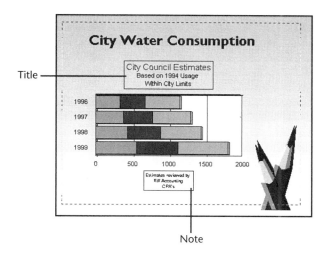

Fig. 6.26
Titles and notes
place additional
information on a
chart so readers
can more easily
interpret the chart.

Setting Up Value Labels

You can place on the chart the actual numbers that bars and lines represent by adding value labels. Value labels appear at the data points along lines or at the tops of bars (see fig. 6.27).

You can turn the labels on and change their formatting by selecting the chart, then choosing Chart, Series Labels. The Labels Properties InfoBox appears (see fig. 6.28).

Fig. 6.27
Value labels
display right on
this line chart.

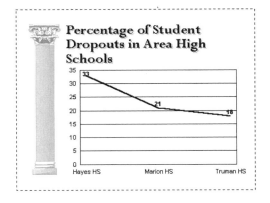

Fig. 6.28
The Series Labels
Properties InfoBox
lets you show
labels as values
and percentages.

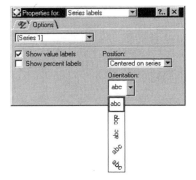

Turn on the display of value labels by selecting the Show Value Labels check box. You can also select the Show Percent Labels check box. Use the Position and Orientation drop-down lists to determine how the labels will fit on your chart.

If you want to change the appearance of the value label font, click the Font tab. Change any of these settings to change the appearance of the value labels.

Formatting Pie Charts

Because pie charts lack the axes, frame, grid, and number grid of bar charts, they have fewer formatting options. Nevertheless, Freelance offers quite a few formatting controls for pie charts.

Changing Slice Colors

Many of the formatting controls for pie charts are in the Pie Chart Properties InfoBox. To open this InfoBox, double-click a pie chart. Two other methods to do this are to right-click a chart and then choose Chart Properties from the pop-up menu, or click the Open InfoBox SmartIcon. Four tabs are available to you:

- *Type*. Allows you to change the pie type to 3D or flat styles.

- *SmartLook*. Changes the color set applied to the pie chart.

- *Lines & Colors*. Allows you to modify the border and background of the chart.

- *Screen Show Effects*. Adjusts how the page displays during a presentation.

Two other formatting options are available if you select Plot in the Properties For drop-down list, which displays the InfoBox shown in figure 6.29.

- *Layout*. Lets you separate the pieces of the pie by exploding them apart. You can shift the direction of the slides, or organize them from smallest to largest.

- *3D*. Appears only if you choose a 3D chart type. It allows you to adjust things like the elevation and rotation of the chart object.

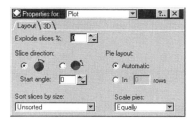

Fig. 6.29
Fine-tuning the angles and position of pie slices adds visual interest to pie charts.

You can use the settings on the Layout tab to explode slices, as shown in figure 6.30. This can help the viewer to see the actual breakdown more clearly.

▶ See "Displaying a Presentation as a Screen Show," p. 311

Tip

If you want to move just one slice away from the others to emphasize it, simply click it and drag it away from the other slices.

The Start Angle setting enables you to rotate the pie. By default, the first pie slice starts at the 3 o'clock position, and other slices are added to the pie in counterclockwise order until the pie is complete. Entering **90**, for example,

III

Adding Charts to Pages

rotates the entire pie 90 degrees counterclockwise. You might want to rotate a pie when the slice labels conflict with another pie's labels or with another graphic object on the page. You can also change the Start Angle if the slice labels are too long to fit on the chart. By rotating the pie, the slices will be at different positions, so the labels will fall at different positions on the chart.

Fig. 6.30
You can explode, or place space between, the slices in a pie chart so each segment shows clearly.

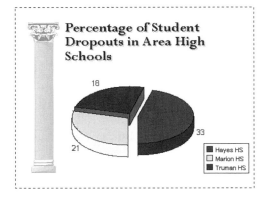

Changing the 3D Depth and Tilt Angle

When you choose to create a 3D pie from the chart gallery, you can change the depth of the 3D effect. Do this by opening the Plot InfoBox for the chart and clicking the 3D tab, then changing the settings for Depth, Elevation, or Shadow Depth and Style (see fig. 6.31).

Fig. 6.31
The effects of making adjustments to the depth, elevation, and shadow effects are previewed on the presentation page as you make them.

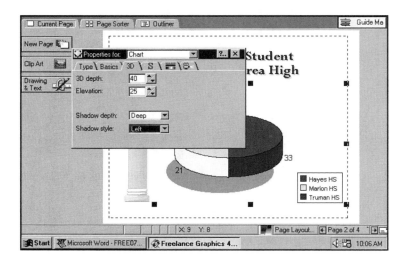

By using the 3D effects controls, you can change the depth of the 3D effect and the tilt or elevation of the pie. The 3D Depth setting is measured as a percentage of the width of the pie (a setting of 50 makes the pie about half as tall as it is wide). The Elevation setting enables you to tilt the pie away from you. Zero degrees creates a two-dimensional pie; 89 degrees, the maximum setting (and a useless one because it basically removes the 3D effect), creates a pie that appears to lie flat. The default setting of 55 produces an attractive tilt. The pie chart in figure 6.31 has a 3D depth of 40 percent and an elevation of 25 degrees.

> **Note**
>
> The more you tilt a pie, the less round it becomes and the less accurately it portrays your data. You can correctly judge the relative sizes of slices only when the pie has no tilt and is truly circular. Don't worry about tilting pies somewhat, though. Viewers can usually interpret the overall proportions.

Using a Legend or Slice Labels

Freelance offers two ways to identify the slices of a pie. A legend shows the color or pattern coding you used, as shown in figure 6.30. Legends are useful when a chart has two or more pies. Slice labels are placed next to slices. If you have only a single pie and the labels are short, slice labels are better because they do not require the viewer to color-match slices with a legend. Figure 6.32 shows the same pie in figure 6.30 with slice labels.

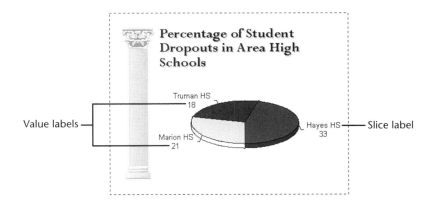

Fig. 6.32
Slice labels make it easy for a viewer to identify parts of your pie chart.

You can decide between a legend and slice labels after you create the chart. Select the chart, then click the Open InfoBox SmartIcon. In the Properties For drop-down list, choose Pie Labels. (If you want to show or hide the legend, choose Legend from the same drop-down list.) The Options tab of the Pie Labels Properties InfoBox appears, as shown in figure 6.33.

Fig. 6.33
Labeling pie slices with a percentage label, value label, or slice label helps the reader understand the data.

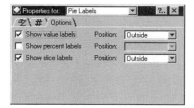

To place the actual number that each slice represents adjacent to the slice label, select the Show Value Labels check box. To display the labels as percentages, select Show Percent Labels. To show the descriptive label for the slice, select Show Slice Labels. Figure 6.32 shows both value labels and slice labels displayed. Each option allows you to also select a position for the label, inside or outside the pie slices, using the Position drop-down list.

To change the format of the label text, open the Font tab of the Pie Labels Properties InfoBox. Depending on what you selected in the Basics page, the font formatting will affect all of that text.

Formatting Multiple Pies

When you choose Multiple Pies from the chart gallery, Freelance might not give you the option of using slice labels. Freelance assumes you will want to use the same colors for corresponding slices in all the pies and that a legend can identify these colors. To create pies with separate colors and slice labels, you must select the multiple pie chart, then click the Open InfoBox Smart-Icon. When the Properties InfoBox opens, choose Pie from the Properties For drop-down list. In the Pie Properties InfoBox that appears, select the Use Independent Data check box to modify each chart separately.

When you select Use Independent Data, Freelance enables you to enter separate slice labels for each pie in the Chart Data & Titles dialog box, as well as different colors and different starting angles for each pie. To choose the colors, double-click the pie to bring up the Properties InfoBox and choose a pie chart before choosing a slice color or starting angle. You can also change the attributes of the value labels independently for each pie.

Setting a Default Chart

While you are working in a presentation, you can set a chart you have created as the default chart for the presentation. Then, whenever you start a new chart for this presentation, you can click Use Default Chart in the New Chart Gallery dialog box to use the formatting of the default chart. If the chart contained data when you set it as the default chart, the same data appears in the new chart, too. You can then edit the data as needed. When you need to create a series of charts of the same design, for example, you can create the first chart, including entering its data, and set it as the default chart. On other pages in the series, you can then use the default chart and simply edit the data to complete the chart.

To set a chart as the default chart, select the chart and then choose Chart, Chart Style, Create. The dialog box in figure 6.34 appears to preview the chart. Click Make This Your Default Chart, then OK to accept this style. Next, enter a style name in the Save As dialog box that follows. Click OK, and the chart type and style, all formatting, and any data are stored as the default chart for the current presentation. When you next create a chart, you'll see this chart style listed along with the basic chart style in the Chart Gallery dialog box.

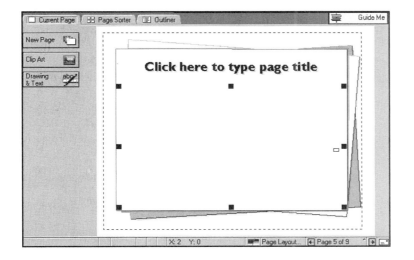

Fig. 6.34
Preview the chart style you want to create.

Ungrouping a Chart

A chart on a presentation page is a single object linked to the data in the chart's Edit Data dialog box. The only way to modify the chart is to change the data or change the formatting of a chart element with the formatting commands and Properties InfoBox you learned about earlier in this chapter.

You can convert a chart to a collection of drawing objects by ungrouping it so you can manipulate each individual shape in the chart as if it had been added with the drawing tools of Freelance. After you ungroup a chart, you gain access to each shape in the chart (each bar, line, or pie slice), and you can move, stretch, copy, recolor, and perform many other actions on them just as you can for any graphic shape. However, you can never regroup these to make them a single chart object, with all the functionality of a chart, again.

▶ See "Grouping and Ungroup-ing Objects," p. 232

After you ungroup a chart, however, you lose access to its data. The chart is now simply a picture of a data chart without the numbers. If you have created a chart by linking the chart to data in another file or application, the link is severed. After you ungroup a chart, you can never regroup it.

If a chart is in a Click Here to Create Chart block, you must press the Ctrl key and drag the chart away from the block before Freelance lets you ungroup it. You will have no problem ungrouping a chart placed on a page if you didn't use a Click Here to Create Chart block, though.

To ungroup the chart, select the chart and then choose Chart, Ungroup. A warning message reminds you of the dangers of ungrouping a chart. Click OK to proceed and ungroup the chart. When the chart is ungrouped, handles surround each shape within the chart. Each shape is now a separate drawing object. Click outside the chart to deselect all the objects, and then click any one object to work with it independently. ❖

CHAPTER 7

Importing the Data for a Data Chart

by Nancy Stevenson

Why retype the numbers for a chart when you can import them into Freelance instead? Retyping is more work and introduces the possibility of human error. By importing the numbers from a file or another program, you can quickly chart data that you keep somewhere else. What's more, you can usually set up a link between the original numbers and the Freelance chart. If the original numbers change, so does your chart.

In this chapter, you'll learn about

- Importing data from common spreadsheet programs
- Linking data
- Importing data from an ASCII file
- Copying data between Windows applications
- Using the Paste Special command

Importing Data from a Lotus 1-2-3 or Microsoft Excel File

Freelance can access two of the most popular spreadsheet programs: Lotus 1-2-3 and Microsoft Excel, and you can selectively pull data into a Freelance Edit Data dialog box. After the data is in the dialog box, one click of the OK button will chart the data automatically.

Identifying the Source and Destination for the Data

For an import from 1-2-3 or Excel to work successfully, you must select the data to import in the spreadsheet program and then identify how the data will be used in Freelance. During the import process, you actually see the 1-2-3 or Excel worksheet in a window within Freelance, and you can then identify the parts of the worksheet to use for various parts of the chart. You can mark worksheet cells that contain legend entries, for example, so that the contents of the cells are used as legend entries in a Freelance chart. You can even set up a link between the 1-2-3 or Excel data and the Freelance data chart so that changes to the 1-2-3 or Excel data update the chart automatically.

To import data from a 1-2-3 or Excel worksheet, you must open the Edit Data dialog box for a chart (see fig. 7.1). You get to the Edit Data dialog box whenever you do one of the following:

- Start a new data chart by choosing Create, Chart, and then select a chart type and click OK.

- Select an existing data chart and choose Chart, Edit Data.

- Create a new page, select a page layout with a chart in it, and click the Click Here to Create Chart block.

Fig. 7.1

You start at the Edit Data dialog box to import data from a spreadsheet program.

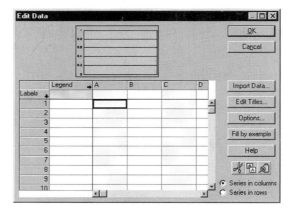

When the Edit Data dialog box appears, select the type of file to import from the drop-down list of File Types, and then use the File Name and Directories controls to find the file.

After you select a worksheet file, the Edit Links dialog box opens (see fig. 7.2). Data from the worksheet you have chosen appears in the dialog box, along with controls on the left that let you identify the cells that contain the title, legends, labels, and chart data. A preview above these controls shows a sample bar chart as soon you begin to designate which parts of the imported data should be used.

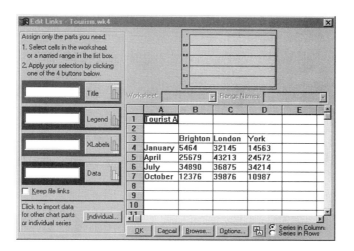

Fig. 7.2
The contents of
the spreadsheet
you want to
import appear in
the Edit Links
dialog box.

If you have not selected the correct worksheet, click the Browse button to return to the Open dialog box so that you can select a different file.

Note

If you have already used the Import Data dialog box to select a worksheet, the same
worksheet will appear in that dialog box the next time you click Import Data.
Freelance assumes that you want to import data from the same worksheet again. To
choose a different worksheet, click the Browse button to get to the Open dialog box.

When the worksheet data appears in the Edit Links dialog box, you can
choose which data to import to Freelance and what part of the chart it will be
used for. You may want to import only certain sets of numbers, or you may
want to import only the row headings from the worksheet to use as legend
entries and type the numbers from another source. Imagine that you need to
chart the sales results of 10 salespeople whose names happen to appear in a
1-2-3 worksheet. You can import only the names from the worksheet as label
entries, so the names will appear along the x-axis and under the bars of a
bar chart.

To identify the range of cells that contains the chart title, legend entries,
x-axis labels, or chart data, select the range by clicking and dragging your
mouse across the cells, and then click the Title, Legend, X-axis Labels, or Data
buttons. The cells you select will become color coded with the background
color of the button you select. For example, the title entry cells will be

outlined in red, the label entry cells will be outlined in green, and the chart data cells will be outlined in blue. These colors are also reflected in the pre-view of the chart within the dialog box, as shown in figure 7.3.

Tip

If you don't want to see the preview of the chart in this dialog box because it's taking a while to draw on-screen, click Options and deselect Show Chart Preview in the dialog box that appears.

Legend button and selected legend

Title button and selected title

Fig. 7.3
After you desig-nate the different pieces of the chart, a preview appears above the worksheet.

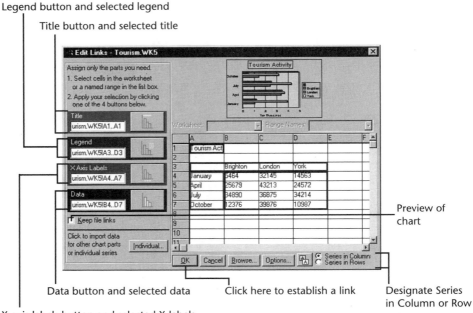

Preview of chart

Data button and selected data

Click here to establish a link

Designate Series in Column or Row

X axis labels button and selected X labels

If you have named ranges in the 1-2-3 or Excel worksheet, you can automati-cally go to and select a named range by clicking the Individual button and then choosing the range name from the list that appears.

If you identify a range of cells as chart data but do not identify which cells hold labels or legends, Freelance will not be able to determine whether the columns in the Edit Data dialog box should be filled with numbers from worksheet columns or worksheet rows. You can use the Series in Column and Series in Rows radio buttons to designate this (refer to fig. 7.3).

Linking the Data

By clicking the Keep File Links check box in the Edit Links dialog box, you can create a link between the data in the 1-2-3 or Excel worksheet and the data in Freelance. After a link is created, the chart will update if the worksheet is changed. You can determine whether this update will be automatic or manual by using the Manage Links dialog box, which is discussed later in this chapter.

After you click OK to import the worksheet data, you are returned to the Edit Data dialog box, where linked data is shown underlined in light blue (see fig. 7.4).

Imported data is
underlined

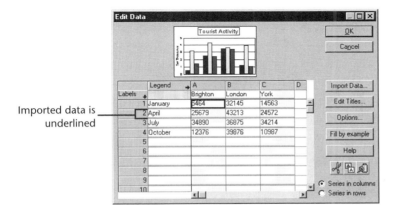

Fig. 7.4
The Edit Data dialog box now contains the imported worksheet data.

Tip

To open the actual worksheet to change any of the original data, double-click any data that is linked (underlined in light blue).

When you click OK in the Edit Data dialog box, your chart is placed on your Freelance presentation page, as shown in figure 7.5.

Troubleshooting

I followed all the steps, but when the chart appeared, the legends and X-axis labels I typed in from the Edit Data dialog box didn't appear at all. Where did they go?

You may need to specify that you want to display the legend and labels in the Chart Properties InfoBox. Select the chart, then click the Open InfoBox SmartIcon. In the Properties For drop-down box, choose Legend, and then click Show Legend. Repeat this process for the X-axis, clicking the Show Labels Every check box.

III

Adding Charts to Pages

Fig. 7.5
The new chart appears based on the data imported from the worksheet.

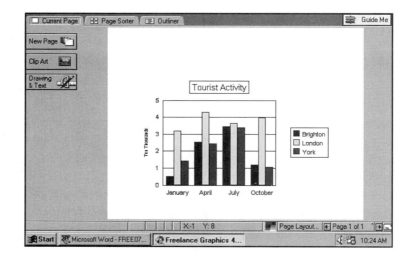

To change the type of link established between a worksheet and a chart, select the chart in Current Page view and then choose Edit, Manage Links. A Manage Links dialog box, similar to the one shown in figure 7.6, shows the current link settings for the selected chart.

Fig. 7.6
Manage links between your Freelance chart and a 1-2-3 or Excel worksheet from this dialog box.

With the Update controls, you can choose whether the link will be Automatic, updating every time the data changes, or Manual, updating only when you click Update Now in the Links dialog box. To delete the link but leave the data for the chart in Freelance, click Break Link. To edit the link, click Edit Chart Links. The Edit Chart Links dialog box appears (see fig. 7.7).

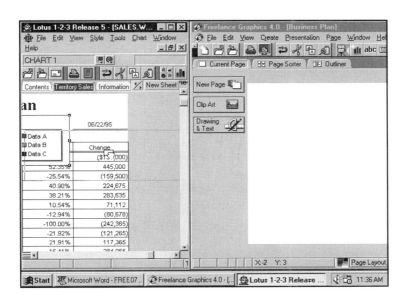

Fig. 7.7
Cell ranges are
displayed so that
you can edit
linked data.

Under <u>L</u>ink, you find a list of the chart parts that can be linked. If a link exists for that chart part, information about the link is presented under Source. The source list includes the range from which the data was imported. Type lists the name of the application from which the data was imported.

Click an object and then click <u>E</u>dit Link to modify the data that the link has been made to. To delete a link but leave the current data in Freelance, click the link and then click <u>B</u>reak Link.

If you want to entirely change the file that you're linking to, click <u>E</u>dit Link. An Edit Link dialog box opens that allows you to browse through directories and files to select a new file to which you can link your chart.

The <u>O</u>pen Source button is available only when you have linked data from a Windows application by using Object Linking and Embedding (OLE). If the application is OLE 2.0 compliant, this gives you access to the source application and allows you to make changes to your worksheet from within Freelance. If you are using an application based on OLE 1.0, the source application itself is opened, but not within the Freelance window. To update your chart to reflect any changes you make in the application, click <u>U</u>pdate All Now. Click OK when you finish using the Edit Links dialog box. Then click Done if you have finished changing the links in the chart.

III

Adding Charts to Pages

Using Drag and Drop to Copy a Chart

One of the simplest ways to take data from another program and move it into Freelance is to simply use the drag-and-drop functionality that object linking and embedding (OLE) support allows. Using this method, you can simply open two windows, such as an Excel or 1-2-3 chart and a Freelance presentation page. Click the spreadsheet chart and drag it over to Freelance. A small fist cursor appears in the Freelance window.

When the fist cursor appears, just release the mouse button to drop the chart onto the Freelance page. The chart now appears in both windows (see fig. 7.8). In Freelance the chart is now a *metafile*. A metafile is a generic file that can be read by any application that is metafile compliant. These files can contain drawing objects, like a chart, that can be manipulated in certain ways in Freelance. When you select the chart, you get a <u>M</u>etafile menu that you can use to make changes to the chart object.

Fig. 7.8

The chart is copied from one application to another using drag and drop.

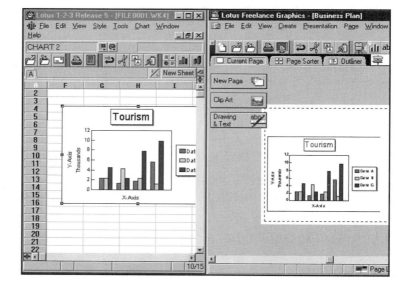

Importing Data from Another Windows Application

When the data you need to chart is in another Windows application, you can easily copy it into the Edit Data dialog box. With certain other Windows applications, you can even set up an active link between the original data and the data in Freelance. The active link causes the chart in Freelance to update immediately when you make any change to the original data in another application. The active link is called a *DDE link*. (DDE stands for a Windows capability called *Dynamic Data Exchange*. DDE is one part of another Windows capability, OLE.)

The benefits of DDE linking are enormous. You don't have to worry about updating a Freelance presentation if any of the data it depends on is updated. Even if you didn't know about a change that somebody made to the 1-2-3 for Windows data on which a Freelance data chart is based, your data chart will still accurately reflect the 1-2-3 for Windows changes.

Copying Data from a Windows Application

To copy data from another Windows application to a Freelance chart when you don't care whether the chart is updated if the original data changes, you can use the drag-and-drop method described earlier, or you can use the Windows Clipboard with the Copy and Paste commands. After selecting the data in the other application, use the application's Copy command to copy the data to the Windows Clipboard. Then switch to the Edit Chart dialog box of a Freelance chart. There you can use the Paste SmartIcon to retrieve the data from the Windows Clipboard. This performs a one-time-only transfer of the data and does not set up a link.

You can use this method to copy and paste a table from a Windows word processor such as WordPro, Word for Windows, or WordPerfect for Windows. You can use the method to also copy a range of numbers from a Windows spreadsheet, such as 1-2-3 for Windows, Excel, or Quattro Pro for Windows. Simply make sure that the data is set up in the cells of a table, in tab-separated columns, or in the cells of a spreadsheet. Then select the data to chart and use the Copy command in the application's Edit menu to copy the data to the Windows Clipboard.

When you plan to perform a one-time-only copy and paste of data into Freelance, the data in most Windows applications can be arranged either in rows or columns. The data sets that you will represent with lines or sets of bars can be arranged vertically in columns or horizontally in rows. After the data is pasted into the Edit Data dialog box, you can use the Series in Columns and Series in Rows buttons to switch the orientation of the chart elements. Figure 7.9 shows a 1-2-3 for Windows worksheet range that can be copied easily to Freelance. Figure 7.10 shows the same worksheet with the data arranged in columns, just the way it was formatted when the information was brought in. Figure 7.11 shows the same data; however, in this case the Series in Rows option was selected in the Edit Data dialog box after the data was imported.

Fig. 7.9

A simple Lotus
1-2-3 spreadsheet
can be cut and
pasted into the
Edit Dialog box.

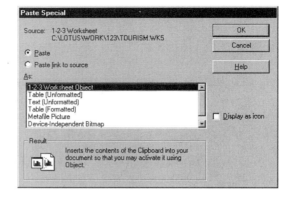

Fig. 7.10

The data in figure
7.10 comes in
organized by
columns, as it was
in the spreadsheet.

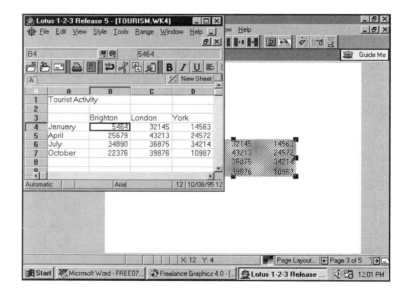

To copy and paste data from another program into the Edit Data dialog box
of Freelance, follow this procedure:

1. Open the other application containing the data.

2. Select the data to copy to a Freelance Graphics chart.

3. From the Edit menu of the other application, choose the Copy
   command.

4. Switch to Freelance Graphics for Windows.

5. Position the cell pointer in the Edit Data dialog box where you want the data to appear. Place the pointer in the gray cell at the top of the Axis Labels column and to the left of the Legend row if you have also selected the column and row headings in the other application. Place the pointer in the first blank cell if you have selected only the data without selecting the column and row headings.

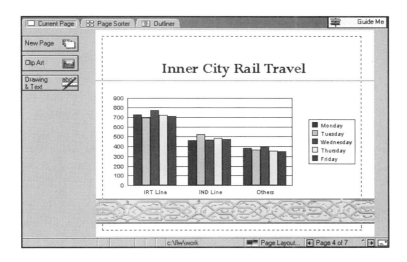

Fig. 7.11
With a click of the Series in Rows button in the Edit dialog box, the display of data is switched to rows.

6. Click the Paste SmartIcon, or from the Edit menu of Freelance, choose Paste.

Creating and Editing a DDE Link

If you want to import data for a chart in Freelance using a link, you should use the import function in the Import Data dialog box, which you access through the Edit Data dialog box. With this process, you use data in a Freelance chart format, which was discussed earlier in this chapter. However, you can also bring in data from another OLE application and paste it directly on a Freelance page as, for example, a table. You can also establish a DDE link to such a table of data by using the Paste Special function.

After selecting the data in the other application and then copying it to the Windows Clipboard, switch to Freelance and choose Edit, Paste Special. If Freelance has recognized that the data in the Windows Clipboard is from an application that supports OLE, it will display the Edit Paste Special dialog box (see fig. 7.12).

Fig. 7.12

You can paste data and establish a link with the Paste Special dialog box.

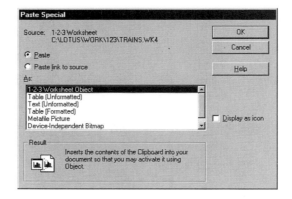

The source of whatever data is in the Windows Clipboard is displayed at the top of this box. Select Paste Link to Source to bring this data in with a link to the file you copied it from. You can select the type of object to paste in the As list, and you also have the option of displaying the pasted data as an icon by clicking that box.

When you select the Paste link option and then click OK, your data appears. After you create the link, updates to the data in the other application will update the Freelance chart if you have automatic updating turned on. If not, you must manually update the link using the Manage Links dialog box (refer to fig. 7.6).

Each row within the dialog box lists a link between a Freelance chart or data and another application. Click one of the links and then make sure that Automatic is selected under Update. To change a link to manual updating, click Manual. To update the link manually, you need to open this dialog box, select the link to update from the list, click the Update Now button, and then click OK.

To delete a link, select the link and then click Break Link. The link will be broken, but the data will remain as imported in Freelance. If any changes occur to the data in the original application, they will not be reflected in Freelance, though.

When you select data that has been inserted using the Paste Special function with a link, there is a special menu available. For example, if you cut and paste a section of a 1-2-3 file, when you select it, a 1-2-3 Worksheet menu appears along with the regular menus at the top of the Freelance window. Using this, you can choose to edit the linked data. Doing so will actually open up the application that the data is linked to in a window above Freelance. Then, you can use all the original application's tools to edit it.

Tip

Also edit an object inserted with a Paste Special link by double-clicking it to open the linked application.

When you finish editing, click back on the Freelance page to close the other application and display the changed data. ❖

CHAPTER 8

Creating Organization Charts

by Nancy Stevenson

Organization charts depict the structure of an organization, showing with boxes and connecting lines who is subordinate to whom in a hierarchy. Also called *org*, *staff*, or *pyramid charts*, organization charts are easy to make and modify.

Freelance Graphics 96 for Windows 95 can create an organization chart automatically from a simple list of names that you type. In this chapter, you'll learn about the following:

- Choosing a style for your chart
- Entering information about the organization
- Adding to the detail in the chart
- Editing names, titles, charts, and connecting lines
- Making changes to the organizational structure
- Formatting text in the organization chart

Building an Organization Chart

An organization chart is an excellent way to give your audience an at-a-glance overview of the structure of a company, department, or even project team. It's also simple to create. Figure 8.1 shows a sample Freelance organization chart.

If you plan to include an organization chart in a presentation, you can add a page for the chart by clicking on the New Page button, and then selecting the Organization Chart page layout. A page containing the Click Here to Create Organization Chart block appears, as shown in figure 8.2. Using this approach, you can create a page with the organization chart automatically sized and positioned to fit the Click Here block.

Fig. 8.1

See how people in an organization interact with a Freelance organization chart.

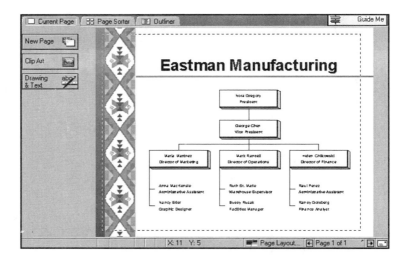

Fig. 8.2

The Organization Chart page layout gives you two Click Here blocks.

You can also add an organization chart to an existing page that may have text or other charts by choosing Create, Organization Chart.

When you either click the Click Here block from the Organization Page Layout or select it through the Create menu, the Organization Chart Gallery dialog box appears, as shown in figure 8.3.

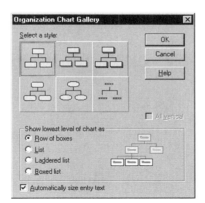

Fig. 8.3
Make choices from
among several
styles in the
Organization
Chart Gallery.

Choosing an Organization Chart Style

You use the Organization Chart Gallery dialog box to make some design
decisions about the chart before entering any data. After you type names
and titles, Freelance draws the chart with the design you've specified.

One of the six chart style buttons is already pressed when this dialog box
opens. You may want to click another button to choose a variation on the
basic organization, though. With these style buttons, you can choose a chart
design with shadowed boxes, 3-D boxes, rounded rectangle boxes, elliptical
boxes, or no boxes at all. The choice is purely aesthetic, and you can always
change it later.

You use the Automatically Size Entry Text check box to determine whether
Freelance will automatically resize the text within the boxes if you resize the
entire organization chart. Unless you need text of a particular size within the
boxes, you should leave this box checked so that Freelance can keep the text
proportional to the chart size.

A list of choices at the bottom-left of the Organization Chart Gallery dialog
box enables you to choose how the lowest level of the chart will be visually
depicted. The Row of Boxes option is the most familiar choice (an example of
this is shown in figure 8.4, which also shows special tools that are available to
you when you are working on an organizational chart), but not necessarily
the best. When you choose Row of Boxes, Freelance displays the individuals
at the lowest level of the structure as side-by-side boxes, making it clear that
they are equals. These groups of boxes require more horizontal space, though.

III

Adding Charts to Pages

Fig. 8.4
This organization chart depicts its lowest level as a row of boxes.

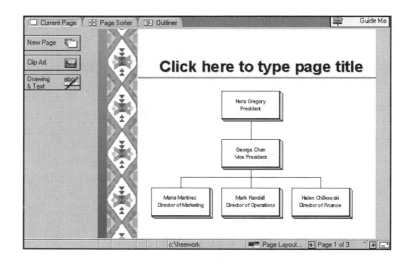

Compounding the problem, the pyramid shape of most organizations places more people at the lowest levels. Therefore, to fit all the people, the boxes and names must be small, and all the other boxes and names in the chart become small accordingly. The result is a chart with small boxes and hard-to-read names. Choosing any of the other choices—List, Laddered List, or Boxed List—solves this problem by placing the names in a vertical list. As you choose one of these options, a small diagram in the dialog box demonstrates the choice.

Entering Organization Members

When you make your choices in the Chart Gallery and click OK, Freelance opens the Organization Chart Entry List dialog box, as shown in figure 8.5. The next step after choosing the design of a chart is to enter the data for it here. This data can include a name, title, and comment for each person for whom an entry should appear in the chart.

The dialog box shows a lined text-entry area that looks much like a piece of ruled paper. Within this area, you enter information about the people in the organization, from the top down. Prompts that appear dimmed show you where to enter the name, title, and comments about the head of the organization first. When you first open this dialog box, the cursor is at the Enter name here prompt.

Choose Edit, Promote or Demote to change
an individual's level in the chart

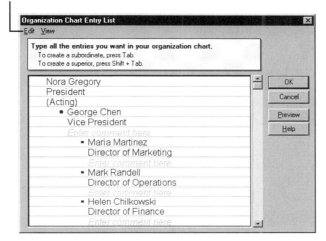

Fig. 8.5
Building an
organization chart
is just a matter of
typing in the
details.

To begin entering the organizational structure, just follow these steps:

1. Type the name of the person at the top of the organizational structure and press Enter to move to the next line.

2. Type the title of the person and press Enter. This step is optional. You can press Enter without entering a title to get to the comment line.

3. Type a comment about the person, if you want, and then press Enter. Typing a comment is optional. You can press Enter to skip the comment as well. The comment line is open for any use, though. You may want to use this space to enter a telephone extension, for example.

You can have only one head of an organization. After you enter information about him or her, the cursor moves down to the next line and to the right one level, as shown in figure 8.5. The subordinates of the first entry (the vice presidents in a standard corporation) are indented one level. Each level of indent is a lower level in the diagram of the organization. You can chart up to 12 levels. The third level in the chart (used for directors of various departments, for example) is indented twice (two steps to the right) and so on.

Troubleshooting

We have two CEOs who run the company jointly. How do I create two top-level boxes in my organization chart?

Sorry, but there's only one top dog in a Freelance organization chart. However, you might try either of these options: give the top spot over to the company name, then create two boxes at the second level for your two bosses; or, use the top level for one of the partners, and draw a simple box with text using Freelance's drawing tools and place it next to the top level box on your completed organization chart.

As the instructions at the top of the dialog box suggest, before or after you enter the name of an individual, you can press Tab to make the individual subordinate to the one immediately above in the list. Pressing Tab moves the prompt text one level to the right. You also can press Shift+Tab to move a subordinate up to the level of the individual immediately above in the list. You can also choose Edit, Promote to move a name to the left, and Demote to indent it to the right in the structure.

Tip

You can leave an empty box in the structure to fill in later. Just press Enter to pass the prompts for an individual without typing a name, a title, or comments.

Changing the Level of Detail in the Chart

Freelance assumes that you will enter the name, title, and comments about each member of the organization. Your chart may need only names, though, or only names and titles without comments. To remove prompts that you don't need from the entry list, use the View menu in the Organization Chart Entry List dialog box.

From the View menu within this dialog box, you can choose Names Only, Names and Titles, or All. The prompts in the text-entry area are automatically readjusted. Figure 8.6 shows the Organization Chart Entry List dialog box when Names and Titles is selected.

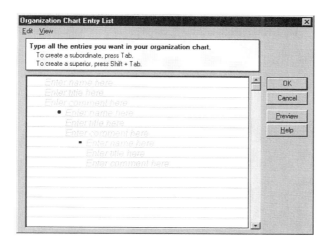

Fig. 8.6
When you have nothing else to say about people, just view Names and Titles and get rid of comments.

Adding a Staff Position

All the members of the organization depicted are in line positions. Each member reports in line to the manager above in the hierarchy. In any organization chart, you can add one special assistant to the head of the organization, and that assistant is in what's called a staff position. Each chart can have only one staff position, and the person in that position must report to the individual at the top of the organization. Usually this is either an advisor or executive assistant.

To add a staff position, choose Edit, Staff. The Organization Chart Staff dialog box opens, as shown in figure 8.7. Enter as much information about the individual as you want, then click OK. Figure 8.8 shows the staff position that results from the information you entered.

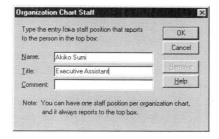

Fig. 8.7
An Executive Assistant's name is often entered as a Chart Staff position in the Organization Chart Staff dialog box.

III

Adding Charts to Pages

Fig. 8.8
The Staff nodule
is placed off to
the side of the
President.

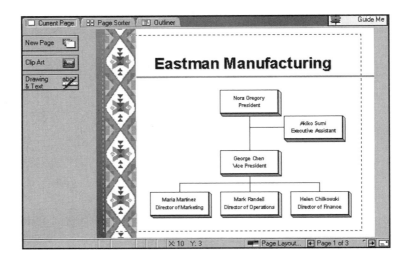

To remove a staff position no longer needed, return to the Organization
Chart Staff dialog box and click <u>R</u>emove.

Editing the Names, Titles, and Comments

◀ See "Editing
Text," p. 52

If a personnel replacement requires you to change the information in a box,
you can easily edit text in the Organization Chart Entry List dialog box by
double-clicking that text with the mouse. A typing cursor appears where you
click, and you can make editing corrections as you would in any text. In fact,
you can use all the cursor-movement and text-selection techniques you use
when editing any text in Freelance. For example, you can press Home to
move the cursor to the beginning of a line. Press Shift+End to highlight to
the end of the line, and then type new text to replace the highlighted text.

Note

When the <u>A</u>utomatically Size Entry Text check box is checked in the Organization
Gallery Chart dialog box, Freelance may wrap part of a name to the next line to
better fit all the entries in the chart. A person's second name may appear on the line
below the first name, for example. To keep the entire name on one line, press Enter
once or twice at the end of the name to add blank lines below the name. This "uses"
the second and third lines in the box, forcing the name to shrink so that it fits on the
first line.

After you have instructed Freelance to draw the chart based on the information provided in the Organization Chart Entry List dialog box by clicking OK, you can also make direct changes to the text in the boxes instead of returning to that dialog box. To do so, click the box that holds the text to be modified. You'll see that the chart is selected and the box is subselected (large handles appear around the entire chart, and smaller handles appear around the box you clicked). Then click the text again to place a typing cursor. When the typing cursor appears, you can use all the cursor-movement and text-editing keys to edit the text. You cannot use the text-formatting keys or the commands in the Text menu (such as Font & Color) to change the appearance of the text. You must change the attributes of the text in the boxes globally instead. Changing attributes is covered later in this chapter in the section "Changing the Organization Chart's Attributes."

Modifying the Organizational Structure

The Organization Chart Entry List dialog box is not only the place to enter the data shown in the chart, but also the place to make changes in response to hirings, firings, or reorganizations in the structure you are representing. You can insert new members in the organization, delete members who have left the organization, and rearrange the positioning of members in the chart.

Demoting or Promoting Members

Once you've created an organization chart, you can still demote or promote an organization member. After the member has been demoted, he or she can also be promoted back to the previous level. To demote a member, in the Organization Chart Entry List dialog box, place the cursor anywhere on the member's name, title, or comment, and then press Tab or choose Edit, Demote. To promote a member who has been demoted, press Shift+Tab or choose Edit, Promote instead.

If an organization member has subordinates, the procedure is quite a bit different because you cannot promote or demote a member who has subordinates without also affecting the subordinates. To promote or demote a member with subordinates, you must select the member and the subordinates by clicking the symbol in front of the member's name. When you do, a rectangle appears that encloses the member's information and the information of all the subordinates below the member. You can then press Tab or Shift+Tab to demote or promote the entire group, or you can choose Demote or Promote from the Edit menu. Figure 8.9 shows the selection rectangle that appears when you click the symbol in front of a name.

Fig. 8.9
You can promote a manager and subordinates all at one time.

Select a group by clicking on this symbol

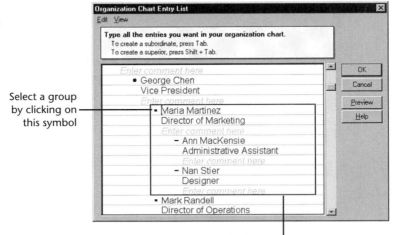

This rectangle shows a group has been selected for promoting or demoting

Moving Members

You can move members in an organization chart if they have been moved in the organization—for example, if they have been reassigned to a different manager. To move a member or a member along with subordinates, click and hold down the mouse button on the symbol in front of the member's name. While still holding down the mouse button, move the triangle to the new position for the member and then release the mouse button. As you move the triangle on the list, a dark horizontal bar appears between names to show where the member will be dropped if you release the mouse button. If the member you are moving has subordinates, the subordinates will also be moved.

Troubleshooting

Mike Smith is being moved into Sales, but I don't want all the people working for him in Marketing to move with him! How do I just move Mike?

If you want to move a manager without taking his or her subordinates along, first promote the subordinates to the same level as the manager, insert a new manager for them, or move them to report to another manager. Once Mike has no subordinates, you can move him without dragging the rest of Marketing along for the ride.

When you move a member, he or she stays at the same level in the new position. If a member at the third level is moved (a department director, for example), the member will appear at the third level when placed below a different second-level member. If there is no second-level member, though, the third-level member will become a second-level member.

Caution

You cannot move someone at the third level to the first level. The third-level person will move but will be "promoted" to the second level so that a level is never skipped.

Inserting, Copying, and Deleting Members

Adding and removing members in an organization chart is far easier than adding and removing employees in real life. To insert a new member in the chart, place the cursor on the last line of data for the member immediately above where you want the new member to be, and then press Enter. Press Tab if you want the new member to be a subordinate.

To delete a member or group of members:

1. Click the symbol in front of the member's name. A selection box surrounds the member and any subordinates.
2. Press the Delete key to permanently clear the members.
3. Press Ctrl+X or Shift+Delete to cut the members from the chart.

When you cut rather than delete, you can paste the members back into the chart at another position by moving the pointer to that position, clicking, and then pressing Ctrl+V or Shift+Insert.

> **Tip**
>
> You can also use the Cut, Copy, Paste, and Clear commands from the Edit menu in the Organization Chart Entry List dialog box to move personnel around or get rid of them.

To copy members and subordinates from one position to another, select their names and press Ctrl+C or Ctrl+Insert. Move the cursor to the destination for the copy, click, and press Ctrl+V or Shift+Insert.

Making Other Changes

Changing the arrangement of names in the Organization Chart Entry List dialog box offers only a limited array of changes to the chart. You may need to depict a structure that is not a simple, top-down, pyramid shape. Unfortunately, Freelance offers no automatic way to create such nonstandard diagrams. What you must do instead is use the Organization Chart feature of the program to create a few boxes and lines (the central core of the chart); duplicate and modify those boxes; and add additional lines, arrows, and other graphic shapes with the drawing tools of the program. With the drawing tools, you can create virtually any diagram you want.

If you will be adding boxes and lines, you can simply draw them onto the existing chart. But you may want to convert the chart to a collection of drawing objects that you can move, duplicate, and redesign. To convert the chart, select it and then choose Org Chart, Ungroup from the main menu. Freelance warns you that ungrouping the chart will convert it to a collection of drawing objects. Click OK to proceed. Then you can begin working with the individual pieces of the chart (the lines, boxes, and text). Figure 8.10 shows the chart after it has been ungrouped. Notice that each element of the chart has its own set of handles because it is an individual drawing object.

▶ See "Understanding Drawn Objects," p. 205

> **Caution**
>
> Once ungrouped, the parts of the organization chart lose their connection to the data you used to create them. You won't be able to use the Organization Chart Entry list to modify the entries, or any of the Org Chart Properties InfoBox functions. If you regroup the elements, they are simply treated as a group, with group attribute functions available, but they will never be an organization chart again.

A Collection menu replaces
the <u>O</u>rg Chart menu

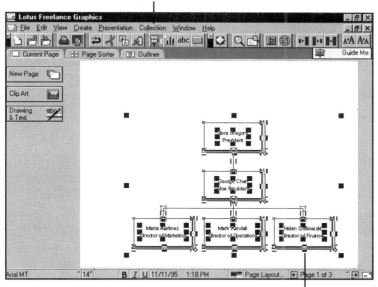

Fig. 8.10
Once ungrouped,
the individual
nodules of the
organization chart
can be modified as
drawing objects.

Individual handles for each object

Modifying the Style or Entry List at a Later Time

You can get back into the Org Chart Properties InfoBox to make changes to
your organization style at any time. Select the chart, then click the Open
InfoBox SmartIcon on the Universal toolbar, or choose <u>O</u>rg Chart, <u>O</u>rg Chart
Properties from the main menu. When the InfoBox opens, make sure the
Properties For selection at the top of the box has Organization Chart selected,
then click the Layout tab, which appears in figure 8.11. Use the pop-up list of
layout styles to choose a new look for your chart.

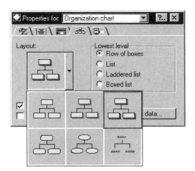

Fig. 8.11
The Lotus InfoBox
for org charts is
where you change
chart layout
settings.

III

Adding Charts to Pages

To get back to the Entry List to make changes in content, simply right-click the chart object and choose Edit Data from the shortcut menu. The Organization Entry dialog box appears. You can also select Org Chart, Edit Data from the main menu. If the chart was created without the use of a Click Here box, you must go through the Edit menu to change its content.

Changing the Organization Chart's Attributes

The steps you have completed so far have provided the content and basic design for the chart. To modify the appearance of individual elements of the chart (the text, connecting lines, or frame), you must change the properties of the elements.

As always, you must select the element by clicking on it before you can make any changes to it. You can then use the tools that appear on the toolbar (refer to fig. 8.4), the Org Chart menu, or the shortcut menu that appears when you click the right mouse key to modify the chart in the Properties InfoBox.

The Open InfoBox SmartIcon opens the Organization Chart InfoBox, which enables you to change the appearance of the part of the chart you clicked. Figure 8.12 shows this InfoBox.

Fig. 8.12
This is the Properties InfoBox for Organization Chart, where you can change several of the chart's attributes.

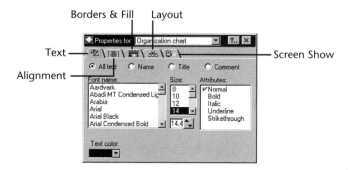

You can use the Properties For drop-down list to choose to make changes to the whole chart, Connecting Lines, Frame, or, if you selected an individual box in the chart before opening the Properties InfoBox, just a single box's contents.

When you're making changes to the entire organization chart, the five tabs available affect—from left to right—Text, Alignment, Border and Fill, Layout and Screen Show. These choices change somewhat if you choose to affect properties for Connecting Lines or Frame. In that case, you get a single tab for each of those specific functions.

Changing the Appearance of Text

To change the appearance of the text within the chart, simply use the Text tab of the Properties InfoBox shown in figure 8.12.

You can choose a different typeface, type size, color, or justification for the text and apply character attributes such as boldfacing and underlining. Depending on whether the Properties For drop-down list says Organization chart or the name of an individual box in the chart, you can make changes globally or for just one person in the organization. By using the radio buttons boxes along the top, you can choose to make changes to all text, or just the name, title, or comment text.

> ### Caution
>
> Freelance automatically controls the sizing of the text in the boxes if Automatically Size Entry Text is checked in the Organization Chart Gallery dialog box. Overriding the automatic sizing of the text by changing the Size setting turns off automatic sizing of the text. The text then remains at its current size even if you change the size of the chart.

Modifying the Look of the Boxes

The organization chart style you chose when you started the organization chart determines the overall design of the boxes in the chart—whether they are plain, three-dimensional, shadowed, or not shown.

By choosing Frames in the Properties InfoBox, you can change the color, width (thickness), and line style of the edge of the boxes and the colors of the interior of the boxes.

You can fill the boxes with a color gradient by choosing a gradient pattern from the list of available patterns. The lower-half of the patterns that appear when you open the Pattern drop-down list are gradients.

To quickly create a box filled with a solid color and with no discernible edge, click the Same Color as Border check box.

Changing the Connecting Lines

The choices for connecting lines are pretty straightforward: you can change only the width (thickness), style, and color of lines that connect the boxes in an organization chart. Simply choose Connecting Lines in the Properties For drop-down list, then use the three drop-down lists shown to make changes to these features.

Using Diagrams

In addition to organizational charts, which are traditionally used to show the hierarchy of people who make up a group or company, Freelance Graphics 96 for Windows 95 offers another option for creating diagrams that are perfect for showing processes. This diagramming feature allows you to use the built-in drawing shapes and connectors to make your own custom diagram from scratch. But its real power comes from dozens of polished-looking, built-in diagrams that show everything from processes to timelines in visually interesting ways (see fig. 8.13).

Fig. 8.13
Show the flow of activities in a process using a built-in diagram.

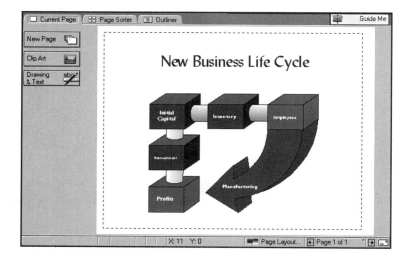

Building Diagrams Using Drawing Tools

One way to build simple diagrams yourself is with the Drawing & Text tools. These tools, shown in figure 8.14, include various shapes (including Shapes with Text blocks built in). There are also different connector line styles so you have maximum flexibility in drawing the lines that link the various pieces of a diagram. Figure 8.15 shows an example of a simple diagram built with these tools.

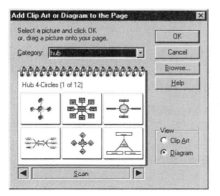

Fig. 8.14
The floating Drawing and Text palette of tools can be moved on-screen wherever you need it.

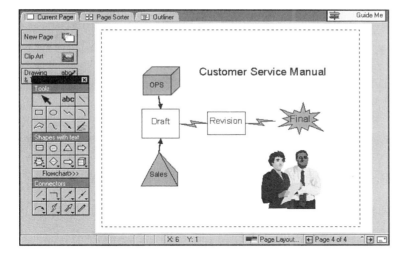

Fig. 8.15
Use a combination of shapes, text boxes, and connector line shapes to create your own diagrams.

To create a diagram using Drawing & Text tools, follow these steps:

1. In Current Page view, click the Drawing & Text button, which reveals the toolbox shown in figure 8.15.

2. Click a drawing tool, such as a square or circle, or on any of the Shape with Text tools in the middle of this palette.

3. Place your cursor on the current page and click, then, holding down the mouse button, drag to draw your shape. You can always resize and move it later, so don't worry about its placement or size as you draw.

III

Adding Charts to Pages

► See "Drawing
the Objects,"
p. 208

4. After you've drawn several shapes, click a connector line tool.

5. Click near the edge of one shape, then drag your mouse to the edge of another shape.

The connector line now indicates a flow between one shape and another. If you'd like to put text within any of the shapes in your diagram, there are two methods:

1. If you've drawn a Shape with Text object, just double-click on the shape and a text block opens, ready for editing.

2. If you've drawn a shape with the tools at the top of the Drawing & Text palette, first click the Text SmartIcon in the Universal toolbox at the top of the screen, then click in the shape. A text block opens, and you can now enter and edit text.

► See "Adding
Text Blocks,"
p. 179

Using Ready-Made Diagrams

Even simpler than using drawing tools to create a diagram from scratch is using the pre-drawn diagrams that Freelance offers. These diagrams come with fancy shapes, connectors, and even background colors and patterns built in.

To create a SmartDiagram, follow these steps:

1. From the Current Page view, select Create, Drawing/Diagram. The dialog box in figure 8.16 appears.

2. Select Use a Ready-Made Diagram to get to the pre-drawn diagrams.

Tip
If you select Make Your Own Diagram with Elements from the Drawing & Text Palette in the dialog box in figure 8.16, Freelance simply returns you to the screen with the Drawing & Text palette open.

Fig. 8.16
Get to the list
of ready-made
diagrams by
clicking the Use
a Ready-Made
Diagram radio
button.

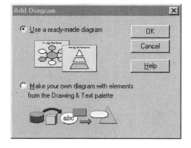

3. The dialog box in figure 8.17 now appears. Use the <u>C</u>ategory drop-down list to select a category of diagrams, such as Hub, Flow, Pyramid or Timeline.

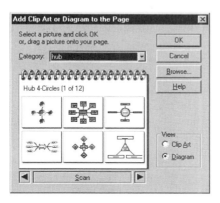

Fig. 8.17
Clicking the <u>S</u>can button will scan through images until you click the button again.

4. Then, using the <u>S</u>can button or arrows at the bottom of the screen, look through the various diagrams until you find one that suits your need. When you click the <u>S</u>can button once, Freelance begins to scan through all the diagrams, and the <u>S</u>can button turns into a <u>S</u>top Scan button. Click it again to stop the scan.

5. Click the diagram you want, then click OK.

The diagram appears on your page, with Click Here text blocks ready for you to enter text, as in figure 8.18.

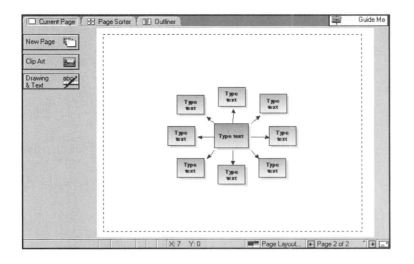

Fig. 8.18
Just click any box and type your text.

III

Adding Charts to Pages

To enter text, just click any piece of the diagram, and the text editing block opens up. Type your text, then click anywhere outside of the text block to see the text in place.

You can edit this text to make it larger or a different font by selecting the diagram, then clicking the Open InfoBox SmartIcon to see the Group Properties InfoBox in figure 8.19.

Fig. 8.19
Change the text and other elements of your chart using the Group Properties InfoBox.

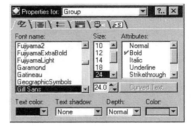

You can click the Text tab on the far left of this InfoBox and use the settings there to change text size, font, attributes, or color. A finished version of the original diagram, with all text boxes filled in and the text enlarged slightly, is shown in figure 8.20.

Fig. 8.20
Show the relationship of parts of an organization with a Hub diagram.

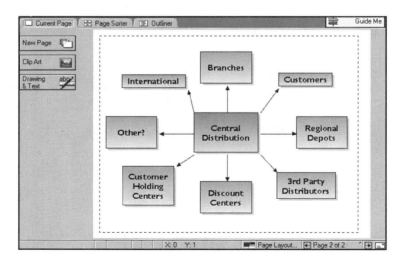

Note

If you want to create a custom diagram that you can use again and again, select all the parts of a diagram you made yourself, then choose Collection, Group. Choose Create, Add to Library, then from the pop-up menu, select Diagram Library. An Add to Diagram Library dialog box appears and allows you to save your custom diagram to a file. Then it will be available to you on the list of ready-made diagrams under the category of Custom.

▶ See "Formatting Text Blocks," p. 185

Editing Ready-Made Diagrams

If you find a perfect diagram, but it has one too many boxes, that's okay. Just create it and enter and format all text. When it's ready, choose Group, Ungroup. The various elements of the diagram are now separate, and each can be treated as a separate object. That means you can delete one or more elements or rearrange them in relation to the other pieces of the diagram. Be aware, however, that if you regroup them, they will not reassume the attributes of the ready-made diagram. Grouping them simply means they can be moved around again as a single unit. ❖

▶ See "Grouping and Ungrouping Objects," p. 232

III

Adding Charts to Pages

CHAPTER 9

Creating Table Charts

by Nancy Stevenson

Table charts hold text and numbers in a grid of cells. This helps you present a lot of information in a concise and easy-to-read format. Tables resemble spreadsheets, and just like spreadsheets, they use the intersection of columns and rows to show unique information, such as dollar sales by month, or inches of rainfall by region.

Freelance makes these charts easy to create and modify. When you start a table chart, you select a chart design from a visual gallery. After you move from cell to cell, entering text and numbers, you may be perfectly satisfied with the chart you get. But to place your own design stamp on the chart, you can click any cell or click the entire chart and choose formatting from the clearly presented alternatives.

In this chapter, you learn how to

- Create table charts
- Enter and edit text
- Add and delete columns and rows
- Resize columns and rows and resize tables
- Format table charts

Creating a Table Chart

To start a table chart, you can create a new page that has a table chart Click Here block, or you can add a table chart to an existing page in the presentation.

To create a new page with a table chart Click Here block, begin by clicking the New Page button at the left side of the Freelance window. Then, select the Table page layout from the list of page layouts in the Choose Page Layout dialog box that opens. A page with Click Here to Type Page Title and Click Here to Create Table blocks appears, as in figure 9.1. The new page will have whatever background you've chosen for your entire presentation.

Fig. 9.1
The Click Here block gives you access to everything you need to create a Freelance table.

To add a table chart to any page of the presentation, turn to that page and choose Create, Table from the main menu. The Table Gallery dialog box in figure 9.2 appears. You use this dialog box to choose a basic design and size for the table.

Fig. 9.2
The Table Gallery offers four styles to choose from.

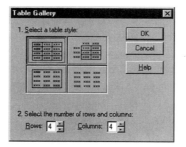

The dialog box shows two numbered steps: Select a Table Style, and Select the Number of Rows and Columns. Default selections of a basic style and four columns by four rows have already been made. To accept the default selections, simply click OK. Or follow these steps to set the basic table design:

1. Click one of the four table style buttons that depict basic table designs to choose how the grid lines in the table should appear. You can always return to this dialog box to choose a different table style for a table you've created.

2. Use the increment and decrement buttons under the Rows and Columns prompt to increase or decrease the number of rows and columns in the table. Again, you can always add and delete rows and columns later.

3. Click OK. A blank table chart appears, as shown in figure 9.3.

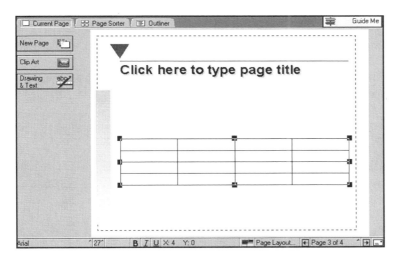

Fig. 9.3
This blank table chart is ready for you to enter data.

Caution

You can create a maximum of 30 columns and 50 rows for a single table in Freelance Graphics. However, be careful to make sure that the details of a larger table are readable by your audience during a presentation.

Entering and Editing Table Text

When the blank table chart appears, the entire table is selected, and special tools for working with tables appear on the main toolbar (see fig. 9.4).

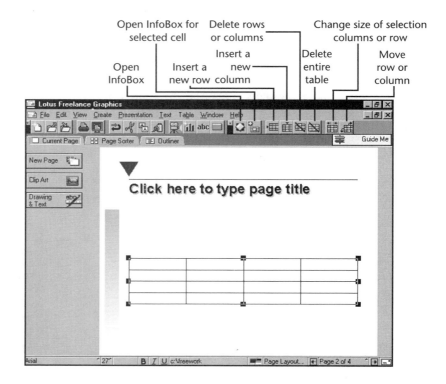

Fig. 9.4
The table tools
make editing and
formatting tables
quick and easy.

To begin entering text and numbers into cells of the table, you must click on a cell. This produces a blinking typing cursor in the cell.

As you type, the text automatically wraps words within each cell. Freelance fits as many words as it can in the cell and then increases the row height and moves the cursor to the next line within the row. To avoid word wrapping, you must either make the text smaller or increase the width of the cell. Both techniques are discussed later in this chapter in the "Reformatting Tables" and "Resizing Columns and Rows" sections.

After you type an entry, press the Tab key or Ctrl+→ to move one cell to the right, or press ↓ to move one cell down. To start a new line in the current cell, press Enter. To move the cursor to the left, press Shift+Tab or Ctrl+←. To move the cursor to the upper-left corner cell of the table, press Ctrl+Home. To move to the lower-right corner cell, press Ctrl+End. Of course, you can always click any cell with the mouse pointer to move the cursor to that cell. Table 9.1 summarizes the keyboard combinations for moving the cursor in a cell.

Table 9.1 Moving the Cursor in a Table Chart	
Key(s)	**Action**
Tab or Ctrl+→	Moves right one cell
Shift+Tab or Ctrl+←	Moves left one cell
↓	Moves down one cell
↑	Moves up one cell
Ctrl+Home	Moves to upper-left corner cell
Ctrl+End	Moves to lower-right corner cell
End End	Moves to the last cell in the row
End End End	Moves to the end of the first line in the last cell in the row

Tip

By default, text is left-aligned in cells, and numbers are right-aligned. To change this, select text, then choose Table, Table Properties and use the alignment tab.

To edit the contents of a cell, click the text in the cell. A typing cursor appears. Then use the standard text-editing keys to revise the existing text. Any text that you highlight in a cell, for example, will be replaced by the new text you type. You can double-click an entry to highlight it and then type new text or numbers.

◀ See "Editing Text," p. 52

Adding and Deleting Columns and Rows

When you first create a table chart, you select the number of rows and columns you'll need. But plans often change, and table charts can too. Adding more rows or columns to a table chart is easy. Simply follow these steps:

1. Click a cell in the table. This inserts a typing cursor in the cell next to where you want the new column or row to appear. Also, the table buttons will become available to you on the toolbar (refer to fig. 9.4).

2. Click the Insert Row or Insert Column button on the toolbar.

That's it! If you are inserting a row, it appears *after* the row where your cursor rests, which means below. If you are inserting a column, *after* means to the right.

III

Adding Charts to Pages

If you want to add multiple columns or rows, or you want to add both rows and columns in a single action, you might be better off using the Insert Column/Row dialog box.

Follow these steps to insert new rows or columns:

1. Place your cursor in a cell of the table.

2. From the Table menu, choose Insert.

3. From the pop-out Insert menu, choose Row/Column. The Insert Column/Row dialog box opens, as shown in figure 9.5.

Fig. 9.5
The Insert Column/Row dialog box lets you change your mind about your table's size.

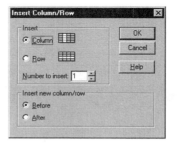

> **Tip**
>
> An alternative to steps 2 and 3 is to right-click the table and choose Row/Column from the shortcut menu.

4. The first thing to do is click one of the buttons at the top of the box to indicate whether you want to insert a Column or Row.

5. Next, choose whether the new column or row will appear Before or After the selected cell.

6. Use the increment or decrement arrows to change the number of columns or rows to insert; then click OK.

Deleting rows and columns works pretty much the same way. Select the table, then place your cursor in a single cell, or highlight a range of columns or rows to delete more than one at a time. Use the Delete Column/Row button or select Table, Delete, Row/Column to get the dialog box in figure 9.6. Simply select Row or Column, and click OK.

Fig. 9.6
Delete as many
columns or rows as
you have selected.

Resizing Columns and Rows

The easiest way to change the width of a column or the height of a row is to
drag the boundary of any cell in the column or row. You can drag the boundary between two columns to the left or right and drag the boundary between
two rows up or down. The entire column or row resizes. As you increase the
size of columns and rows, the entire table grows or shrinks accordingly.

To drag a boundary, place the mouse pointer on the line at the edge of the
cell, click and hold down the left mouse button, and then drag. When you
place the pointer over the boundary of the cell, the cursor becomes a double
arrow that points in the directions you can drag the boundary. Figure 9.7
demonstrates the process of changing the width of a column.

	Major Import	Major Export	GNP (millions)
Tanzania	Steel	Tanzanite	$101,310
Thailand	Rice	Sapphires	$98,010
Turkey	Automobiles	Wool	$198,120

Fig. 9.7
A dashed line and
double-headed
arrow cursor
appear as you drag
boundaries.

Tip

Try increasing the width of a column that contains word-wrapped text. You might
create enough space in each cell of the column so all the text fits on one line.

To set exact column widths and row heights, you must use the Cell Properties
InfoBox. From here, you can set all the columns of a table to exactly the same
width, for example. First select the rows and columns you want to adjust. To
get to the InfoBox you can select Table, Cell Properties, or right-click on the
row or column. When the Table InfoBox appears, click the fifth tab to get to
the Column/Row size settings (see fig. 9.8).

III

Adding Charts to Pages

Fig. 9.8
Change all kinds of settings for tables from this InfoBox.

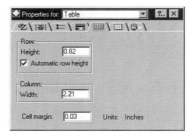

Highlight the current measurement and type a replacement number. When you click the close button in the upper-right hand corner, the new measurements are put in effect.

Tip

The default measurement unit is inches; to use a different measurement unit choose View, Set Units & Grids (you can choose from Inches, Points, Picas, Millimeters, and Centimeters).

Adding Column and Row Spacing

To add some space between successive columns or rows in a table, you can use the same tab in the Table InfoBox you used to change the cell height and width. You can get there in a couple of ways:

- Click the Table: Size Column/Row button.
- Or, select the table or click any cell in the table and then choose Table, Size Column/Row. The dialog box in figure 9.8 appears.

Troubleshooting

I selected my table, then went through the menu to choose the Size Column/Row command, but the InfoBox that appeared looks different than the one here. The same tabs aren't available. What's going on?

Notice that at the top of the Properties InfoBox for tables, you can use a drop-down menu to choose to work on properties of either the entire table or just selected cells. By changing this, you will get different tabs to choose from. The tab used for sizing columns and rows still exists, but it may not apply to this element of the object you selected. For example, if you click somewhere on the table rather than its frame, then choose Properties, the Select Cell(s) InfoBox appears, showing four tabs (refer to fig. 9.8). However, if you had simply clicked the table to select the whole thing, the InfoBox would have appeared set to Table (see fig 9.9). With this setting, there are seven tabs. Although this can be a little confusing when you first start using the InfoBox, it allows you to change settings for a multitude of features all from one place.

Fig. 9.9
The Table Properties InfoBox appears when you select an entire table, then click the Open InfoBox SmartIcon.

Use the Cell margin boxes to enter new settings for the spacing between successive rows and columns. The spacing for all the rows and columns in the table will be adjusted.

Moving Columns and Rows

Sometimes it's helpful to rearrange columns or rows of information into a more logical order for the content. Or perhaps you inserted a row or column at the wrong place by mistake. You can move columns one position left or right and move rows one position up or down easily. Select the column or row you wish to move and do one of the following:

- Click the Table Move Column/Row button.
- Choose Table, Move Column/Row.

The Move Column/Row dialog box appears, as shown in figure 9.10.

Fig. 9.10
You can move
columns or rows
over one place
using this dialog
box.

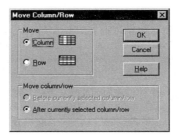

Within the dialog box, use one of the Move options (Column or Row) to choose whether to move the column or row where the cursor is located. Then use one of the two Move Column/Row options at the bottom on the dialog box to choose whether to move the column or row Before or After the currently selected column/row. With rows, Before moves the row up and After moves it down. With columns, Before moves the column one space to the left and After moves it one space to the right. Click OK to finish. The table is then updated.

Resizing the Entire Table

After you have added as many columns and rows as you need and you've stretched them to fit the data, you may need to adjust the overall size of the table to fit the design of the page. By clicking and dragging a side handle (the handles along the four sides of the table), you can make the overall table wider, narrower, taller, or shorter. By dragging a corner handle, you can make the table larger or smaller in two directions simultaneously, and keep its size proportional.

▶ See "Moving
and Sizing
Objects,"
p. 230

As you change the size of the table, the text and numbers inside do not change size. As you widen the table, more text can fit across each cell, so the word wrapping may change. To cause the text size to change proportionately with the table size, press and hold down the Shift key as you drag a corner handle. As the table size increases, the size of the text and numbers in the cells increases too, so the word wrapping may be affected.

Figure 9.11 shows a table after it has been resized by dragging a corner handle. Notice that the text size remains the same even though the table has been enlarged. Figure 9.12 shows the same table resized by holding down the Shift key while dragging a corner handle. Notice that the table shape has remained the same and the text has increased in size along with the table. Also, the increased text size has caused some words to wrap differently.

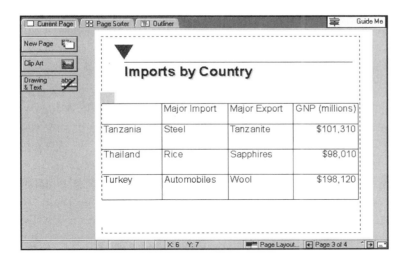

Fig. 9.11
Simply resizing a
table doesn't affect
the size of text
in it.

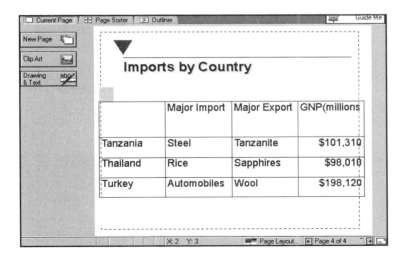

Fig. 9.12
Resizing a table by
dragging a corner
handle while
holding down
Shift resizes both
table and text.

Formatting the Table

Tables can be formatted to be more attractive, or to be easier for your audience to read. You can change the appearance of the text and numbers within
the cells, the colors and borders of the cells, and the color and border design
of the overall table. You can even return to the table gallery and select a different overall table design.

III

Adding Charts to Pages

Formatting Text in the Table

To format all or part of the text in a cell or to format all the text in a group of cells, select the cells. To select the cells, click a single cell to place a typing cursor in the cell. Then position the pointer on the cell again and hold down the mouse button while moving the pointer to adjacent cells. You can select a group of cells in a column, row, or rectangular region. Cells that are selected become highlighted. Once cells are selected, use the Text Font and Text Size buttons at the bottom of the Freelance window to format those cells to your liking.

▶ See "Formatting Text Directly," p. 194

You can also click the Text or Cell buttons, or select Table, Table Properties and use the text tab shown in figure 9.13 to make changes.

Fig. 9.13
The Table Properties InfoBox is the place to make all types of changes to text at once.

From this InfoBox you can change font, size, attributes such as bold and italic, add a shadow to text, or change the text color.

> **Tip**
>
> You can also make text bold, italic, or underlined using the buttons in the status bar at the bottom of the page.

Formatting the Table Background and Border

To format the table background color and the border surrounding the entire table, select the table or any cells in the table and then select Table, Lines & Fill Color to get the InfoBox page shown in figure 9.14.

Fig. 9.14
Apply borders or change fill colors here.

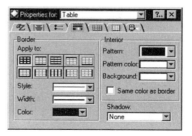

The dialog box shows controls for changing the background and border settings. You can click one of the Apply To: images to apply a border to a single side or set of lines in the table. Select a line style, width, and color that you prefer. There's an additional control for placing a shadow behind the table. Select None to show no shadow. A shadow gives the page a subtle three-dimensional look. Finally, you can change the background color and pattern for your cells using the Interior section of this sheet.

Caution

Be careful when using dark fill colors for the background of a table. You may need to adjust the color of the text to be lighter to ensure that's it's readable against a darker background.

Selecting a Different Table Design

To select a different overall design for a table, you can use the Layout page in the Table Properties InfoBox. Simply select the table and then click the Table button. Click the tab marked Layout. It contains a drop-down menu of the same choices offered in the Table Gallery dialog box that appears when you first create a table. Click the design of your choice. When you close the InfoBox, the new design is in place.

Caution

The new table design selected from the Table Gallery may override some of the cell-border formatting you have applied.

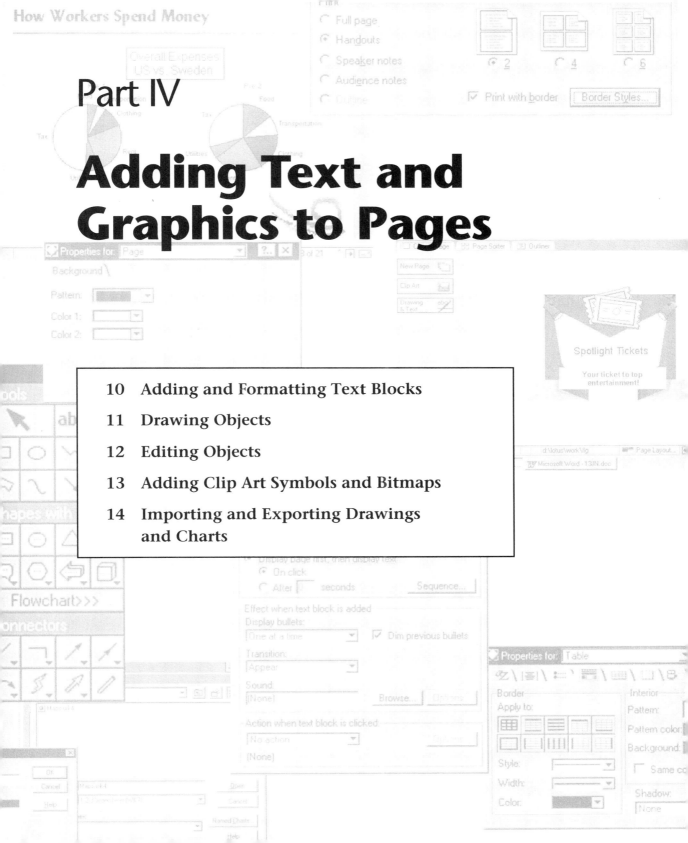

Part IV

Adding Text and Graphics to Pages

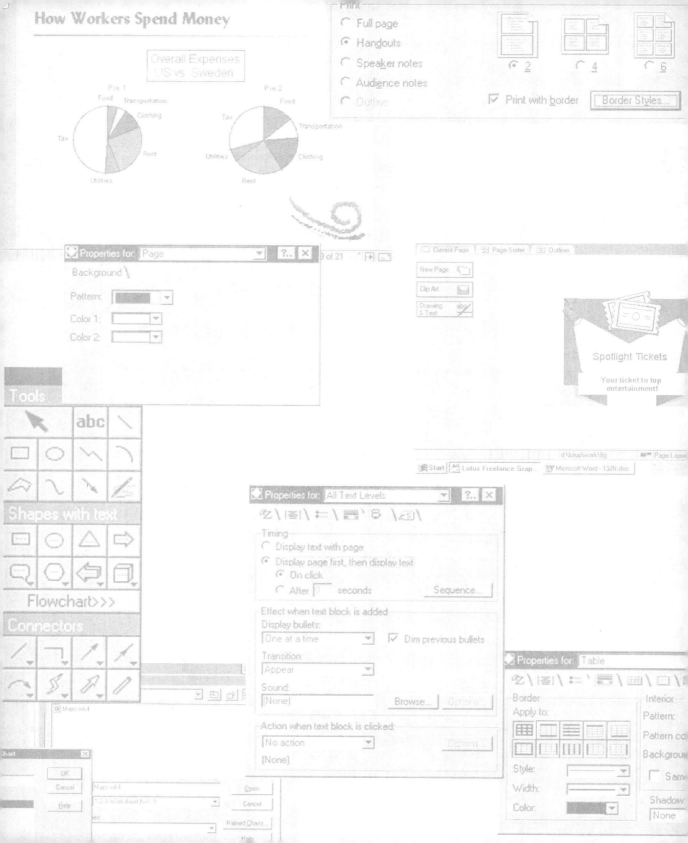

CHAPTER 10

Adding and Formatting Text Blocks

by Elizabeth Eisner Reding

Even after you fill in the Click Here to Type blocks on the page layouts you chose, something might still be missing from the presentation. You might want to add more text and position it in different places on the page. You might want to change the appearance of some of the text you already entered. Or you might want to get creative and turn text on some of the pages into design elements by curving the text or combining it with a symbol or an object.

This chapter tells you how to add and format the simplest or most elaborate text. You learn how to change the way text looks by doing the following:

- Adding wrapping and non-wrapping text blocks
- Formatting text blocks
- Creating curved text

Adding Text Blocks

Each type of text—whether it's a title or bulleted list has its own Click Here message. Clicking the Click Here to Type text blocks enables you to add text to a page quickly. But you can add additional text to any page by manually creating text blocks after you click the Text SmartIcon. You can place a text block anywhere on the page and then set its appearance, but you might find it easier to create a text block, format it in a clear area of the page, and then position the text.

In Freelance, you can create two types of text blocks: wrapping and non-wrapping. The text in a *wrapping* text block fits neatly in a box you draw on the page. When the words you type can no longer fit in the width of the box, they wrap to the next line. Using wrapping text lets you designate the precise area of the screen in which the text should appear. The text in a *non-wrapping* block starts at a point you designate and runs across to the right until you press Enter to start a new line. Non-wrapping text does not fit in a rectangular area of the page. It just starts at the point you specify. You can easily make non-wrapping text into wrapping text, though.

Creating Wrapping Text Blocks

To create a wrapping text block, first outline the boundaries of the text block by drawing a box with the Text SmartIcon. Then you can type text in the box.

To make a wrapping text block, follow these steps:

1. Open the toolbox by clicking the Drawing and Text button.

2. Click the Text SmartIcon in the toolbox.

3. Place the pointer where you want one corner of the text block to be.

4. Hold down the mouse button and drag diagonally from the upper-left corner to the lower-right corner to create a box (see fig. 10.1).

Fig. 10.1
Drag a box that marks the boundaries of a wrapping text box before you begin typing.

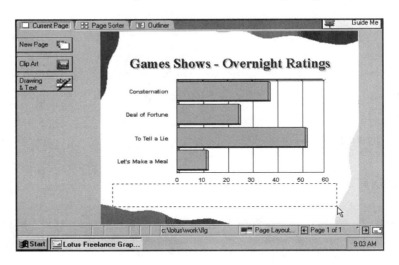

5. Release the mouse button. When you release the mouse button, the text entry box (shown in fig. 10.2) appears. The insertion point is blinking in the text box, ready for you to type.

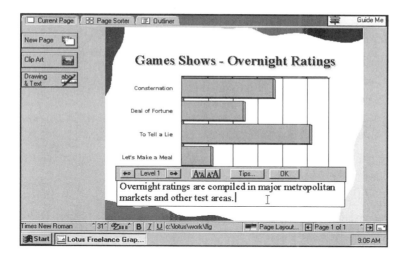

Fig. 10.2
Type text into a
text block created
by dragging the
mouse.

6. Type text in the box. The text fits into the area you defined.

7. When you finish typing, click OK or click outside of the text box.

Creating Non-Wrapping Text Blocks

To place a line of text on the page without specifying a box into which it should fit; the text will not wrap to the next line unless you press Enter. Follow these steps to create a non-wrapping text block:

1. Click the Text SmartIcon in the toolbox.

2. Click at the point where the text should begin.

   A text block, identical to the text block created for wrapping text, but without a predefined size, opens.

3. Begin typing.

4. When the text is complete, click the OK button in the text block or click elsewhere on the page.

> **Tip**
>
> You can turn non-wrapping text into wrapping text at any point by simply resizing the non-wrapping text (dragging a handle at a corner of the text block).

> **Note**
>
> To delete a text block after creating it, just select the text block by clicking it and then press the Delete key.

Creating Wrapping and Non-Wrapping Text Blocks

You can easily create text blocks that are both wrapping and non-wrapping. Follow these steps to create wrapping and non-wrapping text blocks:

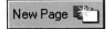

1. Click the New Page button at the bottom of the Freelance window to open the New Page dialog box.

2. Select the Basic Layout page layout.

3. Click the Click Here to Type Page Title text block.

4. Type the title you want and click anywhere on the page outside the text block when you finish. This closes the text block.

5. Click the Text SmartIcon in the toolbox and create a wrapping text box by dragging the mouse directly below the title. A text block appears on the page.

6. Type the text you want and click anywhere on the page outside the text block. A non-selected block of wrapping text appears on the page. This text block on your screen might have wrapped differently from the text block shown in figure 10.3; the size of your text block might be larger or smaller. Your text will be word-wrapped in the rectangle you created.

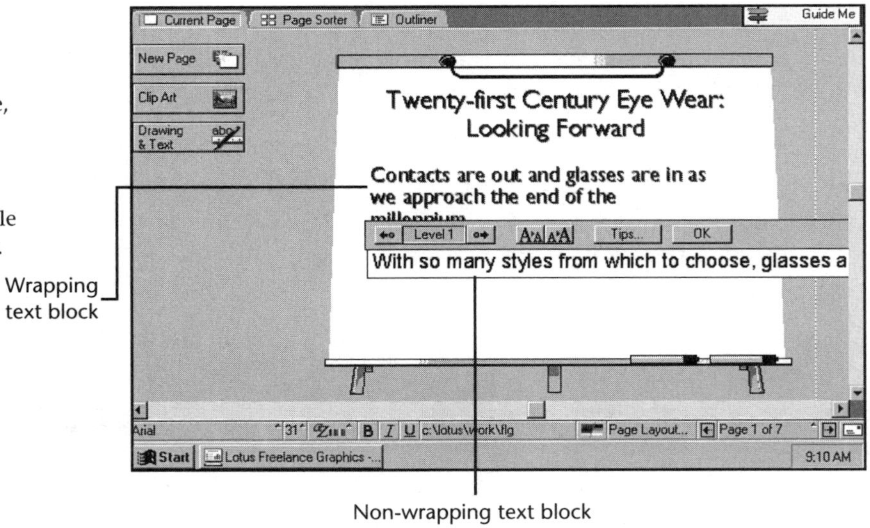

Fig. 10.3
A wrapping text block has a controlled shape, unlike a non-wrapping text block, which continues a single long line of text.

Wrapping text block

Non-wrapping text block

7. Click the Text SmartIcon in the toolbox and click once below the first text block. A non-wrapping text block in edit-text mode appears on the page.

8. Type your new text in the text block and click anywhere in the blank area of the page. You just created a non-wrapping text block, and it is selected on the page. Figure 10.3 shows both a wrapping text block and a non-wrapping text block.

9. Click and drag the bottom-right corner handle of the non-wrapping text block down and to the left to make a taller, narrower rectangle that fits on the page. This turns a non-wrapping text block into a wrapping text block. Figure 10.4 shows the dragging of a corner handle to resize a non-wrapping block into a wrapping block.

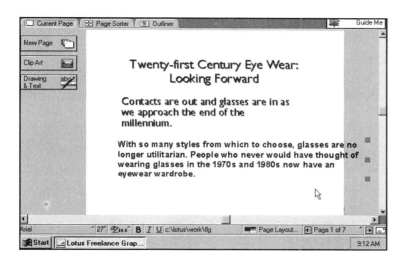

Fig. 10.4
Turn a non-wrapping text block into a wrapping text block by dragging its handles.

10. Click in the text block after the last word. The text block goes into Edit-Text mode.

11. Type additional text in the text block. Notice that the text automatically wraps in the text block.

12. Click anywhere on the page outside any text block. You now have a Basic Layout page with two wrapping text blocks (see fig. 10.5).

Fig. 10.5
Both text blocks
look like they
wrap, even though
the bottom one
was a non-
wrapping text
block.

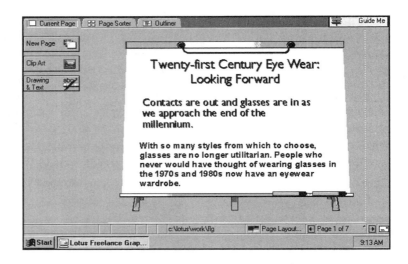

Importing Text into a Text Block

Instead of typing text in a text block, you can import text from another application. If the text is from another Windows application, you can select the
text, copy it to the Windows Clipboard, and then paste the text into a presentation page. Follow these steps:

1. In the other Windows application, select the text and click the Copy
   button, choose Edit, Copy, or press Ctrl+C. This copies the text to the
   Windows Clipboard.

2. Switch to Freelance Graphics.

3. Click a Click Here to Type text block or position the cursor in an
   existing block at the point where you want to insert the text. If you
   don't position the cursor in a text block, the text will be pasted onto
   the presentation page in its own text block.

4. Choose Edit, Paste, or click the Paste SmartIcon to paste the information from the Windows Clipboard.

If the text is in an ASCII file, you can import that file just as easily. Simply
follow these steps:

1. Click a text block or position the cursor in an existing block at the
   point where you want to insert the text. If the cursor is not positioned
   in a text block, the text will be pasted into the presentation page in its
   own text block.

2. Choose File, Open.

3. From the File Types drop-down list, choose ASCII (TXT).

4. Use the File Name and Directories controls to find and then select the appropriate file name. The File Name control will display only files with a TXT file extension unless you edit the *.TXT filter at the top of the control. The filter *.* displays all files, for example.

Imported text takes on the attributes of the paragraph style that is in effect at the insertion point. You learn about paragraph styles next in this chapter.

Formatting Text Blocks

The difference between editing text and formatting text is simple. When you edit text, you change its content; when you format text, you change its appearance.

The default formatting of the text in a presentation is controlled by the paragraph styles in the SmartMaster set you choose. Every SmartMaster set has a variety of paragraph styles that applies different formats to text, although every new text block automatically gets the first paragraph style. You can switch a text block to any other paragraph style, and you can change the settings of all the paragraph styles.

As an alternative to changing the paragraph styles, you can change the formatting of text by selecting the text and then using the commands on the Text menu. This is called *direct formatting* of text.

Formatting Text Blocks with Paragraph Styles

To change the appearance of a text block, you can choose a different paragraph style for the block (there are five to choose from). Or, if none of the paragraph styles is suitable, you can change the attributes of the paragraph styles.

Choosing a Different Paragraph Style for a Text Block

To change the paragraph style applied to a text block, use the Indent and Outdent buttons in the editing box to change levels or paragraph styles. Place a typing cursor in the text block by clicking the text block, pausing for a moment, and clicking again. Then click the Indent button at the top of the text block to change the entire block to the second paragraph style. Click again to switch to the next paragraph style. Clicking the Outdent button returns to the previous paragraph style. Clicking again returns to the first paragraph style. Changing levels can affect text in the Outliner view. Figure 10.6 shows the Indent and Outdent buttons.

Indent button promotes
text to the next level

Outdent button
demotes text to
the previous level

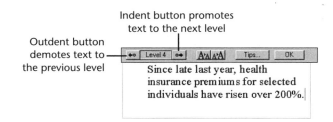

Fig. 10.6
Change the style
of text using the
Indent and
Outdent buttons.

If you place the typing cursor before the first character of text in the block, you can also press Tab to move to the next level, or press Shift+Tab to promote the text to the previous level. It is only a coincidence that the Tab key causes an indent; in fact, it can be used to change levels, in addition to the Indent and Outdent buttons.

> **Note**
>
> Unless the three paragraph styles have different attribute settings, you might see no difference in the text when you apply a different paragraph style.

Editing Paragraph Styles

If you don't like how the default paragraph styles that come with a SmartMaster set format a particular text block, you can override them by creating your own paragraph styles. Changing the attributes in the paragraph styles changes the look of only one block of text without affecting the rest of the text in a presentation.

To change the level styles for a text block, click the Text Properties SmartIcon to open the Text Properties dialog box. You also can right-click a text block to open the pop-up menu and then choose Text Properties. Either way, the Text Properties dialog box opens (see fig. 10.7). Among the tabs in the Text Properties dialog box are text attributes and bullet attributes.

Fig. 10.7
Change the
font and bullet
appearance for the
contents of a text
block.

To change the attributes of specific text levels, select the text you want to change, then choose Text, Text Properties by Level, and click the level you want to change from the cascading menu. You can also choose Text Properties by Level from the shortcut menu that appears when you right-click the text. Make sure the Text page is showing.

The pull-down arrow in the Property dialog box lets you select which text level you'd like to change. First, you must choose the level to modify (first through fifth). By choosing All Text Levels from the Properties For pull-down list, you can apply the same change to all five paragraph styles simultaneously. Then select the properties you want to change from within the Property dialog box.

You can, for instance, change the settings of the Font controls and color and shadow qualities.

In the Font Name list box, you can select from among the available typefaces installed in your computer. The Size and Text Color controls let you select a point size and color for the text. The Font Name and Size controls might display Mixed if you changed all paragraph styles and two or more styles use different faces and sizes.

Use the Attributes list to turn on or turn off any available features (such as bolding, italics, or underlining) for all the text in the text block.

Bullets are dramatic punctuation marks that grab your attention. They are such a valuable device for presentations that Freelance has four different page layouts with built-in bulleted text and lists.

You can make changes in the way bullets display by opening the Bullet page in the Text Properties dialog box (see fig. 10.8). Use the Bullet Attributes pull-down lists to change a bullet's style, color, size, and start number (if your bullets are numbers). A different bullet shape can be selected from a display of common shapes. You also can select Clip Art from the list of possible bullet shapes if you want to retrieve artwork and use it as a bullet. The None setting displays no bullet point before a text block. You use the Color and Size controls in the Property dialog box to choose a color and size for the bullet.

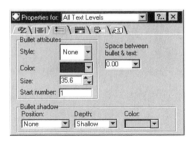

Fig. 10.8
Change the appearance of bullets using the Bullets page of the Property dialog box.

Bullets are traditionally round or rectangular, but you can choose numbers, letters, or Roman numerals from the Style pull-down list, shown in figure 10.9. New number and letter bullets automatically progress in numerical or alphabetical order, so for every new paragraph, your text will automatically be bulleted with the next number or letter.

Fig. 10.9
Choose a bullet from a variety of symbols or clip art.

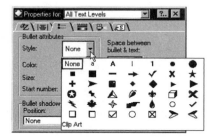

Changing Text Justification

The Alignment page in the Property dialog box offers four buttons that you can click to left-justify, center, right-justify, or full-justify text. The button faces show a sample justified paragraph. With the Vertical control, you can vertically justify text so it is placed along the top edge, in the vertical center, or along the bottom edge of the text block.

The Wrap Text check box turns on or off word wrapping in the text block.

To add a frame around a text block, click the Drawing & Text SmartIcon. Click the SmartIcon for the shape you want to create, then drag the mouse around an object in the dimension you'd like. A frame can add a dramatic highlight to a text block, giving it the appearance of a sign. Change the properties of a shape by double-clicking the shape or right-clicking the shape, then selecting Rectangle Properties. The shape's properties dialog box opens. The Rectangle Properties dialog box is shown in figure 10.10.

Fig. 10.10
Change the color, width, or shadow of a shape using the Property dialog box.

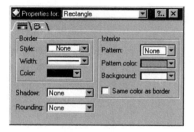

You use the Border controls to choose a Color, Width, and Style for the border of the frame surrounding the text block. To see the border, you must choose a style other than None. When you choose a style, the Shadow control becomes active, enabling you to choose a direction in which a subtle background shadow extends from the frame. The Interior controls let you choose a Pattern, Pattern color, and Background color for the interior of the frame.

To determine how to use these colors, choose a pattern from the Pattern list box. The pattern displays in the two colors. If the pattern is a gradient, the gradient shows a transition from the first color to the second color. To make the box a solid color, select the Same Color as Border check box to make the interior of the box the same color as the border.

Figure 10.11 shows a text block with a shadowed frame.

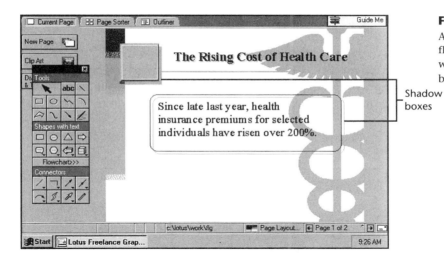

Fig. 10.11
Add drama and flare to a shape with a shadow box.

Shadow boxes

To change the horizontal positioning of the text in the block and to change the spacing between successive lines and successive paragraphs, click the Alignment tab in the Properties dialog box (see fig. 10.12).

Change the horizontal and vertical alignment by clicking the button for the way you want your text to look. Use the Space Between and Indent controls to change the current measurements. The Lines setting determines the spacing between successive lines in a paragraph; increase this setting to space out the lines a bit and make the text look a little airier. The 1st Line setting lets you set a special indent for the first line of a paragraph. The Left and Right settings determine the left and right margins in the text block (the interior distance between the text and the edge of the block).

Fig. 10.12
Control align-
ment, spacing,
and indents in
this Property
dialog box.

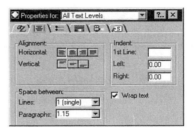

If you change the paragraph styles of text in a Click Here to Type Text block, two additional check boxes appear in the Paragraph Styles tab in the Property dialog box. Apply to SmartMaster makes the same change to all other Click Here to Type Text blocks on all other pages that use the same page layout. Reset to Style removes the changes you made to the paragraph styles and resets the paragraphs to the default styles in the SmartMaster set.

After modifying any or all of the settings in the Paragraph Styles dialog box, click OK to view the changes.

Formatting a Text Block with Paragraph Styles

Try formatting a text block using level styles. Before getting started, check the measurement units for the indents. Make sure the measurement units are set to Inches by choosing View, Units & Grids to open the Set Units & Grid dialog box. If the units aren't set to Inches, select the Inches radio button and click OK. Then follow these steps:

1. Click the New Page button on the Freelance window to open the New Page dialog box.

2. Double-click Blank Page to make a new page without Click Here to Type Text blocks.

3. Click the Text SmartIcon in the toolbox and create a rectangle on the page. A text block in edit-text mode appears.

4. Type the text you want to add and click OK. Figure 10.13 shows the text block on the page.

5. Right-click the text block to open the Properties dialog box.

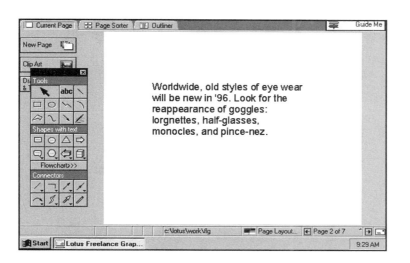

Fig. 10.13
A wrapping text
block is added to
a blank page.

Now, begin making changes to the styles that control the appearance of the
block. Follow these steps:

1. Make sure All Text Levels appears in the Properties For drop-down list.

2. In the Font tab, click the Font Name list, choose Arial; in the Size list,
   choose 36 pt; and choose dark blue as the Text Color.

3. Click the Alignment tab.

4. Click the Center Vertically button to center the text vertically.

Change the spacing and level of the text block by following these steps:

1. Make sure the Alignment tab is exposed.

2. Choose Level 1 Text from the Properties For drop-down list, then click
   the Alignment tab.

3. Choose 2 from the Paragraphs drop-down list.

4. Make sure Lines is set to 1 (single).

5. Enter **0.5** in the 1st Line box, Left box, and the Right box.

6. Change the text level to Level 2 using the Indent button.

7. Set Paragraph Spacing to 2 (double).

8. Set Line Spacing to 1.5.

9. Enter **0.5** in the First Line Indents box.

10. Enter **1.0** in both the Left and Right Indents boxes.

11. Click OK to save your settings and return to the Paragraph Styles dialog
    box. Figure 10.14 shows the screen with these changes made.

Fig. 10.14
Change the appearance of a text block using spacing and level styles.

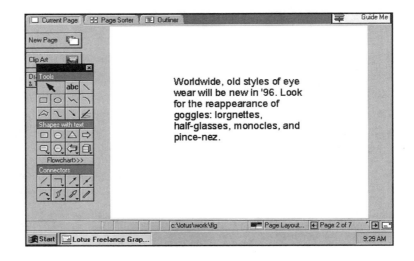

Add and format a frame for the text block by following these steps:

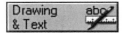

1. Click the Drawing & Text SmartIcon, then click the rectangular shape under the Tools palette and enclose the text block with the shape.
2. Right-click the shape, then open the Rectangle Properties InfoBox.
3. In the Properties dialog box, click the Border tab.
4. Choose a new Interior Pattern color from the Pattern Color drop-down list.
5. Choose a new width from the Width drop-down list.
6. Choose a new line style from the Style drop-down list.
7. Choose a dark gray color from the Color list box.
8. Choose Below Left from the Shadow drop-down list.
9. Close the Properties For InfoBox.

Now try using the paragraph styles. Follow these steps:

1. Place the cursor in front of a word at the beginning of a sentence and the text block goes into edit-text mode. Press Enter, and the sentence becomes the beginning of a new paragraph (see fig. 10.15).
2. Click the Demote button. The text in the newly created paragraph is reformatted in the Level 2 style with wider margins.
3. Click anywhere outside the text block. The final framed text appears deselected on the page (see fig. 10.16).

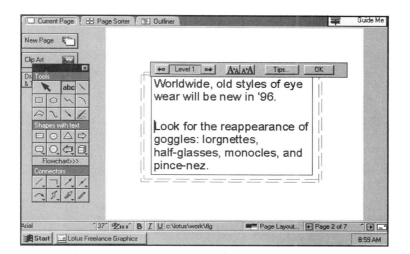

Fig. 10.15
Create a new paragraph while the text block is in Edit mode.

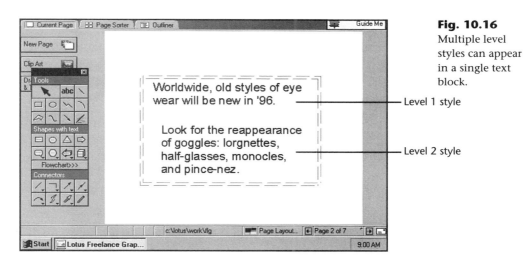

Fig. 10.16
Multiple level styles can appear in a single text block.

— Level 1 style

— Level 2 style

4. If you want to change the size, shape, or placement of the framed text, you can click and drag the text block or its handles until you adapted it so it is pleasing to you. Notice that narrowing the text block changes the placement of the text. Click anywhere outside the text block to deselect it when you are through.

Changing the Default Paragraph Styles

Each SmartMaster set contains two sets of default paragraph styles: one set for the title page layout and one set for the rest of the page layouts. By changing the default paragraph styles, you can change how every new text block will be formatted, because each new text block takes on the attributes of the default paragraph styles. You might want to change the default paragraph styles if you want every new page title in a presentation to be a different color or a larger size, for example.

Changing the default level styles will not change text blocks that have already been formatted by paragraph styles, though. Nor will it change text blocks that you have formatted by editing their paragraph styles. Changes to the paragraph styles of a text block override the default settings.

To revise the default level styles, double-click the Text SmartIcon in the toolbox.

Formatting Text Directly

Paragraph styles control the overall look of a text block, but changing them is somewhat involved, as the previous sections have shown you. Sometimes, if a text block needs only one quick formatting change, you can select the block and then apply a formatting change directly. At other times, you might need to emphasize a few characters or words in the block by changing their styling (boldfacing them or changing their font, for example). To format specific text in a block, select only that text and then choose formatting that will override the paragraph style.

Whether you want to quickly format a block of text, a word, or a phrase, you use the same direct formatting techniques. You can use the method that is most comfortable for you: if you're a keyboard person, you can use the shortcut keys, and if you're a mouse person, you can use SmartIcons or the right-mouse button.

To directly format an entire text block, click the block to select it. To directly format a passage of text in a block, click the block, pause a moment, and then click at the beginning of the passage in the block. A typing cursor appears in the text where you clicked. Drag across the text to be selected, or press and hold down the Shift key while pressing the right-arrow key. Selected text appears in reverse video (when the text and background colors display in reverse).

Choosing Text Fonts

After you select text to format, you can use any of the following methods to change the font and size:

- Click the Text Font and Text Size buttons at the bottom of the Freelance window.

- Right-click the mouse, choose Text Properties, and then choose the font name and size you want to use from the Font tab.
- Choose Text, Font & Color.

If you added the Change Font SmartIcon to the SmartIcon palette, you can click it to get to the Font dialog box.

Changing the font and size of text is covered in detail in Chapter 3, "Making Basic Changes to the Presentation."

Tip

Freelance provides a visual way to size the text in a selected text block. Simply hold down the Shift key, click and hold down the mouse button on a corner handle of the text block, and then drag the handle diagonally. When you release the Shift key and mouse button, the text resizes according to the next size of the block.

Choosing Text Character Attributes

The fastest way to choose text character attributes is to select the text to format and then use accelerator keys. Table 10.1 lists these keys.

Table 10.1 Accelerator Keys for Text Character Attributes

Character Attribute	Accelerator Key
Bold	Ctrl+B
Italic	Ctrl+I
Underline	Ctrl+U
Normal	Ctrl+N
Undo	Ctrl+Z

You can use text character attributes alone or in any combination. If you want to reverse an attribute you just applied, press Ctrl+Z to undo the last command or action. If you want to remove all the character attributes you added to selected text, press Ctrl+N to return the text to Normal.

The character attribute SmartIcons are another quick way to choose character attributes. SmartIcons work like toggle switches; you can click them on or off. Click the Bold SmartIcon to apply boldface to text, the Italic SmartIcon to italicize text, and the Underline SmartIcon to underline text.

Adding Text Bullets

Adding bullets to text is easy. To add a bullet to only one paragraph in a text block, place the typing cursor anywhere in the paragraph. To add a bullet to every paragraph in a text block, select the entire text block. Then right-click the text block to open a shortcut menu. Choose Text Block Properties, then click the Bullet tab (see fig. 10.17).

Fig. 10.17
Use the Bullet tab of the Properties dialog box to change its style, color, and size.

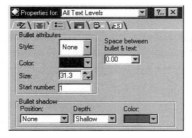

Choose the style of the text bullet from the Style drop-down list and the color of the text bullet from the Color drop-down list. Choose the size of the text bullet from the Size drop-down list or enter a custom point size.

To use a symbol as a bullet, select Clip Art from the list of available bullet styles. Then select a symbol from the clip art gallery. A miniature of the artwork appears as a bullet before each paragraph. Figure 10.18 shows a hand symbol used as a bullet in a text block.

Fig. 10.18
Available clip art can be used as a bullet symbol.

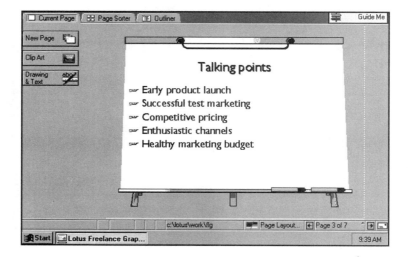

Setting Indents with the Text Block Ruler

With the text block ruler, Freelance provides an easy, visual method for changing the indents in a block of text. To turn on the text block ruler, choose View, Set View Preferences from the main menu and select the Text Block Ruler check box in the Set View Preferences dialog box.

Then, when you place a typing cursor in a text block, the text block ruler appears at the top of the block. Small triangular-shaped markers in the ruler indicate the first-line, left, and right indents. To change the indents, you can drag these markers along the ruler. The marker at the right, which indicates the right indent, is a solid triangle. The triangular marker at the left is composed of two smaller halves (although it looks like a single triangle). Drag the top half to set the first-line indent and drag the bottom half to set the left indent. You can drag the top marker to the left of the bottom marker to set a hanging indent, for example. Figure 10.19 shows the markers in the text block ruler as they are set to create such a hanging indent.

Left indent marker can be used to create a hanging indent

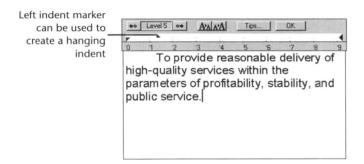

Fig. 10.19
By simply dragging the left indent marker, you can create a hanging indent.

Justifying Text

The only way to change the alignment—rather than the level—of text without changing the paragraph style for a block is to use the accelerator keys for alignment. Table 10.2 lists these keys. Select the text block and then use the appropriate accelerator key.

Alignment affects all the text in a block, even if the block contains more than one paragraph.

Table 10.2 Accelerator Keys for Text Alignment	
Alignment	**Accelerator Key**
Left	Ctrl+L
Right	Ctrl+R
Center	Ctrl+E
Full Justify	Ctrl+J

Framing Text

You can only frame an entire text block; you cannot frame selected text in a block. After you select the block, open the Text Frame Properties dialog box by choosing Text, Text Properties (you can also right-click the block, choose Text Properties, and choose the Border tab—the fourth tab from the left). On this page, you can choose the style, width, interior color, and pattern of a frame.

Creating Curved Text

Freelance Graphics 96 has a new text-formatting capacity that can really jazz up your presentations. Curved text lets you mold text into any shape you want. Or you can choose from among the many predesigned shapes in the Curved Text dialog box. With curved text, you can make text into a design element that stands on its own, or you can even shape the text around an object or a symbol.

You can curve any text block on a presentation page. You can even use the same procedure when editing page layouts to curve a Click Here text block. Then, text blocks you create by clicking the curved Click Here text block will appear with the curve you created. You learn how to edit page layouts in Chapter 22, "Modifying the Default Settings."

Creating Curved Text with Predesigned Shapes

You don't need to custom-design a text shape to turn your text into something special. Freelance offers so many predesigned text shapes that you can probably find what you want in the extensive menu of curves, ovals, circles, rectangles, squares, and triangles. The only text element you can't curve is a bullet.

To curve text by using one of the predesigned text shapes, click the text block you want to shape, and then choose Text, Curved Text to open the Curved Text dialog box (see fig. 10.20).

In the Curved Text dialog box, you can scroll through many pre-designed text shapes, click a text shape, and then choose Pre_v_iew to see how the text will look. If the new text design passes inspection, click OK.

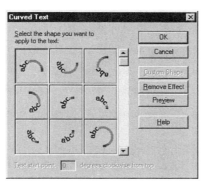

Fig. 10.20
Create dramatic text effects using the Curved Text dialog box.

IV

Adding Text and Graphics

Caution

Be careful when using the Curved Text Preview button. Once you click the Pre_v_iew button, the selected text is automatically curved. To return to the original text, click the _C_hange button, which reopens the Curved Text dialog box. If you click OK after previewing the curved text, the only way to return the text to its previous condition is to click _E_dit, _U_ndo, or press the Undo SmartIcon.

Note

You can edit curved text like any other text. Click the text to enter edit-text mode. The text reverts to a straight line so it is easier to edit. Remember to click the right mouse button for quick access to font style, size, and so on. You cannot underline or strike out curved text, though. When you finish editing, click OK. The text becomes curved again.

Tip

To alter the size and shape of curved text, drag the text block by any of its handles until you have the look you want.

To remove the curving from curved text, select the curved text on the page, open the Curved Text dialog box, and choose _R_emove Effect.

Try curving text around a shape by following these steps:

1. Click the New Page button in the Freelance window to open the New Page dialog box.

2. Double-click Blank Page to make a new, blank page.

3. Click the Text SmartIcon in the toolbox and create a rectangle on the page. A text block in edit-text mode appears.

4. Type the text you want to shape and click OK.

5. Choose Text, Click Curved Text. The Curved Text dialog box appears.

6. Scroll through the menu of predesigned shapes until you find a shape you like and click OK. The text takes on the selected shape.

7. Move and enlarge the newly curved text by clicking and dragging the text block by its handles. Figure 10.21 shows the curved text.

Fig. 10.21
Ordinary text can be shaped to look like an oval using the Curved Text dialog box.

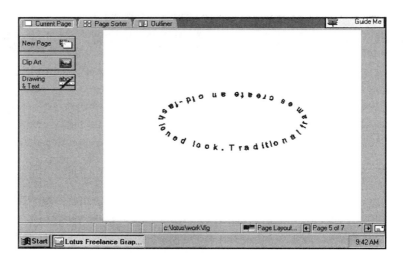

Custom-Shaping Text

What if none of the predesigned text shapes in the Curved Text dialog box suit your taste? Perhaps you want a text shape that is more spontaneous, irregular, or asymmetrical. You can custom-design curved text to follow exactly the contours you want.

To custom-design curved text, follow these steps:

1. Draw a graphic shape with one of the tools from the toolbox.

2. Create the text block.

3. Select both the graphic shape and the text block.

4. Choose Collection, Collection Properties, then click the Curved Text in the Text tab. The Curved Text dialog box appears.

5. Choose Custom Shape.

The text is redrawn, following the edge of the graphic shape you drew. The text is also resized so that the text block fits the length of the edge of the graphic shape.

You can leave the graphic shape, or you can delete it to leave behind only the reshaped text.

First create the text to be custom-shaped by following these steps:

1. Click the New Page button in the Freelance window to open the New Page dialog box.

2. Select Blank Page to make a new, blank page.

3. Click the Text SmartIcon in the toolbox and create a rectangle on the page. A text block in edit-text mode appears.

4. Type the text you want to shape and click OK.

Next, create the graphic object around which the text will reshape by following these steps:

1. Click the Curve icon in the toolbox.

2. Position the pointer near the left side of the page, press and hold down the mouse button, and drag the pointer to a second spot above and to the right.

3. Release the mouse button to create the first part of the curve.

4. Press and hold down the mouse button again, and then drag the pointer to a third spot below and to the right.

5. Release the mouse button to create a second segment of the curve.

6. Press and hold down the mouse button again, and then drag the pointer to a fourth spot up and to the right.

7. Release the mouse button to create the third curve segment.

8. Click the right mouse button to end the curve.

Tip

Remember that you can always delete the shape and try again by selecting the curve and either choosing Edit, Clear or pressing the Delete key.

IV

Adding Text and Graphics

Now shape the text along the curve by following these steps:

1. Select both the curve and the text block by clicking one, holding down the Shift key, and clicking the other. Figure 10.22 shows the completed text block and selected curve.

Fig. 10.22
An individual text block and curve can be combined so the text follows the curve.

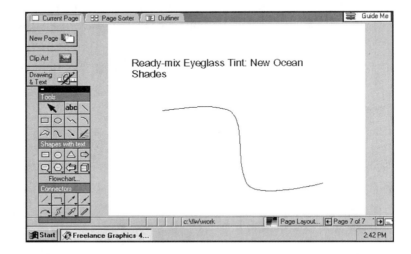

2. Choose Collection, Collection Properties, then click Curved Text from the Font tab.

3. Choose Custom Shape in the Curved Text dialog box. Figure 10.23 shows the final shaped text.

Fig. 10.23
Combine text and a unique shape for a dramatic effect.

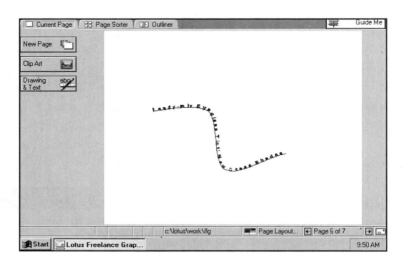

Custom-Curving Text around a Symbol

You can also use Freelance to mold text so it curves around an object to create a unified design statement.

To start, create a text block or select the text block you want to curve. Then click the Symbol icon in the toolbox to open the Add Symbol to Page dialog box. There you can browse through the symbol categories until you find a predesigned symbol you like. Click the symbol and then drag the shape on the presentation page. Click and drag the handles to move and size the symbol, if you want.

For the text to follow the shape of the object, you must ungroup the symbol and then select the principle shape. Then choose Text, Curved Text to open the Curved Text dialog box, and choose Custom Shape. The text curves to fit the contours of the object on the page.

Curving Text around an Object

The following steps show you how to curve text around part of one of the symbols in the symbol library:

1. Click New Page in the Freelance window to open the New Page dialog box.

   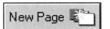

2. Select Blank Page to make a new, blank page.

3. Click the Shapes With Text SmartIcon in the toolbox to open the Shapes palette.

4. Choose a shape from the palette and drag the mouse to the desired size.

5. Click anywhere else on the page to deselect the shape.

Now create the text to curve around the symbol by following these steps:

1. Click the Text SmartIcon and create a rectangle on the page. A text block in edit-text mode appears.

2. Type the text you want around the shape and click OK.

3. Click the shape, press and hold down Shift, and click the text block. Figure 10.24 shows both objects selected.

4. Choose Text, Text Properties, then click the Basics tab in the Properties For dialog box.

5. Click the Shrink Shape Text to Fit Shape check box. The selected text shapes itself around the hexagon, changing the type size to fit completely around the hexagon.

Fig. 10.24
Text and hexagon
can be combined
so the text wraps
around the shape.

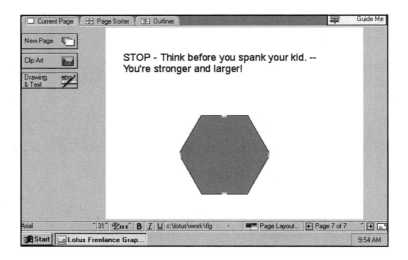

To remove the hexagon and leave just the text, follow these steps:

1. Click anywhere outside the hexagon and text so that neither is selected.

2. Choose Edit, Select, Cycle.

3. When the Cycle Selection dialog box appears, click Next until Polygon/
   Shape appears in the dialog box.

4. Choose Select to select only the hexagon and then click OK.

5. Press Delete to delete the hexagon.

You might want to add a second text block in the center of the shaped text
with the large word "STOP" to create a dramatic sign. ❖

CHAPTER 11

Drawing Objects

by Elizabeth Eisner Reding

Page layouts and Click Here blocks make it easy to create presentation pages that hold text, charts, and symbols, but often you may need graphic drawings on pages as well. A presentation might not be complete, for example, without a client's logo at the lower corner of each page or without an arrow pointing to an important bar or pie slice.

This chapter describes how to add basic graphic shapes by using the drawing tools and how to change the attributes that control the appearance of the objects. It also tells you what you need to know to set up the drawing aids of Freelance, such as the rulers and grid.

In this chapter, you learn how to

- Understand drawn objects
- Change the attributes of drawn objects
- Draw the objects
- Change the drawing environment
- Use Freelance as a drawing program

Understanding Drawn Objects

Freelance gives you the tools to draw and edit graphic shapes on the pages of a presentation. The drawing tools are powerful enough to make Freelance an impressive stand-alone drawing program. For example, you can start with a blank page and draw a diagram, such as an office floor plan or a map with directions to an event, as shown in figure 11.1. Another example of drawn objects is shown in figure 11.2, which illustrates a presentation page with both a client's logo and a chart annotation. The logo and the arrow were added as drawn objects.

Fig. 11.1
You can create
a map using
Freelance
Graphic's drawing
tools.

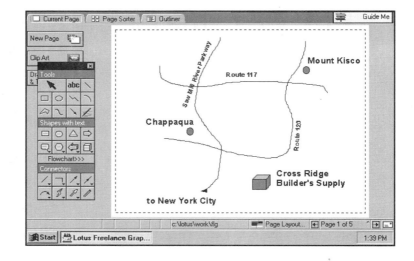

Fig. 11.2
A presentation
page can be
enhanced by
adding drawn
objects.

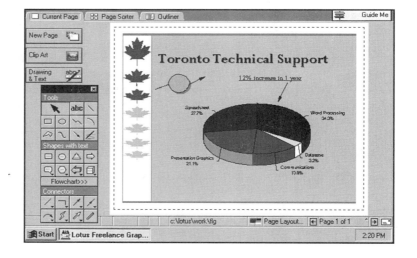

The toolbox holds a set of tools that you can use to draw various graphic shapes, such as lines, rectangles, and circles. After choosing a tool from the toolbox, you must follow the specific drawing procedures that apply to that tool. These techniques are a variation of the general procedures that you follow when using all tools, such as clicking the tool, dragging the pointer to draw the object, clicking the mouse to place points on the page, and releasing the mouse button to finish an object.

Each graphic shape that you add is a separate drawn object on a Freelance page. You can select the objects independently and then move, resize, or edit them. You can also perform a wide range of actions to change the appearance of the objects by using the commands on the Text Shape menu or by using the Properties for Text Shape InfoBox. You can place a graphic object behind a text block created with a Click Here text block, for example. The next chapter covers these commands.

Changing the Attributes of Drawn Objects

After you have drawn a text shape, you can click the object, then choose Text Shape, Text Shape Properties to gain access to the object's Properties InfoBox. You can also click the object with the right mouse button and then choose Text Shape Properties from the pop-up menu. The Properties InfoBox for a polygon is shown in figure 11.3.

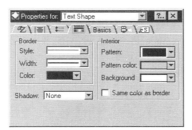

Fig. 11.3
The Text Shape Properties InfoBox enables you to make changes to your text.

Using the Properties InfoBox

Pages within the Properties InfoBox for drawn objects contain settings that enable you to change such basic design aspects as edge thickness and interior color. The InfoBox pages for most drawn objects have groups of settings labeled Border and Interior:

- *Border.* Enables you to change the Color, Width, and Style of the line along the border of an object. Click the pull-down button to the right of each setting to see the available choices. Choosing None as the Style setting draws no line along the edge of the object and displays only the interior color.

- *Interior.* Enables you to change the first and second colors used within the object. If you set the Pattern to solid (the first choice at the upper-left corner of the menu of patterns), Freelance uses the first color to fill the object. If you choose a pattern, the pattern is composed of the first and second colors. If the pattern is a gradient, the transition it displays runs from the first color to the second. Clicking Same Color As Border fills the object with the Pattern color; the object then appears to be made up of a solid color.

> **Note**
>
> The tabs for some objects have other settings that are applicable to the object type, too. The Properties sheet for a rectangle has a Rounding setting, for example.

You can see the effect of your changes immediately by moving the Properties InfoBox so it's not covering the selected object, or by closing it. It's a good idea to just move the sheet out of the way so you can continue to make changes, however.

Any other settings specific to an object type appear below the Border and Interior settings.

Changing the Default Object Attributes

Change the default properties for an object to match an existing object by right-clicking the object, then clicking the Change Default Properties message box. Figure 11.4 shows the Change Default Properties message box.

Fig. 11.4
The Change Default Properties message box enables you to further customize your object.

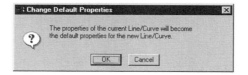

> **Caution**
>
> Changing any default properties affects all new objects drawn in the current presentation. Changes to the settings are not carried over to the next presentation you create.

Drawing the Objects

Drawing objects with the drawing tools usually requires choosing a tool from the toolbox, dragging the pointer across the page, and clicking the mouse button. The specific steps you follow depend on the object type. The following sections describe these object types.

Drawing Rectangles and Squares

You draw both rectangles and squares by clicking the Rectangle tool in the toolbox and then dragging the pointer on the page. Simply press and hold down the Shift key while you draw to keep the rectangle a perfect square.

To draw a rectangle, follow these steps:

1. Click the Rectangle tool in the toolbox.

2. Place the pointer where you want one corner of the rectangle to be.

3. Press and hold down the mouse button.

4. Drag the pointer to the opposite corner of the rectangle. A dashed box marks the rectangle's position, as shown in figure 11.5.

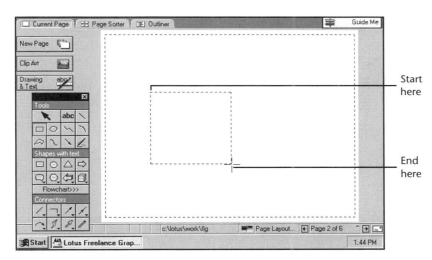

Fig. 11.5
Draw a rectangle by dragging the crosshair pointer from one end of the shape to the other.

Start here

End here

5. Release the mouse button. The rectangle then appears with the default rectangle attributes. The Rectangle tool in the toolbox is deselected, and the Selector tool is selected.

When you double-click the drawn rectangle, the Properties InfoBox shown in figure 11.6 appears.

The Rounding setting offers four settings: None, Low, Medium, and High. Figure 11.7 demonstrates each of these settings.

Fig. 11.6
Double-click the object to open its Properties sheet.

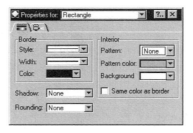

Fig. 11.7
Use rounding to change the appearance of a rectangle.

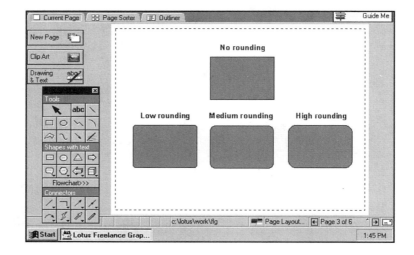

Tip

By holding down the Shift key as you draw the rectangle, you can constrain its shape to a perfect square.

The Shadow setting enables you to choose a direction in which a subtle shadow should extend behind the rectangle or to display no shadow (None).

Drawing Lines

Drawing a line on a page is just like drawing a line on a piece of paper. After clicking the Line tool, you drag the pointer across the page in a straight line.

To draw a line, follow these steps:

1. Click the Line tool in the toolbox.

2. While holding down the mouse button, drag the pointer from the start to the end points of the line, shown in figure 11.8.

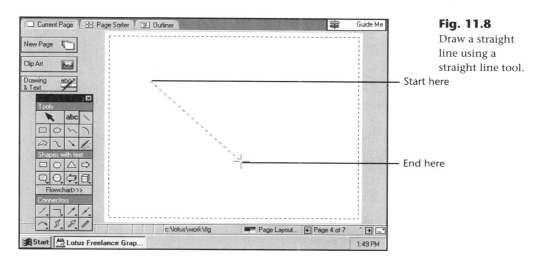

Fig. 11.8
Draw a straight line using a straight line tool.

Start here

End here

3. Release the mouse button.

> **Tip**
>
> To constrain the line to exactly horizontal, diagonal, or vertical, press and hold down Shift while you draw the line.

Double-clicking a line brings up the Properties Line & Curve InfoBox. This InfoBox works similarly to the Properties for Rectangle InfoBox.

By using the Line settings, you can determine the color, width, and line style of the line. The Marker setting enables you to place a graphic shape at the beginning and end of the line; click the pull-down list next to Marker to display the available shapes. By clicking the Shadow pull-down list, you can add a shadow above or below the line and make the line appear to float above the page.

By using the Arrowhead setting, you can change its location to the Start of Line, End of Line, Both, or None. The Size setting lets you to make the arrowhead larger or smaller.

Drawing Arrows

Drawing an arrow is just like drawing a line except that Freelance automatically puts an arrowhead at the end of the line. To draw an arrow, follow these steps:

1. Click the Arrow tool in the toolbox.

2. While holding down the mouse button, use the pointer to draw a line on the page, or click the starting and ending points of the arrow.

3. Release the mouse button. Your arrowhead will look similar to the one shown in figure 11.9.

Fig. 11.9
Create a large, thick arrow to draw the reader's attention to a particular item.

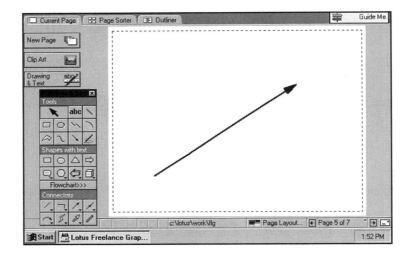

Tip

As with lines, pressing the Shift key as you draw an arrow constrains the arrow to horizontal, diagonal, or vertical.

When you double-click an arrow, its Properties InfoBox looks just like a line's Properties InfoBox. End of Line is the automatic setting for Arrowheads. To convert an arrow to a line, choose None for the Arrowheads setting.

Drawing Polylines

Polylines are lines composed of two or more straight segments. To draw a polyline, follow these steps:

1. Click the Polyline tool in the toolbox.

2. Click a point, hold down the mouse button, and draw a line segment. Then click at the end of the segment, hold down the mouse button, and draw the next segment.

3. Click the right mouse button, double-click, or press Esc after you draw the last line segment to finish the polyline. Figure 11.10 shows a completed polyline shape.

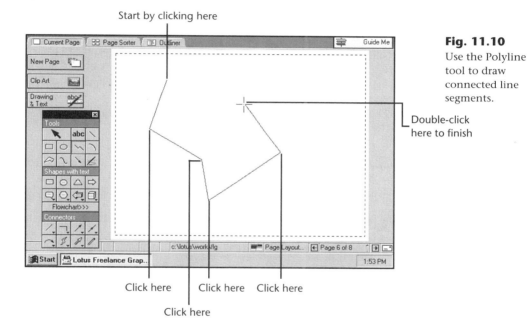

Start by clicking here

Double-click here to finish

Click here   Click here   Click here

Click here

Fig. 11.10
Use the Polyline tool to draw connected line segments.

Rather than draw each line segment, you can click at the end of each segment and then right-click the end of the last segment.

Tip

Holding down the Shift key as you add each segment constrains the segment to a horizontal or vertical line.

Double-clicking the completed polyline opens its Properties InfoBox, which has the same settings as the Properties InfoBox for lines. To learn about these settings, refer to the section "Drawing Lines" earlier in this chapter.

> **Tip**
>
> While a polyline is being created, you can delete line segments one by one in the reverse order in which they were drawn, by pressing the Backspace key repeatedly. Each time you press Backspace, Freelance deletes the previous line segment.

To draw an object that has both straight and curved segments, you complete a polyline segment and then use the Curve tool to draw the next segment. A later section in this chapter describes how to use the Curve tool.

Drawing Polygons

▶ See "Drawing Curves," p. 216

Polygons are shapes with three or more straight sides which form a closed object. Polygons can be filled, unlike *polylines* which are not closed objects and cannot be filled. To draw a polygon, follow these steps:

1. Click the Polygon tool in the toolbox.

2. Click a point, hold down the mouse button, and draw a line segment that serves as a polygon side. Then click at the end of the segment, hold down the mouse button, and draw the next side.

3. Click the right mouse button, double-click, or press Esc after you draw the last side. Freelance joins the ends of the first and last sides to close the polygon. Figure 11.11 shows the process of drawing a polygon.

Fig. 11.11
Draw a polygon using your mouse, which can be filled if you choose.

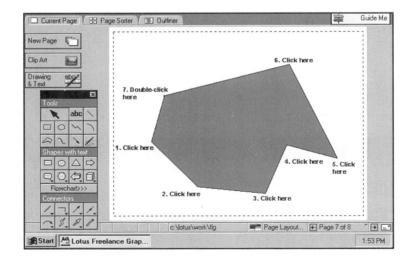

Rather than draw each side, you can click at the end of each side and then right-click at the end of the last side.

> **Tip**
>
> Holding down the Shift key as you add each side constrains the segment to horizontal or vertical.

Double-clicking the completed polygon brings up the attributes InfoBox for polygons (see fig. 11.12). Polygons have both edges and interior areas, so the sheet has both Border and Interior settings. You can fill a polygon with a gradient, for example, by choosing different first and second colors and then choosing a gradient design from the menu of palettes. To place a shadow behind the polygon, use the Shadow setting.

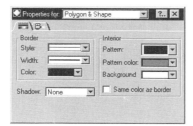

Fig. 11.12
Change the Properties of a polygon using its Properties InfoBox.

> **Tip**
>
> To delete the sides of a polygon one by one in the reverse order in which they were drawn, press the Backspace key repeatedly. Each time you press Backspace, the previous side is deleted.

To draw a polygon that has both straight and curved sides, you complete a polygon side and then switch to the Curve tool. Switch back to the Polygon tool to complete the polygon. The next section describes the use of the Curve tool.

> **Tip**
>
> A polyline can be converted into a polygon once it has been selected. Choose Drawing, Convert, To Polygons, and the polyline object becomes a polygon. Any unconnected lines in the polyline object will be connected when the object is converted into a polygon.

Drawing Curves

▶ See "Changing the Shape of Curves," p. 243

A *curve* is a continuously curving line that passes through at least three points which you place on the page. Technically, the shape created by the Curve tool is called a *Beziér curve* because you can change its shape after it is drawn by using special controls at each point along the curve. You learn how to draw the basic curve here.

To draw a curve, follow these steps:

1. Click the Curve tool in the toolbox.
2. Click the starting point of the curve.
3. Click the first point that the curve should pass through. A dashed, straight line connects the two points temporarily, as shown in figure 11.13.

Fig. 11.13
The first part of the curve looks straight, but it will soon become a curve.

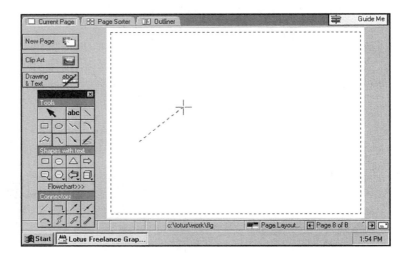

4. Click the next point that the curve should pass through. A dashed, curved line now passes through the second point to the third, as shown in figure 11.14.
5. Continue clicking points.
6. Click the right mouse button, double-click the final point on the curve, or press Esc when you have clicked the ending point for the curve.

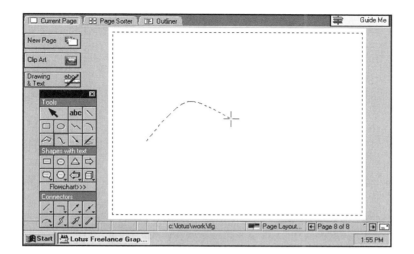

Fig. 11.14
Click again, and complete drawing the curve.

> **Tip**
>
> While drawing the curve, press the Backspace key to delete the last point you placed. Continue pressing Backspace to delete earlier points in reverse order.

Double-clicking a completed curve opens the Properties InfoBox for curves. This sheet holds the same settings as the one for lines. Refer to the earlier section "Drawing Lines" for a description of these controls.

Drawing Circles and Ellipses

After you click the Circle tool in the toolbox, you can draw either a circle or an ellipse. Simply hold down the Shift key while dragging to draw a perfect circle.

To draw circles and ellipses, follow these steps:

1. Click the Circle tool in the toolbox.

2. Click a point on the page and hold down the mouse button.

3. Drag in any direction to size the circle or ellipse, as shown in figure 11.15.

4. Release the mouse button.

Fig. 11.15
Use the Circle tool to create a circle or ellipse.

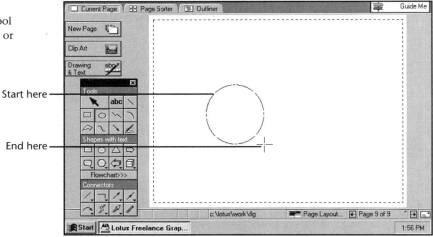

Start here

End here

To draw a perfect circle, press the Shift key while dragging the pointer diagonally away from the first point.

Double-click the circle or ellipse to open the attributes dialog box for the circle. The dialog box contains Edge and Area settings and a Shadow setting.

Drawing Arcs

An *arc* is a segment of a circle or ellipse. To draw an arc, follow these steps:

1. Click the Arc tool in the toolbox.
2. Click a point on the page, hold down the mouse button, and drag to a second point. A dashed, straight line appears, as shown in figure 11.16.
3. Place the pointer anywhere along the line, press and hold down the mouse button, and drag away from the line. A dashed arc then appears, as shown in figure 11.17.
4. Release the mouse button when the arc is correctly shaped.

The arc that forms when you follow these steps is a segment of a circle. To make the arc *elliptical* (a segment of an ellipse), you must reshape the arc by dragging the side handles.

Double-clicking the arc produces the Properties InfoBox for lines and curves. The arc attributes are the same as those for lines and curves. Refer to the earlier section "Drawing Lines" to learn about the settings in this InfoBox.

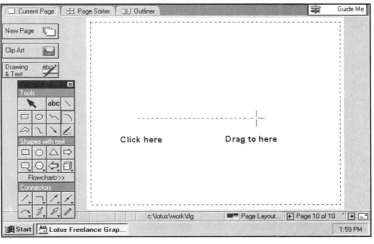

Fig. 11.16
An arc starts out looking like a straight line.

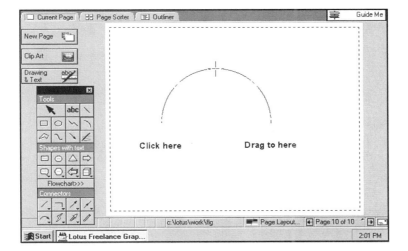

Fig. 11.17
Pull on the line with your mouse, and it becomes an arc.

Drawing Freehand

By clicking the Freehand tool and then holding down the mouse button as you drag the pointer around the page, you can draw freehand shapes. Figure 11.18 shows a freehand shape.

Double-clicking the freehand shape produces the same Properties InfoBox used for lines and curves, because the properties are the same.

Fig. 11.18
The Freehand tool lets you create freeform designs.

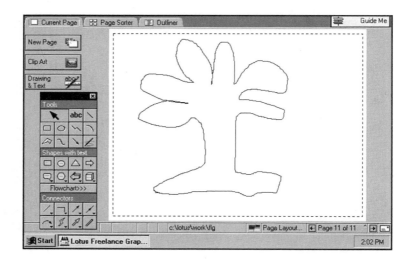

Changing the Drawing Environment

Freelance Graphics 96 for Windows 95 offers a number of aids you can use to make drawing objects easier. The program also offers several settings you can change to modify how drawing is accomplished. The following sections discuss these settings.

Using the Drawing Rulers

The *drawing rulers* are a pair of rulers that run across the top and down the left side of the main page viewing area. As you move the pointer, yellow lines in the rulers display the pointer's position. Blue lines in the rulers display the widest or tallest points of any object or group of objects that is selected. Along the top ruler, for example, blue lines mark the left and right edges of a selected object. Figure 11.19 shows the Freelance window with the drawing rulers turned on.

To turn on or off the drawing rulers, choose View, Set View Preferences. Then click the Drawing Ruler check box.

You can also select and deselect the Show Ruler command on the View menu to perform the same procedures.

To change the units displayed in the drawing ruler, choose View, Set Units & Grids. Then choose Millimeters, Centimeters, Inches, Points, or Picas.

Drawing rulers

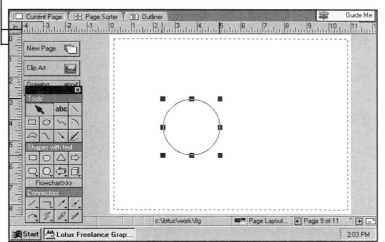

Fig. 11.19
Rulers and
position pointers
add perspective to
your page.

Showing Coordinates

By clicking the Coordinates check box in the View Preferences dialog box,
you can display the current X and Y cursor positions in the edit line at the
bottom of the window. When you are drawing an object, the coordinates also
show the current size of the object. When you are resizing an object, a second
set of numbers shows the change in the width and height of the object. Figure 11.20 shows the coordinates as they look when you are resizing an object.
Notice that the object has been stretched so that it is slightly more than one
inch wider.

The units of measurement used by the coordinates are determined by the
current Units setting in the Set Units & Grid InfoBox.

Using a Grid

The *grid* is a series of regularly spaced dots that you can choose to display
across the page. You can use these dots to align objects visually. You can also
have the pointer snap to the nearest grid dot while you are drawing objects.
This makes placing objects a very exact science.

To turn on the grid, choose View, Set Units & Grid and then choose Display
Grid in the Units & Grid dialog box that appears (see fig. 11.21). The Horizontal Space and Vertical Space settings enable you to change the spacing
between grid points.

Fig. 11.20
Displaying coordinates lets you see an object's size as it changes.

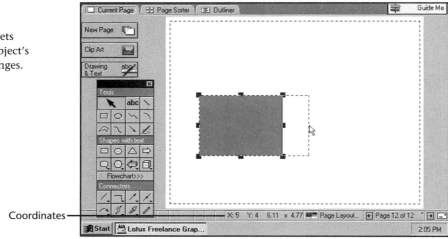

Coordinates ——

Fig. 11.21
Change the unit of measurement and grid properties to settings like Inches or Snap to Grid.

To have the pointer snap to the nearest grid point while you draw, choose Snap to Grid. Snap to Grid keeps objects perfectly aligned by pulling them towards an invisible grid.

Changing the Crosshair Size

By default, a small crosshair appears while you are drawing objects, but you can have a large crosshair appear. Choose View, Set View Preferences and then click Big Crosshair. You also can press Shift+F4 to switch between a big and small crosshair. A large crosshair can help you align objects and is easier to see while you're working.

Keeping a Drawing Tool Active

By default, the Selector tool is chosen in the toolbox, and the cursor reverts to a pointer the moment you finish drawing an object with a drawing tool. To keep the drawing tool active so that you can easily draw another object of the same type, choose File, User Setup, Freelance Preferences and then click Keep Tool Active. Keep Tool Active is one of the Drawing tool's settings in the User Setup dialog box. Revert to Pointer returns the cursor to a pointer when you finish drawing an object. The Freelance Graphics Preferences dialog box is shown in figure 11.22.

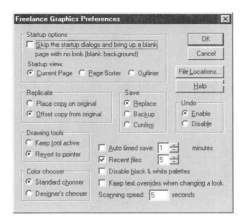

Fig. 11.22
Change the settings of drawing tools using the Freelance Preferences dialog box.

Using Freelance as a Drawing Program

By adding graphic objects to presentation pages, you are already using Freelance as a drawing program, but you also can instruct Freelance to display a blank drawing page every time you start the program. Then, on the blank page, you can add drawing objects just as you would with any software dedicated to drawing.

To have Freelance display a blank page whenever you start the program, follow these steps:

1. Choose File, User Setup, Freelance Preferences.
2. Click the check box next to Skip the Startup Dialogs and Bring Up a Blank Page with No Look (Blank Background).
3. Click OK.

The next time you start a new presentation or when you next start Freelance, you will see a blank page without the usual dialog boxes that ask you to choose a SmartMaster set and page layout.

Even though you see a blank page, a SmartMaster set is still formatting the presentation. When you create a new page, you must choose `[Blank Page]` from the list of page layouts to get another blank page. You can always change the SmartMaster set and choose a page layout with a background and Click Here blocks by choosing Presentation, Choose a Different SmartMaster Look and then clicking the <u>S</u>can left or right button. ❖

CHAPTER 12

Editing Objects

by Elizabeth Eisner Reding

Freelance Graphics offers a full arsenal of tools and commands you can use to make editing changes to the objects you draw. Most of these commands are on the Drawing menu.

With some editing commands such as Group, Priority, Align, and Space, you can make basic changes in the way objects appear on the page. Other commands, such as Rotate, Flip, and Convert, enable you to change the appearance of individual objects. Freelance even includes a special feature—points mode—for modifying the precise shapes of objects.

In this chapter, you learn how to

- Select objects using your mouse
- Change the location and size of objects
- Turn many objects into one object
- Modify the spacing and rotation of objects
- Change the shape of a curve
- Connect non-joining lines

Selecting Objects

Freelance works according to the consistent practice that you must first select an object and then choose a command that edits the object. Because selecting the correct object to edit is so important when you're working with complex drawings that may be made up of many objects, Freelance offers several ways to select objects easily and accurately.

Selecting Objects with the Pointer

The simplest way to select a single object is to click it. Handles then appear around a selected object. The simplest way to select more than one object is to hold down the Shift key while you click each object. Handles then appear around each selected object.

Sometimes clicking each object in a drawing can be difficult and time-consuming. After you ungroup a complex symbol into dozens of component objects, you might find that clicking each object is virtually impossible. To select multiple objects in this case, use the pointer to draw a selection box that entirely encloses them. Every object completely inside the selection box is then selected. If part of an object sticks outside the box, *that object is not selected*.

To draw a selection box, move the pointer to a spot to the left or right of a group of objects and either above or below the group. Then hold down the mouse button and drag the pointer to a spot that is diagonally across the group of objects and outside the group. When you release the mouse button, every object in the selection box is selected. Figure 12.1 shows a selection box that selects the circle and rectangle, but not the triangle.

Fig. 12.1
Draw a selection box that selects some, but not all, objects.

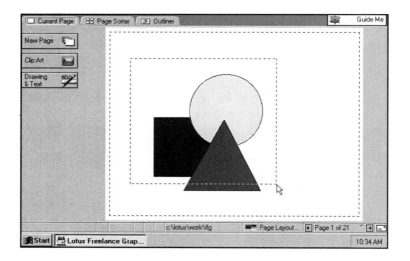

When you release the mouse button, you see handles surrounding each of the selected objects.

Selecting Objects Using the Edit, Select Command

An alternative to selecting objects by clicking them or drawing a selection box is to choose Edit, Select. These commands enable you to select objects according to a variety of schemes. The following sections discuss the commands in the Edit, Select menu.

Selecting All Objects

To select all objects on the presentation page, click the Select All button on the toolbar, or choose Edit, Select, All. The keyboard alternative is to press F4 (Select All). All objects on the current page are selected, including objects in Click Here blocks.

Deselecting All Objects

To deselect all objects on the presentation page, choose Edit, Select, None. This command is helpful after you deselect several objects. After you deselect them all, you can then select any individual object for editing.

> **Tip**
>
> Another way to deselect a group of objects is to click anywhere on the page—and not on any object. You can even click in the gray area around the page.

Cycling Through the Objects

When you create a complex drawing with many objects, you might have difficulty distinguishing among the objects, especially if they overlap. By choosing Edit, Select, Cycle, you can have Freelance highlight each object consecutively. The Cycle Selection dialog box enables you to choose the object you want. Then you can select an object or a combination of objects as you cycle through them.

Freelance cycles through the objects in the order of their priority on-screen. You learn about changing the priority of objects later in this chapter, but usually the priority is the order in which the objects were placed on the page—from first to last. Freelance draws a dashed rectangle around the object and describes it in the Cycle Selection dialog box (see fig. 12.2). Once the object you want is listed in the dialog box, click Select.

Fig. 12.2
Switch the focus
of objects in an
area using the
Cycle Selection
dialog box.

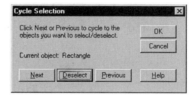

Click Select to select the currently highlighted object; click Next or Previous to move the focus to a different object in the cycle. You can select more than one object as you cycle through them. When you select an object, the Select button becomes the Deselect button so that you can use it to deselect the object. After you select the objects you want, click OK.

Selecting Like Objects

After you select one object, you can choose any combination of the object's attributes and then select all other objects that have the same combination of attributes. You might, for example, want to select all objects having the same interior color or pattern. Choose Edit, Select, Like to open the Select Like Objects dialog box (see fig. 12.3).

Fig. 12.3
Objects with
similar characteris-
tics can be selected
using the Select
Like Objects
dialog box.

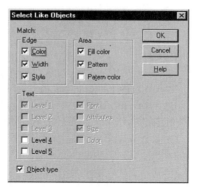

The selected check boxes in the Select Like Objects dialog box represent the attributes of the currently selected object. You can click as many check boxes as suits your needs. Freelance then finds objects whose properties match those that are checked. If the object is a graphic shape and you check only the Fill Color check box, for example, Freelance selects all other objects that have the same fill color. If you also click the Style check box, Freelance selects only those objects that have the same fill color *and* the same edge style.

Select the Object Type check box if you want to match only other graphic objects of the same type. When you select a circle, Freelance matches only circles that have the combination of attributes selected. Click OK after you select the attributes of the first object, and Freelance then selects all matching objects.

> ### Tip
>
> If the object you want to match is text and you checked a text style check box (Style 1, Style 2, or Style 3), Freelance matches only other entire paragraphs to which the same style has been applied. You might, for example, want to select all paragraphs having the same color. If only some text in the paragraph has the same style, the paragraph is not matched.

Selecting Objects Inside the Selection Box

By default, when you draw a selection box, you select all objects entirely inside the box. Inside is the default setting when you choose Edit, Select. Any objects with parts that stick outside the selection box are not selected. As a guideline, this means that when you draw a selection box, all objects entirely within its borders will be selected.

Selecting Objects Touching the Selection Box

If you choose Edit, Select, Touching, Freelance selects objects that have any part in the next selection box you draw—not just the objects entirely inside the selection box (see fig. 12.4). After you draw the selection box, Freelance returns to its default setting of Inside. You must choose Touching again to make the next selection box select all objects inside or touching the box.

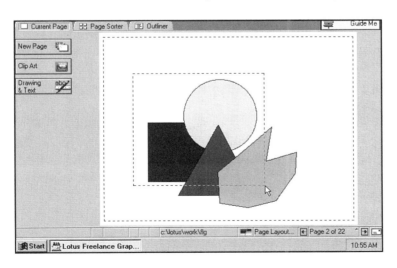

Fig. 12.4
Freelance selects all four objects because they all touch the selection box.

Zooming In

Full Page view gives you the overall picture of a drawing, but zooming in on a specific portion can give you the detail you need. To zoom in closer on a drawing, choose View, Zoom In, or click the Drag to Zoom In on an Area button on the toolbar and draw a box around the area of the drawing to magnify it.

By choosing View, Zoom In, you can zoom in eight times. Choose View, Zoom Out to zoom out one level. Choose View, Last Zoom to return to the last zoom level you used. To return to viewing the full page, choose View, Zoom to Full Page or click the Show Whole Page button on the toolbar. When you've exhausted either the Zoom In or Zoom Out commands, the menu item will become dim.

When you zoom in on an area, you can slide the entire page in the Freelance window to expose parts no longer in view. To move the page, select the Page Sorter tab, click the Move Page button on the Page Sorter toolbar, place the cursor (which now looks like a hand) on the page, and then hold down the mouse button and drag the page up, down, left, or right.

Moving and Sizing Objects

The most basic change you can make to an object is to move or size it. You move an object by placing the pointer on it, holding down the left mouse button, and dragging the object to a new location. You size an object by selecting the Selector tool from the Tools palette, clicking the object, placing the pointer on one of the handles that appear around the object, holding down the left mouse button, and dragging the handle. All objects resize proportionally (retaining their shape) if you hold down the Shift key while you drag a corner handle.

Figure 12.5 shows two possible results when you size an object. The bottom cube on the right is a proportionally enlarged copy of the cube on the left. I made the copy by dragging a corner handle while holding down the Shift key. The top cube is a copy that was stretched lengthwise by its side handle and flattened by its top handle. The concept of changing the size of an object while preseving its proportion is called *maintaining* (or *constraining*) *the aspect.*

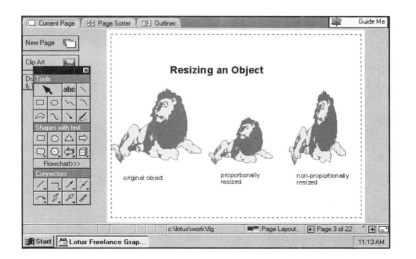

Fig. 12.5
You can resize an object proportion-ally and non-proportionally.

Replicating Objects

To make a duplicate of objects on-screen, select the object or objects, choose Edit, Copy, and then choose Edit, Paste. The Copy command places a copy of the object on the Windows Clipboard; the Paste command retrieves the copy from the Windows Clipboard. An easier method (because it requires only one command) is to select the object and then choose Edit, Replicate or press Ctrl+F3 (Replicate). You also can click the Replicate button. The Replicate method does not overwrite the contents of the Windows Clipboard.

When you use Replicate, a copy of the object appears slightly offset on top of the original. To make the copy appear directly on top of the original, choose File, User Setup, Freelance Preferences, Place Copy on Original, then click OK.

If you move and resize a replicated object after you replicated it and then use the Replicate command again, the second copy of the object is moved and resized proportionally to the first replication. If the first replication is half the size of the original, for example, the second replication will be half the size of the first replication. Figure 12.6 shows an object that was moved and resized after the first replication and then replicated repeatedly.

Fig. 12.6
Choosing Edit,
Replicate
command is an
easy way to
duplicate an
object.

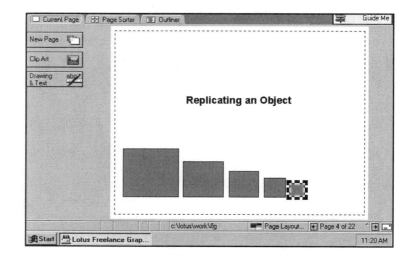

Grouping and Ungrouping Objects

 After you arrange a number of objects together to form a picture, you can choose Drawing, Group to join more than one object into a single object, or click the Group Objects button. Then, when you click the group, only one set of handles appears around the group. Figure 12.7 shows an example of grouped objects and ungrouped objects. (When both grouped *and* ungrouped objects are selected, the Collection menu appears on the menu bar, instead of the Drawing menu.) You can use the handles to move and size all the objects in the group as though they were one object. When you stretch the group, all objects in the group stretch in the same proportion.

 To group objects, select all the objects you want in the group and choose Drawing, Group. You also can click the Group button on the toolbar.

 After you group objects and made a change to the group, you can ungroup the group to select and edit an individual object. To do this, select the group and then choose Group, Ungroup or click the Ungroup button on the toolbar.

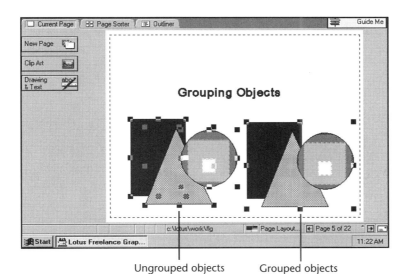

Ungrouped objects   Grouped objects

Fig. 12.7
You can turn
many objects into
a single object.

IV

Adding Text and Graphics

Why should you group objects?

Grouping objects can make working with more than one object easy—in more ways than you can imagine!

Suppose you use the drawing tools to create a logo: you might have several shapes in your design, each with a different pattern and fill color. After you arrange the shapes just the way you want them, it's a good idea to group them into one object. That way, if you find you need to move the design, you can move it as one object and not disturb the arrangement of the shapes.

If you are using shapes to create a logo, grouping the objects means the design will have consistency from one page to the next, because you can duplicate the object using the Copy or Replicate command. When you resize the object, all the shapes in it will be enlarged or reduced in proportion to one another.

It makes good sense to group several objects if, when together in a design, they become a separate entity, such as a logo.

When all the objects in the group are the same type, you can modify a group's properties by double-clicking the group. When the objects in the group are of different types (such as a polygon, some lines, and a circle), clicking the group opens the Group Properties sheet (see fig. 12.8). You can also open the Properties sheet for the Group by right-clicking the mouse on the object.

Fig. 12.8
A group's property sheet can be opened by right-clicking the object.

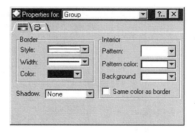

The Properties For drop-down list in the title bar lets you select specific selected objects whose properties you want to change. When All Selected Objects displays in the title bar, any changes you make to the Border and Interior properties affect all objects in the group. To change objects of only one type, select the appropriate object type from the drop-down list and then make changes to the settings in the Properties sheet.

When objects in the group have different property settings, the setting for that property appears blank. If you change the object type to Selected Rectangles, as shown in figure 12.9, properties for the rectangle only appear.

Fig. 12.9
Use the Properties sheet to select a specific object whose properties you want to change.

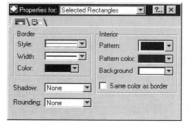

Changing the Priority of an Object

Drawing objects on-screen is similar to placing paper cutouts on a desktop, in that the last cutout you put down will overlap the other cutouts already on the desk. But what happens when you place two cutouts on different areas of the desk and then slide them together so that they overlap? Which cutout will end up on top?

When you're working with cutouts, you decide which one overlaps the other. When you're working with Freelance drawing objects, however, the object that was drawn last is the one that overlaps all others. In Freelance terminology, the last object you draw has the highest *priority*. You can test this concept by drawing three objects of different colors on different areas of a blank page. Then drag the objects together so they all overlap. You will see that the first drawn object is on the bottom and the most recently drawn object is on top. Freelance maintains this bottom-to-top order for the life of the drawing.

You can change the priority of objects in a drawing, by moving an object forward or back a level, or by moving an object all the way to the top or bottom of the pile. You see the change immediately if the object is already in a pile. You see the change later if the object appears alone and you then move it into a pile. Even the last-drawn object will slide into a pile at the bottom when you use the Priority command to send it to the bottom. Figure 12.10 shows a collection of objects before and after the 3-D rectangle is sent back one level.

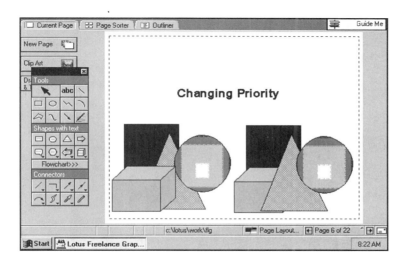

Fig. 12.10
The Priority command enables you to change the sequence of objects.

To change the priority of an object, select the object and choose Drawing, Priority. Then choose one of these choices from the cascading menu: Bring to Front, Send to Back, Bring Forward One, or Send Back One. You also can press Shift+F8 (Bring Forward One) or F8 (Send Back One), or use the Bring to Front or Send to Back toolbar buttons to manipulate objects. The Drawing menu only appears for objects that are governed by its commands—which excludes TextShapes. If you create and select a Shape with Text triangle, for instance, the Drawing menu does not appear.

Aligning Objects

The Align command gives you the power to align objects relative to one another. To align objects, select all the objects to align and then choose Drawing, Align. If objects of the same type are selected, the Drawing menu appears. If objects of different types are selected, the Collection menu appears: in this case, choose Collection, Align. The Align Objects dialog box opens (see fig. 12.11). You can also right-click the mouse when the objects to be aligned are selected, then click Align.

Fig. 12.11
Line up objects using the Align Objects dialog box.

As you click each option in this dialog box, a diagram illustrates the effect of the option. Figures 12.12 through 12.14 show the effects of all the options. When you choose to align the sides of objects, they align with the side of the object that extends the most.

Fig. 12.12
Create objects that you can align later.

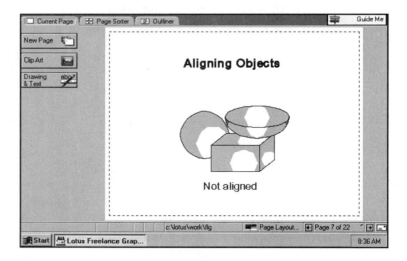

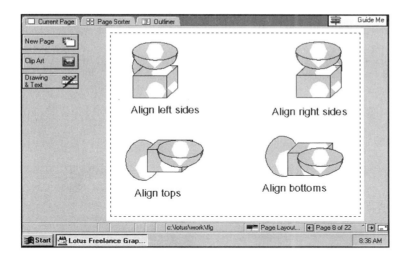

Fig. 12.13
You can align objects to the top, bottom, left, or right.

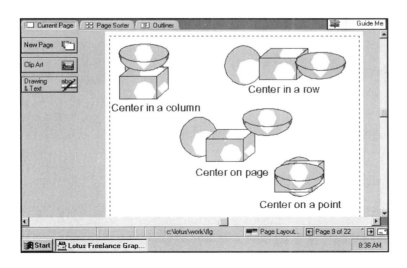

Fig. 12.14
You can center objects around a line or point.

In the Align Objects dialog box, you can select Center on Page in addition to any of the other options so that the group of objects align relative to one another and then move to the center of the page.

Spacing Objects

The Space command enables you to evenly space three or more objects on a page. You must select at least three objects for this command to become available.

After you select the objects and choose Drawing, Space, you can use the Space dialog box to evenly space the objects vertically, horizontally, or both. Figure 12.15 shows the effects of spacing objects horizontally.

Fig. 12.15
You supply the objects; let Freelance horizontally space them for you.

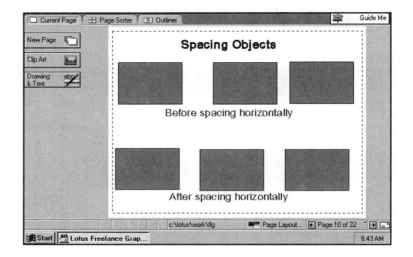

Rotating an Object

To rotate objects around their center, select the object or objects, and choose Drawing, Rotate or click the Rotate button. The cursor changes shape to show an arrow curving around a plus sign, and the edit line shows the angle of rotation of the objects.

Place the cursor at a point near the object and drag in a circle around the object in the direction you want to rotate the object. If you selected one object to rotate, you see its outline rotate (see fig. 12.16). When you select two or more objects to rotate, you see a dashed outline of a box rotate, outlining the area of the objects. The objects rotate around a point that is the center of the set of objects.

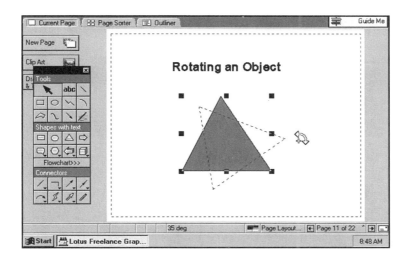

IV

Adding Text and Graphics

Fig. 12.16
You can create novel effects by rotating an object.

You can rotate text, but not charts or tables. Text is rotated by choosing Text, Rotate. When you edit a rotated text block, it becomes level temporarily while you edit the text. It then returns to its previous rotation when you finish editing.

By holding down the Shift key as you rotate objects, you can force the objects to rotate in 45-degree increments. Bitmaps can rotate in 90-degree increments only.

> **Tip**
>
> By placing the rotate cursor far away from the object or objects, you gain finer control of the rotation angle when you drag the cursor.

Flipping an Object

Flipping an object turns it upside down or left to right. You can flip only graphic objects—you cannot flip charts, tables, text blocks, linked or embedded objects, or metafiles.

To flip an object, select the object and then choose Drawing, Flip. From the cascading menu, you can choose to flip the object Left-Right or Top-Bottom. Figure 12.17 shows a picture made from a symbol that has been replicated and then flipped Left-Right.

Fig. 12.17
After you place an object on a page, you can replicate and flip it.

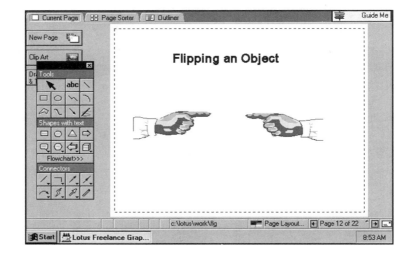

Using Points Mode to Edit Points

Most objects are made up of lines, sides, or curves that connect points. By moving, adding, and deleting points in Points mode, you can change the shape of the objects.

To enter Points mode, choose Edit, Points Mode or press Shift+F6. Freelance stays in Points mode until you choose Edit, Points Mode or press Shift+F6 again. While Freelance is in Points mode, a check appears next to the Points Mode option in the Edit menu. Freelance also displays an outline cursor with a small, unfilled point inside.

While the program is in points mode, you can work with the points of all drawing objects except rectangles and circles. You must first convert rectangles and circles to lines or polygons by using the Drawing, Convert command (covered later in this chapter). You cannot edit the points of grouped objects.

Moving Points

When you select a drawing object in points mode, a tiny hollow box appears at each of the object's points. When you click a point to select it, the tiny box becomes filled. After you select a point, you can drag the point just as you would any object—by positioning the pointer on it, holding down the left mouse button, and dragging the mouse. When you release the mouse button, the point drops, and the object changes shape accordingly. Figure 12.18 shows a point being moved. Notice the shape of the cursor and that the selected point shows a filled box. The other points show hollow boxes.

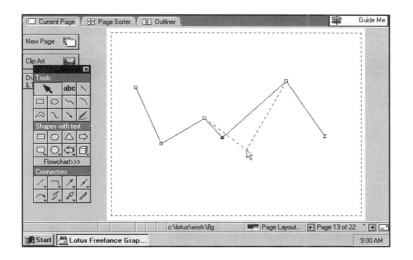

Fig. 12.18
Modify an object
by switching to
Points mode.

By drawing a selection box around two or more points with the pointer, you
can select multiple points. When you drag one of the points, all of the selected points move.

Adding Points

In points mode, you can add a point anywhere on the perimeter of a drawing
object to gain additional flexibility in changing the shape of the object. To
add a point, press the Insert key and then click along the edge of the object
where you want the new point to be. Figure 12.19 shows an object before and
after adding a new point.

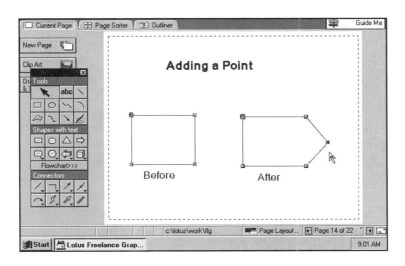

Fig. 12.19
Add a new point to
an existing object
in Points mode.

You also can choose Edit, Edit Points, Add Point, and then click where you want the new point to be.

Deleting Points

It is very simple to delete points. Just select the point and press the Delete key. You can also select the point and choose Edit, Edit Points, Delete Points.

Breaking Objects

While the program is in points mode, you can break a drawing object into two objects with the Break command. If the object is a polyline, you can break the polyline into two separate polylines. The original polyline will still connect the first and last points, but the new polyline will start at the break point and follow the shape of the original polyline to the end point. If the object is a polygon, the result will be two separate, smaller polygons.

To break a line, you must select a point along the line. If the line is a single segment, you must add a point to the line first and then select that point. You then choose Edit, Edit Points, Break at Points. The original line will connect the first and last points, and the new line will connect the break point and the last point. Figure 12.20 shows the steps for breaking a line into two lines.

Fig. 12.20
Use Points mode to create a break, and then split a line.

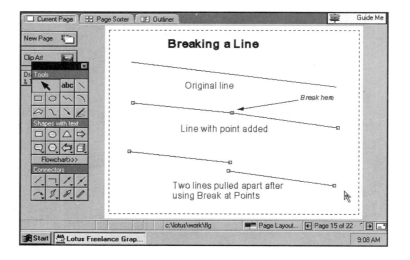

To break a polygon, you must select two points that are separated by other points and then use the Break at Points command. The polygon then splits into two objects. The first polygon connects all the points. The second polygon connects the original first point of the polygon, the two selected points, and the points between the selected points. Figure 12.21 shows one polygon being broken into two polygons.

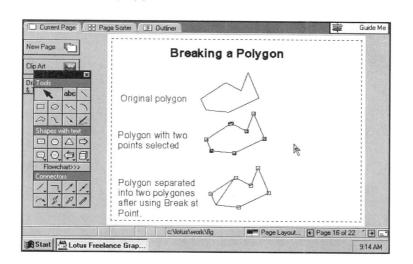

Fig. 12.21
Break an existing object by using Points mode.

Changing the Shape of Curves

When the object you select in points mode is a curve or an arc, clicking one of the points along the curve or arc produces a pair of handles at that point. You can drag each handle to change the shape of the curve as it approaches or departs from the point. You also can drag the point as you would drag a point of any object.

When you drag a handle, the handle pulls the bend of the curve. A dashed curve shows how the curve will look when you release the mouse button. When you press Shift and drag a handle, the handle on the other side of the point moves an equal distance in the opposite direction. As a result, the curve remains smooth as it passes through the point. When you press Ctrl and drag a handle, a sharp angle called a *cusp* forms at the point.

Figure 12.22 shows a curve with handles at a point and the same curve after dragging one of the points.

Fig. 12.22
Drag a handle in Points mode to alter the shape of a curve.

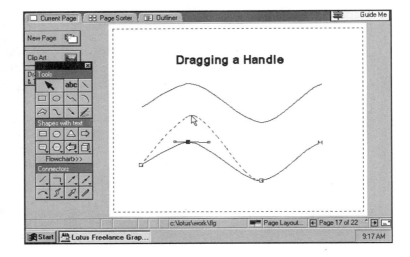

Figure 12.23 shows a curve that has had a handle dragged while the Shift key was pressed.

Fig. 12.23
Use the Shift key to drag a handle proportionally.

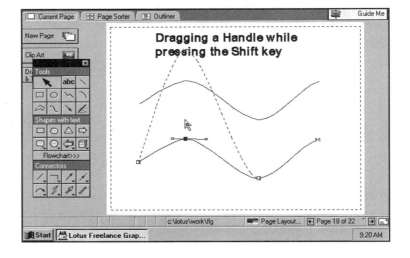

Figure 12.24 shows a curve that has had a handle dragged while the Ctrl key was pressed. Notice that the curve forms a cusp at the selected point.

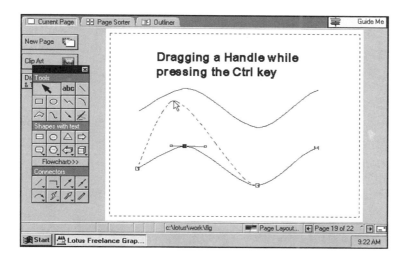

Fig. 12.24
The Ctrl key
creates a different
effect than the
Shift key.

Converting Objects to Lines or Polygons

You can convert objects to lines or polygons with the Convert command.
You must convert rectangles and circles to lines or polygons before you can
edit them in Points mode. Before converting an object, it must be selected.
Then you can choose Drawing, Convert, To Polygons or To Lines.

When an object is a polygon, you can convert it to a line. Converting a filled
polygon removes the fill and disconnects the line between the first and last
points of the polygon. In points mode, you can then move the points of the
line, add or delete points, or break the line. Figure 12.25 shows a polygon before and after I converted it to lines. In points mode, I moved the first point
away from the last point to show that the lines are no longer connected.
Once a filled polygon is converted into lines, the fill is no longer displayed.

Converting an object to a polygon connects its first and last points; the object becomes closed and you can fill it with a color, gradient, or pattern.
When you convert a line that has arrowheads to a polygon, the arrowheads
are removed. Figure 12.26 shows a line before and after being converted to
a polygon.

Fig. 12.25
A polygon can be
converted to lines;
then the object
can be separated
in Points mode.

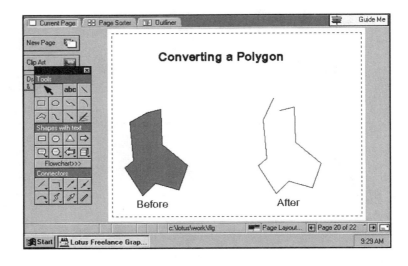

Fig. 12.26
A line can easily
be converted into
a polygon using
the Convert
command.

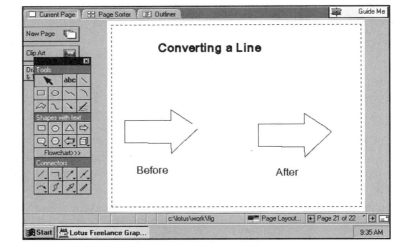

Connecting Lines

To join the ends of lines or curves, select the objects and choose the Drawing,
Connect Lines. The closest two ends of the selected objects are joined by a
new line segment. When you select more than one line to connect, Freelance
connects each line to the nearest line. When you connect straight line segments, you create a polyline.

Figure 12.27 shows three line segments before and after I connected the lines.

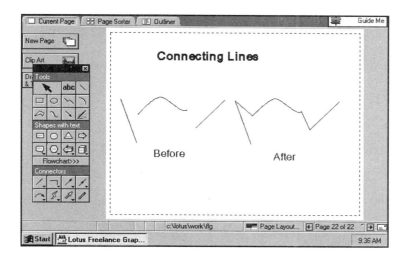

Fig. 12.27
Connect lines and
curves using the
Connect Lines
command.

CHAPTER 13

Adding Clip Art Symbols and Bitmaps

by Joyce J. Nielsen

Rather than draw every picture you need to by hand, you can take advantage of the library of pictures that comes with Freelance. These pictures, called *clip art*, were drawn by professional artists, so they can add polish to any presentation.

Another type of graphic image is a bitmap. A *bitmap* is a pattern of dots of different colors, much like the pattern of dots that makes up a television picture. You cannot create bitmap images in Freelance, but you can add them to a Freelance presentation by importing them from other sources, such as Paint, a program provided with Windows 95.

Bitmaps are important because they are the type of file generated by scanning software. After you scan a picture with an electronic scanner, the scanning software generates a bitmap file. To incorporate a photograph into a presentation, you must import the bitmap file.

In this chapter, you learn how to do the following:

- Add a clip art symbol to a presentation page
- Use clip art symbols as text bullets
- Add individual clip art symbols or new symbol categories to the Freelance clip art library
- Import and crop a bitmap image
- Modify the attributes of a bitmap image

Using Clip Art Symbols

Adding pictures can give any presentation more impact, but original drawings, photos, and copyrighted art cost lots of money and take time to purchase or produce. For these reasons, clip art has long been part of a graphic artist's repertoire. Clip art, in books of pictures and decorative images, can be purchased so that you may use it in your page layouts copyright-free.

Freelance Graphics has its own library of clip art, sometimes called *symbols*. The Freelance clip art symbols are copyright-free pictures covering a wide range of subjects. Figure 13.1 shows just a few examples of clip art provided with Freelance Graphics. For a comprehensive list of the symbols in each category, refer to Appendix C, "The Symbol Library."

Fig. 13.1
Freelance Graphics provides a variety of clip art for use in your presentations.

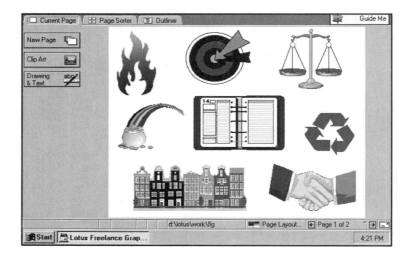

Freelance clip art, no matter how simple or complex, is composed of groups of drawn objects. Just as you can draw and edit your own art objects in Freelance, professional artists have used various drawing tools to draw, arrange, and group together objects to make the Freelance symbols. You can also pull out and use only one part of a symbol, or draw additions to the existing symbols with the Freelance drawing tools. Refer to Chapter 11, "Drawing Objects," for more information on drawing objects within Freelance.

Tip

You cannot ungroup bitmapped objects such as BMP, PCX, TIF, GIF, or TGA files. This is because bitmapped files do not contain any information about the individual objects represented in them.

Because you know that Freelance symbols are groups of drawn objects, you can ungroup them to edit their components and modify a symbol to fit your needs. If the symbol is simple, you can select it and change its attributes, such as its edge style and color. If the symbol is more complex, you must ungroup the component objects and then edit each object separately. Figure 13.2 shows a selected symbol before and after it is ungrouped.

◀ See "Grouping and Ungrouping Objects," p. 232

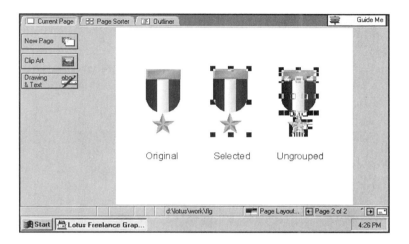

Fig. 13.2
Three forms of the same symbol: original, selected, and ungrouped.

> **Note**
>
> Be careful not to use copyrighted art without permission. Many different packages of clip art exist on disk; some of the packages are copyright-free, and some of them are copyrighted. Look for copyright information within the documentation or on the disk itself. If you don't see any, it is probably safe to use the art without permission.

Adding Clip Art to a Presentation

Clip art can be such an important part of a presentation that many of the page layouts in Freelance have built-in Click Here To Add Clip Art blocks. These blocks enable you to easily place and size clip art that you choose. You also can add clip art to other selected presentation pages, or to every page in the presentation. You can then enlarge, reduce, move, or copy the clip art, and change their attributes.

> **Tip**
>
> If you do not use a Click Here to Add Clip Art block, you don't need to delete the block from the presentation page. The words Click here to add clip art will *not* appear when you print a presentation or view a screen show.

Adding Clip Art with a Click Here Block

Some of the page layouts in Freelance include a Click Here to Add Clip Art block (see fig. 13.3). This is the easiest method to add clip art to a presentation page. If you want to add a clip art symbol to a page that does not have a Click Here to Add Clip Art block, refer to the section "Adding Clip Art to a Page Without a Click Here Block," later in this chapter.

Fig. 13.3
A Click Here to Add Clip Art block usually appears on a title page.

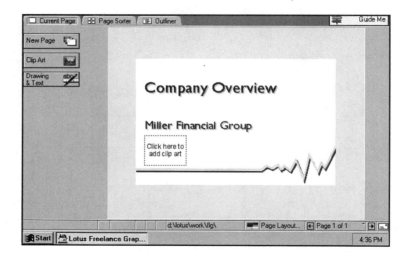

◀ See "Using the Ready-Made Business Diagrams," p. 158

To add clip art using a Click Here block, follow these steps:

1. Display the presentation page that includes a Click Here to Add Clip Art block.

2. Click the Click Here to Add Clip Art block. The Add Clip Art or Diagram to the Page dialog box appears (see fig. 13.4).

3. Select the Clip Art option button (if it isn't already selected).

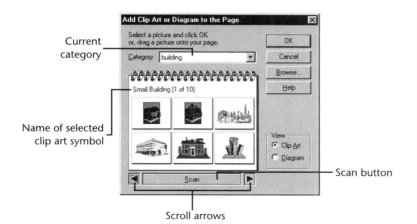

Current category

Name of selected clip art symbol

Scan button

Scroll arrows

IV

Adding Text and Graphics

Fig. 13.4
Use the Add Clip Art or Diagram to the Page dialog box to select a clip art symbol to add to a presentation page.

Tip

You also can click the arrows on either side of the Scan button to manually scroll through the clip art categories.

4. Choose a category from the Category drop-down list.

   Or, click the Scan button to have Freelance automatically scan through all categories. When you begin scanning, the Scan button changes to Stop Scan, which you can click when you see a category that interests you.

Note

The default scan rate when using the Scan button to view the clip art categories is five seconds. To change the scan rate, choose File, User Setup, Freelance Preferences. Then, change the number of seconds in the Scanning Speed text box at the bottom of the dialog box, and click OK. You can enter a number between .1 and 100 in this text box.

5. Click the clip art symbol that you want to use in your presentation. The name of the symbol you select appears at the top of the notebook, inside the dialog box.

6. Click OK. The clip art you chose now appears on the presentation page (see fig. 13.5).

Fig. 13.5
The clip art
symbol has been
added to the
presentation page.

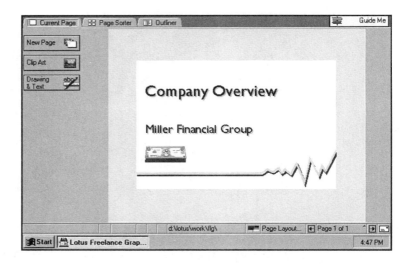

Fig. 13.5
The clip art
symbol has been
added to the
presentation page.

After you add a clip art symbol to your presentation page, you can move the
symbol by selecting and then dragging it to another area of the page. You
also can resize the clip art by selecting the symbol and then dragging one of
the selection handles. Use the Shift key while resizing to keep the graphic
proportional.

Editing Clip Art in Click Here Blocks

You can edit the basic attributes of simple clip art symbols in "Click here..."
blocks. For example, you can change the style, width, and color of the clip
art's border, add a drop shadow surrounding the clip art, or modify the fill
color and pattern used in the clip art symbol.

To edit a simple clip art symbol in a Click Here block, follow these steps:

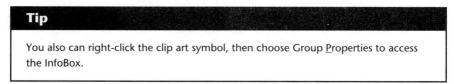

Tip

You also can right-click the clip art symbol, then choose Group Properties to access
the InfoBox.

1. Double-click the clip art symbol. The Group Properties InfoBox appears
   (see fig. 13.6).

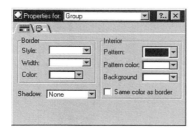

Fig. 13.6
Use the Group
Properties InfoBox
to modify a clip art
symbol.

2. Edit the Border, Interior, and Shadow options, as desired.

    Use the Border options to edit the Style, Width, and Color of the clip
    art's border. Use the Interior options to edit the Pattern, Pattern Color,
    and Background of the selected clip art. Use the Shadow option to add a
    drop shadow to the clip art symbol.

    If you want to make the interior color of the clip art symbol the same
    color as the border, click the Same Color as Border option.

3. Click the Close button of the InfoBox when you have made all the
    changes you want.

Complex clip art symbols must be ungrouped into component objects so that
each object can be edited individually. You cannot ungroup a symbol in a
Click Here block. You can, however, remove the symbol from the Click Here
block and then ungroup it. Follow these steps:

1. Click the clip art symbol to select it.

2. Choose Edit, Cut; then choose Edit, Paste. Now, you can ungroup the
    symbol.

3. Choose Group, Ungroup. Handles appear around each object within the
    symbol.

4. Click anywhere else on the page to deselect all the objects and remove
    the handles. Then select the object you want to edit.

5. Use the Group Properties InfoBox to edit the object as desired.

6. When you finish editing the clip art symbol, select all the objects that
    make up the symbol, and then choose Collection, Group to rejoin them
    into one object.

    To select a group of drawn objects, use the Selector tool in the Tool-
    box to draw a box around the group. All objects that are completely
    enclosed within the box are selected.

Troubleshooting

I would like to modify a bitmap image I imported, but when I select the bitmap so that I can ungroup it, the Group menu option does not appear on the main menu.

You cannot ungroup a bitmap file. You only can ungroup clip art images that are composed of objects; these are called *vector graphics* because the program stores the information as mathematical formulas for the vectors (lines) that compose the image. This makes it easier for the graphic to be modified or resized without resulting in distortion to the image. Consider using a clip art image from Freelance's Clip Art Library; these images can be ungrouped and easily modified.

Adding Clip Art to a Page Without a Click Here Block

You may want to add more than one clip art symbol to a presentation page, or add clip art to existing pages of a presentation that do not include a Click Here to Add Clip Art block. For example, you may want to add clip art to a chart page.

To add a clip art symbol to a page without using a Click Here block, follow these steps:

1. Display the page where you want to add the clip art.
2. Choose Create, Add Clip Art. The Add Clip Art or Diagram to the Page dialog box appears (refer to fig. 13.4).

Tip

You also can click the Clip Art button on the left side of the screen to quickly access the Add Clip Art or Diagram to the Page dialog box.

3. Select a clip art symbol from the library, and click OK; or double-click the clip art symbol in the dialog box.
4. Move and resize the clip art symbol, as desired.

Note

To help you place and align clip art on a presentation page, you may want to display a grid on the Freelance desktop. Choose View, Set Units & Grids to display the Set Units & Grid dialog box. Select the Display Grid check box and click OK. A grid appears on the desktop. You also can select the Snap to Grid check box (or press Shift+F7) to have the cursor snap to the nearest grid point while you place or align symbols.

Using Clip Art as a Text Bullet. When using Freelance Graphics, you can add any clip art symbol to a presentation as a text bullet. To use a clip art symbol as a text bullet, follow these steps:

1. Display the presentation page that includes a bulleted text box, and click the bulleted text block.

2. Choose Text, Bullets & Numbers. The Text Properties InfoBox appears (see fig. 13.7).

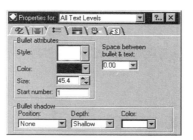

Fig. 13.7
Use the Text Properties InfoBox to select clip art symbols for bulleted text.

3. Under Properties For, select the desired text level (for example, All Text Levels, Level 1 Text, etc.).

4. Under Style in the Bullet Attributes box, select the word Clip Art (at the bottom of the drop-down list). The Choose Clip Art for Bullet dialog box appears.

5. Select a clip art symbol from the library.

6. Click OK.

7. Close the InfoBox. A miniature of the clip art you selected will appear as a bullet before each paragraph (see fig. 13.8).

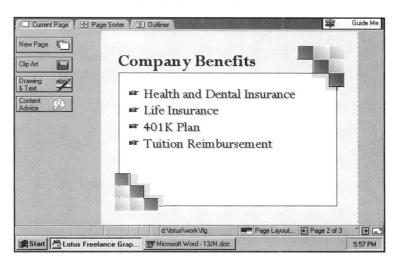

Fig. 13.8
The clip art symbol you chose appears as a bullet.

Adding a Logo or Clip Art Symbol to Every Page

Freelance enables you to easily add a logo or clip art symbol to every page in your presentation that uses the presentation backdrop, except for the title page. You can use a clip art symbol from the Freelance clip art library, or draw or import a company logo.

To add a logo or clip art symbol to every page of a presentation, follow these steps:

1. Choose Presentation, Add a Logo to Every Page. Freelance switches to the Current Layout view (see fig. 13.9).

Fig. 13.9

The Current Layout view enables you to add, draw, or import a logo to be used in each page of a present-ation.

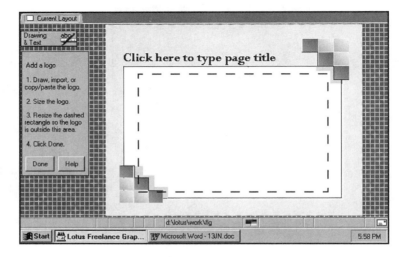

Tip

Choose Create, Add Clip Art if you want to use a clip art symbol from Freelance's clip art library on every page.

2. Import, copy and paste, or draw the logo on the presentation page.

3. Move and size the logo, as desired.

4. Move and size the placement block guide, as desired.

5. Click Done in the instruction box when you are finished. The logo or clip art will appear in every page of the current presentation.

Troubleshooting

I added a logo to every page of my presentation, but I decided not to use it. How do I remove the logo?

Choose Presentation, Add a Logo to Every Page. In Current Layout view, click the logo to select it. Press Delete to remove the logo. Click Done to return to the presentation.

Adding Symbols to the Clip Art Library

The Freelance clip art library is a collection of symbols, categorized by subject. Each of these categories has an individual file name.

When you find or create new art that you think you might want to use again, add the art to the clip art library so that you can quickly retrieve it and add it to a presentation. You can add objects drawn in Freelance, edited symbols, charts, and imported bitmap images. Figure 13.10 shows a new clip art symbol created by editing and combining existing Freelance clip art symbols.

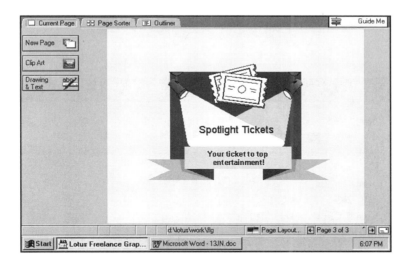

Fig. 13.10
A new clip art symbol is created with several different Freelance Graphics clip art symbols and a text block symbol.

To add art to the clip art library, follow these steps:

1. Display the page containing the graphic object that you want to add to the clip art library.

2. Click the object to select it.

> **Note**
>
> If your clip art includes more than one object, you must first group the objects into one object by holding down the Shift key as you click each object. Then choose Collection, Group, or click the Group button.

3. Choose Create, Add to Library, Clipart Library. The Add to Clip Art Library dialog box appears (see fig. 13.11).

Fig. 13.11
The Add to Clip Art Library dialog box enables you to add a selected object to the Freelance clip art library.

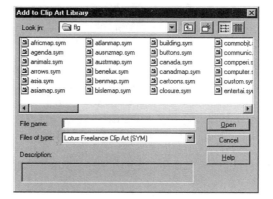

> **Tip**
>
> Use the CUSTOM.SYM file to store your clip art in the Custom category. The Custom category contains no clip art symbols until you add clip art to it.

4. In the middle of the Add to Clip Art Library dialog box is a scrolling list of the file names of all the Freelance Graphics clip art categories. Scroll through the list and select the clip art category where you want to store your new clip art symbol.

5. Click Open. The object you selected is then added to the selected clip art category file.

Adding a New Category to the Clip Art Library

Adding new clip art category files is a great way to keep your clip art symbols organized. You can keep all the clip art pertaining to a subject together in one clip art category file, and you can make special clip art category files for special projects. The more clip art that you acquire from different sources and use in Freelance Graphics presentations, the more useful your new clip art categories become.

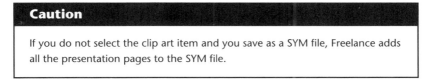

To create a new clip art category file, follow these steps:

1. Add at least one clip art object to a blank page in a new presentation.

2. Choose File, Save As to open the Save As dialog box.

> **Caution**
>
> If you do not select the clip art item and you save as a SYM file, Freelance adds all the presentation pages to the SYM file.

3. In the Save as Type drop-down list, select the Lotus Freelance Clip Art (SYM) file type.

4. If necessary, use the Save In drop-down list to switch to the drive and folder where the Freelance clip art categories are stored (C:\LOTUS\ SMASTERS\FLG).

5. Type a new file name in the File Name text box (see fig. 13.12).

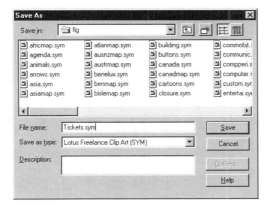

Fig. 13.12
The Save As dialog box shows the new symbol category filename TICKETS.SYM.

6. Click Save. The next time you open the clip art library, you will find the new category in the list.

Using Bitmap Images

Bitmap images are stored in a variety of common bitmap file formats. Many paint and scanning programs can generate any or all of the common bitmap file formats. Other programs generate their own exclusive brand of bitmap file format. Fortunately, Freelance can accept most of the popular bitmap file formats you may encounter. These bitmap file formats include the following:

- Windows/PM Bitmap (BMP)

- Hewlett-Packard Graphics Gallery (GAL)
- Zsoft PC Paintbrush Bitmap (PCX)
- Tag Image (TIF)
- Targa Bitmap (TGA)

Importing a Bitmap

To use a bitmap file from another application in your presentation, you need to use Freelance to import the bitmap.

To import a bitmap file, follow these steps:

1. Display the presentation page where you want the bitmap to appear.

2. Choose <u>F</u>ile, <u>O</u>pen. The Open dialog box appears.

3. If necessary, use the Look <u>I</u>n drop-down list to switch to the drive and folder where the bitmap file is stored.

4. Under Files of <u>T</u>ype, select the bitmap file format from the list of available file types (see fig. 13.13).

Fig. 13.13
Use the Open dialog box to select the bitmap file you want to import.

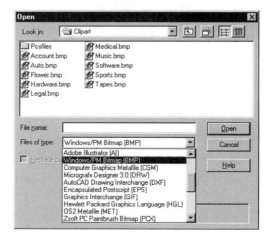

5. From the list of files in the middle of the Open dialog box, select the file you want to import.

6. Click <u>O</u>pen to import the image.

7. Depending on the bitmap file format you chose in step 3, you may be prompted to do one of the following: embed the image with the file, include the image as a PostScript object, or make a template background (to override the SmartMaster look).

After responding to the prompt, the bitmap appears on the current page (see fig 13.14).

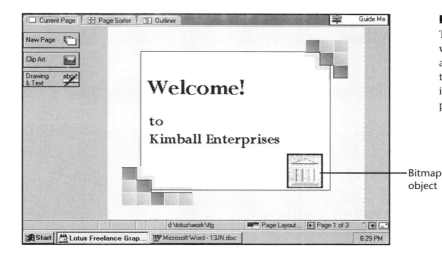

Fig. 13.14
The bitmap, which was created in another applica-tion, has been imported to a presentation page.

Note

Because bitmap files can be extremely large, you may not want to include the data from the bitmap file in the Freelance file. If you do not include the bitmap data, Freelance refers to the image data from the separate bitmap file when you need to view the image in the presentation.

If you plan to give the Freelance presentation file to another user (or run the screen show on a different computer), you should embed the image with the Freelance file. You also could provide the separate bitmap file(s) along with the presentation files. Otherwise, Freelance will not be able to find the bitmap images on the other user's system when the program needs to refer to the data.

The bitmap appears on the page at the same size the bitmap was created. If the bitmap is too large to fit the page, the bitmap will be halved in size repeatedly until it fits the page.

A bitmap can be moved and resized just like any other object on the Free-lance page. Holding down the Shift key while you drag a corner handle will maintain the proportions of the bitmap as you resize it. Bitmaps change resolution when they are sized, though. As you enlarge or decrease the size of a bitmap, Freelance must use more or fewer dots to form the image; it may, therefore, become distorted. You will have to judge for yourself how the bitmap looks after you resize it. If you are unhappy with the appearance of the picture after resizing it, immediately choose Edit, Undo Stretch, click the Undo SmartIcon, or press Ctrl+Z.

Cropping a Bitmap

You can display any rectangular portion of a bitmap image on a presentation page by using the Bitmap, Crop Bitmap command. This command enables you to cut out any portions of the picture that you don't want the viewer to see.

To crop a bitmap, follow these steps:

1. Select the bitmap in Freelance.

2. Choose Bitmap, Crop Bitmap. The Crop Bitmap dialog box appears.

3. A rectangle bounded by handles appears at the corners of the bitmap in the Crop Bitmap dialog box. Drag the handles to position the rectangle over the portion of the bitmap that you want shown (see fig. 13.15).

4. Click OK. The selected portion of the bitmap fills the space on the page that was previously occupied by the entire bitmap.

Fig. 13.15
You can crop a bitmap image in the Crop Bitmap dialog box.

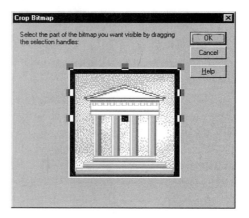

Even after you crop a bitmap, the data for the entire bitmap is still available. You can, therefore, select the bitmap and use the Bitmap, Crop Bitmap command again to choose a different portion of the image or to display the entire image.

Modifying the Attributes of a Bitmap

When color bitmaps are printed by Freelance to a color output device, the bitmaps appear in color. When the output device is black and white, Freelance maps color images to shades of gray. You can modify the attributes of a bitmap to change its look. For example, you can change the contrast, brightness, and sharpness of a bitmap. You also can make a bitmap transparent or invert a black-and-white bitmap.

Changing the Contrast, Brightness, and Sharpness of a Bitmap

Free-lance can import black-and-white bitmaps (2-bit), 16-color or grayscale bit-maps (4-bit), 256-color bitmaps (8-bit), or 16.7-million color bitmaps (24-bit). When you import grayscale images (various shades of gray with no colors), you can adjust their contrast, brightness, and sharpness. When you import color images, you can change only their contrast and brightness.

To change the contrast, brightness, or sharpness of a bitmap, follow these steps:

1. Double-click the bitmap image. The Bitmap Properties InfoBox appears (see fig. 13.16).

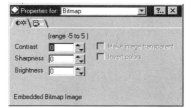

Fig. 13.16
The Bitmap Properties InfoBox enables you to adjust the contrast, brightness, or sharpness of a bitmap.

Tip

You also can right-click the bitmap image, then choose Bitmap Properties to access the InfoBox.

2. Enter values between -5 and 5 (zero is the default) in the Contrast, Sharpness, and Brightness text boxes (or use the scroll arrows beside the text boxes). As you change each setting, the changes are reflected in the bitmap.

Note

The Contrast setting changes the ratio of black to white in the image. The Brightness setting changes the overall luminous intensity of the image. The Sharpness setting changes the clarity of the lines and borders in the bitmap.

3. Click the close button of the InfoBox when you are finished.

Making a Bitmap Transparent

Another control in the Bitmap Properties InfoBox enables you to make all dots except black dots in the image transparent. Then objects behind the bitmap will show through the bitmap. To make a bitmap transparent, click the Make Image Transparent check box. The bitmap's border disappears.

Inverting a Black-and-White Bitmap

If the bitmap is black and white only, you can make all black dots white and all white dots black by clicking the Invert Colors check box in the Bitmap Properties InfoBox. You will see a negative of the bitmap. (If the bitmap is already a negative, you will see a correct display of the image.) ❖

CHAPTER 14

Importing and Exporting Drawings and Charts

by Joyce J. Nielsen

Freelance is certainly not the only graphics program that can create drawings. Many drawing programs, such as Visio, Adobe Illustrator, and Micrografx Designer, have even more sophisticated drawing tools than those in Freelance, so the drawings those programs create have special effects that are impossible to create in Freelance. You can use the File, Open command in Freelance to import these sophisticated drawing files. The drawings appear on the Freelance page just as if they were created in Freelance.

Freelance also enables you to export completed presentation pages as graphics files. Then you can incorporate the pages in designs created in other graphics programs, such as bitmap-editing programs or desktop publishing software.

In this chapter, you learn how to do the following:

- Link and embed objects from other applications in a Freelance presentation
- Link and embed a Freelance page in another application
- Export a Freelance page to a graphic file
- Import a graphics file
- Import a named chart created in 1-2-3

Transferring Graphics Between Freelance and Other Windows Applications

Transferring graphics between Freelance and other Windows applications is particularly easy. You can simply select the graphic, choose Edit, Copy,

◀ See "Importing Data from Another Windows Application," p. 135

switch to the other application, and choose Edit, Paste Special. A behind-the-scenes translator in Windows converts the graphic so that its data transfers correctly from one application to another. You can use this technique to import graphics into or export graphics out of Freelance. You can use the copy-and-paste operations to copy a chart from Freelance into a word processing or desktop publishing document, for example.

Linking a Graphic to a Presentation Page

Windows also enables you to establish a link between a graphic in another application and the graphic in Freelance. The link works both ways, whether you're pulling the graphic from the other application to Freelance or referencing a Freelance graphic from another application. To create the link, you must follow these steps:

1. In the other application, save the graphic to a file (normally, you would choose File, Save). This step is required, or you will not be able to create a link.

2. Select the graphic in the other application (in most cases, you click a graphic to select it).

3. From the other application's menu, choose Edit, Copy.

4. Switch to the Freelance presentation in Current Page view.

> **Note**
>
> If the Windows 95 Taskbar appears at the bottom of your screen, click the Lotus Freelance Graphics button to switch to Freelance. If the Taskbar does not appear, press Alt+Tab to cycle among the open applications until Freelance appears on-screen.

5. Choose Edit, Paste Special. The Paste Special dialog box appears. The name of the source document or file containing the graphic appears at the top of the dialog box.

6. Select Paste Link to Source (see fig. 14.1).

> **Caution**
>
> If the Paste Link to Source option appears dimmed in the Paste Special dialog box, the source application containing the graphic you want to copy does not support linking. Choose the Paste option and continue to step 7. Refer to the following section, "Embedding a Graphic in a Presentation," for more information.

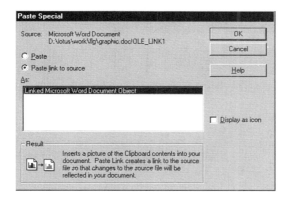

Fig. 14.1
The Paste Link to Source option enables you to establish a link between the graphic in another application and Freelance.

> **Tip**
>
> The formats in the As list differ depending on the source of the graphic you are linking.

7. One of the formats in the As list of formats describes the graphic as an object. Choose this format and then click OK. The object then appears in Freelance.

You can move and resize the graphic as you would any other object. If you edit the graphic in the original application, the changes appear in Freelance, too.

◀ See "Moving and Sizing Objects," p. 230

> **Caution**
>
> When you link a graphic from another application to a Freelance presentation, you must be aware that the data for the graphic still resides in the other application. If you transport the Freelance presentation to another computer, the graphic will not be displayed in the presentation because its data is not stored in the presentation file. You must also transport the file (but not the application) in which the data is stored. To avoid this problem, you can instead embed the graphic in your presentation. This topic is covered in the next section.

Troubleshooting

I created a link to a graphic in another application, but the next time I opened the presentation in Freelance, the graphic did not appear.

Be sure to save the object in the source file before you copy the object and link it. Otherwise, Freelance is unable to reference the graphic when you open the presentation again.

I need to delete an application that I used as a source for objects that I linked to my Freelance presentation. How do I unlink the graphic so that it won't be lost when I delete the source application?

You can break a link if you no longer want it connected to its source. Choose Edit, Manage Links. Select the link you want to break. Click Break Link, and then click Close.

Embedding a Graphic in a Presentation

To ensure that the data for an imported graphic will become part of the Freelance presentation file, you can embed the graphic. You can use embedding only when the other application is a Windows program also. The disadvantage of this approach is that changes you make to the graphic in the original application will not appear in the Freelance presentation. The advantage is that you can still double-click the graphic and then edit it from within Freelance. The original application in which you created the object opens so that you can use its tools to modify the object.

To embed a graphic from another Windows application, follow these steps:

1. Select the graphic in the other application.
2. From the other application's menu, choose Edit, Copy.
3. Switch to the Freelance presentation in Current Page view.
4. Choose Edit, Paste Special. The Paste Special dialog box appears.
5. Select Paste.
6. One of the formats in the As list of formats describes the graphic as an object. Choose this format and then click OK. The object then appears in Freelance.

Figure 14.2 shows a graphic that was created in Windows Metafile Format (a standard drawing format used by many Windows applications) and embedded on a Freelance page with a presentation title and subtitle.

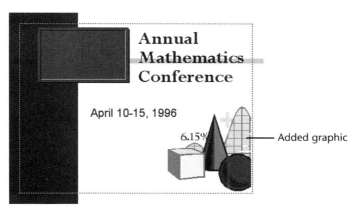

Fig. 14.2
An embedded graphic appears in a Freelance presentation.

To edit an embedded graphic in its original application, follow these steps:

1. Double-click the graphic on the Freelance page. The original application opens with the graphic loaded.

> **Note**
>
> If the original application from which you copied the graphic does not appear on-screen, try double-clicking the graphic again.

2. Edit the graphic, as desired.

3. Choose File, Exit to close the graphic and return to Freelance.

Linking or Embedding a Freelance Presentation Page in Another Application

You can easily copy an individual text or graphic object from a Freelance page to another application by selecting the object and then choosing Edit, Copy in Freelance and Edit, Paste in the other application. To link or embed a Freelance presentation into another application, however, you must link or embed an entire presentation page, one page at a time. You do this in Page Sorter view.

▶ See "Embedding Presentations in Other Windows Applications," p. 290

To link or embed a Freelance page in another application, follow these steps:

1. In Freelance, save the presentation file.

2. Switch to Page Sorter view.

3. Select the page you want to link or embed.

4. From the Freelance menu, choose Edit, Copy.

5. Switch to the other application.

6. Place the cursor where you want the Freelance page to appear.

7. From the other application's menu, choose Edit, Paste Special.

8. To link the data, select Paste Link. Or, to embed the data, select Paste.

9. In the As list, select Lotus Freelance 96 Presentation Object (see fig. 14.3).

10. Click OK to link or embed the object. The Freelance page appears in the other application (see fig. 14.4).

Fig. 14.3
You can link or embed a Freelance Presentation page to another application.

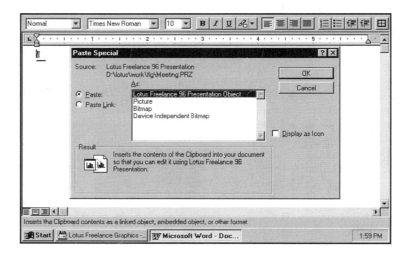

When you link a Freelance Presentation page to another application (using the Paste Link option), any edits you make will appear in the other application, too. The data is stored in Freelance, though; if you transport the file from the other application, the data will not be taken unless you also transport the Freelance presentation file.

When you embed a Freelance page (using the Paste option), the data becomes part of the other application's file. To edit the presentation page from within the other application, you double-click the page to open Freelance. If the other application's file has been moved to another computer, you can edit the Freelance Presentation page by double-clicking it as long as the other computer also has Freelance installed on it.

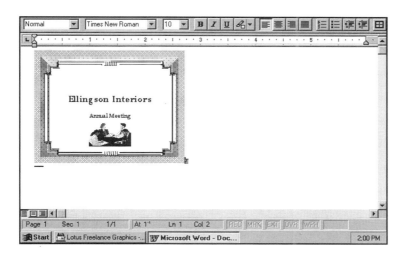

Fig. 14.4
A Freelance page has been embedded in a Microsoft Word document.

Troubleshooting

I used several links in a Freelance presentation, but the presentation takes forever to load whenever I want to make changes to the presentation.

By default, Freelance automatically updates all links when you open a presentation. You can switch to manual updating, which enables you to choose when you want to update the links. Choose Edit, Manage Links. Select the link you want to change, and click Manual. Click Close. After you finish editing your presentation, you can update all the links at once. Choose Edit, Manage Links. Then click Update Now, and click Close.

Exporting a Presentation Page to a Graphics File

If you want to use a Freelance page in a non-Windows application, such as WordPerfect for DOS, you can export the page as a graphics file and then import the file into the other application. You also can export a page to a file for use in a Windows application on another system. After you export the page, you can take the file to the other system and then import it there.

To export a Freelance page, follow these steps:

1. Display the Freelance page you want to export in Current Page view.

2. Choose File, Save As. The Save As dialog box appears (see fig. 14.5).

Fig. 14.5
Use the Save As dialog box to export a Freelance page to a non-Windows application.

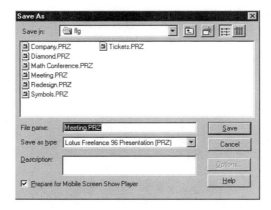

3. Select the file type you want to export from the Save as Type drop-down list.

4. Type the file name for the export file in the File Name text box (or accept the suggested file name). If necessary, use the Save In drop-down list to switch to the drive or directory where you want to save the file.

5. Click Save. Freelance exports the page to a graphics file with the default set of options for that file type.

Certain file types in the Save as Type drop-down list enable you to customize the output for the export file. You can view or change these options by clicking Options before you click Save. If the Options button appears dimmed when you select the Save as Type file type, then you cannot change any options for that file type.

When you click the Options button in the Save As dialog box, an Output Filter Setup dialog box appears. Figure 14.6 shows the dialog box that appears when you choose PCX as the export file type.

Many Output Filter Setup dialog boxes have Format, Resolution, Size, and Color Translation settings.

You can use the Format settings to determine how many colors appear in the export file. Bi-Level shows only black and white, for example.

The Resolution settings enable you to choose the density of dots in a bitmap export file. You cannot modify the resolution settings for all file types. Choose Screen to match the current resolution of the screen. Choose Printer to match the resolution of the printer that is currently selected in Windows. Choose Source to let Freelance select the optimal resolution. You also can type your own resolution by clicking the button next to the two Pels/In text boxes and then typing a number of horizontal pels (dots) per inch in the first box and the number of vertical pels per inch in the second box.

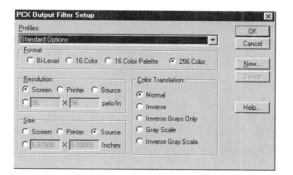

Fig. 14.6
The PCX Output Filter Setup dialog box enables you to customize the settings before you export the file to PCX format.

To limit the size of the image in the output file, use the Size settings. Choose Screen to use the size of the image as it appears on-screen, Printer to limit the image to the size of the current page selected for the current printer, or Source to export the image at the size it is created in Freelance. You can enter a custom size for the image by first clicking the button next to the two text boxes that hold the current size of the image in inches, and then typing new horizontal and vertical sizes.

The Color Translation settings tell the output filter to translate the colors shown on a color presentation page when the export file is created. Here are the color translation alternatives:

Option	How Colors Are Translated
Normal	As they are shown in Freelance
Inverse	To their opposite RGB values
Inverse Grays Only	Blacks, whites, and shades of gray in the image are inverted to their opposite color. For example, blacks are shown as whites.
Gray Scale	As shades of gray
Inverse Gray Scale	As shades and then inverted to their opposite colors

Certain file types have special options settings. When you choose Adobe Illustrator (AI) as the export file type, for example, an output setting called Line Cap Mode appears in the AI Output Filter Setup dialog box. This setting enables you to choose whether the export file has Device line caps (Freelance line endings that Adobe Illustrator supports) or Stroked line caps (Freelance line endings that are not directly supported by Adobe Illustrator but are represented in a style that Adobe Illustrator can accept).

For several export file types, Freelance offers a list of Profiles that correspond to several popular applications in which you might use the export file. Select a profile to choose an appropriate combination of options settings. The default profile is called Standard Options. You should check the list of Profiles to see whether there is another profile that better suits your needs.

If you find yourself using a custom combination of settings often, you can save it in a custom profile. To create a custom profile in an Output Filter Setup dialog box, choose the settings you want, click New, and then enter a name for the profile in the Profile Name text box that appears (see fig. 14.7). Then click OK. The profiles that you create appear preceded by an asterisk on the list of Profiles.

Fig. 14.7
Use the New
Profile Menu
dialog box to save
custom profile
settings.

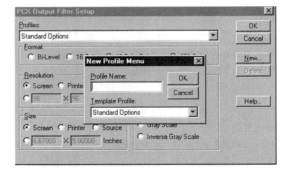

Importing a Graphics File

◀ See "Importing
a Bitmap,"
p. 262

In the preceding chapter, you learned how to import a bitmap and add it to a presentation page. You also can import graphic drawings that were created in other presentation graphics programs or in drawing and illustration software. These images are composed of collections of drawn objects just as Freelance images are. When you import these images, Freelance converts the objects into Freelance-drawn objects.

To import a graphic, follow these steps:

1. Choose File, Open. The Open dialog box appears.
2. Select the import file type from the Files of Type drop-down list (see fig. 14.8).

3. Switch to the drive and directory containing the file you want to import (if necessary), then select the file name.

4. Click Open to import the image.

> **Note**
>
> Depending on the import file type you choose, you may see a message box which asks if you want to embed a copy of the image file. Choose Yes to embed the image in the presentation; or choose No if you want Freelance only to refer to the image as a link.

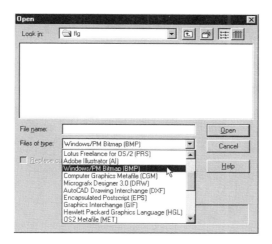

Fig. 14.8
The Open dialog box enables you to import graphics files created in a variety of file formats.

Importing a Named Chart from 1-2-3

If you have created a named chart in 1-2-3, you can import the chart into a Freelance presentation. Follow these steps:

1. Within Freelance, choose Create, 1-2-3 Named Chart.

2. Under Files of Type, select the 1-2-3 Worksheet option.

◀ See "Importing Data from a Lotus 1-2-3 or Microsoft Excel File," p. 127

> **Note**
>
> You can also import a chart created in Freelance for OS/2. Select the Freelance for OS/2 option under Files of Type and continue with the rest of the procedure. You cannot, however, use this method to import a chart created in Excel. To use an Excel chart in Freelance, you must link or embed the chart. See "Transferring Graphics between Freelance and Other Windows Applications" earlier in this chapter.

IV

Adding Text and Graphics

3. Switch to the drive and directory containing the 1-2-3 file, and select the worksheet file that contains the chart (1-2-3 worksheet file extensions begin with WK).

4. Click Named Charts. The Import Named Chart dialog box appears (see fig. 14.9).

Fig. 14.9
Select the 1-2-3
chart you want
to open in the
Import Named
Chart dialog box.

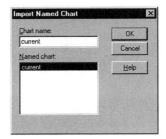

5. Select the desired chart from the Named Chart list.

6. Click OK.

7. Click Open. The chart appears on the Freelance page.

When you import a named chart, the chart remains linked to its original data. Therefore, if you change the data in the other application, the chart changes in Freelance. ❖

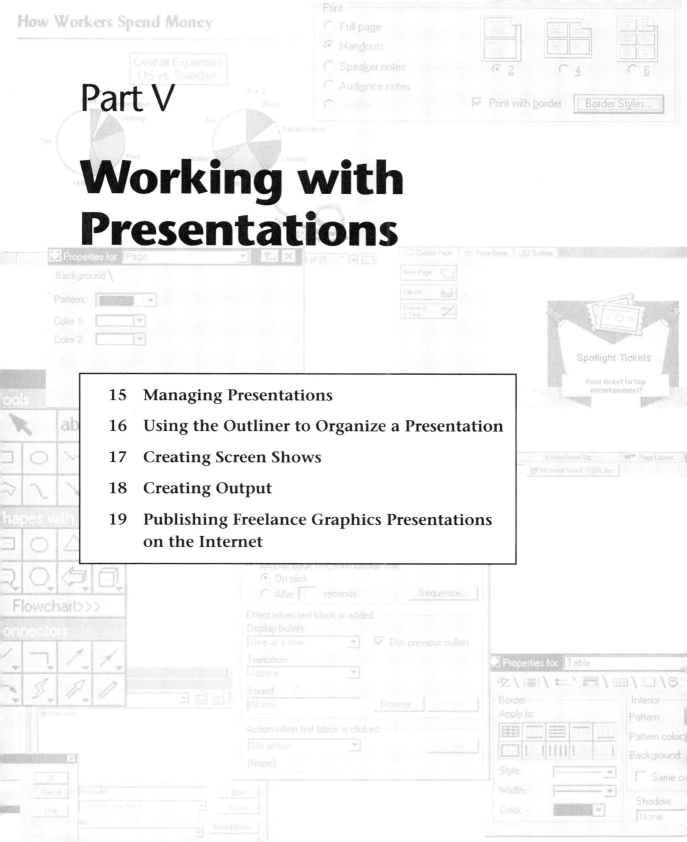

Part V

Working with Presentations

CHAPTER 15

Managing Presentations

by Nancy Stevenson

After you finish the page-by-page construction of a presentation, you may want to take advantage of some of the tools and commands that Freelance offers for managing the presentation. These tools allow you to polish the presentation by checking for mechanical issues, like spelling errors. With Freelance Graphics, you can also manage multiple presentations by copying pages from one presentation into another, or by copying embedding presentations as a whole into other programs. But beyond putting the finishing touches on your presentation, Freelance also lets you begin to prepare for the moment when you must face an audience.

In this chapter, you learn how to

- Check the spelling in the presentation
- Create speaker notes to guide the person at the podium
- Copy work between presentations
- Embed a completed presentation in another Windows application

Using Spell Check

Freelance does not require or even suggest that you check the spelling of a completed presentation, but a typo can be most embarrassing when it is exhibited in five-inch high letters before an audience of your peers. Always take a moment to use the program's Spell Check feature before you project your presentation.

> **Caution**
>
> As with all computer spell checkers, Freelance's Spell Check only warns you about words that are not found in its dictionary. Spell Check does not detect when you have dropped a word from a sentence or used the wrong word inadvertently (such as "they're" rather than "their"). Be forewarned that careful proofreading of a presentation is also a good idea.

How Spell Check works depends on the part of the program you are using. Table 15.1 summarizes the possibilities.

Table 15.1 How Spell Check Works

Activity or View	What Spell Check Checks
Editing text	The word at the typing cursor
Viewing the current page with no text selected	Text on the current page or the entire presentation (your choice)
Page Sorter view	The entire presentation, including text in charts, speaker notes, and metafiles; or the text on the selected page (your choice)
Outliner view	Visible text in the outline (not collapsed text, which is detailed level outline text that can be hidden from view)

To start Spell Check, press Ctrl+F2, or choose Edit, Check Spelling. A Spell Check dialog box like the one in figure 15.1 appears.

Fig. 15.1
Check for spelling errors by using this dialog box.

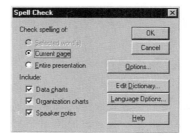

The Spell Check dialog box allows you to determine the scope of the spell checking: whether to check only Selected Word(s), the Current Page, or text throughout the Entire Presentation. The dialog box also enables you to specify whether to check the spelling in Data Charts, Organization Charts, or Speaker Notes. You can choose any combination of these.

> **Note**
>
> If you are in the Outliner view when you initiate Spell Check, you will not have the option of Current Page or the Entire Presentation. Your options here will be Selected Words or the Outline.

After you click OK, Spell Check finds words that are not in its dictionary, displays each word in context, and suggests alternative spellings (see fig. 15.2).

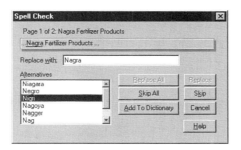

Fig. 15.2
Possible options are given for solving or ignoring the spelling problem.

Choose the correct spelling from the list of alternatives and then click Replace to replace only this occurrence of the word. Other options include:

- Click Replace All to replace the word wherever it appears in the current presentation.

- Click Skip if the word is spelled correctly (often when it is a proper name or acronym).

- Click Skip All to ignore all further occurrences of the word.

- If the word is used frequently in presentations, you may want to add it to the user dictionary by clicking Add To Dictionary.

> **Troubleshooting**
>
> *I can't seem to get to the Add to Dictionary button—it's gray and doesn't seem available to me. Why?*
>
> Once you click one of the suggested alternatives, the alternative spelling is placed in the Replace With text box, and the option to Add to the Dictionary is not available to you anymore. Basically, Freelance figures if you're choosing to change the word, you're choosing not to add it to the dictionary. This is true even though the word will not actually be replaced in your presentation until you click the Replace All or Replace button. However, if you change your mind and decide to add the original word to your dictionary after you've clicked on an alternative, you're going to have to cancel and begin the Spell Check all over again.

Changing the Spell-Checking Options

By clicking Options in the Spell Check dialog box, you can change how Spell Check works. The Spell Check Options dialog box, shown in figure 15.3, shows four options that are described in table 15.2.

Table 15.2 Spell Check Options	
Option	**Description**
Check for Repeated Words	Finds and flags any words that you may have inadvertently typed twice in succession.
Check Words With Numbers	Checks the spelling of words that contain ordinal numbers, such as 2nd or 3rd.
Check Words With Initial Caps	Checks words that start with capital letters. You can turn this option off to prevent Spell Check from flagging proper names as incorrect, for example.
Include User Dictionary Alternatives	Displays words you have entered in the user dictionary as alternative spellings when Spell Check deems they are appropriate.

Fig. 15.3
Have a lot of proper names in your presentation? Deselect the initial caps option here.

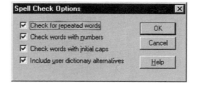

Adding Words to the User Dictionary

You may want to add to the user dictionary any words such as acronyms like ESP, terms that are common to your profession, or proper names that you frequently use. These words will not be flagged as misspellings. For example, you may want to add your company name, its abbreviation, and your own name. To add words, start Spell Check and then click Edit Dictionary in the Spell Check dialog box. The Spell Check User's Dictionary dialog box opens, as shown in figure 15.4.

To add a new word to the dictionary, type it in the New Word text box and then click Add. To delete words, select them from the Current Words list and then click Delete. When you are finished, click OK.

Setting the Spell Check Language

Do you correspond regularly with a friend in France? Or perhaps you're fond of using Spanish proverbs here and there in your presentation to make a point. Freelance has several language dictionaries built in. You can change to a different dictionary by clicking the Language Options button in the Spell Check dialog box and then selecting the dictionary from the list that appears (see fig. 15.5).

Fig. 15.4
Add frequently used terms and names to your dictionary so Check Spelling won't flag them in the future.

Fig. 15.5
Check spelling based on any available language dictionary.

> **Note**
>
> You even have the option of American or British—two amazingly divergent versions of English—at your command. For example, the British spelling "colour" is flagged as an error when you use the American dictionary, but left alone with the British version.

Switching to a Black-and-White Version of a Presentation

Each SmartMaster set in Freelance Graphics 96 for Windows 95 comes with a pair of internal palettes that determine all the colors used in a presentation. One palette assigns colors to the various parts of a presentation. The other palette assigns shades of gray instead. You can use the color palette to create color slides or a screen show and then, after the color presentation is complete, temporarily switch to the black & white palette to print the presentation with a black-and-white printer. If you are using a black-and-white printer, you can create the presentation by using the black & white palette to see on-screen how the presentation will look when you print it.

 To switch easily from the color palette to the black & white palette, click the Display in Color/B&W button in the status bar at the bottom of the Freelance window or press Alt+F9. Another method is to choose Presentation, Switch Palette.

You can edit the colors in the color palette within each SmartMaster set, but you cannot edit the shades of gray in a black & white palette.

▶ See "Editing a Color Palette," p. 378

> **Tip**
>
> If you're going to print in black and white, use the black-and-white display to see how your color set is likely to translate to grayscale. If it's not so hot, try a different SmartMaster look.

Copying Work Between Presentations

Freelance makes it easy to copy charts, text blocks, graphic objects, and even entire pages from one presentation to another so that you can easily reuse items rather than recreate them. If a chart that you made for a presentation last month is appropriate for tomorrow's presentation to a different client, for example, you can copy the chart to the new presentation.

  To copy a chart, text block, or graphic object from one presentation to another, select the object, and then choose Edit, Copy or click the Copy SmartIcon. Next, switch to the other presentation and either choose Edit, Paste or click the Paste SmartIcon.

An even easier way to do this is to simply drag elements from one presentation to the other while both are open. To have two presentations open at the same time, follow these steps:

1. Open one first and then the other.

2. When you click the Window menu, a list of all the open presentations appears. Click a presentation name in the list to switch to it.

3. To place two open presentations side by side, choose Window, Tile Left-Right.

4. To arrange two open presentations so that they overlap one another, click Cascade.

Tile Left-Right and Cascade work only with presentation windows that are maximized or restored. If a presentation is minimized to an icon, it is not affected. Figure 15.6 shows two tiled presentation windows.

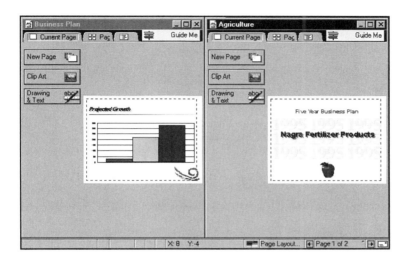

Fig. 15.6
When they're side by side, it's easy to move pieces between presentations.

When SmartMaster look objects, such as text or background graphics, are copied or moved from one presentation to another, they are reformatted by the color palette and page layout of the presentation to which they are copied. A chart copied from one presentation to another may have very different colors when it appears in the second presentation. The content remains the same.

To move a presentation page between presentations, place two presentations side by side and switch them both to Page Sorter view, as shown in figure 15.7. Then select a page in one presentation and drag it over to the second presentation. The page then appears after the selected page in the second presentation and takes on the formatting of the second presentation's SmartMaster set. To make a copy of a page, simply press Ctrl, then click on the page to select it and drag it to the other presentation. The page will remain in the original presentation, and a copy of it will also appear in the second presentation.

V

Presentations

Fig. 15.7
It's easy to drag elements from one presentation to another.

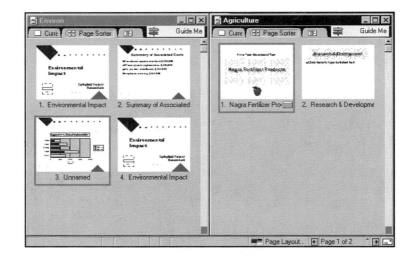

Creating Speaker Notes

You can attach a speaker note containing comments about the contents to each page in a presentation. Speaker notes can come in handy at a lectern; they can summarize each slide and remind you of possible discussion topics relevant to the slide. When you print speaker notes in Freelance, you actually get an image of the slide's content along with the notes so you have a comprehensive guide to the content of the presentation. However, if you show a presentation on-screen, speakers notes won't appear.

To create a speaker note for a page, turn to the page in Current Page view. Then click the Speaker Notes button on the far right of the Outliner view toolbar. A blank speaker note page that looks like a 3 × 5 card appears. Figure 15.8 shows a speaker notes page with notes typed in it.

Begin typing notes about the contents of the page, or copy and paste the notes from a presentation page or another Windows application. By default, the text appears without bullets, but you can change that.

The appearance of the text and bullet is controlled by the settings in the Text menu within the Speaker Note window. The options in this menu enable you to choose a typeface for all the text, a bullet shape, and a text point size. The changes you make to the default settings affect all text you type in other speaker notes in that presentation. Text that you have already typed is not affected. To change some or all of the text in a particular speaker note, select the text and then use the commands in the Text menu to apply standard character attributes such as bold-facing, or to change the typeface, apply bullets, or change text point size.

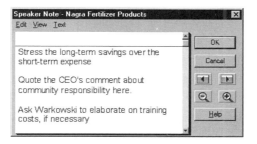

Fig. 15.8
Remind yourself of important things to cover in a speaker note.

Tip

To return to the default settings for speaker note text, choose Text, Reset to Default.

The Edit menu within the Speaker Note window supplies standard editing commands, such as Copy and Paste, which you can use on the text inside the window.

To add a speaker note to the next page or to switch to the speaker note for previous page, click the right or left arrows to the right of the note text.

When you finish a speaker note and you view the presentation in Page Sorter view, a speaker note icon appears below the page thumbnail, as in figure 15.9. Double-click this icon to view the speaker note.

After you finish a presentation, you can print the speaker notes. Freelance prints a small version of the current page and the speaker note on the same page. To print speaker notes, choose File, Print and then select the Speaker Notes radio button from the Print dialog box. As you can see in figure 15.10, there are three options in the Print section of this box for how many pages and corresponding speaker notes you want to print on a page. The 6 option, for example, provides six images: three pages and three speaker notes. You can also choose to apply a border to the notes here.

Click the Print button to begin printing.

V

Presentations

Fig. 15.9
The small note
card icon below a
page indicates an
associated speaker
note.

Speaker Note icon

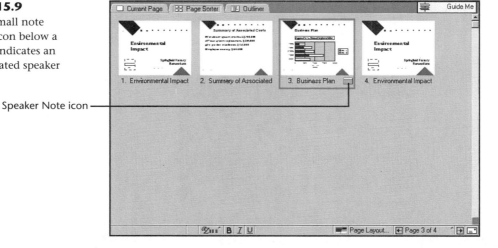

Fig. 15.10
You can fit as
many as three
pages with
associated speakers
notes on a page
from here.

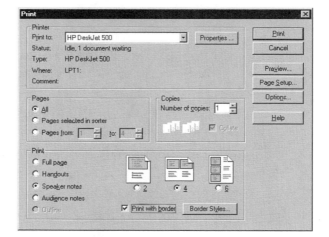

Embedding Presentations in Other Windows Applications

A special feature of Windows, called Object Linking and Embedding (OLE, pronounced O-LAY), gives you the capability of embedding a Freelance presentation page in a file within another application that supports OLE (specifically, that can act as an OLE client). After you have created a presentation, you can copy any number of presentation pages from it to another application. Then you can access the whole Freelance presentation from within the other application by double-clicking the presentation page, as long as Freelance and the original presentation are also available. That way, you can take the Freelance presentation wherever the other application's file goes.

Embedding a presentation page makes it possible to view a Freelance presentation from within another program. You can embed a Freelance presentation page, for example, in a report created in Word Pro or Word for Windows, two popular Windows word processors. Then you can send the word processor report file to a distant location by mail or modem and know that the presentation page is also embedded in the report file. As long as the recipient has Freelance, he or she can view the presentation page while examining the report on-screen. If they have Freelance and a copy of the presentation file, they can open the presentation up from the word processed document and see all the pages from there.

> **Tip**
>
> If the user you want to view your presentation doesn't have Freelance on his or her computer, consider providing them with the Mobile Screen Show Player. This allows people without Freelance to view Freelance presentations.

There are two ways to embed a presentation page:

- From within the other application, which requires that you temporarily switch to Freelance and create the presentation page when it is needed.
- Create the presentation and then copy selected pages to another application, instructing the application to embed the presentation page with a link to Freelance.

The first method, creating the presentation from within another application (explained in the following section), is best when you are working in a report and you need to create a Freelance presentation on-the-fly. The second method is preferable when you want to embed a page from a presentation you have already completed in a new document.

Embedding a Presentation from within Another Application

To use Freelance only long enough to create a presentation while you work in another application, you must use the application's Insert Object or Insert New Object command. Consult the application's manual or help system to locate the Insert Object command. With the Insert Object command, the application displays a list of the embedded objects that the applications in your system can provide. Freelance Presentation is the object that Freelance provides. Using this command, you can actually open up Freelance, create a page, then place it in the document created by the first application as an object. To insert a Freelance presentation page into the other application (in this case, a Word Pro document), choose Freelance Presentation and click OK. After a moment, Freelance opens so that you can create a presentation.

When you complete the new presentation, choose File, Exit and Return to (the other application) to return to and embed the presentation in the original application. The Freelance window closes, and the last page you were working on appears in the other application.

With many applications, you can resize the picture of the presentation page. Figure 15.11 shows a presentation page embedded in an Word Pro document.

Fig. 15.11
Give the pizzazz of a Freelance chart to your document by embedding a Freelance page in it.

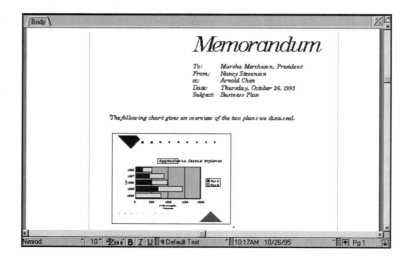

Tip

If you create several pages in Freelance, you can switch to Page Sorter view and then click on a page before exiting back to the other program. The page you've selected will be the page that appears in the other application.

Embedding an Existing Presentation

The second way to embed a presentation is to copy it as an embedded object to another application. This method allows you to embed a page from a presentation you've already created.

To embed a presentation page, open the presentation in Freelance, switch to Page Sorter view, and click the page you want to see in the other application. Then choose Edit, Copy. This copies information about the presentation to the Windows Clipboard.

Open or switch to the other application's window and then place the cursor where you would like the image of the selected presentation page to appear. Then choose Edit, Paste Special. If you're working in Ami Pro or Word Pro, choose Paste Link to Source in the Paste Special dialog box, as shown in figure 15.12. The selected Freelance presentation page then appears in the open document. Although the Paste Special commands and the wording of choices in the Paste Special dialog box may differ slightly among applications, you should have no trouble finding and using them; the basic procedure is the same.

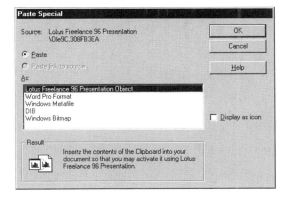

Fig. 15.12
If you want to be able to edit the Freelance presentation from the new application, choose Paste Link to Source.

V

Presentations

> **Note**
>
> If you want to just place the image of the Freelance page in the other application and you don't want to link it to the original presentation, choose Paste. It appears as a bitmap image, but you won't be able to edit it in Freelance by double-clicking it. Also, it won't update if you make changes to it back in Freelance.

Using the Embedded Presentation

To provide access to the embedded presentation page, the computer that you are using must have Freelance Graphics Release 2.0 for Windows or a more recent version installed. Then you can get to the presentation page in a Freelance window by double-clicking the presentation page that you've embedded in the other application. Freelance Graphics then opens, and the presentation page opens within Freelance. If the full Freelance presentation file is also available to the user, the whole presentation will open up when they click on the embedded page. You can view the presentation pages one by one or view the screen show in the presentation. You can also make editing changes to the presentation, using the capabilities of Freelance. When you're done, choose File, Exit Freelance Graphics and be sure to save the changes when prompted. You are then returned to the other application, and these changes are reflected in the embedded copy of the presentation page.

Now that you have a link between applications, you may see special messages when you open the files that have links, telling you that the link is being updated. Also, if the other file is missing, Freelance will give you an error message indicating that it can't find the file to which the link was made.

Embedding Objects in Freelance

You can also embed objects from other applications in Freelance and access the other application by clicking on that embedded object. It's basically the same process given earlier but in reverse:

1. Select something in another application—say, a bullet list from a Word for Windows document, for example.
2. Use the Copy command in Word, then open Freelance.
3. In Freelance, go to the Current Page view for the page where you want to place the object, then choose Edit, Paste Special.
4. Choose to Paste Link to Source in the Paste Special dialog box, then click OK.

The object appears on your current page. If you double-click it, you can access the source application. To update or break a link, use the Manage Links dialog box in Freelance. Select Edit, Manage Links to see the dialog box depicted in figure 15.13.

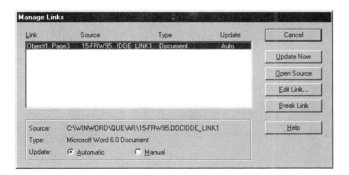

Fig. 15.13
If you make
changes to a linked
file, you can up-
date the linked file
manually using the
Manage Links
dialog box.

If you choose <u>A</u>utomatic Update by clicking that radio button in this dialog
box, then every time you open this Freelance file, if the source file is available, updates will be made. That way, if someone changes the original
bulleted list in Word, for example, the changes will be reflected in your
Freelance object as well. If you'd rather only update the Freelance presentation when you choose, click the <u>M</u>anual radio button in the Manage Links
dialog box. Then when you want to update, click on the <u>U</u>pdate Now button
in this same dialog box.

To break or edit the link, use the <u>E</u>dit Link or <u>B</u>reak Link buttons and make
the changes you want in the dialog box that appears. ❖

Presentations

CHAPTER 16

Using the Outliner to Organize a Presentation

by Nancy Stevenson

No top-notch presentation graphics software these days is worth its salt without a built-in, integrated outliner function that focuses on the content of a presentation rather than the design.

The other two views, Current Page view and Page Sorter view, offer different functions. Current Page view enables you to work on both the content and design of individual pages. Page Sorter view gives you an overall look at a presentation and enables you to rearrange the order of main topics. Only Outliner view distills the presentation into its text content and gives you the tools to concentrate on the text.

In this chapter, you learn about

- Switching to Outliner view
- Adding and editing text in Outliner view
- Adding, deleting, and moving pages in Outliner view
- Viewing different levels of detail in your outline
- Importing outline text from word processors
- Changing page layouts and making columns of text in Outliner view

Working with Text in Outliner View

Many people think in terms of outlines as they gather and organize the thoughts they will express in a presentation. They like to formulate a list of themes, rearrange the flow of ideas toward a conclusion, and then fill in the detail. Freelance's Outliner view is the perfect tool for these people. In an outline, you can create and organize the presentation's text and then switch to Current Page view to concentrate on the design of each page in detail.

Other people will use Outliner view after they have created presentation pages one by one in Current Page view. The Outliner can filter out charts, drawn objects, and design elements and display only the presentation text. Then users can edit individual topics and work with the overall flow of concepts. Either way, the Outliner view is always available as an alternative view of a presentation.

Switching to Outliner View

Outliner view displays a presentation's text on a representation of a familiar yellow pad. Figure 16.1 shows the Outliner view of a presentation. A page number and page icon in the left margin denote each new page. The text content of the page (text that appears on the page in text blocks) is shown to the right. The image on the page icon represents the content of the page. Figure 16.1 shows the different page icon designs and tools.

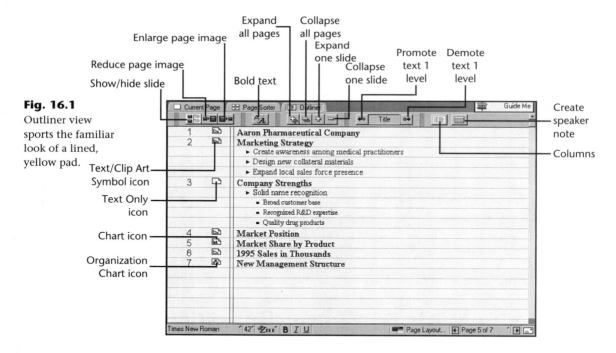

Fig. 16.1
Outliner view sports the familiar look of a lined, yellow pad.

In Freelance Graphics 96 for Windows 95, you can also display the graphical representation of pages next to the text in Outliner view, as shown in figure 16.2. To show or hide the slide images, click the Show/Hide Pages button on the Outliner View toolbar. To go back to page icons and stop displaying page images, click the button again.

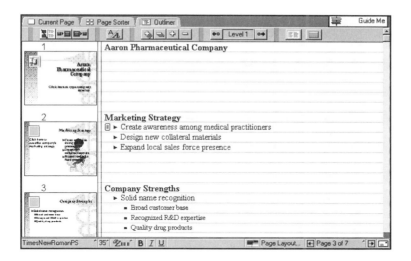

Fig. 16.2
New in Freelance
Graphics 96 is a
display of pages in
Outliner view.

To switch to Outliner view at any time while working with a presentation, click the Outliner tab that is always present, though sometimes shifted behind either the Current Page or Page Sorter tabs. You can also choose View, Outliner.

Moving among the views is easy. If you want to return to Current Page view or Page Sorter view at any time, just select the appropriate tab at the top of the view pages, just below the toolbar. You can also select the View menu and choose either Current Page or Page Sorter.

If you prefer to start a new presentation in Outliner view every time, change the Startup View setting by choosing File, User Setup, then select Freelance Preferences from the side menu. The Freelance Graphics Preferences dialog box in figure 16.3 appears. Click Outliner under Startup Options, and Freelance will always open to that view.

Troubleshooting

My User Setup is set for opening a presentation in Current Page view, but when I re-opened this file it opened in Outliner view. Why?

Your User Setup determines in what view a new presentation will first appear. However, after you save a presentation, when you reopen it, it reopens in the view you were using when you last saved it. If you've finished working with one view and know you'll want to work in another when you come back to the file, just click the tab to bring up the other view before saving the file.

Fig. 16.3
Preferences for
what appears at
startup, and how
copies, drawings,
and save functions
work are all here.

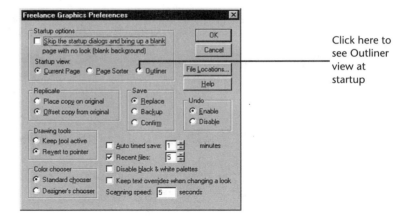

Click here to
see Outliner
view at
startup

To the right of the page icon, the page title appears. If the page has text
blocks, the text in the first two Click Here text blocks are shown indented
and bulleted beneath the page title. If the text is in other text blocks added
with the Text icon, only the first of these is shown in Outliner view.

Notice that the way items are indented in Outliner view reflects a hierarchy,
just like outlines you may have created in the past. By indenting text one
level (called *demoting*), it moves over to the right, which indicates a subordinate position to the heading above and to the left of it. In this way, you get a
visual representation of the flow from major points, down through the levels
of indent to detail points in your presentation. Although you can have several levels of indent in Outliner view, it usually a good idea to stick to no
more than one or at the most two levels of indentation, because any more
would be difficult for those watching your presentation to see and read.

By default, all text in Outliner view is shown in the same typeface that's applied to the text in the Current Page view. To display the text in boldface
type, click the Bold Text button. This is a toggle function: to go back to plain
text, click this button again.

Adding and Editing Presentation Text

You can edit the text of a presentation page in both Current Page view and
Outliner view. While in Outliner view, you can move the cursor and edit text
by using all the standard cursor-movement and text-editing keystrokes and
commands of Freelance. For example, you can press the Delete key to delete a
character at the cursor position, or use the Copy and Paste commands to

copy selected text to and from the Windows Clipboard. Table 16.1 summarizes the cursor-movement keystrokes you can use in Outliner view.

Table 16.1 Cursor-Movement Keystrokes in Outliner View	
Keystroke(s)	**Action**
Home	Moves cursor to the beginning of the current line
End	Moves cursor to the end of the current line
Ctrl+Home	Moves cursor to the beginning of the outline
Ctrl+End	Moves cursor to the end of the outline
Page Up	Moves cursor up one screen
Page Down	Moves cursor down one screen
Up arrow	Moves cursor up one line
Down arrow	Moves cursor down one line
Tab	Demotes text one level
Shift+Tab	Promotes text one level
Ctrl+Page Up	Moves cursor to the beginning of the preceding page
Ctrl+Page Down	Moves cursor to the end of the next page
Ctrl+left arrow	Moves cursor left one word

Use the vertical scroll bar at the right edge of the window to scroll the text in Outliner view.

Remember that you can replace text by simply selecting it and then typing new text in its place.

Tip

To add a new line of text in Outliner view, move the cursor to the end of an existing line and press Enter. A new line appears just below the existing line, and the cursor moves to the beginning of the new line. You can then type new text.

As you create the outline, you can use five levels of indents under the page titles. These levels correspond to the five paragraph styles in the presentation. Text indented to the second level in Outliner view appears in the second paragraph style in Current Page view. Text indented to the third level appears in the third paragraph style, and so on. Press Shift+Tab or click the Promote icon to move the text up one level. If the text is already at the first level and you press Shift+Tab, you start a new page, and the text becomes a page title. You can also use the Demote button to move the bullet item to a deeper level of detail in your outline. Figure 16.4 shows text at various levels of indent in Current Page view. Compare it to figure 16.5, which shows the same corresponding text levels in Outliner view.

Fig. 16.4
Different levels of text are formatted automatically in Current Page view.

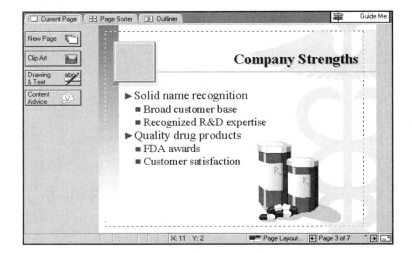

Fig. 16.5
Levels of text are shown as indented in Outliner view.

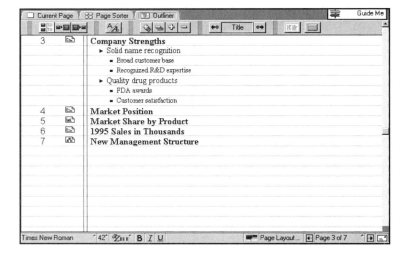

Tip

To create a new line for more text without giving the new line its own bullet point, from either Current Page or Outliner view, press Ctrl+Enter at the end of a line rather than Enter.

Adding, Moving, and Deleting Pages

Although the ability to add and edit text in Outliner view is useful, you don't have to stop there. Outliner view also gives you the freedom to add whole new presentation pages, move existing pages, and delete pages you no longer need. In fact, you can build your entire presentation and organize it right from Outliner view, if you prefer.

◀ See "Rearranging the Order of Pages," p. 66

Adding and Deleting Pages in a Presentation

If you start a new presentation and switch to Outliner view, the number 1 and a blank page icon appear in the left margin. Type a line to the right of the page icon, press Enter, and type a subordinate line of text on the next line. To add the next page, press Enter again and then press Shift+Tab or click the Promote icon.

To add a new page in the middle of a presentation, click on any of the text on a page. Then press F7 or choose Create, Page. The new page dialog box appears, allowing you to choose a page layout. Once you've made your choices and clicked OK, the new page appears after the page the cursor is on. You can also click at the end of the last line of a page, press Enter, and then press Shift+Tab or click the Promote icon.

You can delete pages using one of three methods. First, select the page by clicking the page icon. Then do one of the following:

- Press the Delete key
- Choose Edit, Clear
- Click the Cut SmartIcon

Moving Pages in a Presentation

Although you can also rearrange pages in Page Sorter view, it's often difficult to read the text on those miniature page images. Moving pages in your presentation when you can clearly see the text of each page is an advantage to reorganizing in Outliner view.

To move a page or group of pages, you must select the pages first. To select an entire page, click its page icon once. A border surrounds the page, as shown in figure 16.6.

Fig. 16.6

A border around a page indicates it's ready to be moved elsewhere.

Original position

New position marker

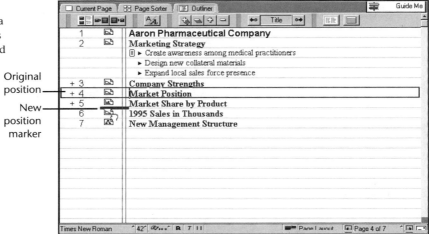

To select adjacent pages in the presentation, hold down the Shift key while you click the icon for the next or preceding page. The border you see in figure 16.6 will simply expand to include all the pages you've selected. You must click a group of adjacent pages, such as pages 2, 3, and 4. You cannot select page 2 and page 4, for example.

Another method of selecting several pages is to place the cursor at the left edge of the left margin and then drag to draw a box that includes the page icons you want included in the group, as shown in figure 16.7. The box does not have to completely surround an entry for it to be included; the entry is included if any of its text falls inside the box. If you do not get the correct pages included in the group, click any single page to deselect the group and then try again.

After you select a page or group of pages, click on a page icon (if you've selected a group of pages, click any of the page icons) and drag the pointer up and down the list of pages. The mouse cursor disappears, and instead a dark line appears where the page or pages will end up when you release the mouse button, as you saw in figure 16.6. When you let go, the selected block of text appears in its new location. If you don't like where you moved the text, you can use the Undo button or Ctrl+Z to undo it.

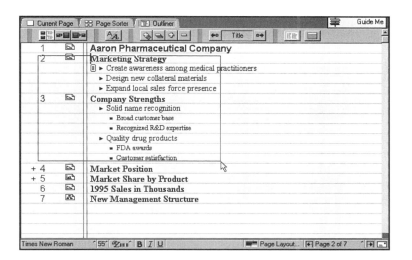

Fig. 16.7
Multiple pages can be selected by dragging across them with the mouse.

Hiding and Showing Text in Outliner View

If Outliner view is where you'll formulate a presentation, you may want to step back a moment and consider the big picture while working on the text for a single page. By collapsing the text at lower levels of the outline, you can view text only at higher levels to make sure your main points are in the right order. You can view only page titles, or all the levels of text by collapsing or expanding all the text underneath.

Use the tools in table 16.2 to collapse and expand text.

Table 16.2	SmartIcons Used to Expand and Collapse Outlines
Icon	**Function**
	Collapse all subtopics under a single page
	Expand all subtopics of a single page
	Collapse all subtopics under all pages
	Expand all subtopics of all pages

Notice that a plus sign appears in the left margin next to a collapsed page (see fig. 16.8 for an example of this).

Fig. 16.8
Plus signs to the left of a slide title indicate hidden detail points underneath.

Plus sign ──────

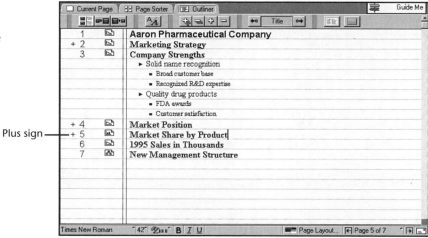

Tip

The equivalent menu commands—Collapse, Expand, Collapse All, and Expand All—are in the View menu.

Printing the Outline

You may want to print an outline to review your presentation's content away from the computer, or to use as speaker notes. You can print a presentation's outline by choosing File, Print. Choose Outline as the format. An even faster method is to click the File Print SmartIcon while in Outliner view and then choose Outline from the Print File dialog box.

▶ See "Determining What to Print," p. 338

When you print an outline, collapsed entries do not print. To print a list of page titles, you can click the Collapse All SmartIcon and then click the File Print SmartIcon.

Importing an Outline from a Word Processor

Rather than type an outline in Outliner view, you can create an outline in your favorite word processor and then import the outline into a new presentation's Outliner view. Each outline entry at the first level becomes the title of a new page. Entries indented under the main entry in the word processor become indented entries in Outliner view, too.

One option is to use Word Pro 96 for Windows 95, or an earlier version of the product with the Ami Pro name. This Windows word processor from Lotus makes copying an outline into Freelance especially easy:

1. Simply create the outline in Word Pro, using the outlining features of the software, or by placing a tab for each level of indent in a simple type list.

2. Select the portion of the outline text you want to use in your presentation and copy it to the Windows Clipboard by choosing Edit, Copy.

3. Switch to Outliner view of a presentation in Freelance.

4. Position the typing cursor on a line in the outline, and choose Paste from the Freelance Edit menu.

Level-one entries in the Word Pro outline become page titles and take on the first paragraph style on presentation pages. Level-two and level-three entries become indented entries under the page title and take on the second and third paragraph styles on presentation pages, and so on through the five indentation levels. Figure 16.9 shows a simple outline in Word Pro. Figure 16.10 shows the same outline after it has been copied and pasted into Outliner view of a new presentation.

> **Note**
>
> This cut-and-paste functionality works with any major word processor, such as Word for Windows or WordPerfect. If a word processor doesn't have an outliner function, just type the text using tabs to indicate each level of indentation, and your list should come in as an outline with no problem.

V

Presentations

Fig. 16.9
Here's a list of items formatted as an outline created in Word Pro 96 for Windows 95.

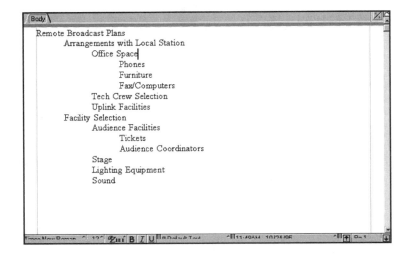

Fig. 16.10
Here's a portion the same outline pasted into Outliner view of Freelance.

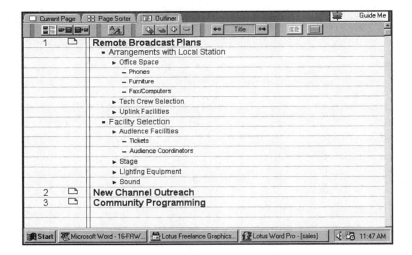

Making a Second Column of Bulleted Text Entries

Sometimes when you have lists of items you'd like to compare, or just a long list, it's helpful to arrange the bullet points in more than one column.

When a page has the 2-Column Bullets page layout, Outliner view displays two special symbols at the start of each column of bullets. You type the text entries for the first column to the right of the symbol with only one line in it, which is the first column marker (see fig. 16.11). Then, move the cursor to the right of the symbol with two lines on it—the second column marker—and type the second column of text entries. If you've entered text in a single column and want to convert it to two columns, simply select the text and click the Column tool. To reassign a new page layout to the Outliner entry, put the cursor on the page to be changed, click the Page Layout button on the status bar, and choose 2 Column Bullet page layout from the pop-up menu.

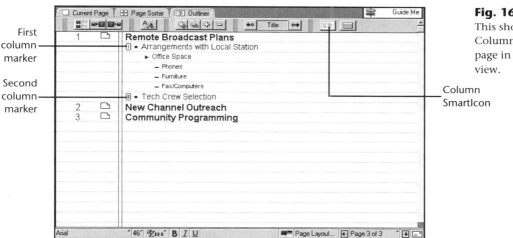

Fig. 16.11
This shows a 2-Column Bullets page in Outliner view.

Using Spell Check in Outliner View

By using Spell Check in Outliner view, you can check only the spelling of the text that appears in Outliner view. Spell Check does not check the spelling of collapsed text, nor does it check the spelling of text in charts, speaker notes, or metafiles in the presentation. If you try to spell check a collapsed page, the spell checker will check the word directly to the right of the cursor.

To check the spelling in a presentation, choose Edit, Check Spelling. The Spell Check dialog box appears, as shown in figure 16.12.

Fig. 16.12
Check for spelling
errors in Outliner
view using the
Check Spelling
function.

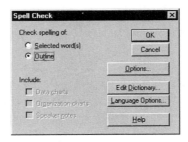

◀ See "Using
Spell Check,"
p. 281

Spell Check gives you the option of checking Selected Word(s) or the entire
Outline. To check selected words, place the typing cursor in the word to
check before starting Spell Check. ❖

CHAPTER 17

Creating Screen Shows

by Nancy Stevenson

After you complete all the pages of a presentation, you can print the presentation, send it to a service that will make slides, or display the presentation on-screen as an automated screen show.

A *screen show* is a sequential display of the pages of a presentation. The pages can simply replace one another on-screen, or they can appear with fancy transition effects, such as fades, splits, pans, or rolls.

Screen shows put the liveliness into a presentation that slides simply cannot offer. And when screen shows are projected before an audience with a good-quality video projection system, they can have even more visual impact than slides, particularly when animation or video clips are added.

In this chapter, you learn to

- Create a slide show and add transition effects
- Make bulleted list charts build point-by-point on-screen
- Add music, sound, and video to a presentation
- Use animation features, including animated clips
- Add buttons to give your show interactive possibilities
- Use the new Rehearse mode

Displaying a Presentation as a Screen Show

After you finish a presentation, you can display it as a screen show by simply clicking the Run Screenshow from the Beginning SmartIcon, or pressing Alt+F10. You can also choose Presentation, Run Screen Show. When the screen show starts, it advances to the next page each time you click the mouse button, press Enter, or press Page Down. To return to the preceding page, right-click, press Page Up, or press the Backspace key. You can also choose to display a control panel on-screen, which gives you buttons to click to more forward, backward, to stop the show (see fig. 17.1).

Fig. 17.1
A slide in Screen Show mode, with the Control Panel displayed.

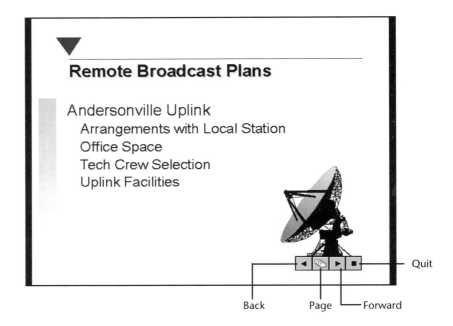

◄ See "Viewing the Presentation as a Screen Show," p. 39

If you have already set up the screen show so that it advances automatically (which you'll learn to do later in this chapter), you can sit back and watch Freelance display page after page at the interval you specified. Or, you can move around the presentation manually. Table 17.1 summarizes the keystrokes you can use while viewing a screen show.

Table 17.1 The Screen Show Keystrokes	
Action	**Keystrokes or Mouse Clicks**
Move to the next page	Click the left mouse button, press Page Down, or press Enter
Move to the preceding page	Click the right mouse button, press Page Up, or press Backspace
Pause or restart an automatic screen show	Press spacebar

Action	Keystrokes or Mouse Clicks
Cancel screen show and display a list of pages	Press Esc
End screen show	Press Esc and click the Quit Screen Show button in the Screen Show Pages dialog box

Setting Up a Screen Show

If you want to do more than run the slides just as they were created, you have several options in Freelance. You can add transition effects that change the way new slides appear on-screen, control the way the entire show runs, and choose to display a special control panel to help you navigate through the show.

Changing the Transition Effect

By default, each page of the screen show appears to simply replace the slide that preceded it. This transition effect, called Replace, is only one of 29 transition effects you can program into a screen show. For example, you can make the next slide in the sequence appear to shift in from the side of the screen or dribble over the other slide in a raindrop-like effect. The new slide can replace the current slide in chunks in a checkboard pattern, or it can spiral onto the screen. And, you can apply these kinds of effects in any combination you like—even having a different transition effect between each slide.

> **Caution**
>
> Transition effects, like color and design elements, should be used judiciously. You don't want the audience looking more to the space between slides than the content of them! Besides, too many effects can be distracting and give your presentation a messy and haphazard look.

To change the effect used to draw each page in a screen show, select the Presentation menu, and then choose Set Up Screen Show. The Set Up Screen Show dialog box appears, with the Page Effects tab on top (see fig. 17.2).

Fig. 17.2
The Set Up Screen
Show dialog box
has three tabs for
controlling screen
shows.

There are three tabs in this dialog box:

- *Page Effects*. Controls transitions between pages in the presentation.
- *Tools*. Includes controls for whether the control panel will display.
- *Options*. Controls the timing and cues for running the show.

The Apply To options at the top of the Page Effects tab enable you to apply
the transition effect you select to All Existing Pages, or only to New pages
only; that is, pages you create going forward.

> **Tip**
>
> To change transition effects for a single page only, choose Page, Screen Show Effects.

To choose an effect, select one from the Transition scrollable list. With the
Display Next Page controls, you can determine whether the show should proceed to the next page manually or automatically. To use a manual advance
choose the On Click or Keypress option (when the left mouse button is
clicked, Page Down is pressed, or Enter is pressed, the presentation will advance). To have the screens advance automatically choose the After *n* Seconds
text box option and specifying the number of seconds your computer should
wait before displaying the next page (the default setting is 3 seconds).

You can select as little as 1 second before advancing, but, especially with animation and video clips, it may take a few seconds for them to actually play
themselves on screen. It's best to stick with at least the 3 second minimum.
On the other hand, too long a wait—say in minutes—may bore a viewer if
there's no discussion by a speaker, as in a trade show setting. If there is a

speaker, it's hard for that speaker to know exactly when the change is coming when they're spaced so far apart. If you need more than, say, 30 seconds between slides, you might consider advancing to the next slide manually.

> **Note**
>
> Don't want a page to display at all? Select the page, then choose Page, Screen Show Effects. At the bottom of the properties dialog box that appears, click Do Not Display This Page During Screen Show. This new feature means you can build one presentation, then, without any more effort than hiding slides in this way, use it in modified versions at any time.

Each page can have a different transition effect. However, you may want to limit the variety of transition effects or use the same transition effect repeatedly until you change subjects in the presentation to give your slide show some visual continuity. To see the transition effect you've chosen for the presentation, click OK, then run the screen show.

Setting Screen Show Options

Select Presentation, Set Up Screen Show. In the Set Up Screen Show dialog box, you can click the Options tab to make three overall changes to the way the screen show will work (see fig. 17.3).

Fig. 17.3
Change the way you move from slide to slide with the Options tab.

Pages can take a moment or two to "draw" themselves on-screen, particularly if you've added animation, sound clips, or even a simple clip art symbol. Your computer may need a few seconds to retrieve and play or draw these elements on-screen. Freelance can signal with a tone or an arrow at the lower right of the screen when the next page is ready to be displayed. By waiting for the tone or arrow, you can avoid the embarrassment of waiting with an audience for the next page to appear. Depending on your preference, you can select the Sound a Tone or Display an Arrow in the Cue for Displaying Next Page area at the top of the Options page. You may even select both options to have both events occur.

You can control the Run-Time of a show by choosing to either have the screen show start automatically whenever the file itself is opened, or running the show in a loop. A loop is a continuous display: it starts at the first slide, runs through to the last, then starts back at the first slide again until you stop it. This is useful for situations such as trade show displays, where the audience comes and goes and the show repeats for each new group of viewers.

Finally, you can override individual page settings you may have made using the Page menu. Using the two checkboxes at the bottom of the Options tab, you can override any timing changes you may have made in the Screen Show Effects dialog box for individual pages, or choose to mute any sounds you've associated with individual pages.

Using Presentation Tools

Tools is the remaining tab in the Set Up Screen Show dialog box (see fig. 17.4). Here you can designate that you want to show the control panel. Placing a control panel on-screen during a screen show (refer to fig. 17.1) gives you a set of controls that you can use to move from one page to another during the screen show. After you click the Display Control Panel check box, you can select one of the preset locations for the control panel. Do this by clicking the arrow on the side of the Position drop-down list and choosing one of the four positions listed there.

Fig. 17.4
The Tools tab of the Set Up Screen Show dialog box has to do with the control panel settings.

If you display the control panel, it offers four buttons (shown on the Tool tab in fig. 17.4) with the following functions:

- Click the button containing a left arrow to turn back a page.
- Click the button containing a right arrow to turn forward a page.
- Click the button with three dots to get a dialog box that displays a list of pages that you can jump to in the screen show.
- Click the square to end the screen show.

There is one other option available to you on the Tools tab of the Set Up Screen Show dialog box. While a screen show is in progress, you can hold down the mouse button and drag the mouse to draw on a page on-screen. The On Screen Drawing controls enable you to set the Color and Width of the line you draw.

You can draw on a screen show to point out certain parts of a chart or diagram, or to underline or circle key text points that merit emphasis.

◀ See "Drawing the Objects," p. 208

Tip

This drawing capability is akin to a freeform drawing tool and may take some getting used to. It's a good idea to practice with it and have an idea of how you're going to use it. Also, use it sparingly. The jagged freeform look of the lines can begin to make your presentation look messy if used too much on any one slide. If you're such that you want to callout an item on a slide, consider drawing such a callout on it before running the screen show.

Creating Special Effects

Sometimes in presentations you want to do more than just go from bulleted list to bulleted list. Transitions provide some variety, but Freelance offers much more. You can use build effects to have each point on your presentation page appear one-by-one, in effect "building" a list of points for your audience.

You can also set your page up so that at the click of your mouse, any on-screen object can initiate a sound, movie, or animated sequence to make your static presentation a multimedia one.

Adding Automatic Build Pages

If your presentation includes a bulleted list, you can have Freelance create a build that will add each item in the bulleted list sequentially during a screen show. As each new bulleted item appears, it is highlighted, and the items already on the page appear dimmed.

The first page in the sequence shows the page title only. When you use any of the options for moving forward in the presentation, such as clicking the mouse, Freelance shows the page title, and the first bulleted item. The next page shows the first bullet point dimmed, and the second item highlighted. The next page shows the page title, the first two items dimmed, and the third item highlighted. Figure 17.5 shows a presentation page with several of the bullets displayed and dimmed.

Fig. 17.5
A presentation page using build effects.

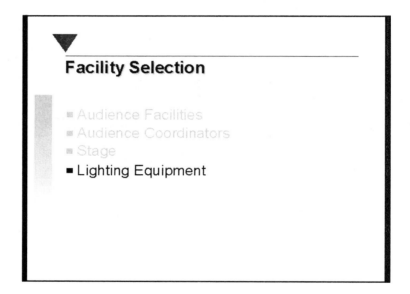

Fortunately, creating a build in Freelance is completely automatic. Simply follow these steps:

1. Create a page with a bulleted list. (Use the Bulleted List, Bullets & Chart, or Bullets & Symbol page layout.)

2. Turn to the page in Current Page view and select the list.

3. Choose Text, Bullet Build. Make sure the Screen Show tab is selected (it has a little projector image on it). Freelance displays the dialog box in figure 17.6.

Fig. 17.6
Make choices
about how bullets
will build on your
page here.

This tab allows you to choose several effects and their timing:

■ The Timing section lets you display bullets as soon as the page appears, or after the page appears either on a mouse click or after so many seconds.

■ In the Effect When Text Block Is Added section, you can choose to display bullet points one at a time and choose whether each new bullet should simply appear, or use some other transition effect.

■ You can choose to have the other bullet points appear dimmed when you move on to the next one by checking that box.

■ You can even have a sound occur when a bullet point is revealed.

■ Finally, you can select to have an Action occur when the text block is clicked, such as having an animation play.

To have each bullet point build on page, follow these steps:

1. Click the Display Page First, Then Display Text radio button.

2. Select the radio button for either On Click or After n Seconds for the timing of the display.

3. Make sure One at a Time is chosen in the Display Bullets drop-down list.

4. To have the previous bullets dim, as in figure 17.5, click the Dim Previous Bullets check box.

You can choose at the top of this dialog box to add each new bullet either by clicking the mouse, or after a set number of seconds. You can also choose to show the previous bullet items dimmed or not by selecting the Dim Previous

Bullets checkbox (fig. 17.5 shows a page with this option selected). You can also use either a transition or a sound concurrent with the revealing of each new bullet item. For example, if you are displaying a list of achievements for the year for your department, you might have the cheering sound accompanying each bullet as it appears.

To use a sound with a bullet point display, follow these steps:

1. Click the Browse button next to the Sound text box.
2. In the Attaching Sounds To Text dialog box, click one of the sounds from Freelance's media folder, or browse to locate another sound file elsewhere on your computer.
3. Click the Open button, and you return to the Screen Show tab of the Text Properties InfoBox.

When you run your screen show, the bullet points in the list you selected will appear with the accompanying sound. This sound will repeat as each bullet point appears.

Creating Screen Show Buttons

You can make any object on any presentation page a screen show button. The object can be text, a drawing object, a chart, a table, or a symbol. Clicking that object during a screen show will turn to a specific page in the presentation, launch another application, or play a multimedia sound, video, or movie selection. You must define each object that you want to act as a button, and then select the action you want the button to perform.

To define an object as a button, select the object. You will actually assign the screen show button properties in the Properties InfoBox for the object. You get to this InfoBox slightly differently, depending on the object you've chosen:

- If you select a bullet list or other text item, choose Text, Bullet Build.
- If you select a clip art symbol, choose Group, Screen Show Effects.
- If you select a Chart, choose Chart, Screen Show Effects.
- If you select a Table, choose Table, Screen Show Effects.
- If you select a drawing object, choose Drawing, Screen Show Effects.

An InfoBox appears. Click the Slide Show tab, as shown in figure 17.7.

Fig. 17.7
The last item in
this box controls
the effects you can
add to any on-
screen object.

The Action When Object Is Clicked area at the bottom of this dialog box
contains a drop-down list with several options. These options are discussed
in detail in the following sections.

Jumping to a Page

To have the screen show jump to a specific page when you click the object,
select Jump from the Action When Object Is Clicked drop-down list. Figure
17.8 shows the options available.

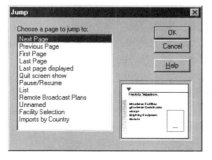

Fig. 17.8
Jump forward,
backward, or to a
particular page.

You might use the Jump feature with a logo that appears on each page. Each
time the logo is clicked, you jump to, say, the first page in the presentation,
which may contain a summary of all key points. Simply select the object—a
bulleted list, title, clip art symbol, or whatever—then click the Open InfoBox
SmartIcon. On the Screen Show tab, choose Jump as the action when the object is clicked. Close the InfoBox and run the show. Whatever page you're on,
when you click the object, you will return to the designated spot in the
presentation.

Presentations

V

Tip

You can ungroup a data chart and then make each bar, line, or pie slice a button that can lead to a page of additional information about the data.

Playing a Multimedia Object

You can also create a button to play a multimedia object. A multimedia object can be a sound file, MIDI music file, or movie file.

When you select Sound from the Action When Object Is Clicked drop-down list, the Play Sound dialog box in figure 17.9 opens.

Fig. 17.9
Add the sound of a trumpet to a new product announcement with a sound file.

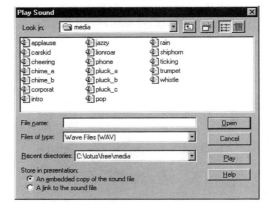

First, select a file type from the Files of Type drop-down list. Available file types include WAV (or "wave") files (with a WAV extension), Midi files (with a MID extension) or Sound Files, which would show both WAV and MIDI files.

WAV files are digital audio files that you can play if you have a sound board installed in your system. Many sound boards available as plug-in devices can reproduce the music and sound effects stored in WAV files. With most of these sound boards, you can use a microphone to record your own WAV files. You can incorporate the voice of an associate or member of your company within a presentation, for example.

MIDI files are digital data files that can control music synthesizers hooked to your system through a MIDI port. Today's synthesizers can reproduce the sounds of an entire orchestra or band, so you can incorporate sophisticated digital music into a presentation using either a built-in synthesizer chip in your sound card, or keyboards or synthesizer sound modules that can play MIDI data.

After you select a file type, use the choices in the Look in drop-down list at the top of the dialog box to find the multimedia file on your system. The MEDIA folder of Freelance contains several sound clips you might try, or find another directory to use sounds from other sources. You can click Play to hear the sound file before you accept it.

Under the Store in Presentation section at the bottom of the Play Sound dialog box, you can choose either A Link to the Sound File or An Embedded Copy of the Sound File. Choosing A Link to the Sound File does not copy the data for the multimedia objects into the presentation file. Instead, the data is read from the disk files and played whenever necessary. As a result, the same multimedia files must be available on a system to which you transfer a screen show in order for the multimedia files to be playable. Choosing An Embedded Copy of the Sound File copies the multimedia data into the Freelance presentation file. This makes a presentation with multimedia data that you can transport to another PC. But it also creates very large presentation files because the presentation files have the multimedia data embedded inside.

When you are satisfied with your selection, click Open to add the sound to your object. You return to the Properties InfoBox, where the Options button next to the Action drop-down list is now available. Click Options to view the Options for dialog box for the selected sound (see fig. 17.10) so that you can decide how many times to play the multimedia file. You can choose the following Play Options: Play *n* Times (play a specified number of times), or Play Continuously.

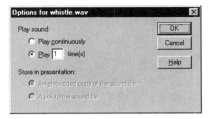

Fig. 17.10
Choose how to play sound clips when an object is clicked in the Options For dialog box.

Troubleshooting

I added a sound to a clip art symbol, but when I click it, the sound doesn't play till several seconds later—which seems like an eternity while I'm waiting for it in front of an audience. What's happening?

With larger sound files, it may take your computer several seconds to load and play the sound. Because of this, especially if you have a computer that doesn't have a great deal of spare memory, you might find that the bells and whistles of too many multimedia effects actually detracts from and slows down your presentation. Until multimedia gets better, or you get a computer with a lot of memory, use these effects sparingly. You should also time them out in the Rehearse mode, discussed later in this chapter, to be sure of exactly how long they'll take.

Playing Movies

Movies are digital video clips or animation sequences that can bring action to the screen. If you select Movies in the Action When Object Is Clicked drop-down box, you will see the Add a Movie dialog box shown in figure 17.11.

Fig. 17.11
Browse through movies and animated clips to add action to your presentation.

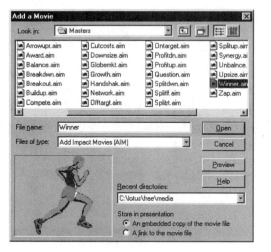

Three file types are available to you in the Files of Type drop-down list: Add Impact Movies (AIM extension), created using AddImpact from Gold Disk; Movies (AVI extension), the Audio Video Interleaved format created with Microsoft Video for Windows; and Animation Works (AWM extension), a Gold Disk animation authoring program that has full compatibility with Freelance Graphics 96 for Windows 95.

Tip

If you have Microsoft Multi-media Movies clips (MMM from Microsoft) or you have Digital Video Interactive (DVI from Intel and IBM) video clips, you also can play them in a screen show.

There are 79 animation sequences (Add Impact Movie clips) stored in Freelance's Masters folder. Click one, and then choose Preview to get an idea of what the movie looks like before clicking Open to select it. Again, you have the option of Refer to File or Embed File to either have Freelance get the graphic from an available source, or store it with the presentation.

Note

Smart Embedding is a new feature of Freelance that knows if you've used the same multimedia clip twice in a single presentation. If you have, Freelance will reference the second instance, rather than actually embedding it in the presentation twice. This reduces the overall size of your Freelance file.

Once you make your selection and return to the Properties InfoBox, you can click the Options button to get the Options for Selected Movies dialog box in figure 17.12. Here, you can determine how many times the movie or anima-tion will play, what should happen when it's finished, and what speed and location it should use.

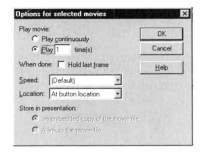

Fig. 17.12
Configure how your movie will play in the Options for Selected Movies dialog box.

Launching an Application

To have an object launch another application, on the Screen Show tab of the Properties InfoBox, select Run Application in the Action When Block Is Clicked drop-down list. The application can be another Windows program or a standard DOS program or batch file. The Launch Application dialog box appears, giving you a text box to enter the path name and file name. A more error-free way to enter the application's file name is to click Browse to the right of the text box and then use the File Name and Directories controls in the Find Application to Launch dialog box to find the application's EXE, COM, or BAT file.

When you click a button that launches another application, the other application opens in Windows. When you quit the other application, you return to the screen show in progress.

> **Tip**
>
> Define a button next to a chart that will open the original spreadsheet file it's based on so you can make changes to the worksheet. If the chart is linked to the worksheet, the chart will reflect the changes.

Producing a Multimedia Show: Sound, Animation, and Movies

One way to include a sound, movie, or animation clip in a presentation is to assign a preexisting multimedia object to a button. You have already learned how to create buttons that will play multimedia objects whenever the buttons are pressed during a screen show. You also can add a multimedia object directly to a presentation page that will play whenever the page is viewed in a screen show.

> **Note**
>
> New to Freelance Graphics 96 for Windows 95 is a built-in animation player. What does this mean for you? You see smoother animations, which run faster. That's because you're not using OLE (object linking and embedding) to go out to a player separate from the Freelance application to run those animations.

You might want to add music that begins when the title page appears, for example, or add a voice-over from the chairman of the board when a profitability data chart appears on-screen. If you have the hardware needed to get a video clip into your system, you can even play a video clip of the chairman of the board with both sound and picture.

Freelance allows you to utilize several types of media programs to record sound. Microsoft Media Player and Sound Recorder are part of Windows 95 and should already be available to you. Others may have come preloaded with your computer, such as the WAV Player from Compaq. With other Windows software, you can even record your own video and animated movie clips and add them to your presentation.

Recording a Sound for a Freelance Presentation

If your PC is equipped with a microphone and a sound board that can record sound, you can use programs like Microsoft Media Player to record audio clips while creating a page for a presentation. You can save each of these clips in a file on disk. You can also embed each clip in the Freelance file so that the clip becomes an integral part of the presentation. An icon for the sound will appear on the presentation page in Current Page view (see fig. 17.14). Double-click the icon, and the sound will play. When the page appears in a screen show, the sound will play automatically.

To record a sound while creating a presentation, choose Create, Object. From the list of object types, select Wave Sound to open Microsoft Sound Recorder. A dialog box opens, as shown in figure 17.13. Also, a new Wave Sound menu will appear on your main menu bar.

Fig. 17.13
Various sound recording programs have similar controls for playing and recording sounds.

The controls in this dialog box look much like the controls on a tape recorder, and are generally common to most of the sound recording programs you might have access to. To start recording, click the Record button and then speak into your microphone. To end recording, click the Stop button. After you record a sound, you can play the sound by clicking the Play button, stop the sound by clicking the Stop button, or fast-forward or rewind the "tape" by clicking the Forward or Rewind buttons.

> **Tip**
>
> To more closely control the quality of your recording, select the Edit menu in the Sound Object dialog box and choose Audio Properties. Here, you can determine the volume level and recording and playback devices you prefer to use. Consult the Help menu of a sound application for more details about recording procedures.

As the sound plays, the slider at the bottom of the controls moves to the right, and the line in the middle of the screen takes shape to indicate the sound visually, with the various forms representing the louder and softer points, as in figure 17.13. You can quickly move to any point in the sound by dragging the slider left or right. To add to the recording, place the slider in the sound where the new recording should begin, and then click the Record button. To remove excess blank space or unwanted sounds, move the slider to the desired point in the sound and click the Record button, then the stop button to record silence over a portion of the sound. A specific position and Length record on either side of the sound display will help you pinpoint such edits.

When you finish recording a sound, click the close control button to embed the sound and return to the Freelance page. The Wave Sound menu disappears. A sound icon will appear on the presentation page, as in figure 17.14. Double-click this icon to play the sound. If you want to return to Sound Recorder to edit the object, select the object, and the Wave Sound menu appears again. You can use the commands here to open the object for editing.

> **Caution**
>
> Multimedia can be complex: there are a variety of sound object formats that can be used and a variety of hardware to play them. The one discussed here is pretty simple to use, but also limited in functionality. If you require more sophisticated sound effects and you run into problems, check the documentation for the sound program and sound card you're using to make sure they are configured properly.

Before you exit the recording program, you can save the sound you've recorded on disk in a WAV file by choosing File, Save As and then entering a file name with an appropriate extension. That way, you can use the sound later in Freelance or in other Windows applications.

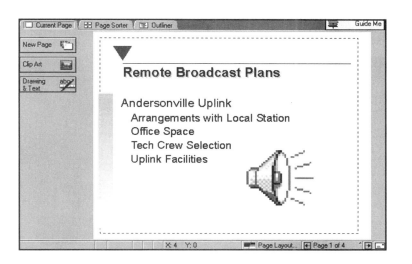

Fig. 17.14
A presentation page with a sound file embedded.

Tip

You can also open existing sound clips and edit them to extend, say, a cheering crowd to run for a minute or more, or to add sounds together. Select File, Open to edit an existing file.

Setting the Play Options for a Sound Object

After you have added a multimedia object to a presentation page, select that object and a new menu will appear on the menu bar at the top of the screen. You can determine how the Microsoft Sound Recorder object will be played in a screen show by selecting the object and then choosing the Wave Sound menu. Select Wave Sound Properties. A dialog box appears, shown in figure 17.15.

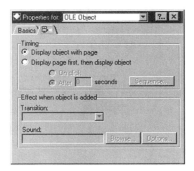

Fig. 17.15
There are a few play options for a sound object.

V

Presentations

The Properties InfoBox for the OLE sound object provides two choices. Choose Static to play the object as soon as the page appears during a presentation. Or choose Active so you can set whether the object will trigger only when you click it, or after a set number of seconds. You also can decide what effect there should be when the object displays—either a visual or audio effect or both.

You can set different play options for each multimedia object in a screen show.

Adding a Movie or Animation to Your Presentation

You can add a movie or animated sequence in a Freelance presentation. If you choose to embed, rather than refer ("link") to the multimedia file, the multimedia data is copied to the Freelance file. You do not need to copy the multimedia files to another computer when you move the screen show file because the data is already within the Freelance file. If the original file changes, though, the update will not be reflected in the Freelance screen show. You will be required to embed the revised multimedia object in the Freelance show, replacing the original.

> **Tip**
>
> If a media clip is being created as you create your presentation or may change over the life of the presentation, you may want to link to it, rather than embed it. Then, as the finishing touches are applied to it, or it is changed in the future, your object will update.

Fortunately, Freelance comes with a quick way to insert a movie clip into your presentation.

Inserting a Multimedia Clip

To insert a multimedia clip, choose Create, Add Movie. The same Add a Movie browser dialog box appears as when you create a movie button out of another on-screen object, described earlier in this chapter. This dialog box was shown earlier in figure 17.11. Simply choose the file type you want from the Files of Type drop-down list. Then use the Look In controls to navigate to the file you want. Select the file from the list and then click Preview to view the file. If the file is the one you want, click Open to copy the multimedia object to the Freelance presentation page.

Troubleshooting

*I placed a movie on one of my pages, but I've forgotten exactly how it looks. Is there
some other way, short of running the presentation, for me to preview it from Freelance?*

You can select a movie or animation object while in the current page view, then
open the Movie menu and select Play. A small window will open, and the movie or
animated sequence will play right there. When it's done, the window will close and
you are back at your presentation page in current page view.

Changing the Options of the Multimedia Object

To change how the movie or animated object will play and how it will be
stored, select the object, then choose Movie, Movie Properties. The menu
choice will be Movie whether the clip is a video or animated sequence.

Use the choices here to determine whether the movie or animation will display as an icon, and whether it will run as soon as the page appears during a
presentation, or after so many seconds.

Using Rehearse Mode

Now that you have everything in place, it's a good idea to practice your presentation. With all the media clips and special build and transition effects
you may have used, the time it takes your individual slides to appear on-
screen won't be easy to estimate. It's also helpful to talk through your comments for each slide and take the time to practice using speaker notes and
drawing on slides, if necessary. All these things add time to a presentation.
A well-rehearsed presentation can make the difference between a bored audience confronted with a confused speaker and an enthusiastic audience
impressed by your confidence and ease.

New to Freelance Graphics 96 for Windows 95 is a Rehearse mode. This is a
very handy tool for running through your show to polish your presentation
before you appear in front of an audience. Rehearsing allows you to:

- Walk through your presentation while a timer adds up the seconds
- Pull up speaker notes while rehearsing
- Draw on your slides exactly as you would during a presentation
- Pause the rehearse timer if you want to make changes, then resume to
  keep your timing accurate

V

Presentations

To rehearse your show, open the presentation. Then follow these steps:

1. Select Presentation, Rehearse.

2. From the drop-down menu next to Rehearse, select Start.

3. A dialog box appears asking if you want to clear any previously recorded times or use the previous times. If you use previous times, Rehearse Mode won't record the actual time this run-through takes.

4. Click OK to accept the default of clearing any previously recorded times and recording this rehearsal.

5. The first page appears, with the Rehearse controls showing at the bottom of the screen, as in figure 17.16.

Fig. 17.16
Control your rehearsal session's timing and display with the tools in Rehearse mode.

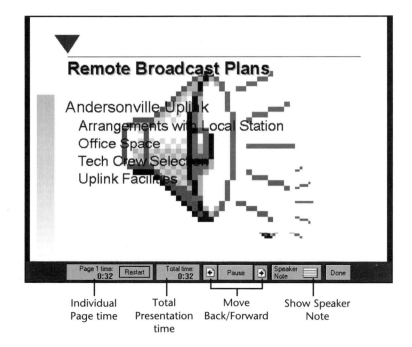

The controls in Rehearse allow you to do the following:

■ At the far left of these controls, the time for the page that's currently displayed is shown. To restart the presentation, click the Restart button.

■ The Total time for the presentation is shown to the right of the Restart button, letting you know the cumulative time of all the pages displayed so far.

■ You can move forward or backward one page at a time using the right and left arrow buttons or pause your rehearsal by clicking the Pause button.

■ To show the speaker note for the page currently being displayed, click the Speaker Note button.

When you're done rehearsing, click the Done button. The Rehearse Summary dialog box shown in figure 17.17 appears, giving the total time by page and cumulatively for the entire presentation.

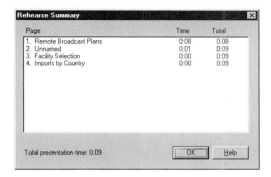

Fig. 17.17
Get an idea of how long your presentation will take with the Rehearse Summary dialog box.

CHAPTER 18

Creating Output

by Nancy Stevenson

When it comes time to create a permanent version of a presentation, Freelance offers a number of choices. You can print the pages on a standard printer to create a paper copy of the presentation. If you have slide-making equipment, you can record the presentation on film that can be made into slides. If you need slides but don't have a film recorder, you can send a completed presentation by disk or modem to a slide service bureau that will return developed slides.

In this chapter, you learn about

- Using Print Preview
- Using Printer Setup
- Printing pages
- Printing speaker notes, audience notes, and audience handouts
- Creating slides

Previewing Your Presentation

Freelance offers the option of taking a look at your printed presentation before you actually print it. The program will either preview in color or black and white, based on whether you're printing to a color or black-and-white printer. This enables you to check for things like backgrounds that are too dark to see text clearly in if printed in black and white, or the balance of objects on the printed page. However, even if you select to print speaker notes or handouts, Print Preview will only preview one full page at a time.

You can get to Print Preview through a SmartIcon or the File menu. While still in Current Page view, you can simply click the Print Preview button on the toolbar. A dialog box appears, like the one in figure 18.1.

Fig. 18.1

You can start your print preview from the current page.

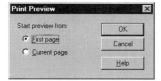

Your choices here are simple: start the preview from the First Page of the presentation, or the Current Page. Choose one, then click OK. A preview appears, as in figure 18.2, which is a preview of the first page in a presentation. From this preview, you can move to the Next or Previous page, or choose to Print.

Fig. 18.2

A preview of a page going to a black-and-white printer.

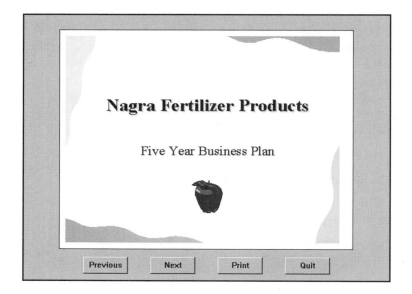

This image represents how your page will look when printed. When you're done with Print Preview, you can choose to either print your presentation, or Quit preview without printing.

Troubleshooting

In current page view, I have a clip art symbol that sits right at the edge of the page and it looks fine, but in Print Preview, half of it gets cut off. What's happening?

Print Preview will show any area around the edges that can't be printed as white space. So, if you have text or an object that extends out of the printable area, it may appear to be cut off in Print Preview. In fact, that's one of the best ways to use Print Preview—to ensure that all objects are fitting on the page properly. Just Quit Print Preview, move clip art on your page and preview again to be sure it will print properly.

The other way to get to Print Preview is to select File, Print Preview. You will be taken to the same dialog box shown earlier in figure 18.1 and proceed in exactly the same way to preview your presentation. Another way to get to Print Preview is to select File, Print. This takes you to the Print File dialog box shown in figure 18.3.

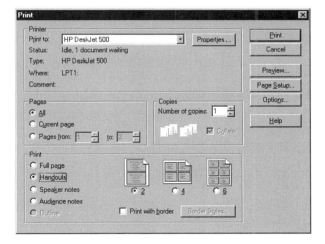

Fig. 18.3
The Print File dialog box allows you to preview your presentation.

If you click Print Preview from here, you go to the same Print Preview dialog box shown in figure 18.1, and proceed in the same way as before.

Determining What to Print

You can print a presentation in a number of ways. You can print one presentation page per printed page, of course, but you can also print the presentation as speaker notes, audience notes, or handouts:

◀ See "Creating Speaker Notes," p. 288

■ *Speaker notes* show a miniature of the page on the top half of a printed page and, on the lower half, whatever speaker notes you entered by choosing Page, Create Speaker Note. The Print Format section of the Print File dialog box gives a preview of this format, as seen in figure 18.4.

Fig. 18.4
Speaker notes can be printed with one, two, or three presentation pages and corresponding speaker notes.

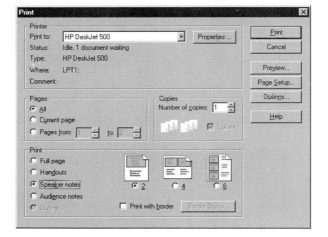

■ *Audience notes* show the presentation page on the top half of a printed page with blank space below for audience members to write their own notes. In the Print Format section of the dialog box, they look similar to the speaker notes, but the grayed-out notes area indicates nothing will actually print there (see fig. 18.5).

■ *Handouts* have two, four, or six presentation pages on each printed page (see fig. 18.6) so that audience members can leave the presentation with a miniaturized, but still readable, version of the presentation.

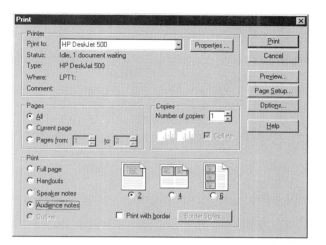

Fig. 18.5
The setup is the same as speaker notes, but the lower portion of the page will be left blank when printed.

Fig. 18.6
Print up to six presentation pages on one printed page.

V

Presentations

Tip

If you have a lot of text on your presentation pages, avoid using the six page print format, as the small images will make that amount of text difficult to read.

Printing any of the styles just listed simply requires making your choices in the Print and Print Format sections of the Print File dialog box. However, before you print the presentation pages as a sequence of standard pages, you should check the Printer Setup and Page Setup settings.

Using Printer Setup

When you build a presentation in Freelance, the presentation is customized for the printer that is currently the selected printer in Windows. To change the selected printer, you must use go to the Start menu on the taskbar and choose Settings, Printers. Then click the Add Printers icon. To set an installed printer as the default, right-click the printer icon in the Printer Window, then select File, Set As Default (see fig. 18.7). If you have a Hewlett-Packard LaserJet III printer, for example, then HP LaserJet Series III is probably the currently selected printer in Windows. When you print from any Windows application, the presentation is printed correctly on the HP LaserJet III.

Fig. 18.7
Click a printer in this window, then select Set As Default in the File menu to set the default printer.

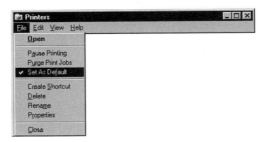

If you are printing the presentation on a printer other than the currently selected Windows printer, you can choose that printer in the Print File dialog box, as shown in figure 18.3. Suppose that you routinely use a laser printer to print word-processed pages, but you want to print the Freelance presentation on a special color printer. You can use the Print To selection in the Print File dialog box to customize the presentation for the color printer without having to change from the black-and-white laser printer in Windows.

You can designate another printer for the current print job by changing the Printer settings in the Print File dialog box. Click the down arrow next to the Print To drop-down list. You can choose a printer from this scrollable list of printers. Freelance automatically adjusts the pages to match the capabilities of the printer selection. The printer selection remains in effect only during the current session with Freelance. When you use Freelance the next time, the current Freelance printer is reset to the default Windows printer.

> **Note**
>
> The printers shown are the printers that are currently installed in your version of Windows. To install a new printer driver, you must use the Windows Printer settings.

To change the current settings for the printer you have selected, click the Properties button next to the Print To box. Another dialog box with settings specific for the selected output device, such as the resolution and paper source, appears. The pages and choices available here will vary depending on the output device you've chosen. For example, if you're printing a fax, a dialog box specific to your installed fax software will appear. If you choose a Rendering subsystem, the dialog box that appears will help you deal with grayscale issues, and so on.

> ### Caution
>
> If you change devices after creating your presentation, you may get a message that says some elements of your pages won't print because they no longer fit on the printable portion of that device's page. Your options here are to scale objects on the page until they all fit, or not modify anything. If you choose to scale the objects, it takes forever: you can't return them to original size to print to another device later on. The recommendation is to not modify anything, but go back and move some objects around yourself until they fit properly. You can use Print Preview to help you do this.

Changing the Page Setup

The Page Setup dialog box, shown in figure 18.8, enables you to set up a header for the top and a footer for the bottom of every printed page. This dialog box also enables you to set the orientation and margins of the pages. You can get here directly from the Print File dialog box, or by choosing File, Page Setup.

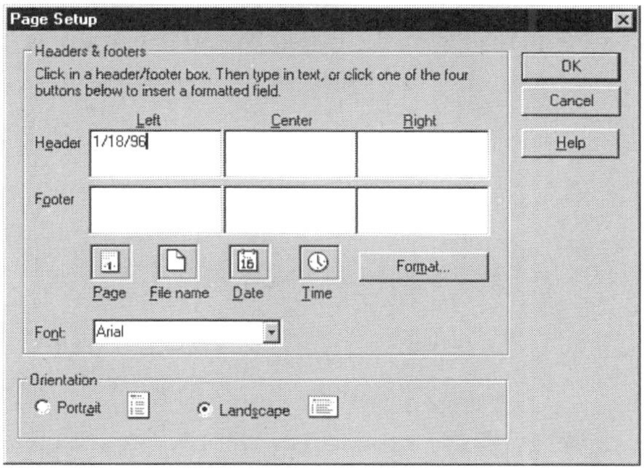

Fig. 18.8
The Page Setup dialog box provides shortcuts to inserting things like the date and time into your headers and footers.

Working with Headers and Footers

To set up headers and footers, you simply enter text in the Header and Footer text boxes. You can enter up to 512 characters for each (but I wouldn't recommend anything that lengthy in a header or footer). Any text that you enter appears on the page with the 8-point Arial MT typeface. If you want to change the typeface, select a new typeface from the Typeface drop-down list in the Headers & Footers section of the Page Setup dialog box. You can also click the Format button to change the way the date and time are formatted (02/03/95 or February 3, 1995 for example).

There are header and footer text boxes for Left, Center, and Right, depending on how you want the text to align on your printed page. To quickly insert Page Number, Date, Time, or the File Name, click in the appropriate Header or Footer box and use the shortcut buttons in the middle of the dialog box. A code in brackets is placed in the text box, for example [PAGE] for page number.

To split a header or footer into more than one line, just press Enter to move to a second line in the Header or Footer text box.

Portrait or Landscape?

If you want to change the orientation used for Freelance presentation pages, click Landscape or Portrait in the Page Setup dialog box. *Portrait* will print an 8 1/2-by-11-inch page with the longer side standing upright. *Landscape* places that longer side across the top of the printed page. Landscape and Portrait override the current setting for the selected Windows printer so that you can see, on-screen, how the presentation will look when printed, even if the printer that will eventually print the presentation is not set as the default printer.

Printing the Pages

 After you check Printer Setup and Page Setup, you can simply click Print in the Print File dialog box to print the presentation. If you are in the presentation window, you can also click the File Print SmartIcon to get to the same dialog box. Before you do, however, there are a few last items to check.

Use the Pages and Copies sections of the Print dialog box to determine which pages and how many copies to print. To print only the selected page, select the Current Page check box. To print the full presentation pages, choose All Pages as the Format setting. To print only a range of pages, select Pages From and use the arrows to select the page numbers to define the range. You can also just type in a first and last page in the boxes next to these arrows. If you want multiple copies to be collated, be sure to select that option.

Choose a format from the list of formats in the Print section (Outline is available only if you are in Outliner view), and then make any adjustments you need to the three Print Format check boxes at the bottom.

If you prefer a border around the pages in your presentation, click Print with border in the Print section. When you do, the Border Styles button becomes available. Click it to see the Choose a Border Style dialog box shown in figure 18.9. Scroll down the list of border styles and choose one you like from its preview. Click OK to return to the Print Files dialog box.

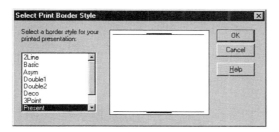

Fig. 18.9
From Basic to Deco, borders can keep the edges of your pages neat and trim.

Exploring Print Options

Before you hit that Print button, there are a few more options available that you might want to know about. These reside behind the Options button in the Print File dialog box. Click it, and you'll see the dialog box in figure 18.10.

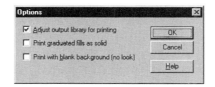

Fig. 18.10
Fine-tune the way graphics and backgrounds will print using Options in the Print dialog box.

Adjusting the Color Library for Color Printing

You can designate a color printer for your output in two ways. One way has both you and the current Windows printer printing to the default printer; the second is to use the Print To option in the Print Files dialog box to select a color printer as the current printer for the presentation. When you make either of these choices, Freelance automatically uses a special color palette that is optimized for the selected color printer. This palette helps match the printed output with the colors you see on-screen. You will want to deselect the <u>A</u>djust Output Library for Printing check box only if you have modified the color library. However, on some printers, the automatic settings don't provide the best effect. You can use the Adjust Output Library for Printing check box to stop Freelance from applying its automatic adjustments and might get better results in some cases.

> ### Tip
>
> You also might want to try turning off the color adjustment if the colors print much lighter than you expected.

Printing Graduated Fills as Solid

◀ See "Changing the Attributes of Drawn Objects," p. 207

Graduated fills modify the saturation of any fill pattern within an object in a range from darker to lighter. This can create a nice graphic effect, but sometimes what works fine on-screen, or on one type of printer, won't look so great on another. By clicking the Print <u>g</u>raduated Fills as Solid check box, you can have Freelance print graduated fills as solid colors on presentation pages. Graduated fills take longer to print, and some older or dot matrix printers are incapable of printing graduated fills or don't print them well.

Printing without the SmartMaster Background

To print only the text, charts, and graphic objects you've placed on presentation pages (and not the background objects that are part of the SmartMaster set), you can click the Print With <u>B</u>lank Background (No Look) check box. This speeds up the printing of draft presentations for proofing text, where the design elements may not be needed. All elements will keep their position on the page. So, for example, if the SmartMaster had a graphic element on the top and the title pushed off to the right, the title will still be off to the right, but the SmartMaster graphic will not appear.

Creating Slides

Freelance provides the capability for creating 35mm slides. Slides have the advantage of very high resolution—their detail is extremely fine, their text looks razor sharp, and their colors and color gradients are rich and smooth. Slides, like printed pages, are static, though. You cannot animate slides as you can pages in a screen show; nor can you add sound, music, or video clips by using the multimedia capabilities of Windows and Freelance as you can if you are running the actual Freelance presentation file off of a computer. Another major disadvantage of slides is that you cannot edit their contents at the very last second, and there is usually some expense to produce them.

Generating Slide Output

To create slides, you would use slide-recording equipment (often called a *film recorder*) that records the pages of a presentation onto 35mm film. After the film is recorded, you develop it as you would develop pictures photographed with a camera. If you do not have slide-recording equipment, you can send a file generated by Freelance to a slide service bureau that records and develops the slides for you and returns them the same day or overnight. You can even use a modem to send the slide file by telephone to a slide service bureau so that you can get the slides back quickly.

Caution

Quick turnaround on slides, like any other service, often carries a heavy premium in rush charges and overnight shipping. Check these costs carefully before ordering the fastest service.

How you set Freelance to create slides depends on how you will have the slides made. If you have a film recorder, you must use the correct Windows printer driver for the film recorder and then print to the film recorder just as if you were printing to any other output device.

Tip

Slide drivers have their own color optimizing system. To let them ensure the best color possible, consider turning off the Adjust output library for printing choice in the Options of the Print dialog box.

If you use a matrix film recorder, which essentially makes a high quality digitized image of your presentation, you can install the Stingray SCODL driver into Windows and then select Stingray SCODL as the current printer. This driver converts Freelance output into a SCODL file that you can send to a matrix camera.

If you are working with a service bureau, the bureau can tell you the format it accepts. You can print the Freelance presentation using a slide driver installed on your computer (see your specific slide driver documentation for details on how to install it), and send the file to a bureau to print. Freelance supports several drivers, including Autographix and Genographics. Or, if you don't have a slide driver available, the bureau can usually take the original presentation file and create the slide file, then generate the slides from that.

Many service bureaus accept Freelance presentation files (PRE files). Others require you to save a presentation in an Encapsulated PostScript (EPS) file, a Postscript format that saves high-resolution images.

Printing a Presentation to an Encapsulated PostScript File

If the service bureau you use asks for an Encapsulated PostScript file (an EPS file), you need to print the presentation as an EPS file. Check with the service bureau about which Windows printer driver you should use so that they can read your file and then follow these steps:

1. Click the Windows Start button.

2. Choose Settings, Printers. The Printers window appears.

3. Install or select the appropriate Windows PostScript printer driver.

4. Right-click the installed printer Icon. Choose File, Set as Default Printer.

5. Select File, Close.

   Switch back to Freelance by clicking the button on the Windows taskbar. From the File menu, choose Print.

6. In the Freelance Print dialog box, select the PostScript printer from the list of Printers and click OK.

EPS files can be very large, so you may have to compress the EPS file with a file compression utility such as PKZIP to fit on a disk for transport to a service bureau.

Tip

If files are bigger than 1.44MB, you may need more than one disk. If you have the capability to create a CD-ROM, it might be a better way to store these large files to get them to your service bureau.

Troubleshooting

I got my slides back and my Freelance charts, which filled the pages on my screen, look smaller. Why?

35mm slides are actually wider than the paper you typically print to. If you don't set the slide driver as the output device in the Print dialog box before you create your presentation, the output may not fill the slide space properly. Before you even begin work on your presentation, select the slide driver, and you should have no problem.

CHAPTER 19

Publishing Freelance Graphics Presentations on the Internet

by Nancy Dykstra

You might be asking the obvious first question: what is the Internet? The answer you receive often depends on the person you ask. One person might provide an answer that includes complicated explanations about how the original Department of Defense experiment mushroomed into a vast global network of computers. Another person might answer that the Internet provides a large collection of resources you can access through those networks. Still another person might answer that the Internet provides a global community of people connected through those networks.

Who is correct? Actually, *all* of these answers are correct. On a simple level, you can tap into the Internet using your PC, a modem, Internet access tools, and a connection to the Internet.

> **Tip**
>
> You can find detailed information about the Internet in Que's *Special Edition Using the Internet with Windows 95*. For more information, call Que's Customer Service at 1-800-428-5331.

Once you access the Internet, your options are virtually limitless. For example, you might want to chat with other people, exchange mail with someone in another country, or browse through a vast collection of information. Maybe you want to catch up on the latest news and weather, or maybe you want to share information with others.

You can take advantage of this electronic exchange of information by publishing your Freelance presentations on the Internet so other people can access them. You might want to publish promotional information about your company's newest product, make an announcement, or publish your company's latest financial results.

In this chapter, you learn how to

- Use the World Wide Web format
- Publish your presentation on the Internet
- View your presentation on the Internet

Using the World Wide Web Format

For years, gaining access to the Internet required mastering difficult, text-based tools. An experiment by a particle physics lab in Switzerland sparked the growth of the World Wide Web, also referred to as *WWW* or *the Web*. The scientists sought an easy way to maintain and distribute hypertext to track research information and allow a group of scientists to share that information. This experiment led to the development of *Mosaic*, the first Internet tool to take advantage of a graphical user interface.

> **Tip**
>
> *Hypertext* refers to electronic documents that you can navigate by clicking specially marked text or graphics. In order to view hypertext documents on the Web, you need a special type of viewer called a *browser*.

In a very short time, many graphical Web access tools, called *browsers*, have appeared on the market. These Web browsers use a universal language called *Hypertext Markup Language (HTML)*. All computers everywhere can understand the HTML language, without worrying about gruesome technicalities like operating systems, network transport methods, and data storage methods.

By concentrating on document structure, instead of document appearance, HTML can display the same information on every computer regardless of whether it is a Mac, PC-based, or UNIX-based. As a result, individuals and businesses all across the globe can connect in ways never before possible.

> **Tip**
>
> You can find a wealth of information about HTML in Que's *Special Edition Using HTML.*

Freelance offers two different ways of publishing your presentation on the Internet:

■ You can publish a stand-alone presentation if you want to distribute copies of the presentation. This works well if you are familiar with your audience, and know they either have access to Freelance or can run the Mobile Screen Show Player.

■ You can also publish your presentation so that those with Internet access can view your presentation, regardless of the type of computer they have. You would use this method for a general audience or when you don't know whether someone's computer can run either Freelance or the Mobile Screen Show Player.

Regardless of the method you choose, Freelance automatically creates the necessary files for publishing your presentation on the Internet.

Publishing Your Presentation on the Internet

How simple is it to publish a presentation on the Internet? Just follow these steps:

1. Open an existing presentation in either Current Page or Page Sorter view.

2. Choose File, Publish to Internet. The Publish to Internet dialog box appears (see fig. 19.1).

When you publish your presentation to the Internet, Freelance creates several files, including one graphic and one HTM file for each page in your presentation. For more information, see "Freelance Internet Presentation Files" later in this chapter.

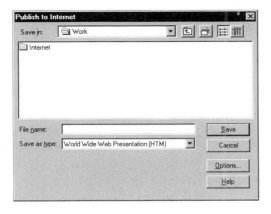

Fig. 19.1
Freelance creates several files that must be transferred to the Internet. You might want to save the files in a separate folder, similar to the Internet folder shown here.

3. Specify a file name.

4. Click Options. The Web Presentation Setup dialog box appears (see fig. 19.2).

Fig. 19.2

You can use these settings to publish a stand-alone presentation, to add additional information to each page, and to create a list of all the pages in your presentation.

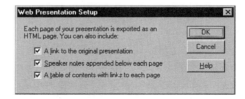

Let's talk about these options. When you create a link to the original presentation, Freelance makes it possible for other people to actually run your presentation. When you select this option, Freelance adds two pictures to the bottom of every page in your presentation.

If you click the Lotus picture, your Web browser displays the Lotus home page so that you can copy the Mobile Screen Show Player to your computer. If you click the Freelance picture, you can either run Freelance or copy the presentation to your computer, depending on how you set up your Web browser.

> **Tip**
>
> Consult your Web browser's documentation or online help for information on configuring the browser to run other applications or copy files. Note that many browsers call these other applications *helper applications*.

This sounds complicated, but it means that you can distribute both your presentation and the Mobile Screen Show Player using the Internet. If you don't want people to have your actual presentation, or you don't know your audience and aren't sure whether their computer can run Windows 95, you should deselect this option.

When you select speaker notes appended below each page, Freelance takes the notes for that page and creates a bulleted list at the bottom of the page. This lets you use the speaker notes to provide additional information about that page or call attention to something on that page. If you don't want other people to see your speaker notes, deselect this option.

When you select a Table of Contents page, Freelance creates a page that contains a list of all the pages in your presentation (see fig. 19.3). You can click any page in this list to jump directly to that page. In addition, that page contains a picture you can click to jump back to the Table of Contents page. This lets people view the pages in your presentation in any order that they want. If you want people to view the pages in order, deselect this option.

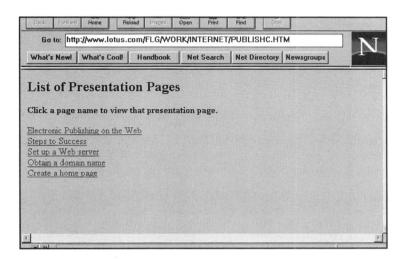

Fig. 19.3
If you specify a Table of Contents page when you publish your presentation, Freelance creates a list of pages in your presentation, similar to this one.

Tip

You can see the list of pages that will appear on the Table of Contents page by clicking the Page Navigator button in the status bar.

Click OK to close the Web Presentation Setup dialog box and then click Save. Freelance creates all the necessary files for publishing your presentation on the Internet. Depending on the number of slides in your presentation, this may take some time. When Freelance finishes creating the files, a message appears telling you so. Click OK, and that's it.

V

Presentations

Freelance Internet Presentation Files

Now take a look at the types of files Freelance creates when you publish your presentation on the Internet. Use the Windows 95 Explorer to go to the folder you saved the files in and view the contents of the folder. You should see the following:

> **Tip**
>
> If you can't see the three-character filename extensions, choose View, Options in the Explorer. On the View tab, uncheck the Hide MS-DOS File Extensions For File Types That Are Registered option. Click OK, and you should see the file extensions.

- One HTM text file for each page in your presentation.
- One GIF graphic file for each page in your presentation. Many of the graphics on the Web are stored in the Graphical Interchange Format (GIF). This format allows most Web browsers to display the graphic.

> **Tip**
>
> Freelance automatically creates file names based on the page number of the presentation. For example, if you publish your presentation using MYFILE as the name, Freelance creates MYFILE.HTM and MYFILE.GIF for the first page in your presentation. Subsequent pages would have the file names MYFILE2.HTM and MYFILE2.GIF, MYFILE3.HTM and MYFILE3.GIF, and so on.

- The files LARROW.GIF and RARROW.GIF are pictures of a left arrow and a right arrow. Freelance adds these pictures to each page in your presentation. You can click these pictures to view different pages in the presentation (see fig. 19.4).

If you selected table of contents in the Web Presentation Setup dialog box (refer to fig. 19.2), you also see the following files:

- An HTM file for the Table of Contents page.

> **Tip**
>
> Freelance automatically creates the file name. For example, if you publish your presentation using MYFILE as the name, Freelance creates MYFILEC.HTM for the Table of Contents page.

Display
Previous —
Page

Display Table of
Contents Page
— Display Next Page

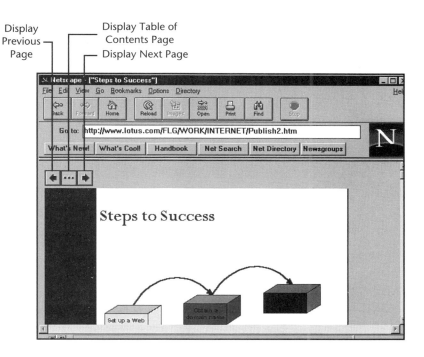

Fig. 19.4
When you publish
your presentation
on the Internet,
Freelance creates a
page similar to the
one here. You can
click the pictures if
you want to view
other pages of the
presentation.

- The file CONTENTS.GIF, which contains a picture of three dots. Freelance adds this picture to each page in your presentation, except the table of contents. You can click this picture if you want to display the Table of Contents page (refer to fig 19.4).

If you selected link to the original presentation in the Web Presentation Setup dialog box (refer to fig. 19.2), you also see the following files:

- One PRZ file contains a copy of your Freelance presentation.

- The file WEBFILE.GIF contains a picture of the Freelance icon. Freelance adds this picture to each page in your presentation, except the table of contents. Depending on how you configure your Web browser, you can click this picture to either run Freelance or the Mobile Screen Show Player, or to copy the presentation to your computer (see fig. 19.5).

- The file WEBHOME.GIF contains a picture of the Lotus home page icon. Freelance adds this picture to each page in your presentation, except the table of contents. When you click this picture, your Web browser displays the Lotus home page so you can copy the Mobile Screen Show Player to your computer (see fig. 19.5).

Fig. 19.5
Depending on the options you specify, Freelance adds pictures to the bottom of your presentation. You can click these pictures if you want to copy the Mobile Screen Show Player to your computer or if you want to access a copy of the presentation.

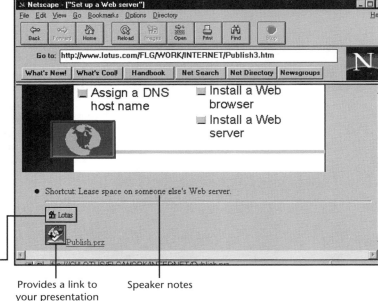

Displays the Lotus home page

Provides a link to your presentation

Speaker notes

Tip

You can edit the HTM files using any text editor, including WordPro. For example, you might want to customize the default Table of Contents page title, "List of Presentation Pages."

Viewing Your Presentation on the Internet

Now that you have published your presentation on the Internet, you are probably eager to see the results. However, there are some things you have to do outside Freelance.

First, you must create a link from your home page to your Freelance presentation. This link can be words or pictures that someone clicks to display your Freelance presentation.

Tip

You can use any text editor, including WordPro, to modify your home page HTML file and add a text link similar to the following:

```
<a href="/user/mydir/presentationtoc.html">My Web presentation</A>
```

For example,

```
<a href="/flg/work/internet/myfilec.html">Electronic Publishing
on the Web</A>
```

For more information about HTML and creating links using pictures, see Que's *Special Edition Using HTML*.

You can't cheat and use your presentation as a home page, because the HTM files Freelance creates only contain instructions for displaying your presentation. Your home page contains other kinds of instructions—for example, the one you just added to display your Freelance presentation.

The next thing you have to do is copy files from your computer to a computer with access to the Internet. How you do this depends on the computer you are copying the files to and the type of access you have to the Internet.

Typically, you need some type of Internet tool to copy these files. This tool copies files, similar to the Explorer, but it uses a special language called *file transfer protocol* (*FTP*). This language allows different kinds of computers to communicate with each other.

After you copy the files, you have to rename the files with the three-character DOS extension HTM to have the four-character UNIX extension HTML. It might seem to be an inconvenience, but you have to do this because most of the computers connected to the Internet use UNIX files, not DOS files. Web browsers expect to see files with HTML, not HTM extensions.

Tip

If you need help copying your files to the Internet, contact your company's system administrator or your Internet provider.

Now for the fun part. Launch your Web browser, connect to the Internet, and display your home page, just as you normally do. Then click the link to your Freelance presentation.

Depending on how you published your presentation to the Internet, either the first page in your presentation or your Table of Contents page appears (refer to fig. 19.3).

Tip

The pictures in these examples show a popular Web browser called Netscape. If you use a different Web browser, your presentation might look slightly different.

Troubleshooting

I selected the Table of Contents option, but my table of contents just lists Unknown Title. *What did I do wrong?*

Check your presentation to make sure you have text in the title block of each page of your presentation.

You can display any page in your presentation just by clicking the title of that page. When Freelance displays that page, you see the pictures for the left and right arrows, as well as the contents page (refer to fig. 19.4).

Troubleshooting

How come my presentation pages don't have the picture of the ellipsis (. . .)?

When you create your presentation, you must select the Table of Contents option.

One of the pages in my presentation just has pictures of the buttons that Freelance adds. What happened to the information on that slide?

The HTML file for that page contains a reference to a GIF file. Either the GIF file is missing, or the name doesn't match the reference in the HTML file.

If you specified a link to the original presentation when you created the presentation, Freelance adds pictures to the bottom of each page of your presentation (refer to fig. 19.5). If you click the picture of the Lotus home page, your Web browser displays the Lotus home page so you can download a copy of the Mobile Screen Show Player.

If you click the Freelance icon, you can access a copy of the presentation. Depending on how you have your Web browser configured, you can either run Freelance or the Mobile Screen Show Player, or you can copy the presentation to your computer.

> **Tip**
>
> If you need help configuring your Web browser, consult your Web browser's documentation or online help.

If you specify speaker notes when you publish your presentation, Freelance adds a bulleted list at the bottom of page with the notes for that page (refer to fig. 19.5). ❖

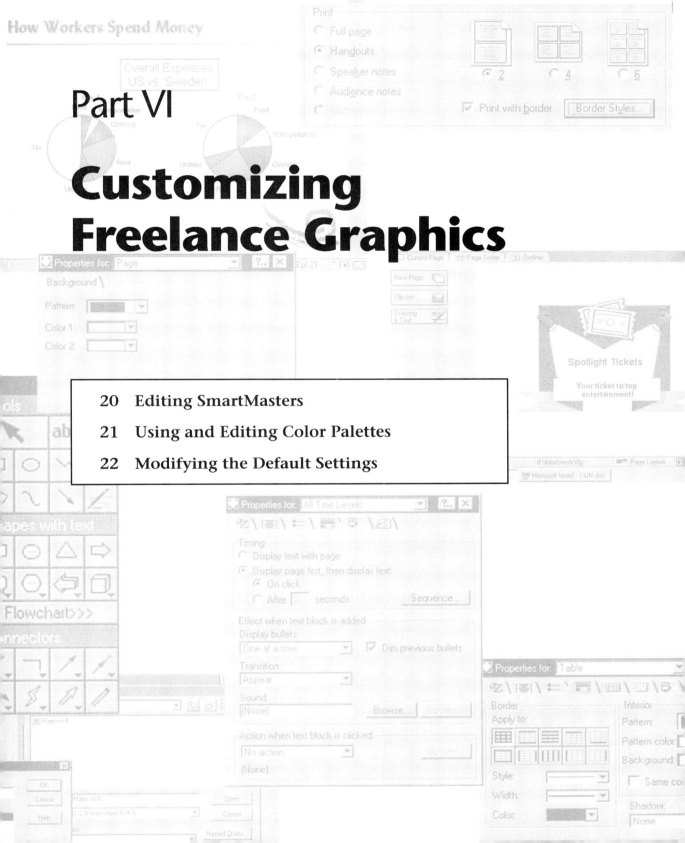

Part VI

Customizing Freelance Graphics

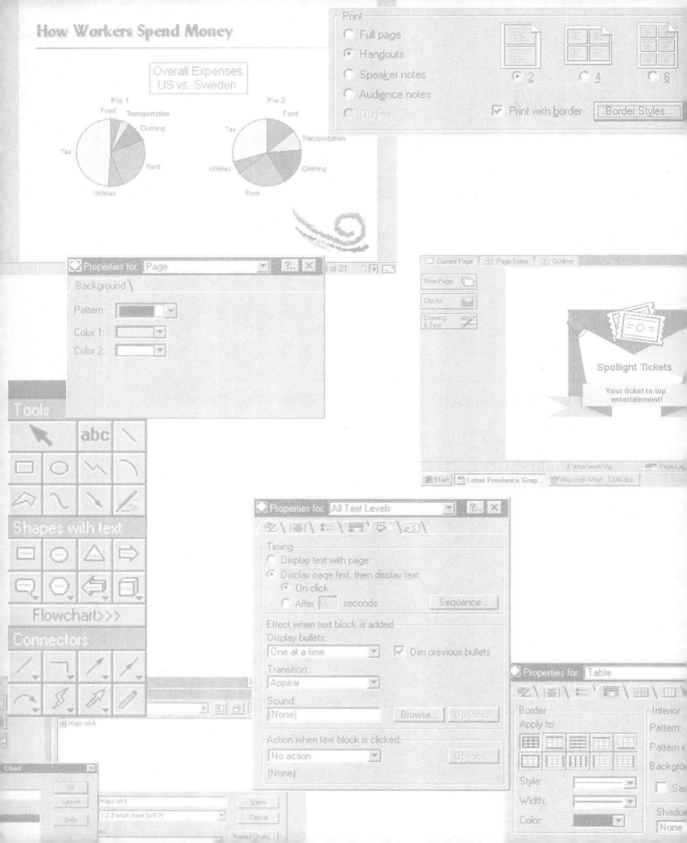

CHAPTER 20

Editing SmartMasters

by Joyce J. Nielsen

As you learned in the early chapters of this book, SmartMasters are the key to the ease of using Freelance Graphics for Windows. SmartMaster looks provide both the background design for a presentation and the page layouts that hold the placement of Click Here blocks. The Content SmartMasters take this one step further by providing suggestions on content for a specific type of presentation, such as a business plan or corporate overview.

The dozens of SmartMasters that come with Freelance provide a wealth of professional presentation designs, but you still may want to create your own SmartMasters, too. By making your own SmartMaster, you can create a template for future presentations that includes your organization's logo, colors, and a design that picks up on the common themes of the presentations you give. If your organization is involved with real estate, for example, the SmartMaster that you design might contain images of homes, blueprints, and office buildings. In addition, its colors and text fonts could reflect those used in your company logo, business cards, and signs.

In this chapter, you learn to do the following:

- Change the background design of a presentation
- Switch to Layout Editing view
- Edit and create new Click Here blocks
- Create a new page layout
- Change presentation colors

Understanding SmartMaster Looks

◄ See "Starting a New Presentation and Choosing Its Look," p. 23

Each SmartMaster look contains two background designs (one for the title page and another for all other pages), twelve page layouts (plus a blank page layout), and two palettes (color and black and white). It is the combination of a background design, a page layout, and a palette that gives each presentation page its look.

Background designs are arrangements of graphic shapes, drawings, symbols, and even text that appear in the background of every page in the presentation. The uniformity of the backgrounds throughout the presentation gives the presentation a consistent, professional appearance. The title page in a SmartMaster has its own background design, to provide a more dramatic look for the start of a presentation. The other page layouts in a SmartMaster (including custom page layouts that you create) are controlled by the presentation backdrop. The *presentation backdrop* consists of the background color and graphic components used in a particular SmartMaster look. The design of the title page and the presentation backdrop used in the remaining page layouts are slightly different for most SmartMaster looks. Figures 20.1 and 20.2 show the title page background and the presentation backdrop of the Capitol SmartMaster.

Fig. 20.1

The Title page design of the Capitol SmartMaster provides a dramatic look.

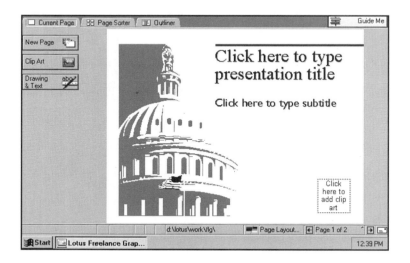

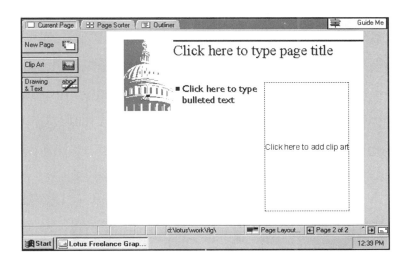

Fig. 20.2
The presentation backdrop used for other page layouts in the Capitol SmartMaster is more subtle. This figure shows the Bullets & Clip Art page layout.

The 12 page layouts in each SmartMaster look contain different combinations and arrangements of Click Here blocks. You click these blocks to quickly add text, charts, clip art, and tables to a presentation. The combination of blocks on a page determines what the completed page will hold. The 1 Chart page layout has two Click Here blocks, for example. One block—a Click Here text block—positions and formats a page title. The other block, a Click Here chart block, positions a chart. Figure 20.3 shows the 1 Chart page layout in the Capitol SmartMaster look.

Tip

To select a page layout for a new presentation page, click the New Page button at the bottom of the screen in Current Page view. Then select the desired page layout and click OK.

The two palettes in each SmartMaster—one that is color and one that is black and white—control the colors or gray shades of all the text, charts, clip art, tables, and graphic objects placed on pages either by clicking Click Here blocks or by creating them manually with the tools in the toolbox. You can use the color palette to see how screen shows, slides, or pages printed with a color printer will look. You can use the black-and-white palette to see how pages printed on a black-and-white printer will look. To switch from one palette to the other while working on a presentation, click the Color/B&W button in the status bar.

VI

Customizing Freelance

Fig. 20.3
The 1 Chart page
layout used in the
Capitol Smart-
Master look in-
cludes two Click
Here blocks.

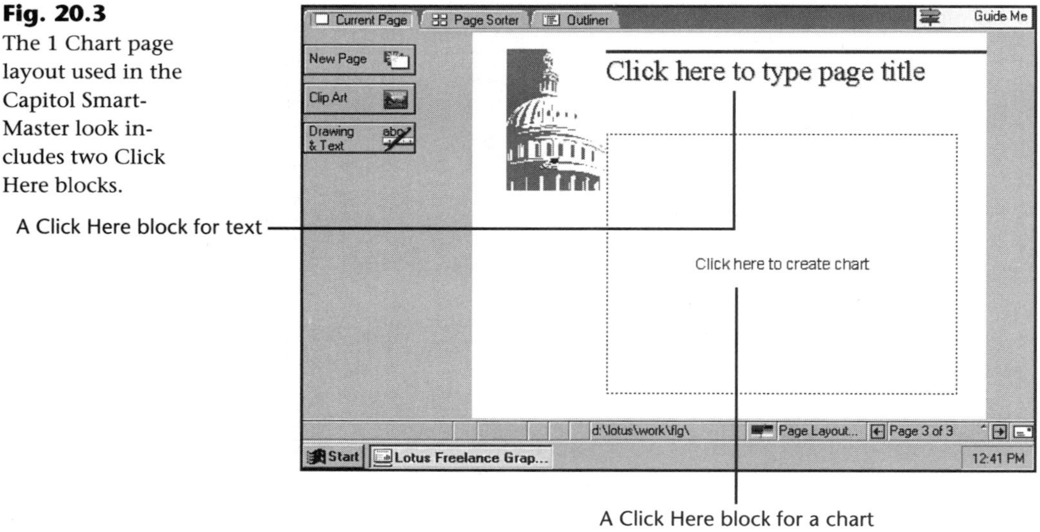

A Click Here block for text

A Click Here block for a chart

Tip

Press Alt+F9 to toggle between the color and black-and-white palettes.

Changing the Background Design of a Presentation

You may find that making a change or two to the background design of an existing SmartMaster adds just the customization you need. Adding your company logo to a corner of every page is one example of a customized design change.

To make the change to every presentation page except the title page, you modify the presentation backdrop. To make the same change to the title page, you must also modify the title page background.

To change the background design of your presentation, follow these steps:

   1. Choose Presentation, Edit Page Layouts. The Edit Page Layout dialog box appears.

Tip

You also can press Shift+F9 to display the Edit Page Layout dialog box.

---

2. Click the Presentation Backdrop layout in the lower-left corner of the Edit Page Layout dialog box (see fig. 20.4). This enables you to change the background of all page layouts in your presentation except the title page. These changes will affect the current presentation only; the SmartMaster look itself will not be affected.

Note

You can modify the background for a specific layout—such as the Title page—or a Bulleted List page only. In the EditPage Layout dialog box, click the specific layout that you want to change from the scrolling list of all page layouts. Then proceed with step 3 below.

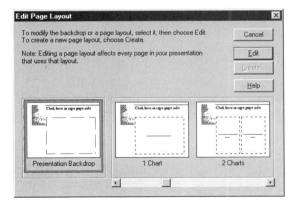

Fig. 20.4
Click the Presentation Backdrop layout to change the background design of all page layouts.

3. Click Edit. Freelance switches to the Current Layout view (see fig. 20.5).

Tip

Click the Drawing & Text button on the left side of the screen to access the Toolbox.

---

4. Make any desired changes to the design of the graphic objects on the page.

Fig. 20.5
You must switch to Current Layout view to make changes that will affect all page layouts in the current presentation.

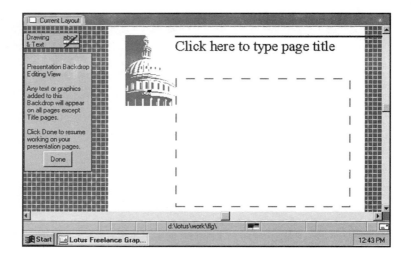

> **Note**
>
> You can draw a logo or add a symbol from the clip art library to the presentation backdrop. If a bitmap graphic or drawn picture that you want exists in a file on disk, choose File, Open to import the file.

---

5. When you finish editing the presentation backdrop, click the Done button, or choose Presentation, Return to Presentation Pages.

To change the color of the presentation backdrop, you must choose Backdrop, Page Properties. The Backdrop command appears on the main menu in Current Layout view. You learn about changing the backdrop color in the section titled "Changing Presentation Colors," later in this chapter.

Adding a Clip Art Symbol to the Background

◀ See "Adding a Logo or Clip Art Symbol to Every Page," p. 258

You can easily add a symbol from the clip art library to the corner of all the pages of a presentation. By adding the clip art to the presentation backdrop, you don't have to add the clip art to each page manually.

All changes you make to the presentation backdrop, including adding a clip art symbol, do not affect the title page. You must edit the title page layout separately.

Modifying a SmartMaster

Previously in this chapter, you learned how to make changes to the presentation backdrop for a specific presentation. These changes affected only the current presentation, not the actual SmartMaster look itself. In this section, you will learn how to make changes to the actual SmartMaster look. Each time you later access the modified SmartMaster look (for a new presentation, for example), the changes you previously made to the SmartMaster look will also appear in the new presentation.

Adding an object to the background of a SmartMaster is only one of the modifications you can make to a SmartMaster. You can also edit Click Here blocks to change their size and position, add new Click Here blocks, add new page layouts, and change the colors of the presentation.

To make any of these changes, you must edit the page layouts of a SmartMaster. While editing the page layouts, you also can make any other design changes you want to a SmartMaster.

Switching to Layout Editing View

Freelance enables you to enter the Layout Editing view to modify a Smart-Master. To edit a SmartMaster, you first open a SmartMaster by choosing File, Open from the main menu. Follow these steps:

1. Choose File, Open. The Open dialog box appears.

2. From the Files of Type drop-down list, choose Lotus Freelance SmartMaster Look (MAS).

3. Use the Look In drop-down list to select the folder containing the Freelance SmartMasters (usually C:\LOTUS\SMASTERS\FLG).

4. Choose a SmartMaster from the list and click Open. The SmartMaster opens in Layout Sorter view.

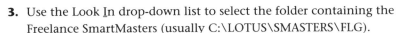

Tip

You can click the Current Layout tab to switch to Current Layout view.

To show that you are in Layout Editing view, Freelance displays small squares across the background of the Freelance window. If Freelance is in Current Layout view, the Done button appears on the left side of the screen.

Troubleshooting

In Layout Editing view, how can I determine if I am editing the current presentation or the actual SmartMaster look?

Look at the title bar at the top of the screen. If the name of the SmartMaster look appears in the title bar, you are editing the actual SmartMaster look.

I want to change the look of my presentation, but keep the SmartMaster look intact for others who may want to use it (without my changes). How do I do this?

Instead of choosing File, Open to open a SmartMaster look for editing, choose Presentation, Edit Page Layouts. In the Edit Page Layout dialog box, select the specific layout you want to modify (or select the Presentation Backdrop layout to modify all layouts except the Title page). Then, click Edit to begin modifying the layout. Refer to the section titled "Changing the Background Design of a Presentation" earlier in this chapter for more detailed information on this procedure.

Editing Page Layouts

When you are in Layout Editing view, the Layout Sorter view enables you to get a bird's-eye view of all the page layouts. In this view, the name of each layout appears under the thumbnail miniature of the layout. Figure 20.6 shows the page layouts in Layout Sorter view.

Fig. 20.6
All of the page layouts appear in Layout Sorter view. As indicated in the title bar, this figure shows the Festive SmartMaster look.

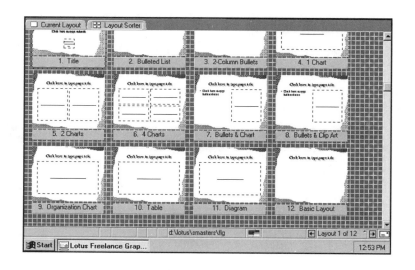

First examine the Basic Layout page layout (see page layout #12 in fig. 20.6). The graphic objects and Click Here blocks on the Basic Layout page layout are also on all other page layouts, except the Title page layout which has its own design. To modify the appearance of the SmartMaster, you should start at the Basic Layout page layout. You can double-click its thumbnail miniature to view it in Current Layout view.

When the Basic Layout page layout appears in Current Layout view, choose Presentation, Edit Backdrop from the main menu. You can now move, resize, or edit existing Click Here blocks, or add new Click Here blocks. Refer to the section titled "Editing Click Here Text Blocks," later in this chapter for more information.

To change the appearance of additional Click Here blocks on other page layouts, switch to the page layout by clicking the Page Layout button near the right end of the status bar and then choosing a layout from the list that appears. You also can click the left or right arrow buttons to move to the next or previous page layout. Another way to choose a different page layout is to switch to Layout Sorter view and then double-click the thumbnail of the page layout.

When you finish editing page layouts, click the Done button (in Current Layout view) or choose Presentation, Return to Presentation Pages.

Editing Click Here Text Blocks

You can move and resize existing Click Here text blocks in page layouts by selecting and dragging them or by dragging their handles just the way you move or resize any text block.

◀ See "Adding Text Blocks," p. 179

To change the prompt text that appears in a Click Here block, click the block (in Current Layout view), pause, and then click again to place a typing cursor inside the block. Then edit the text and type a new prompt. You can change "Click Here to Type Page Title" to "Click Here and Then Type the Name of This Page," for example.

◀ See "Formatting Text Blocks," p. 185

To create a new Click Here text block, follow these steps:

1. In Current Layout view, choose Create, Click Here Block.

2. With the mouse pointer, draw a box on-screen that marks the boundaries of the Click Here text block and then release the mouse button. The words Click here to add text appear in the new text block.

3. Select the text block (if necessary). Choose "Click Here" from the main menu, then choose "Click Here" Properties. The "Click Here" Properties InfoBox appears. Click the Basics tab in the InfoBox (see fig. 20.7).

Fig. 20.7

Use the "Click Here" Properties InfoBox to modify the styles of the selected Click Here block.

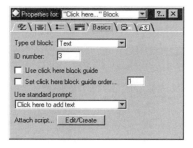

4. Under Properties For, be sure that "Click here..." Block is selected.

5. Under Use Standard Prompt (near the bottom of the InfoBox), select the prompt you want to appear in the Click Here block, or choose Custom Prompt from the drop-down list if you want to enter your own wording.

6. Change other settings in the "Click Here" Properties InfoBox, as desired. For example, you can change the font, text attributes, and color using the first tab of the InfoBox. Switch to other tabs in the InfoBox if you want to change paragraph styles, bullet attributes, and border and fill.

7. After you set all the attributes for the Click Here text block, click the close button of the InfoBox.

8. If you chose Custom Prompt in step 5, click the text block you want to edit, and enter the prompt text you want to use. Then click OK.

9. Click the Done button to return to the presentation pages.

After the text block is on the page, you can still drag the handles of the block to change its size. When you use the Click Here text block while creating presentation pages, the text that you enter will word-wrap within the block you create.

Editing Click Here Blocks for Charts, Tables, and Clip Art

To change the size and placement of the charts, tables, and clip art that you create with Click Here blocks, you change the size and position of the Click Here blocks in the page layouts.

Follow these steps:

1. In Layout Sorter view, double-click the page layout you want to change.

2. Move or size the Click Here blocks in the selected page layout as desired.

3. To change the appearance of the Click Here block or to change the type of Click Here block, click the block and choose "Clic<u>k</u> Here," "Clic<u>k</u> Here" Properties. The "Click Here" Properties InfoBox appears (refer to fig. 20.7).

> **Tip**
>
> You also can display the "Click Here" Properties InfoBox by right-clicking the text block and choosing "Click Here" Block Proper<u>t</u>ies from the shortcut menu.

4. Change any attributes, as desired.

5. Click the close button of the InfoBox.

> **Note**
>
> Changing the settings in the "Click Here" Properties InfoBox does not change the appearance of the chart, table, or clip art that you create by clicking the Click Here block.

To create a new Click Here block for charts, tables, and clip art, follow the procedure for adding a text block (see the previous section, "Editing Click Here Text Blocks"). Then, convert the Click Here text block to another type by clicking the Basics tab in the "Click Here" Properties InfoBox, and selecting a different type in the Type of Block drop-down list.

Creating a New Page Layout

All the SmartMaster looks that come with Freelance have 12 page layouts, and the same 12 page layout names are used in all SmartMaster looks. Therefore, when you apply a different SmartMaster look to a presentation, the new look can reformat the presentation because it has the same page layout names. The page that has the 1 Chart layout gets the design of the 1 Chart page layout in whatever SmartMaster look is chosen.

You can create additional page layouts of your own and give them unique names to accomplish specific page designs. But if you apply a different SmartMaster look that does not have a page layout of the same name, then the page is not formatted by the SmartMaster look. The content of the page will be placed on a blank page with no special formatting.

VI

Customizing Freelance

To create your own custom page design and save it in a new page layout, follow these steps:

1. Switch to Layout Editing view, and choose Layout, New page. The Create New Page Layout dialog box appears (see fig. 20.8).

Fig. 20.8
Use the Create New Page Layout dialog box to add a new page layout to your presentation.

2. Select the Use Backdrop checkbox if you want the new page layout to use the presentation backdrop. This option is selected by default.

3. Enter a new page name in the Page Name text box and change the Number of Click Here Blocks, if desired.

4. Click OK.

5. Add Click Here blocks and other design elements as desired.

6. Click Done to return to the presentation pages.

Changing Presentation Colors

The colors of all objects in a presentation are controlled by one of the two palettes. One palette contains colors; the other palette has black, white, and shades of gray. Each SmartMaster look contains both palettes. You can change the color of presentation objects by modifying the color palette. Refer to Chapter 21, "Using and Editing Color Palettes," for detailed information. In addition to objects, you also can change the color used in the presentation backdrop. The color change you make affects all the pages in the presentation (except the title page).

Note

The changes you make to a color palette affect only the current presentation unless you save the revised palettes in a new SmartMaster look.

To change the color of the presentation backdrop in a presentation, follow these steps:

1. Choose <u>P</u>resentation, Edit <u>B</u>ackdrop. Freelance displays the Current Layout view.

2. Choose <u>B</u>ackdrop, P<u>a</u>ge Properties. The Backdrop Properties InfoBox appears (see fig. 20.9).

3. To select a different background pattern, click the Pattern drop-down button and then select the desired pattern from the drop-down display of patterns.

   To choose a pattern color, click the Pattern Color drop-down button and then select a color from the color palette.

   To choose a background color, click the Background drop-down button and then select a color from the color palette.

4. Click the close button in the InfoBox.

▶ See "Choosing a Different Palette," p. 377

▶ See "Editing a Color Palette," p. 378

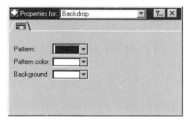

Fig. 20.9
Use the Backdrop Properties InfoBox to change the color of the presentation backdrop.

VI

Customizing Freelance

CHAPTER 21

Using and Editing Color Palettes

by Joyce J. Nielsen

If you plan to deliver your Freelance Graphics presentation either on-screen or using slides or printed color copies, you should understand how the Freelance color palettes work. You need to know about color palettes, for example, if you intend to create your own SmartMaster looks with custom color schemes that match the colors used by your organization or a client.

If you are happy with the colors of the SmartMaster looks that come with Freelance or a customized SmartMaster look that has been provided for you, you may never need to learn about color palettes. After all, the colors in the SmartMaster looks have been coordinated by professional artists, and most of us would have difficulties creating better color combinations.

Even though Freelance can display and print 256 colors, many presentations are printed in black and white. That is why Freelance Graphics includes a black-and-white palette for each SmartMaster look. The black-and-white palette displays the presentation in shades of gray both on-screen and when printed.

In this chapter, you learn how to do the following:

- Choose a different palette
- Edit the colors in a palette
- Create a custom color
- Restore the original color palette

Understanding the SmartMaster Palettes

Each SmartMaster look has two default palettes. One palette chooses colors for the background of each page and for each of the objects on the page. The other chooses shades of gray instead. You can easily switch between the two palettes by clicking the Color/B&W button in the status bar at the bottom of the Freelance window (see fig. 21.1).

> **Tip**
>
> You also can switch palettes by pressing Alt+F9 or by choosing View, Display in Color. A check mark appears beside the Display in Color option when color is selected.

◀ See "Switching to a Black-and-White Version of a Presentation," p. 285

Fig. 21.1
The Color/B&W button in the status bar toggles between the color and B&W palettes.

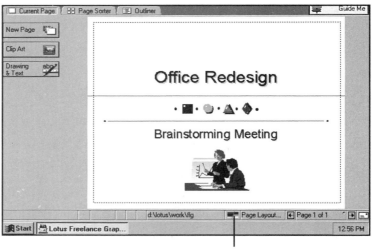

Color/B&W button

Each SmartMaster look uses a separate, predefined palette with 64 colors. There are 48 standard colors that control the different parts of a presentation, and an additional 16 coordinated colors suggested for use with the current palette. One of the 48 colors is used for all bullets in a presentation, for example, and another color is used for all drop shadows. When you choose a different SmartMaster look, different colors may be used for bullets and drop shadows so that they coordinate with the rest of the colors in that particular SmartMaster look. Most other colors in the palette also change, so that the presentation gets a complete color overhaul.

In the section "Editing a Color Palette" later in this chapter, you learn which parts of a presentation are controlled by each position in the color palettes, and how to change the colors.

Choosing a Different Palette

In addition to the two palettes that are built into each SmartMaster look, Freelance provides additional predefined color and black-and-white palettes you can attach to any presentation.

◄ See "Changing Presentation Colors," p. 372

To switch to a different palette, follow these steps:

1. Choose Presentation, Edit Page Layouts (or press Shift+F9). The Edit Page Layout dialog box appears.

2. Click the Presentation Backdrop page (see fig. 21.2).

Presentation Backdrop page

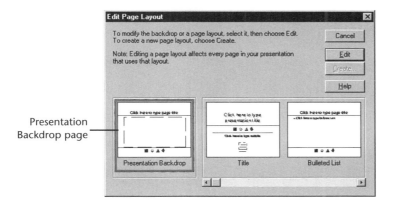

Fig. 21.2
Selecting the Presentation Backdrop enables you to switch the palette used for all layouts in a SmartMaster look.

3. Click Edit. Freelance switches to Presentation Backdrop Editing view. Help information appears on the left side of the screen.

4. Choose Presentation, Switch Palette. The Switch Palette dialog box appears.

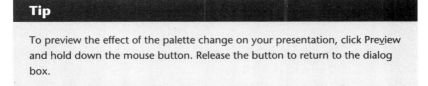

Tip

To preview the effect of the palette change on your presentation, click Preview and hold down the mouse button. Release the button to return to the dialog box.

5. In the Select a Palette list box, select the palette you want to use (see fig. 21.3). The colors in the palette grid change to reflect your selection.

Fig. 21.3

You can select from six pre-defined palettes in the Switch Palette dialog box.

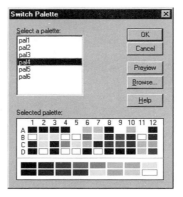

Note

Whether you see the color palettes or the black-and-white palettes in the Switch Palette dialog box depends on whether you were originally viewing the presentation with a color or black-and-white palette.

---

6. Click OK.

7. Click Done.

The palettes that come with Freelance are stored in the same folder in which the SmartMaster looks are stored, usually C:\LOTUS\SMASTERS\FLG. Color palettes have a PAL extension. Black-and-white palettes have a BW extension.

Editing a Color Palette

◀ See "Adjusting the Color Library for Color Printing," p. 343

Many people feel no need to modify any of the colors in a Freelance color palette. The color palettes provided with each SmartMaster look tastefully coordinate all colors used in their presentation.

If you create your own SmartMaster look with a custom background design and logo, however, you may also want to use a modified color palette. The palette can either create a pleasing combination of colors, or match the specific color scheme used for all the printed materials that you generate (in letterheads, logos, and insignias).

When you edit a palette, the colors in the presentation to which the palette is attached change, and any new presentations that you create with the palette show the revised colors. However, presentations that were created with the old version of the palette do not change, unless you specifically select the revised color palette by choosing Presentation, Switch Palette.

To edit a palette, follow these steps:

1. Choose Presentation, Edit Page Layouts.
2. Click the Presentation Backdrop page.
3. Click Edit.
4. Choose Presentation, Edit Palette. The Edit Palette dialog box appears.
5. In the palette grid, select the color you want to change. The name of the selected color appears near the top of the dialog box (see fig. 21.4).

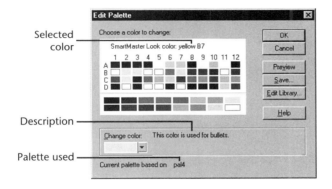

Fig. 21.4
The Edit Palette dialog box enables you to change the selected color to any color in the library of 256 colors.

Note

A description of the selected color in the palette grid appears at the bottom of the Edit Palette dialog box. This enables you to see what elements in the presentation will be affected by changing the color.

Tip

To preview the effect of the color change on your presentation, click Preview and hold down the mouse button. Release the button to return to the dialog box.

6. Click the Change Color drop-down arrow, and select the color you want to use.

7. When you have finished modifying the colors in the palette, click Save.

8. In the Save As dialog box, enter a new name for the palette and click Save again.

9. Click OK.

10. Click the Done button on the left side of the screen.

Table 21.1 identifies the presentation element(s) controlled by each of the positions in the palette. The palette colors are arranged in a grid similar in structure to a spreadsheet with four rows and 12 columns (refer to fig. 21.4).

Caution

Be careful when modifying colors in the positions of A1 through A11 in the color palette. These are the principal colors used in the SmartMaster look.

Table 21.1   The Color Palette Positions

Row 1

Position	Color Used For...
A1	Blank page background
A2	Page background
A3	Page background
A4	Page background
A5	Foreground objects
A6	Foreground objects
A7	Foreground objects
A8	Foreground objects
A9	Foreground objects
A10	Foreground objects
A11	Foreground objects
A12	Shadows of objects, text, and charts

Row 2

Position	Color Used For...
B1	Titles, subtitles, and bulleted text
B2	Titles, subtitles, and bulleted text
B3	Text added with text tool; on-screen drawing
B4	Text in charts, speaker notes, placement blocks, headers and footers, and frame edges
B5	Text in diagrams
B6	Dimmed color in bullet builds
B7	Bullets
B8	Background color for organization chart boxes, tables, and cell backgrounds
B9	3-D organization chart box sides
B10	3-D organization chart box bottoms
B11	Lines and edges
B12	Fills of polygons and diagramming shapes

Row 3

Position	Color Used For...
C1	Chart's first data series
C2	Chart's second data series
C3	Chart's third data series
C4	Chart's fourth data series
C5	Chart's fifth data series
C6	Chart's sixth data series
C7	Chart's seventh data series
C8	Chart's eighth data series
C9	Chart's ninth data series
C10	Chart's tenth data series
C11	Chart's eleventh data series
C12	Chart's twelfth data series

(continues)

VI

Customizing Freelance

Table 21.1 Continued

Row 4

Position	Color Used For...
D1	Edges of diagramming shapes
D2	Plot and background edges of charts; text block and number grid frames
D3	Edges of data charts, organization charts, and organization chart box edges
D4	Grid lines in number grids and data charts
D5	Borders of tables and cells
D6	Frame area for text, data chart text, number grids, organization charts, and placement blocks; data chart background
D7	Second color in a data series grad fill
D8	Second color in a chart frame grad fill
D9	3-D data chart plot walls
D10	3-D data chart plot floor
D11	Foreground objects
D12	Foreground objects

Troubleshooting

I'm familiar with CMYK (cyan, magenta, yellow, black) color values, but not RGB (red, green, blue) values. How do I create a custom color using the CMYK values?

Follow the instructions for creating custom colors earlier in this chapter. Instead of adjusting the scroll bars for Red, Green, and Blue, however (after you click an empty box under Custom Colors), click the CMYK button. Then, type the desired values in the Cyan, Magenta, Yellow, and Black text boxes and click OK.

Creating a Custom Color

The Freelance *color library* consists of 240 defined colors plus 16 custom colors that you can create. Each of the predefined palettes displays 64 of the 256 colors in the color library. If none of the colors in the color library is an exact match of the color you need, you can create a custom color or edit any existing color in the library. Lotus recommends that you create a custom color instead of modifying a color in the color library. Custom colors are available for use with any SmartMaster look. Changes to the color library, however, are part of the current SmartMaster look only. If you do not save the modified color library, the changes appear only in the current presentation.

> **Note**
>
> You must view a presentation in color in order to edit the library colors or create a custom color—you cannot edit the black-and-white color library. You *can* edit colors in a black-and-white *palette*, however.

To create a custom color, follow these steps:

1. Choose Presentation, Edit Page Layouts.
2. Click the Presentation Backdrop page.
3. Click Edit.
4. Choose Presentation, Edit Palette.
5. Click Edit Library. The Edit Library dialog box appears (see fig. 21.5).

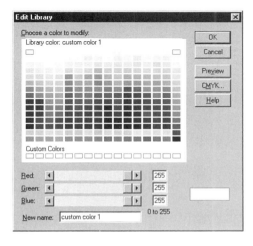

Fig. 21.5
You can create a custom color or modify an existing color in the Edit Library dialog box.

Note

The entire array of 256 possible colors appears in the Edit Library dialog box. It also includes three slider scroll bars that enable you to vary the amount of red, green, and blue (RGB values) in the currently selected color. All colors in the library are a combination of red, green, and blue. The color teal, for example, has 0 parts red, 197 parts green, and 174 parts blue.

---

6. Click any empty box under Custom Colors.

Tip

To choose a custom color more precisely, enter a color number from 0 to 255 in each text box to the right of the slider scroll bars.

---

7. Drag the Red, Green, and Blue slider scroll bars until the desired color appears in the Custom Color box (see fig. 21.6).

Fig. 21.6
Custom colors appear just below the color library.

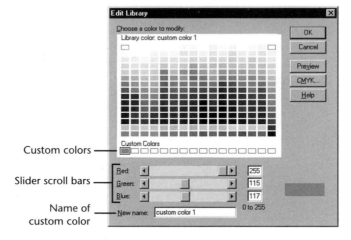

Custom colors

Slider scroll bars

Name of custom color

8. Type the name of the new color in the New Name text box.

9. Click OK.

10. Click OK again.

11. Click Done.

The custom color is now available for selection in any palette you choose. When you edit an existing palette, the custom color will appear in the Change Color drop-down list (see "Editing a Color Palette" earlier in this chapter).

Restoring the Original Palette

To restore the original color palette after you have modified one or more of the colors in a palette, follow these steps:

1. Choose Presentation, Choose a Different SmartMaster Look. The Choose a Look for Your Presentation dialog box appears (see fig. 21.7).

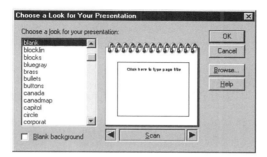

Fig. 21.7
Select the name of the SmartMaster look with the palette you want to restore.

Tip

If you don't remember the name of the SmartMaster, click the Scan button to let Freelance scan through samples until you find the one you want.

2. Select the name of the SmartMaster look.

3. Click OK.

Troubleshooting

When I print a presentation using a black-and-white printer, certain colors appear dithered, or unfocused. How do I avoid this problem?

Freelance provides several non-dithered colors in each color library. Replace the colors that are causing problems with one or more of the following "pure," non-dithered colors: red, yellow, olive, neon green, dark green, turquoise, aztec blue, blue, midnight, hot pink, plum red, scarlet, white, 25-percent gray, 50-percent gray, and black.

CHAPTER 22

Modifying the Default Settings

by Joyce J. Nielsen

The default settings for Freelance are initially set by the manufacturer so that you can be productive from the moment you have the program installed. As you become more familiar with Freelance, however, you may want to change some of these settings to fit the way you like to work.

Many options are available for changing the display of various items in the Freelance window, including the SmartIcons. Other settings enable you to change the way Freelance starts, and how a presentation is saved.

In this chapter, you learn how to do the following:

- Change the look of the Freelance window
- Set Freelance startup and save options
- Modify options for drawing, color, and Undo
- Display and move a SmartIcon bar
- Add and delete SmartIcons
- Create a custom SmartIcon to load an application

Setting the View Preferences

By changing the Freelance View Preferences, you can change settings that determine how some of the elements in the Freelance window look. You can decide whether the drawing rulers display, for example, or whether the coordinates of the mouse pointer location appear on-screen.

To access the Set View Preferences dialog box, choose View, Set View Preferences. The Set View Preferences dialog box appears, as shown in figure 22.1.

Fig. 22.1

The Set View Preferences dialog box enables you to change settings for cursor size, display options, and page borders.

◀ See "Changing the Crosshair Size," p. 222

◀ See "Using a Grid," p. 221

The Set View Preferences dialog box shows three groups of controls. The Cursor Size controls enable you to change the size of the drawing cursor when you are using the drawing tools of Freelance. Click the option you want to use, Big Crosshair or Small Crosshair. By default, the Small Crosshair option is selected.

> **Tip**
>
> Choose View, Set Units & Grid to view or change the current Units selection in the Set Units & Grid dialog box.

◀ See "Showing Coordinates," p. 221

◀ See "Using the Drawing Rulers," p. 220

◀ See "Setting Indents with the Text Block Ruler," p. 197

The Display controls enable you to select three visual displays by clicking the check box next to each control. By default, none of these items are selected. Select the Coordinates option to display the current distance of the mouse pointer from the upper-left corner of the page; this distance is displayed at the bottom of the screen in the current units, as set in the Set Units & Grid dialog box. Select the Drawing Ruler setting to display the drawing rulers across the top and down the left side of the display in Current Page view. The units in the ruler are set in the Set Units & Grid dialog box. Select the Text Block Ruler check box to display the text block ruler at the top of selected text blocks. Figure 22.2 shows all three of these elements.

> **Note**
>
> The point of origin (0,0) of the on-screen coordinates starts, by default, at the top-left corner of the page. To change the point of origin, display the drawing rulers. Then click anywhere in the top and/or left ruler to set a new point of origin.

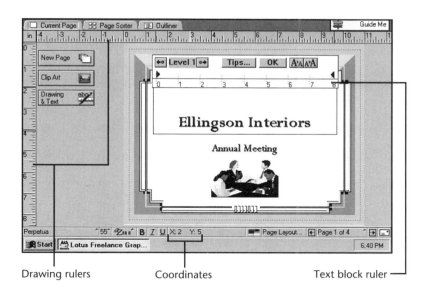

Fig. 22.2
To display these visual elements, change the default settings in the Set View Preferences dialog box.

Drawing rulers   Coordinates   Text block ruler

The Show Page Borders controls enable you to display a dashed line that shows the Recommended Drawing Area or the Printable Area (as determined by the printer selected in the Print dialog box). The third choice, None, displays no page borders. Printable Area is the default selection.

When you have finished selecting desired options, click OK to save your changes and exit the Set View Preferences dialog box.

Changing Freelance Preferences

To access the Freelance Graphics Preferences dialog box with its many controls for changing the way Freelance works, choose File, User Setup, Freelance Preferences. Figure 22.3 shows the Freelance Graphics Preferences dialog box. Following sections describe each of the options in this dialog box. After making your selections, click OK to save your changes and exit the Freelance Graphics Preferences dialog box.

Fig. 22.3

The Freelance Graphics Preferences dialog box enables you to modify settings such as startup options and automatic save.

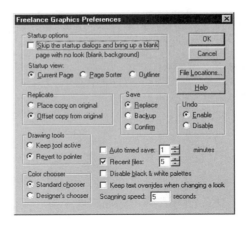

Changing Startup Options

The Startup Options settings (refer to fig. 22.3) determine the screen that Freelance presents when you first start the program. Click the Skip the Standard Startup Dialogs and Bring Up a Blank Page with No Look check box to skip the steps that ask you to choose a SmartMaster and a page layout. Freelance shows a blank page instead. The three Startup View buttons enable you to start up the program in one of the following views: Current Page view, Page Sorter view, or Outliner view.

Choosing Save and AutoSave Options

◀ See "Saving the Presentation," p. 40

With the Save options in the Freelance Graphics Preferences dialog box (refer to fig. 22.3), you can determine whether a presentation that you save replaces the existing saved presentation (Replace), replaces the existing saved presentation and creates a backup copy of the previous saved version (Backup), or prompts you to indicate whether to replace or back up whenever you save a presentation (Confirm).

The Auto Timed Save check box automatically saves a copy of the current presentation at the interval you set with the increment or decrement buttons. You must click the check box next to Auto Timed Save to activate this feature.

The Recent Files check box determines the number of files that are displayed at the bottom of the File menu. These are files that you worked on and saved recently. Clicking any of the file names reopens the file. You can display from one to five files, depending on your selection.

Setting Drawing and Color Options

The Replicate options in the Freelance Graphics Preferences dialog box (refer to fig. 22.3) enable you to specify whether the copies of objects created when you choose Edit, Replicate will appear on top of or offset from the original.

◀ See "Replicating Objects," p. 231

By using the Drawing Tools options, you can decide whether the current drawing tool you are using should remain active when you finish with it (Keep Tool Active) or whether the tool should become inactive in favor of the pointer (Revert to Pointer).

◀ See "Keeping a Drawing Tool Active," p. 223

The Color Chooser options enable you to select either the Standard Chooser colors or the Designer's Chooser colors. The Standard colors include 16 suggested colors plus a 256-color library. The Designer's colors contain all the SmartMaster colors. In most cases, you will only need the colors available in the Standard color set (the default selection). Select the Designer's Chooser option only if you perform a lot of design work, or plan to modify or create SmartMaster looks.

◀ See "Choosing a Different Palette," p. 377

If you select the Disable Black & White Palettes check box, you cannot switch to the black and white palette in each SmartMaster look. Select this option only if you are printing to a color printer or generating color slides or screen shows exclusively.

Setting the Undo, Overrides, and Scanning Options

The Undo options enable you to disable the Undo feature (refer to fig. 22.3). The default, Enable, is almost always preferable because it allows you to undo your last 10 actions by clicking the Undo SmartIcon or choosing Edit, Undo.

If you want to maintain manual text formatting that you applied to characters or levels of text in your presentation when you change to a different SmartMaster look, select the Keep Overrides When Changing a Look check box.

The Scanning Speed text box indicates the number of seconds each page is displayed before scanning to the next page when you use the Scan button. You can enter a number between 0.1 and 100. The default Scanning Speed is five seconds. The Scan button appears when you choose Create, Add Clip Art to add clip art or a diagram to your presentation. It also appears when you choose Presentation, Choose a Different SmartMaster Look, enabling you to easily scan through all the available SmartMaster looks.

VI

Customizing Freelance

Changing the Default File Locations

Clicking the File Locations button in the Freelance Graphics Preferences dialog box (refer to fig. 22.3) leads to the File Locations dialog box, as shown in figure 22.4.

Fig. 22.4

Use the File Locations dialog box to change where you want to store Freelance presentations.

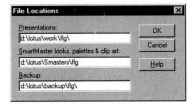

The Presentations folder is where your saved presentations are stored. The SmartMaster Looks, Palettes & Clip Art folder is where these elements are installed during the Freelance installation process. The Backup folder is where backup copies of presentations are saved (when you choose the Backup option in the Freelance Graphics Preferences dialog box).

Using SmartIcons

Freelance provides on-screen icons, called *SmartIcons*, that provide shortcuts to common commands and procedures. Each icon shows a picture of the action that the SmartIcon performs. By default, the SmartIcons appear in a horizontal bar just below the menu bar in the Freelance window, but you can also place them in other positions on the window (see fig. 22.5).

To display a brief description of a SmartIcon, called *bubble help*, move the mouse pointer over the SmartIcon and pause (see fig. 22.5). Move the mouse pointer off of the SmartIcon bar to remove the bubble help.

Freelance normally displays two SmartIcon bars on-screen at one time. By default, the *Universal SmartIcon bar* appears on-screen at all times. This SmartIcon bar includes SmartIcons that you will use most often, such as the Print and Save SmartIcons. In addition to the Universal SmartIcon bar, Freelance provides 22 different *context SmartIcon bars* that contain icons related to common Freelance tasks. The new Task Sensitive Interface (TSI) feature in Freelance Graphics 96 for Windows 95 automatically displays the appropriate context SmartIcon bar based on the task you are performing.

Fig. 22.5
The bubble help feature provides a description of an icon in the SmartIcon bar.

Typically, the Universal SmartIcon bar appears on the left side of the SmartIcons area, and a context SmartIcon bar appears just to the right of the Universal SmartIcon bar. The context SmartIcon bar that appears on-screen depends on what action you are performing. In figure 22.5, for example, the Page SmartIcon bar appears to the right of the Universal SmartIcon bar. If you select a text block in the current page, however, the Text SmartIcon bar replaces the Page SmartIcon bar (and the Universal SmartIcon bar remains on-screen).

You can add SmartIcons from the library of SmartIcons to any existing bar, or create your own SmartIcon bars. These topics are covered in the section "Adding and Deleting SmartIcons," later in this chapter.

Displaying a Different SmartIcon Bar

Although Freelance automatically displays the SmartIcons you most likely will use during a particular task, you always have the option of switching to a different SmartIcon bar.

At the left end of a SmartIcon bar is a button bar with a drop-down arrow. If you click the down arrow in the button bar, a drop-down menu appears. The names of one or more SmartIcon bars appear at the bottom of this menu.

Names of SmartIcon bars that are currently displayed on-screen appear with a check mark beside them (see fig. 22.6). If you want to display another bar in the drop-down list, click the name of that bar. The drop-down list disappears, and the SmartIcon bar you selected appears on-screen.

Note

The SmartIcon button bar also provides access to commands that hide the current SmartIcon bar or all SmartIcons, if you have no need for them. Hiding SmartIcons leaves more space on-screen for the presentation pages.

Fig. 22.6

Active SmartIcon bars show a check mark beside their names in the button bar drop-down menu.

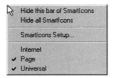

Tip

To quickly access the SmartIcons Setup dialog box, click the down arrow in the button bar, and choose SmartIcons Setup.

Not all SmartIcon bars appear in the button bar drop-down menu. To access the other bars, follow these steps:

1. Choose File, User Setup, SmartIcons Setup. The SmartIcons Setup dialog box appears (see fig. 22.7). The name of the current SmartIcon bar appears near the top of the dialog box.

2. To change bars, click the arrow to the right of the Bar Name drop-down list box and select a different bar from the list. The bar you selected appears at the top of the SmartIcons Setup dialog box.

3. Click the down-arrow to the right of the Bar Can Be Displayed When Context Is drop-down list box and select the desired context for the selected Bar Name. This tells Freelance when to display the Bar Name you selected in step 2.

4. Click OK.

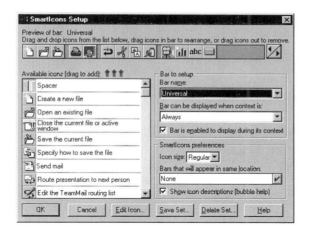

Fig. 22.7
The SmartIcons
Setup dialog box
provides many
options for
customizing your
use of SmartIcons
in Freelance.

Note

In most cases, you will not need to change the SmartIcon bars that display on-screen. This is because Freelance automatically displays the context SmartIcon bar which contains the SmartIcons you will most likely need to use for the current task.

Changing the SmartIcon Bar Position

By default, the current SmartIcon bars appear across the top of the Freelance window. You can move a SmartIcon bar to another position on-screen, however, or place a bar in a floating window that you can move around the screen.

To change the position of a SmartIcon bar, follow these steps:

1. Move the mouse pointer to the button bar at the left end of a SmartIcon bar. The pointer changes to a hand.

2. Click and drag the bar to where you want it to appear on-screen. As you drag the bar, an outline shows the current bar position.

3. Release the mouse button when it is in the desired position.

To create a floating bar, drag the SmartIcon bar to an area near the middle of the screen and release the mouse button. The SmartIcons appear in a small window on-screen, as shown in figure 22.8. You can drag the borders of the window to stretch the window. The SmartIcons then rearrange inside. To move the window, drag the button bar at the left end of the floating SmartIcon bar. To close the bar and hide the SmartIcons, click the down arrow on the left side of the floating bar, and choose Hide This Bar of SmartIcons.

Fig. 22.8

Drag a bar to the middle of the screen to create a floating SmartIcon bar.

Adding and Deleting SmartIcons

The default SmartIcon bars show only a small sample of the available SmartIcons. To make choosing commands that you frequently use easy, you may want to choose other SmartIcons from the library of SmartIcons.

> **Tip**
>
> You can press and hold down Ctrl and drag an individual SmartIcon from one position to another while you are in any Freelance view.

To add or delete SmartIcons, follow these steps:

1. Choose File, User Setup, SmartIcons Setup. The SmartIcons Setup dialog box appears (refer to fig. 22.7).

2. The scrollable list of SmartIcons on the left includes all the SmartIcons built into Freelance. The current SmartIcon bar appears at the top of the screen. Use the scroll arrows to the right of this bar to see additional icons on the current bar (if any).

Tip

By dragging the Spacer SmartIcon to the current bar displayed at the top of the SmartIcons Setup dialog box, you can add spaces that can separate SmartIcons into logical groups.

3. To add a SmartIcon to the current bar, find the icon you want in the Available Icons list and drag it to the desired position in the bar at the top (see fig. 22.9). The SmartIcon then appears in the bar.

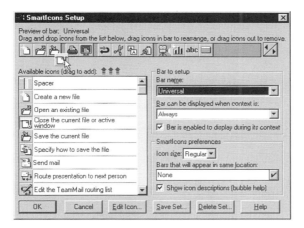

Fig. 22.9
Drag icons you want to add to (or delete from) the SmartIcon bar.

4. To delete a SmartIcon from the current bar, drag it off the bar at the top of the dialog box.

Tip

All SmartIcon bars are automatically saved with the SMI extension.

5. To save the revised SmartIcon bar, click the Save Set button, type a name for the bar in the SmartIcons Bar Name text box, and click OK.

To delete a SmartIcon bar, click the Delete Set button and choose the bar to delete from the list. Then click OK.

6. Click OK again to return to the presentation.

Changing the Size of the SmartIcons

You can change the size of the SmartIcons if they are too large or too small to be useful. Click the Icon Size drop-down list in the SmartIcons Setup dialog box and choose the desired option, Regular or Large. Then click OK.

Creating a SmartIcon to Load an Application or Insert an Object

The SmartIcons built into Freelance carry out Freelance commands and load other Lotus Windows applications. To create SmartIcons that can load other programs or insert OLE objects, follow these steps:

1. Choose File, User Setup, SmartIcons Setup. The SmartIcons Setup dialog box appears.

2. Click Edit Icon. The Edit Icon dialog box appears (see fig. 22.10).

Fig. 22.10
Use the Edit Icon dialog box to create your own custom SmartIcons.

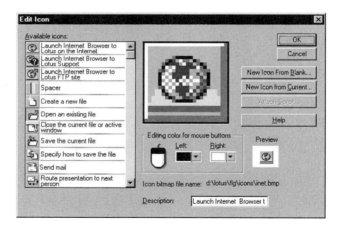

3. To base the new SmartIcon on an existing SmartIcon, choose the SmartIcon from the list at the left and then click the New Icon from Current button. Enter a name for the new SmartIcon when prompted.

   Or, to create a brand new SmartIcon, click the New Icon from Blank button and enter a name for the SmartIcon when prompted (see fig. 22.11).

4. Click OK.

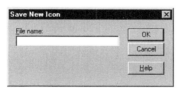

Fig. 22.11
Enter the name of
the new SmartIcon
in the Save New
Icon dialog box.

5. Use the picture editing tools at the bottom center of the Edit Icon dialog box and the mouse to draw the picture that will appear on the SmartIcon's face. A preview of the SmartIcon in progress appears on the right side of the dialog box.

> **Note**
>
> To draw the picture for the face of the SmartIcon, select colors you want to use from the Left and Right drop-down lists. You can switch to another color at any time. Then drag across the large button face that is displayed in the dialog box or click specific dots on the button face. Click either mouse button to place a dot of the color assigned to that button. Continue clicking dots or dragging until you have created the picture you want.

6. Click the Attach Script button. The Add Script dialog box appears (see fig. 22.12).

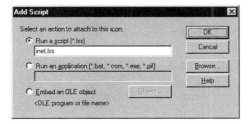

Fig. 22.12
The Add Script
dialog box enables
you to attach a
script to, or run an
application from
the custom
SmartIcon.

7. Select the type of command or program you want to attach by selecting one of the following options: Run a Script, Run an Application, or Embed an OLE Object.

8. Click Browse to select the file you want to attach to the SmartIcon, then click Open.

9. Click OK twice to return to the SmartIcons Setup dialog box. The new SmartIcon now appears in the Available Icons list.

10. Drag the newly created SmartIcon from the Available Icons list to the desired SmartIcon bar, and click OK.

VI

Customizing Freelance

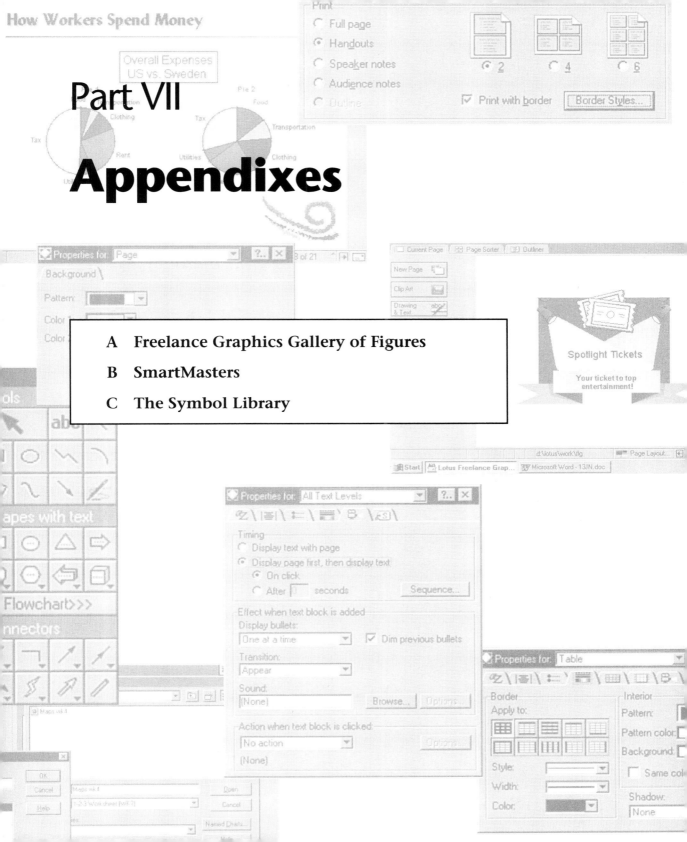

Part VII

Appendixes

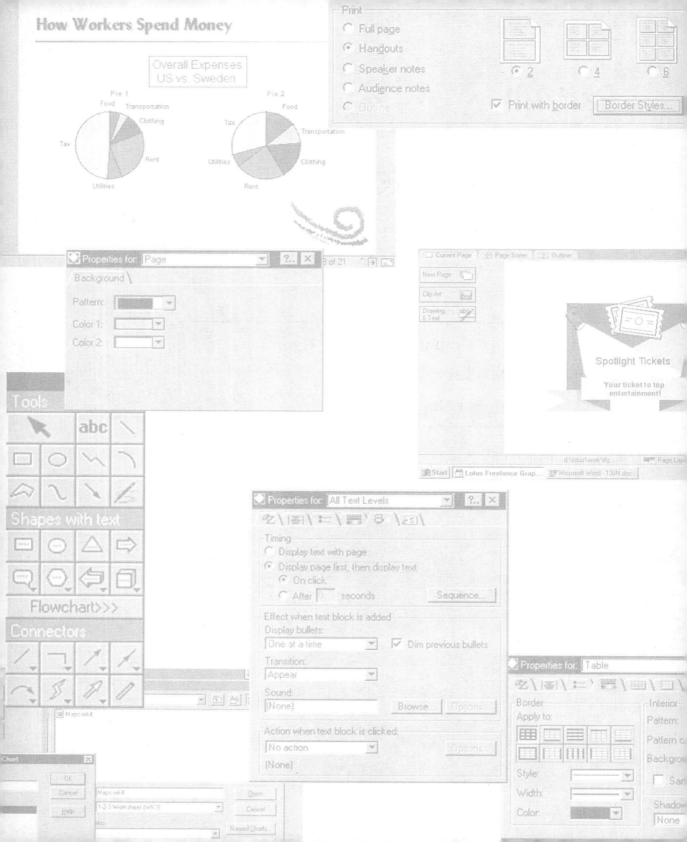

Freelance Graphics Gallery of Figures

by Nancy Stevenson

This gallery of figures was created using Freelance Graphics 96 for Windows 95. Use the images here to get ideas for your own Freelance pages and slides. A brief note accompanying each image highlights some of the features of Freelance that were used to create it, such as the name of the Page Layout or the addition of a clip art symbol or chart. There's also a reference to tell you which chapter in this book might help you learn the features used to create these figures.

Fig. A.1

The Capitol SmartMaster, Bulleted List Page Layout with a Clip Art Symbol added. See Chapter 13, "Adding Clip Art Symbols and Bitmaps."

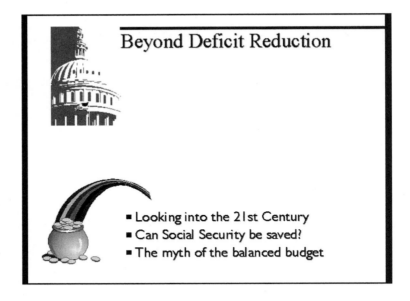

Fig. A.2

The EEC Smart-Master, B&W, 1 Chart Page Layout with 3-D Area Chart, Text Block and Arrow Connector Drawing Object added. See Chapter 11, "Drawing Objects."

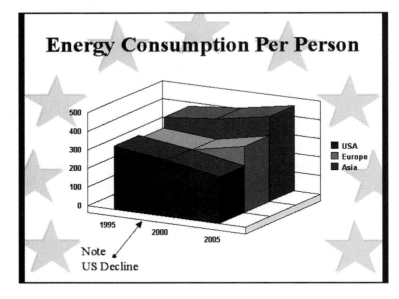

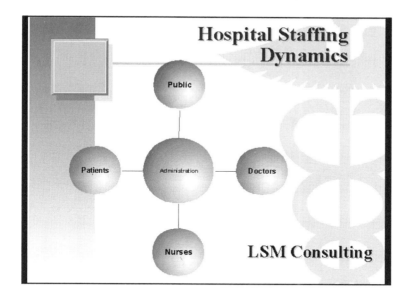

Fig. A.3
The Medical SmartMaster, Title Page Layout with the Hub 4-Circles Diagram added. See Chapter 8, "Creating Organizational Charts."

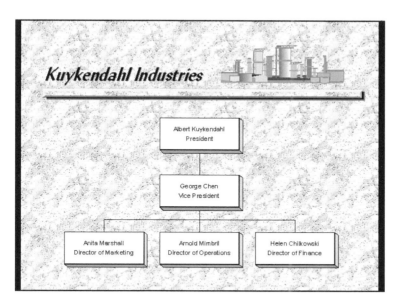

Fig. A.4
The Txmarbwh SmartMaster in B&W, Organization Chart Page Layout with Clip Art Symbol added. See Chapter 8, "Creating Organizational Charts."

VII

Appendixes

Fig. A.5

The USA Flag SmartMaster in B&W, 1 Chart Page Layout with 3-D multiple bar chart. See Chapter 6, "Formatting a Data Chart."

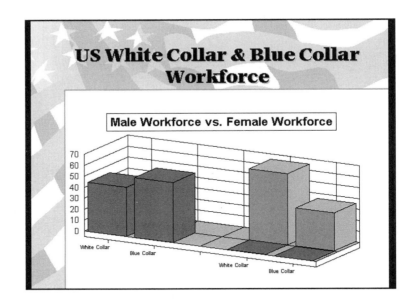

Fig. A.6

The Testtube SmartMaster, Table Page layout with gradient background and added clip art symbols. See Chapter 9, "Creating Table Charts."

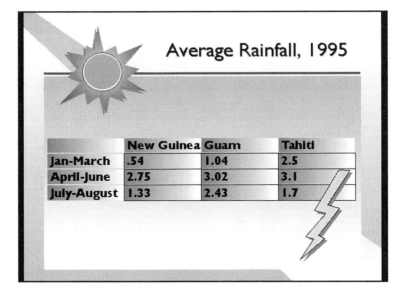

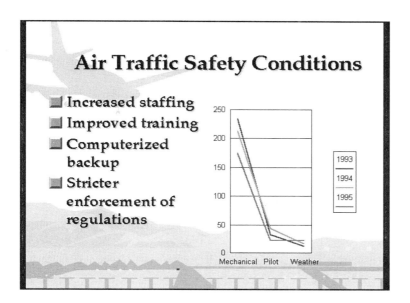

Fig. A.7
The Plane SmartMaster, Bulleted List & Chart Page Layout with Line Chart. See Chapter 5, "Adding a Data Chart."

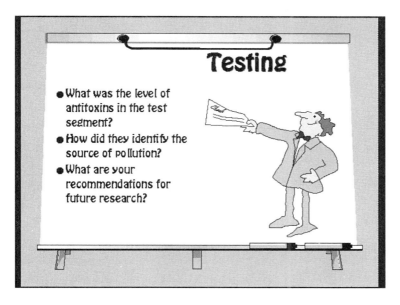

Fig. A.8
Training ContentMaster, Testing ContentPage Layout with SmartMaster background changed to Present. See Chapter 3, "Making Basic Changes to the Presentation."

Fig. A.9
Spotlight
SmartMaster in
B&W, Title Page
Layout with clip
art symbol added.
See Chapter 20,
"Editing
SmartMaster Sets."

Fig. A.10
France
SmartMaster, Two
Bulleted List Page
Layout with
borders applied
to both lists and
clip art symbols
added. See
Chapter 10,
"Adding and
Formatting Text
Blocks."

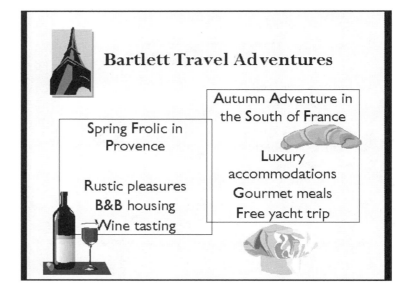

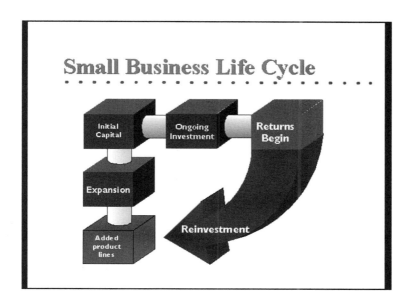

Fig. A.11
Dotline2 SmartMaster, Title Page Layout with Process Diagram added. See Chapter 8, "Creating Organizational Charts."

Fig. A.12
Gears SmartMaster, Title Page Layout with Clip Art Symbol and Text block added. See Chapter 10, "Adding and Formatting Text Blocks."

VII

Appendixes

APPENDIX B
SmartMasters

The samples in this appendix show the designs of the SmartMasters that come with Freelance Graphics 96 for Windows 95. Each sample displays the Bullets & Chart page layout, so you can see the background design, the text, and a chart.

Many of the sets have graduated backgrounds, bitmaps, and symbols that you cannot see in these black-and-white illustrations. To see the full effects of all the designs, refer to your Freelance Graphics documentation or view them on-screen.

Fig. B.1

A sample page from the 1995.MAS SmartMaster.

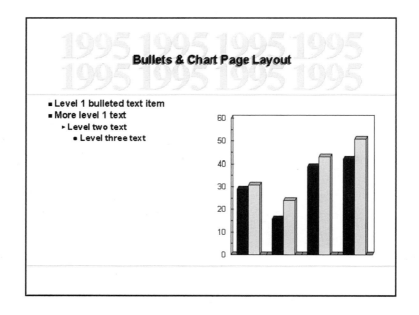

Fig. B.2

A sample page from the 1996.MAS SmartMaster.

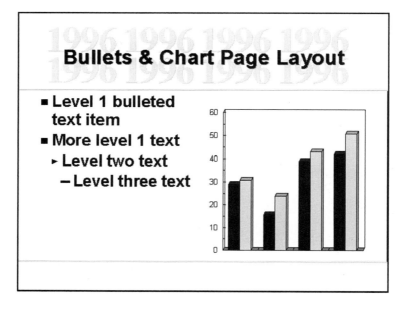

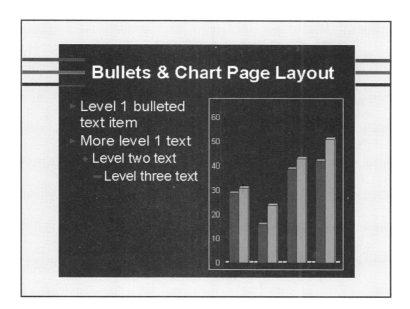

Fig. B.3
A sample page from the 3LINE.MAS SmartMaster.

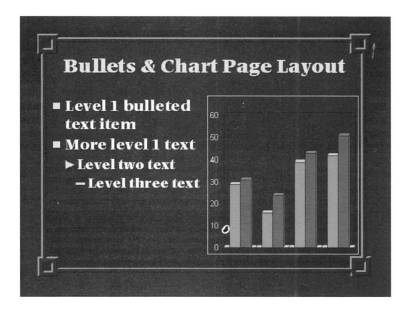

Fig. B.4
A sample page from the 4SQUARE.MAS SmartMaster.

VII

Appendixes

Fig. B.5
A sample page from the ABSTRACT.MAS SmartMaster.

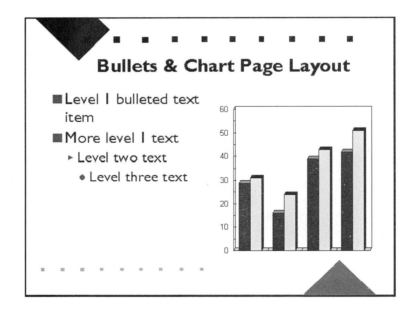

Fig. B.6
A sample page from the ANGLES.MAS SmartMaster.

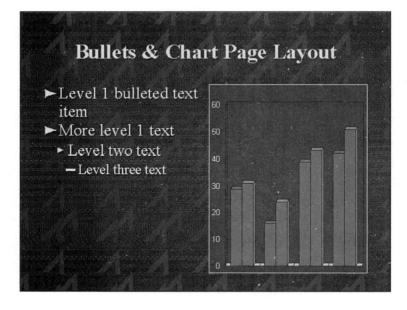

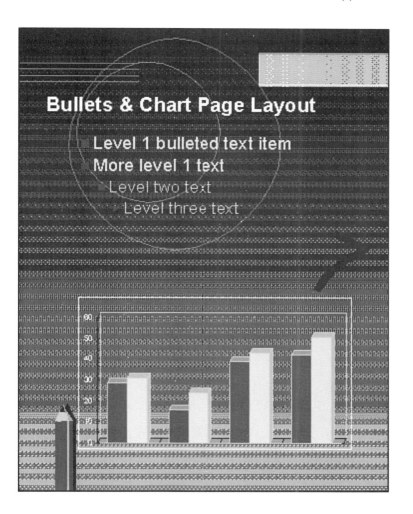

Fig. B.7
A sample page
from the
ARCHITEC.MAS
SmartMaster.

Fig. B.8
A sample page
from the
AUSTRALI.MAS
SmartMaster.

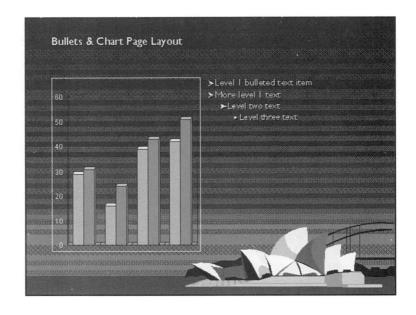

Fig. B.9
A sample page
from the
BASICLIN.MAS
SmartMaster.

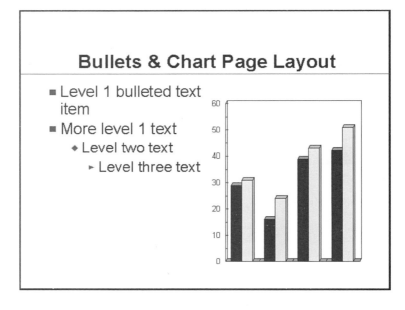

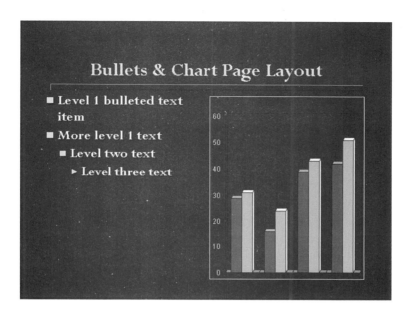

Fig. B.10
A sample page from the BEVRULE.MAS SmartMaster.

VII

Appendixes

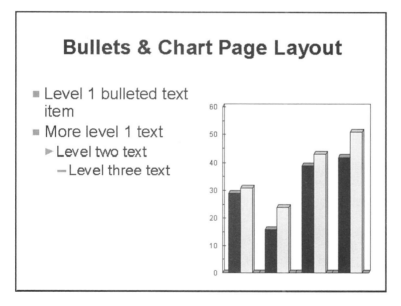

Fig. B.11
A sample page from the BLANK.MAS SmartMaster.

Fig. B.12
A sample page from the BLOCKLIN.MAS SmartMaster.

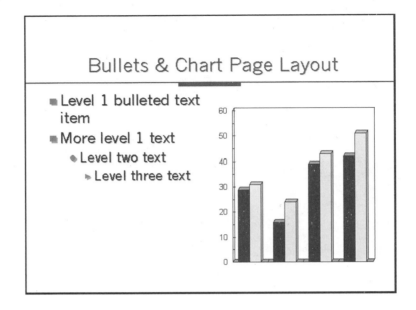

Fig. B.13
A sample page from the BLOCKS.MAS SmartMaster.

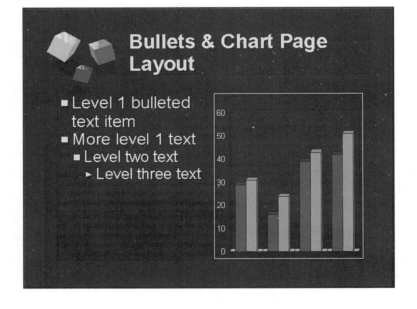

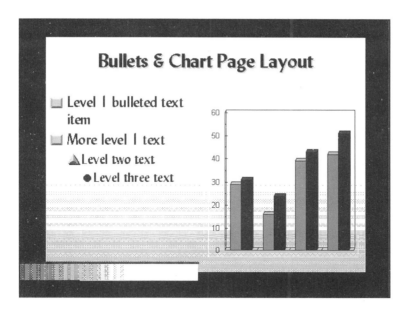

Fig. B.14
A sample page
from the
BLUEGRAY.MAS
SmartMaster.

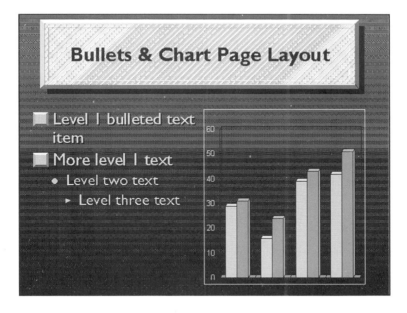

Fig. B.15
A sample page
from the
BRASS.MAS
SmartMaster.

Fig. B.16
A sample page from the BULLETS.MAS SmartMaster.

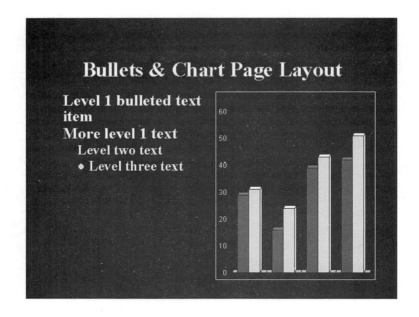

Fig. B.17
A sample page from the BUTTONS.MAS SmartMaster.

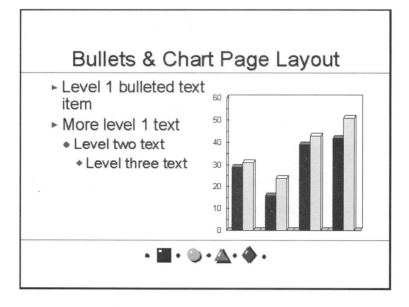

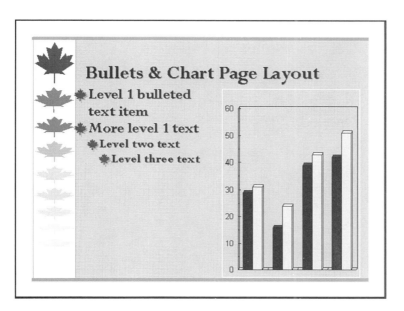

Fig. B.18
A sample page from the CANADA.MAS SmartMaster.

VII

Appendixes

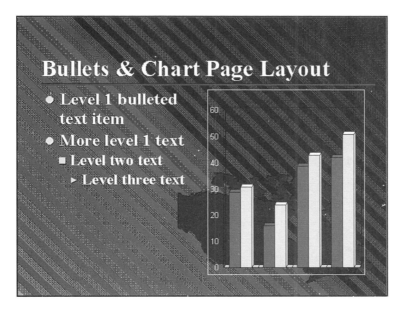

Fig. B.19
A sample page from the CANADMAP.MAS SmartMaster.

Fig. B.20

A sample page from the CAPITOL.MAS SmartMaster.

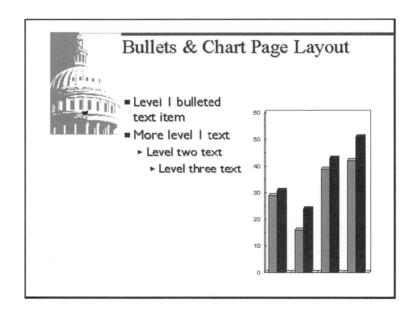

Fig. B.21

A sample page from the CIRCLE.MAS SmartMaster.

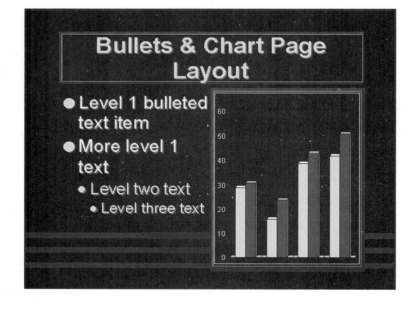

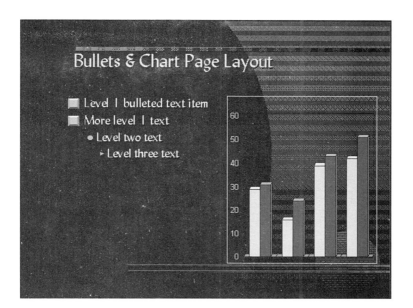

Fig. B.22
A sample page from the CORPORAT.MAS SmartMaster.

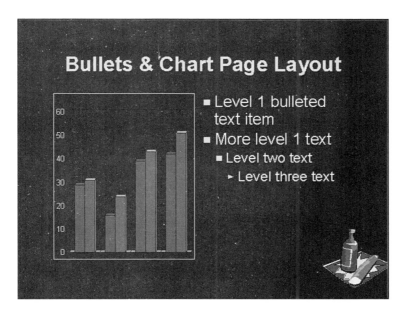

Fig. B.23
A sample page from the CUISINE.MAS SmartMaster.

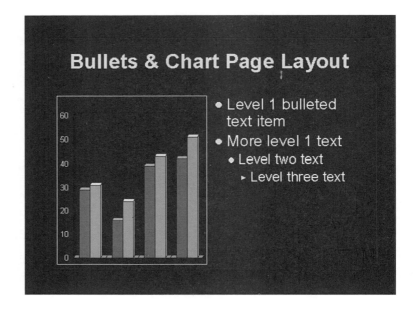

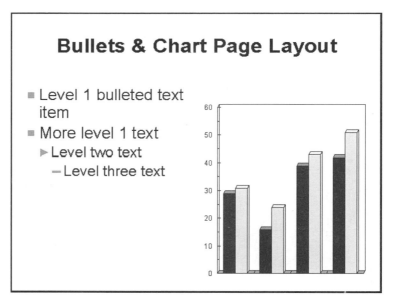

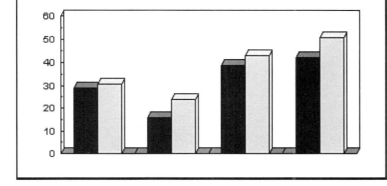

Fig. B.26
A sample page
from the
CUSTOM2.MAS
SmartMaster.

VII

Appendixes

Fig. B.27

A sample page from the DECO.MAS SmartMaster.

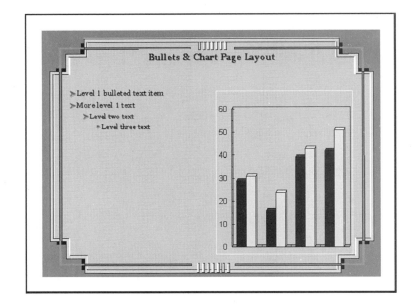

Fig. B.28

A sample page from the DIAMOND.MAS SmartMaster.

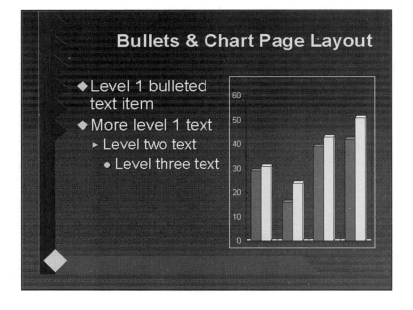

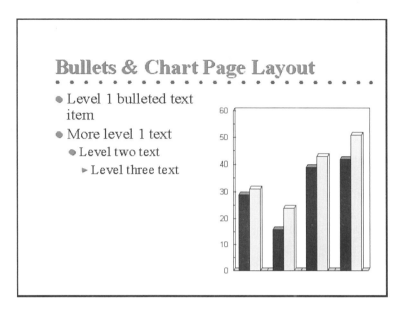

Fig. B.29
A sample page from the DOTLINE1.MAS SmartMaster.

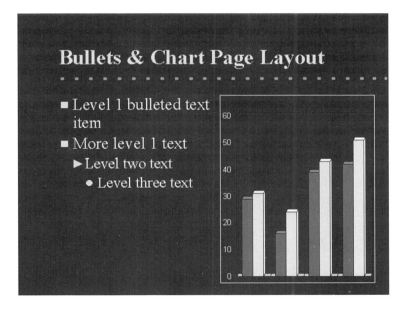

Fig. B.30
A sample page from the DOTLINE2.MAS SmartMaster.

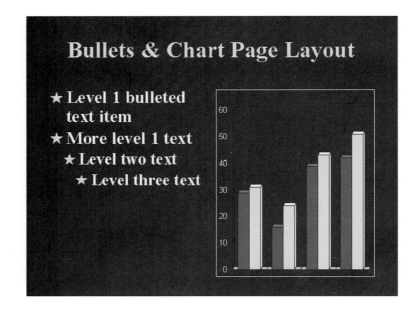

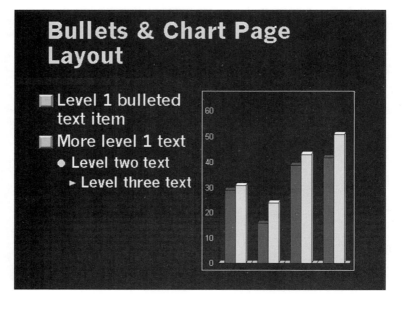

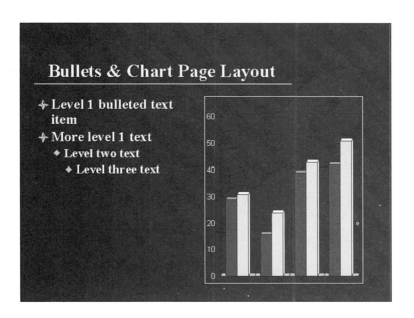

Fig. B.33
A sample page from the EUROPE.MAS SmartMaster.

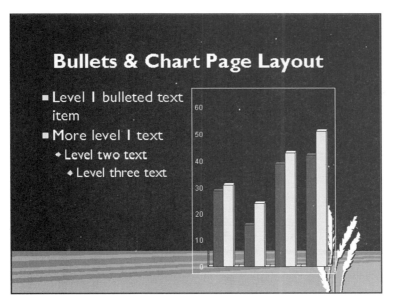

Fig. B.34
A sample page from the FARM.MAS SmartMaster.

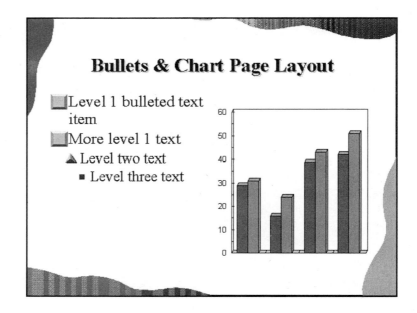

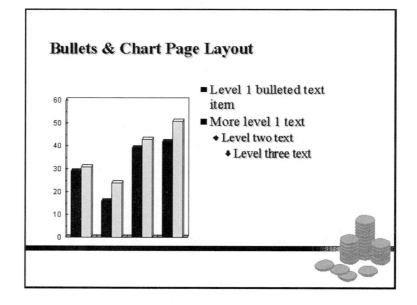

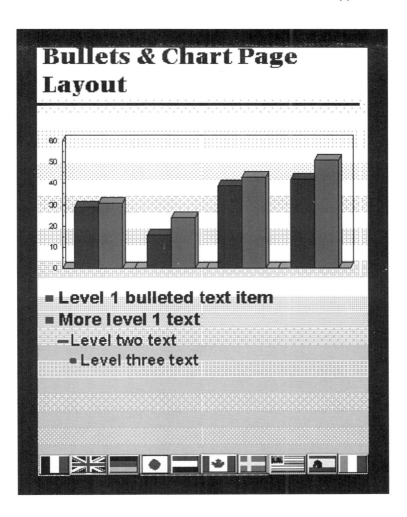

Fig. B.37
A sample page
from the
FLAGS.MAS
SmartMaster.

VII

Appendixes

Fig. B.38
A sample page
from the
FOOD.MAS
SmartMaster.

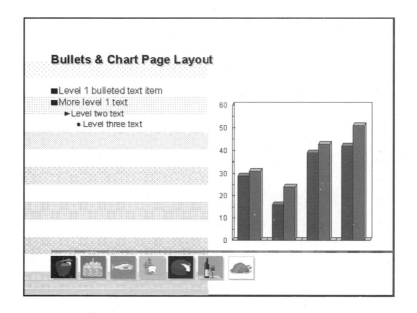

Fig. B.39
A sample page
from the
FOREST.MAS
SmartMaster.

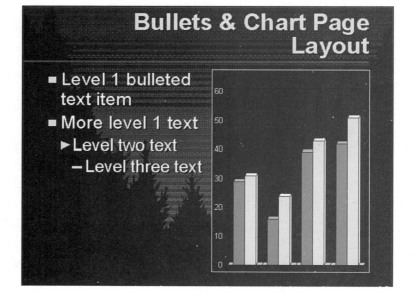

VII

Appendixes

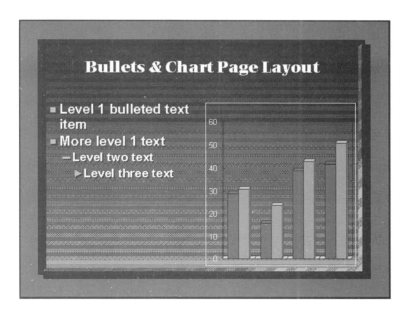

Fig. B.40
A sample page
from the
FRAME.MAS
SmartMaster.

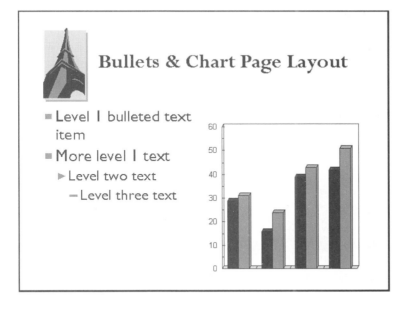

Fig. B.41
A sample page
from the
FRANCE.MAS
SmartMaster.

Fig. B.42

A sample page from the GEARS.MAS SmartMaster.

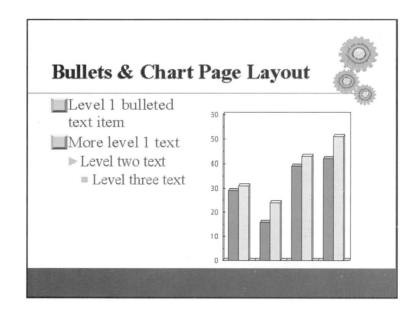

Fig. B.43

A sample page from the GERMANY.MAS SmartMaster.

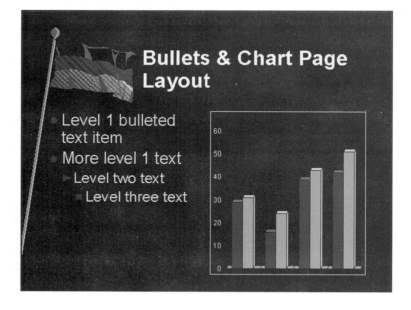

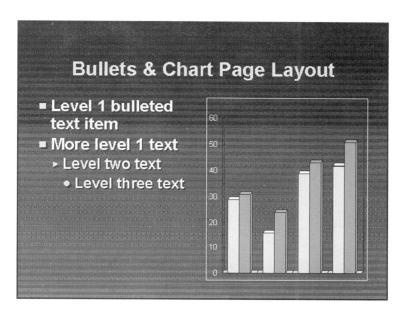

VII

Appendixes

Fig. B.44
A sample page from the GRADATE1.MAS SmartMaster.

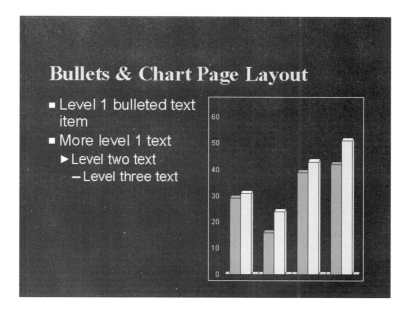

Fig. B.45
A sample page from the GRADATE2.MAS SmartMaster.

Fig. B.46
A sample page
from the
GRADATE3.MAS
SmartMaster.

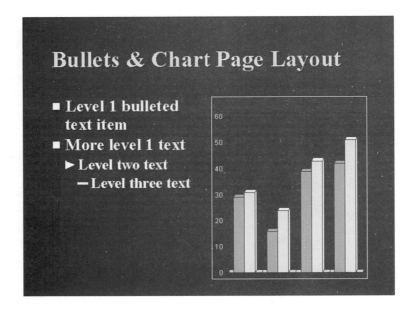

Fig. B.47
A sample page
from the
GRADLINE.MAS
SmartMaster.

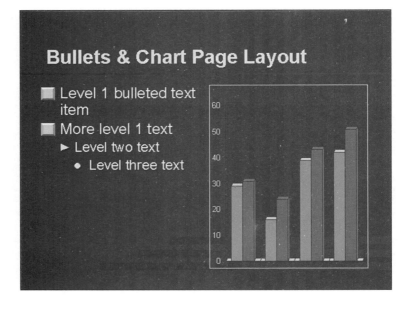

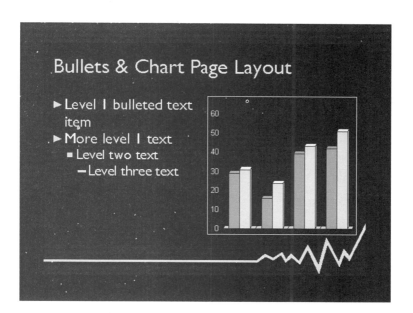

Fig. B.48
A sample page
from the
GRAPHLIN.MAS
SmartMaster.

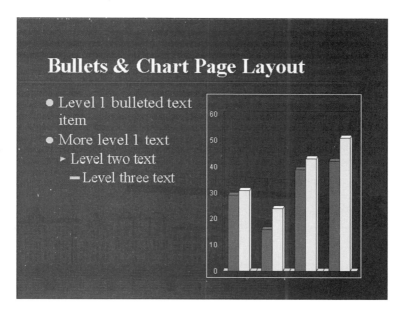

Fig. B.49
A sample page
from the
HOLLAND.MAS
SmartMaster.

Fig. B.50

A sample page from the ITALY.MAS SmartMaster.

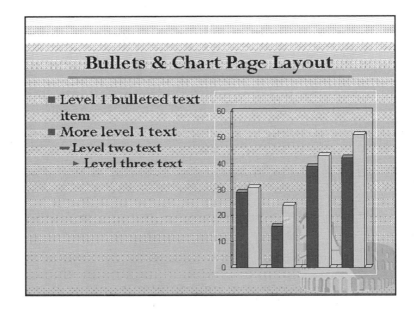

Fig. B.51

A sample page from the JAPAN.MAS SmartMaster.

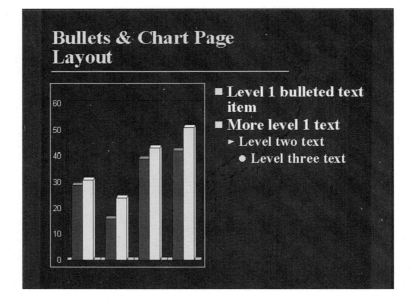

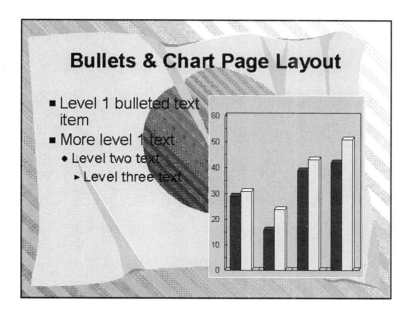

Fig. B.52
A sample page
from the
JFLAG.MAS
SmartMaster.

VII

Appendixes

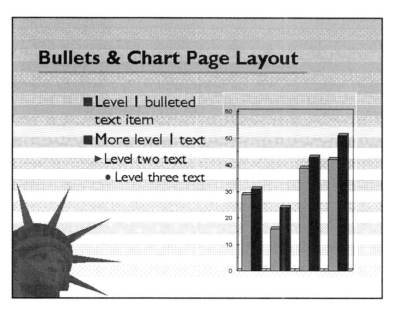

Fig. B.53
A sample page
from the
LIBERTY.MAS
SmartMaster.

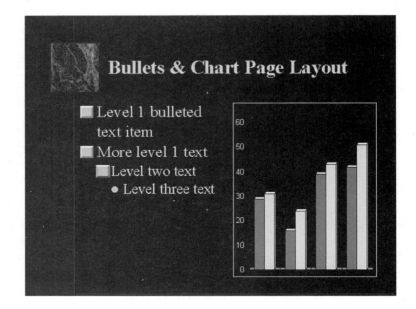

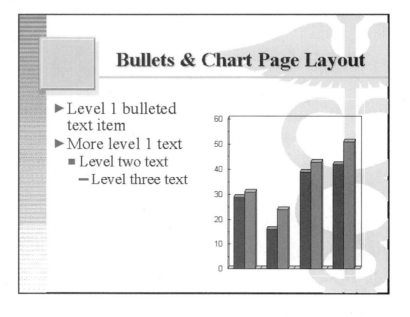

VII

Appendixes

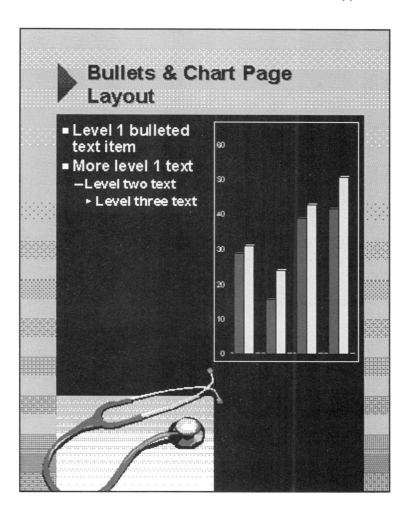

Fig. B.56
A sample page
from the
MEDICAL2.MAS
SmartMaster.

Fig. B.57
A sample page from the MOTION.MAS SmartMaster.

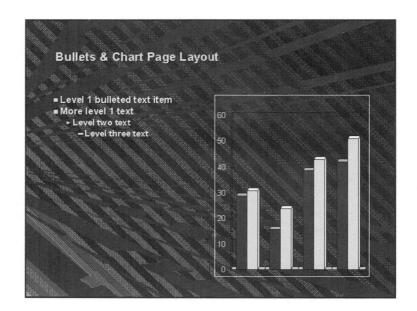

Fig. B.58
A sample page from the MOUNTAIN.MAS SmartMaster.

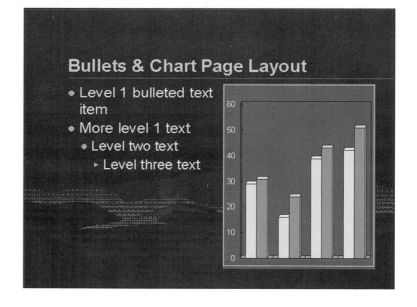

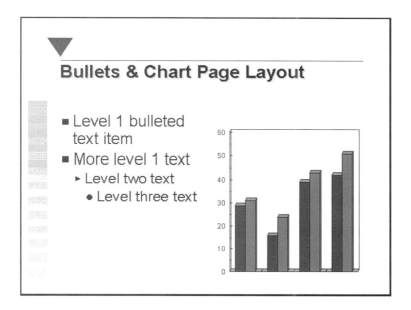

Fig. B.59
A sample page
from the
NEO2.MAS
SmartMaster.

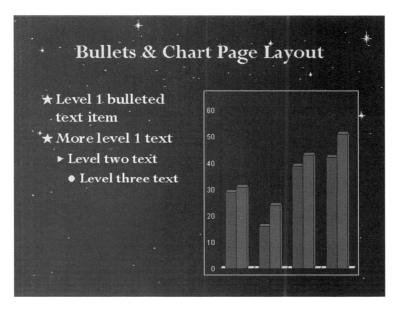

Fig. B.60
A sample page
from the
NIGHTSKY.MAS
SmartMaster.

Fig. B.61
A sample page
from the
NOTEBOOK.MAS
SmartMaster.

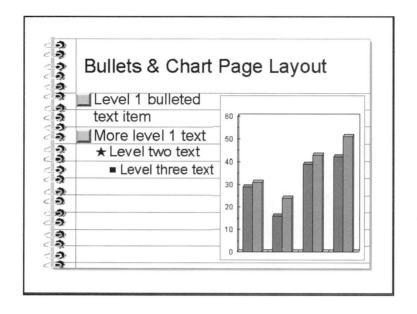

Fig. B.61
A sample page
from the
NOTEBOOK.MAS
SmartMaster.

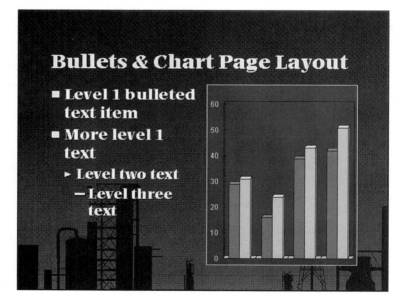

Fig. B.62
A sample page
from the
OILREFIN.MAS
SmartMaster.

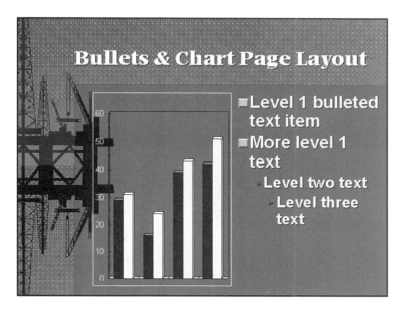

Fig. B.63
A sample page from the OILRIG.MAS SmartMaster.

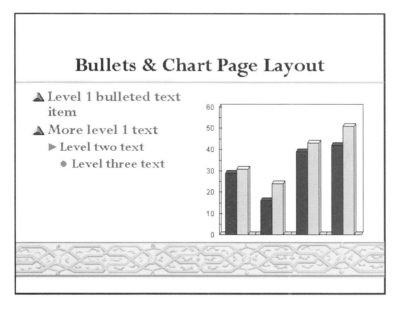

Fig. B.64
A sample page from the ORNATE2.MAS SmartMaster.

Fig. B.65

A sample page from the PACIFIC.MAS SmartMaster.

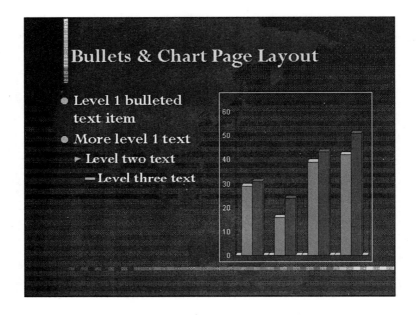

Fig. B.66

A sample page from the PAGE.MAS SmartMaster.

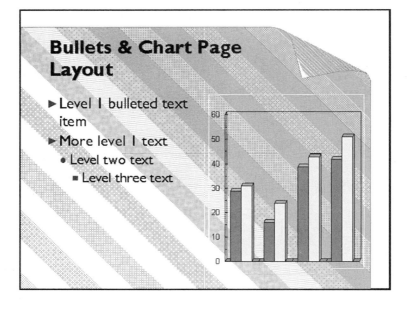

VII

Appendixes

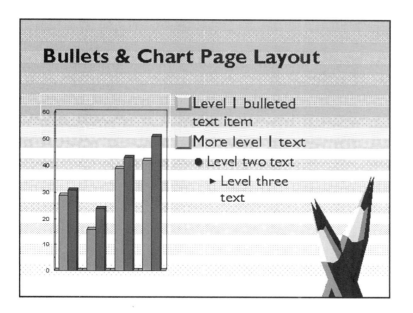

Fig. B.67
A sample page from the PENCIL2.MAS SmartMaster.

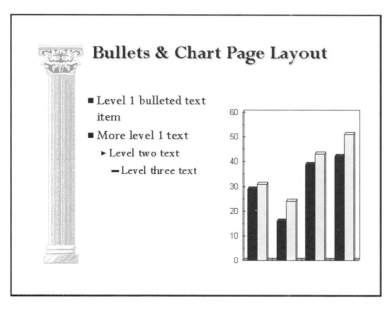

Fig. B.68
A sample page from the PILLAR.MAS SmartMaster.

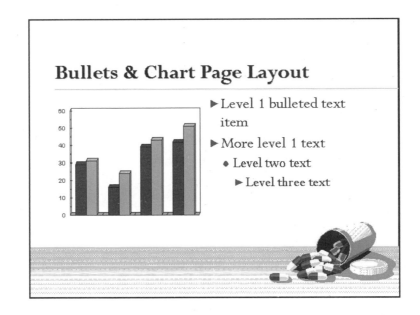

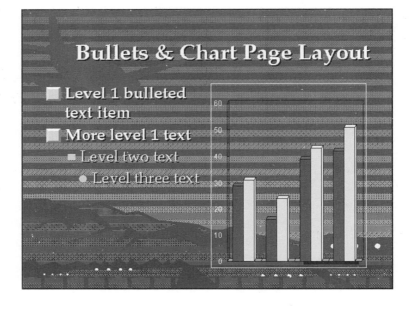

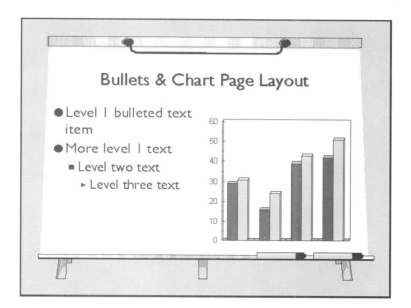

Fig. B.71
A sample page
from the
PRESENT.MAS
SmartMaster.

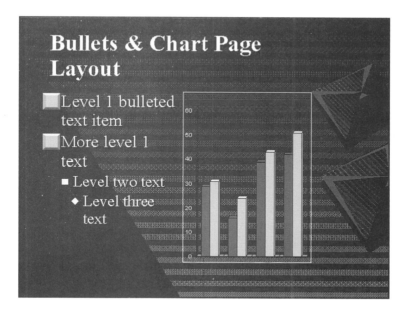

Fig. B.72
A sample page
from the
PYRAMID.MAS
SmartMaster.

Fig. B.73

A sample page from the RAINBOW.MAS SmartMaster.

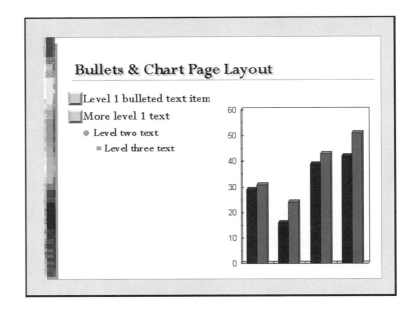

Fig. B.74

A sample page from the REDBOX.MAS SmartMaster.

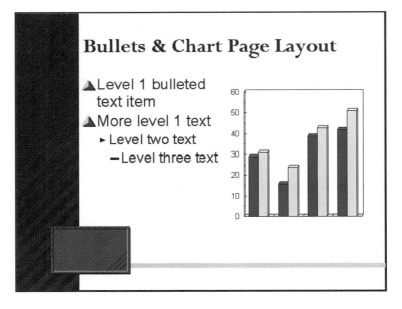

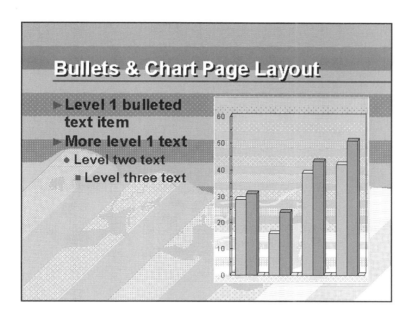

Fig. B.75
A sample page
from the
RUSHMORE.MAS
SmartMaster.

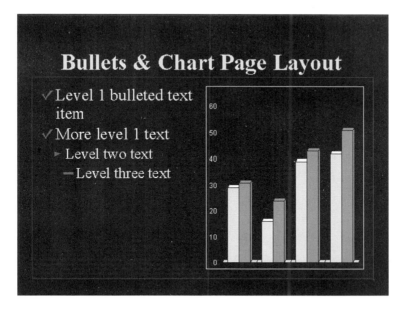

Fig. B.76
A sample page
from the
SCRIM.MAS
SmartMaster.

Fig. B.77

A sample page
from the
SHADOWBOX.MAS
SmartMaster.

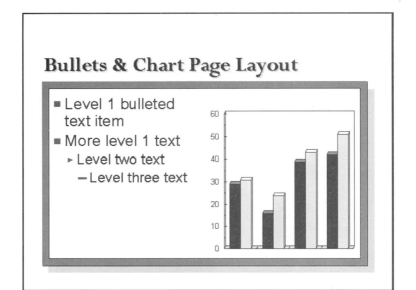

Fig. B.78

A sample page
from the
SHIMMER.MAS
SmartMaster.

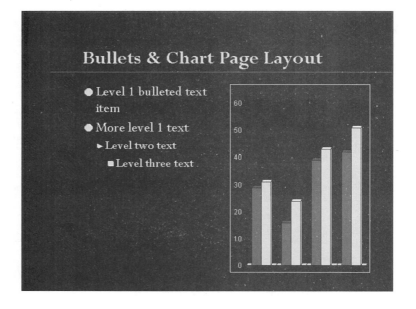

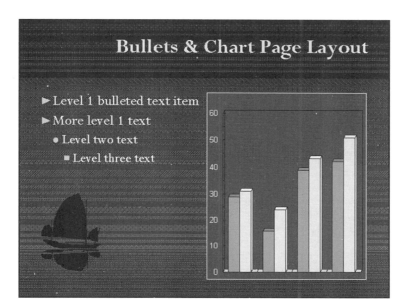

Fig. B.79
A sample page from the SHIP.MAS SmartMaster.

VII

Appendixes

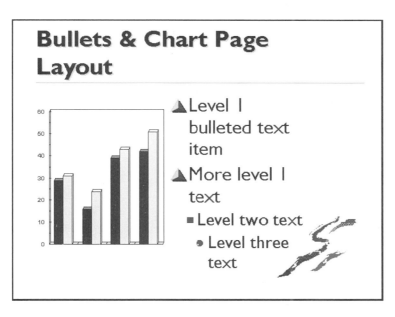

Fig. B.80
A sample page from the SKETCH.MAS SmartMaster.

Fig. B.81

A sample page from the SKYLINE.MAS SmartMaster.

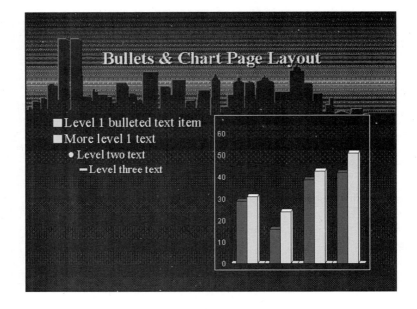

Fig. B.82

A sample page from the SOUTHWEST.MAS SmartMaster.

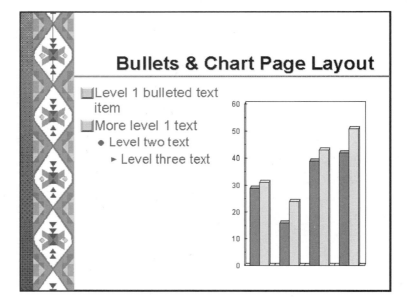

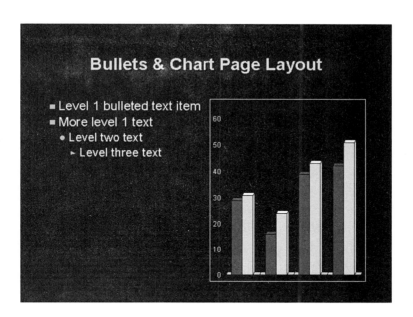

Fig. B.83
A sample page from the SPACE.MAS SmartMaster.

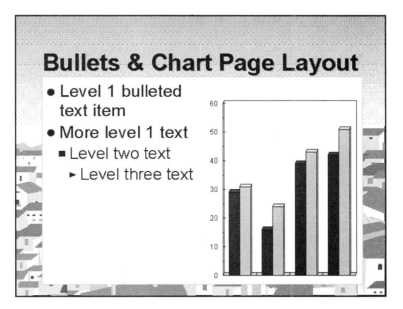

Fig. B.84
A sample page from the SPAIN.MAS SmartMaster.

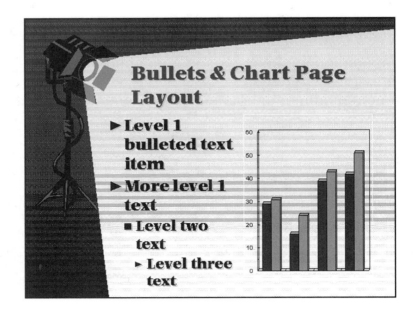

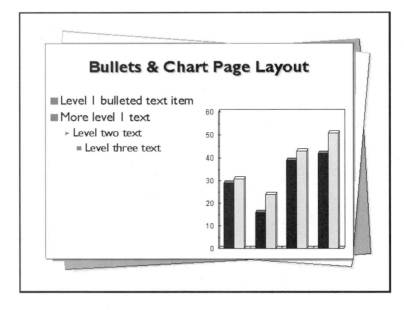

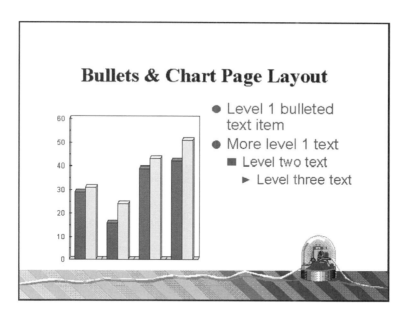

VII

Appendixes

Fig. B.87
A sample page
from the
STOCKMKT.MAS
SmartMaster.

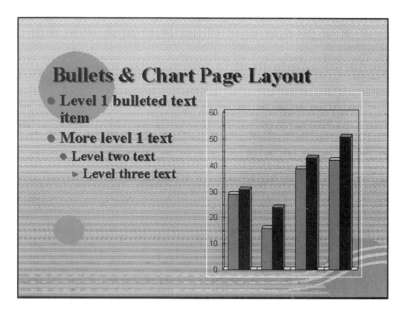

Fig. B.88
A sample page
from the
SWEEP.MAS
SmartMaster.

Fig. B.89

A sample page from the SYMBOLBX.MAS SmartMaster.

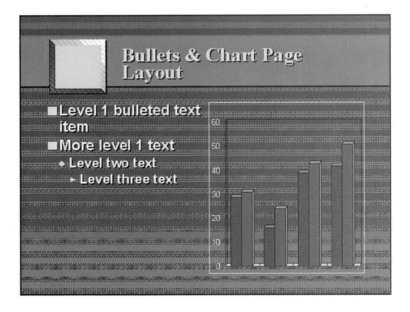

Fig. B.90

A sample page from the TESTUBE.MAS SmartMaster.

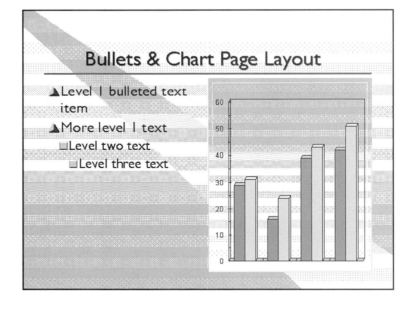

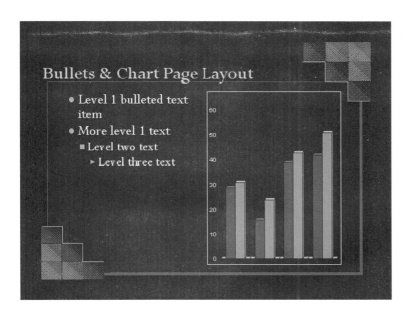

Fig. B.91
A sample page
from the
TILES.MAS
SmartMaster.

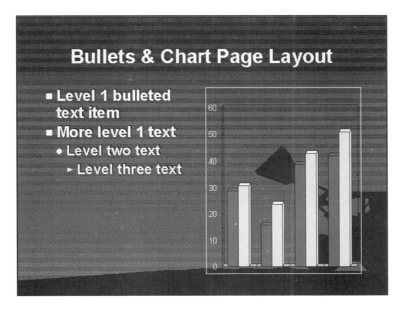

Fig. B.92
A sample page
from the
TRACTOR.MAS
SmartMaster.

Fig. B.93

A sample page from the TUBE.MAS SmartMaster.

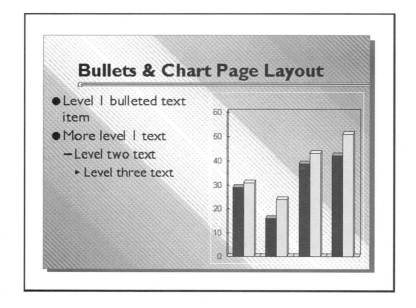

Fig. B.94

A sample page from the UK.MAS SmartMaster.

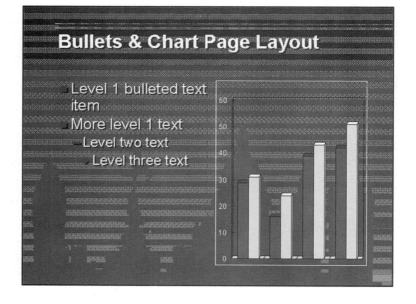

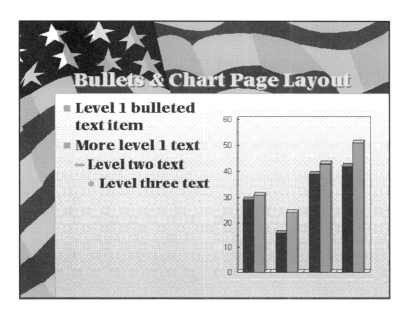

Fig. B.95
A sample page from the USAFLAG.MAS SmartMaster.

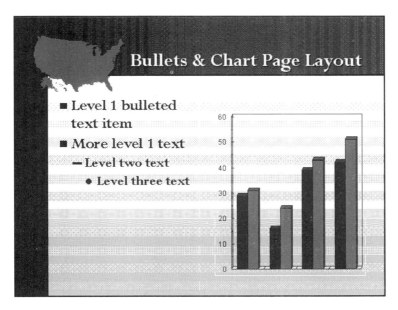

Fig. B.96
A sample page from the USAMAP.MAS SmartMaster.

VII

Appendixes

Fig. B.97
A sample page
from the
VAULT.MAS
SmartMaster.

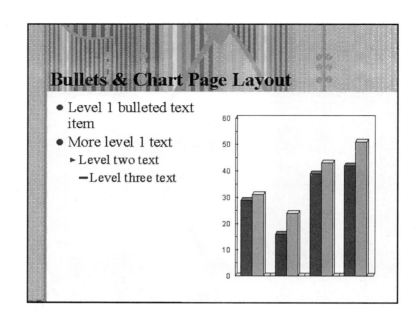

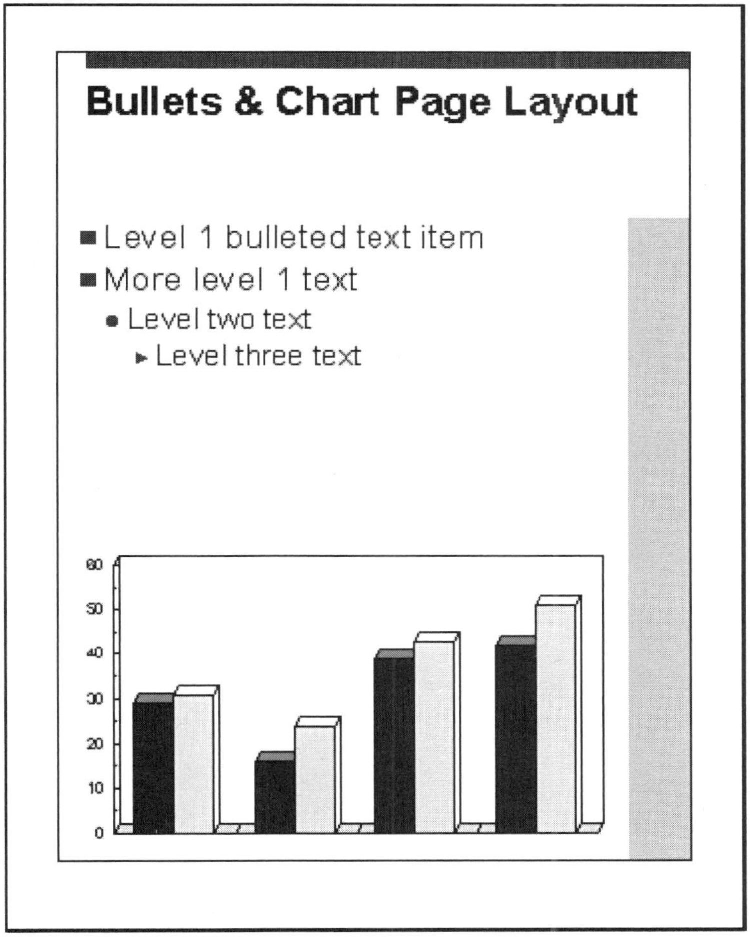

Fig. B.98
A sample page
from the
VERTBAR.MAS
SmartMaster.

Fig. B.99

A sample page from the WAFFLE.MAS SmartMaster.

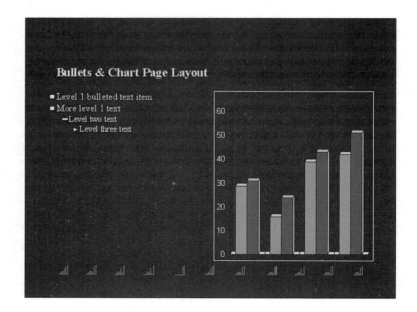

Fig. B.100

A sample page from the WAVE.MAS SmartMaster.

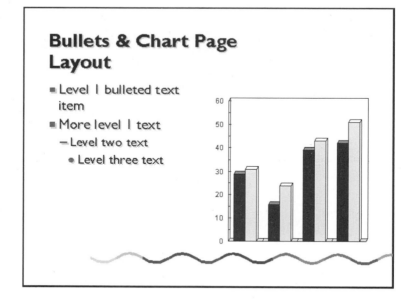

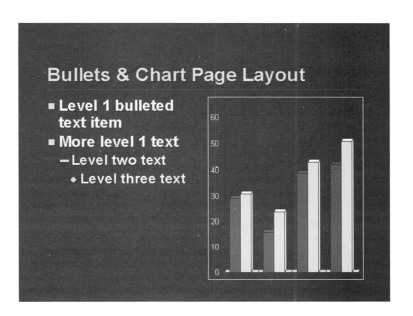

Fig. B.101
A sample page from the WORLD1.MAS SmartMaster.

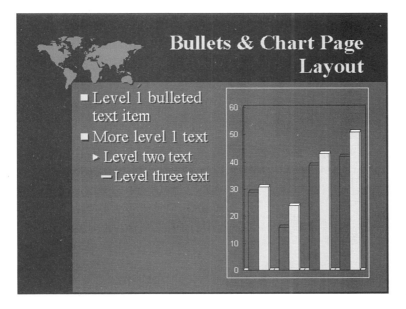

Fig. B.102
A sample page from the WORLD2.MAS SmartMaster.

The Symbol Library

This appendix displays the symbols that are available in the symbol library in Freelance Graphics 96 for Windows 95. The categories are displayed alphabetically by name both here and in Freelance. The symbols within each category are shown in the same order in which they appear in the library.

Fig. C.1
Maps of Africa
contained in the
AFRICMAP.SYM
clip art library.

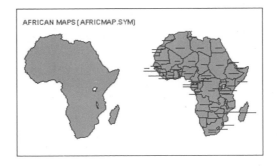

Fig. C.2
Agenda symbols
contained in the
AGENDA.SYM
clip art library.

Fig. C.3
Animal symbols
contained in the
ANIMAL.SYM clip
art library.

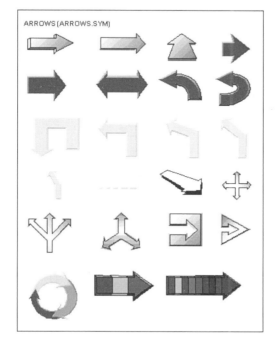

Fig. C.4
Arrow symbols
contained in
ARROW.SYM
clip art library.

Fig. C.5

Asian symbols, and maps of Asia and the Atlantic countries contained in the ASIA.SYM, ASIAMAP.SYM, and ATLANMAP.SYM clip art libraries.

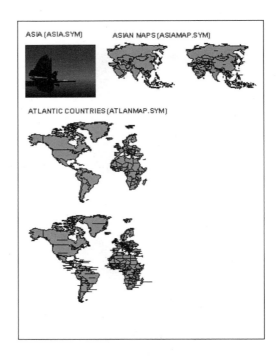

Fig. C.6

Maps of Australia and New Zealand contained in the AUSNZMAP.SYM and AUSTMAP.SYM clip art libraries.

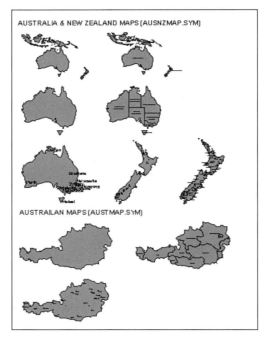

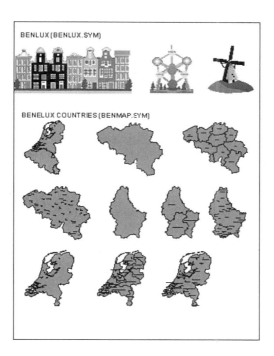

Fig. C.7
Benlux and Benelux map symbols contained in the BENLUX.SYM and BENMAP.SYM clip art libraries.

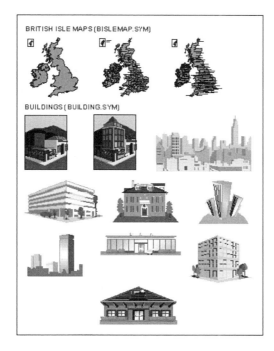

Fig. C.8
Maps of the British Isle and building symbols contained in the BISLEMAP.SYM and BUILDING.SYM clip art libraries.

Fig. C.9
Button symbols
contained in the
BUTTONS.SYM
clip art library.
You can use these
symbols for
attention-grabbing
bullets.

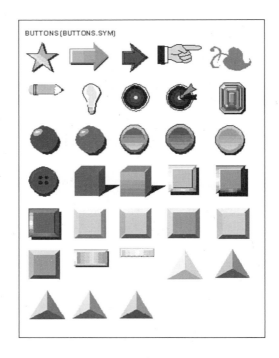

Fig. C.10
Canadian
symbols and
maps of Canada
contained in the
CANADMAP.SYM
clip art library.

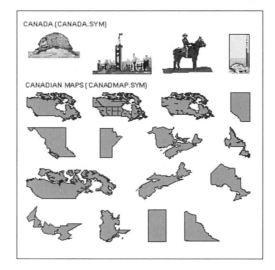

Fig. C.11
Cartoon carica-
tures contained
in the
CARTOONS.SYM
clip art library.

VII

Appendixes

Fig. C.12
Additional cartoon
caricatures
contained in the
CARTOONS.SYM
clip art library.

Fig. C.13
Additional cartoon caricatures and closure symbols contained in the CARTOONS.SYM and CLOSURE.SYM clip art libraries.

Fig. C.14
Symbols of common objects contained in the COMMOBJT.SYM clip art library.

VII

Appendixes

Fig. C.15
Communication and computer peripheral symbols contained in the COMMUNIC.SYM and COMPPERI.SYM clip art libraries.

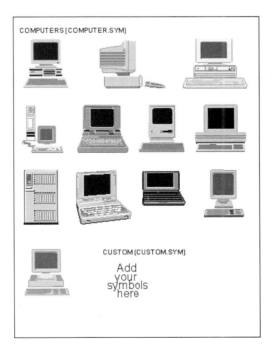

Fig. C.16
Computer symbols contained in the COMPUTER.SYM clip art library. You can use CUSTOM.SYM to build your own clip art library.

Fig. C.17
Entertainment and environmental symbols contained in the ENTERTAI.SYM and ENVIRONM.SYM clip art libraries.

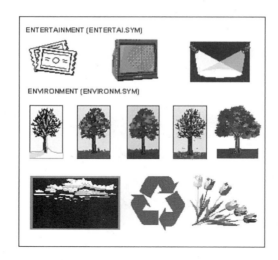

Fig. C.18
Map symbols for European countries contained in the EUROMAP.SYM clip art library.

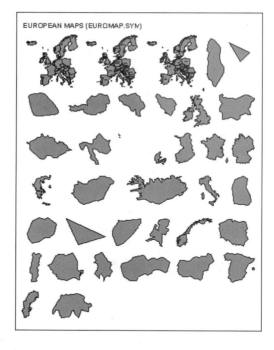

Fig. C.19
Financial symbols contained in the FINANCE.SYM clip art library.

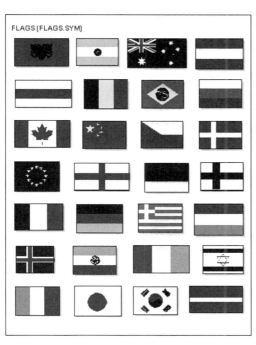

Fig. C.20
Symbols of international flags contained in the FLAGS.SYM clip art library.

Fig. C.21
Additional
symbols of
international flags
contained in the
FLAGS.SYM clip
art library.

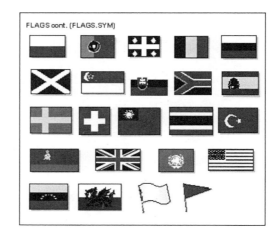

Fig. C.22
Food symbols
contained in the
FOOD.SYM clip
art library.

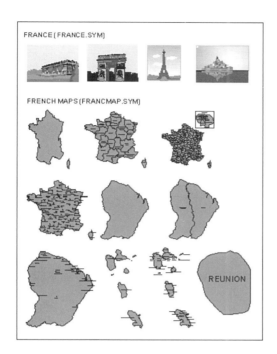

Fig. C.23
French symbols and maps of France contained in the FRANCE.SYM and FRANCMAP.SYM clip art libraries.

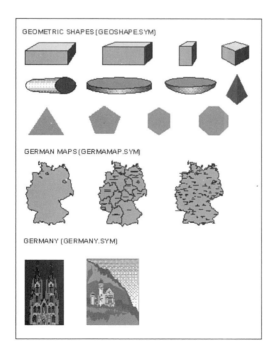

Fig. C.24
Geometric shapes contained in the GEOSHAPES.SYM clip art library. German maps and symbols of Germany contained in the GERMAMAP.SYM and GERMANY.SYM clip art libraries.

VII

Appendixes

Fig. C.25
Hand symbols
and Iberian maps
contained in the
HANDS.SYM and
IBERIMAP.SYM
clip art libraries.

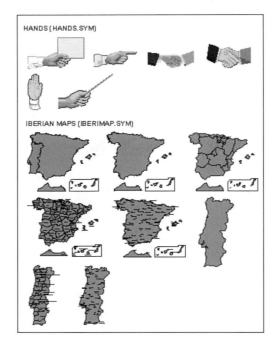

Fig. C.26
Industrial symbols
contained in the
INDUSTRY.SYM
clip art library.
Symbols of Italy
and Italian maps
contained in the
ITALY.SYM and
ITALYMAP.SYM
clip art libraries.

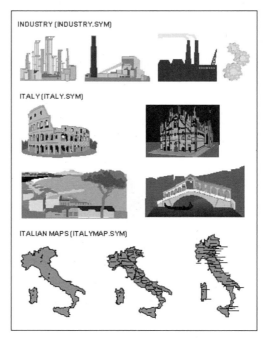

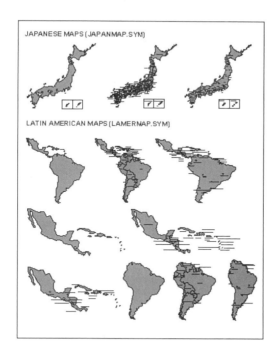

Fig. C.27
Japanese and Latin American maps contained in the JAPANMAP.SYM and LAMERMAP clip art libraries.

Fig. C.28
Map legends, marketing, and medical symbols contained in the LEGENDS.SYM, MARKETNG.SYM, and MEDICAL.SYM clip art libraries.

Fig. C.29
Pictures of men contained in the MEN.SYM clip art library.

Fig. C.30
North American maps and network symbols contained in the NAMERMAP.SYM and NETWORK.SYM clip art libraries.

Fig. C.31
Next step symbols
contained in the
NEXTSTEP.SYM
clip art library.

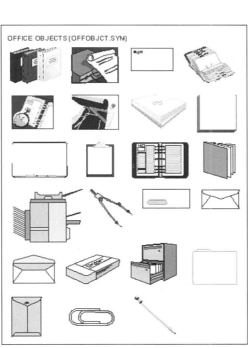

Fig. C.32
Common
office objects
contained in the
OFFOBJCT.SYM
clip art library.

VII

Appendixes

Fig. C.33

Maps of Pacific countries and pictures of people contained in the PACIFMAP.SYM and PEOPLE.SYM clip art libraries.

Fig. C.34

Maps of Poland contained in the POLANMAP.SYM clip art library. Presentation tools and project symbols contained in the PRESEN~N.SYM and PROJECT.SYM clip art libraries.

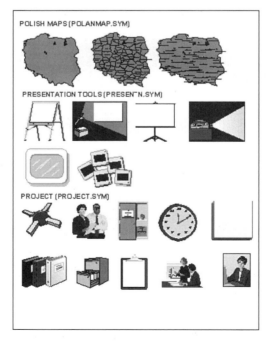

VII

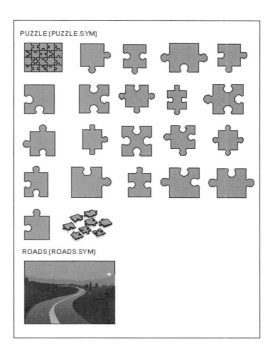

Fig. C.35
Puzzle pieces and a landscape picture showing a road contained in the PUZZLE.SYM and ROADS.SYM clip art libraries.

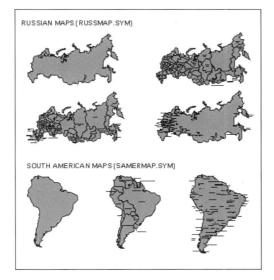

Fig. C.36
Russian and South American maps contained in the RUSSMAP.SYM and SAMERMAP.SYM clip art libraries.

Fig. C.37
Scandinavian
maps contained
in the
SCANDMAP.SYM
clip art library.

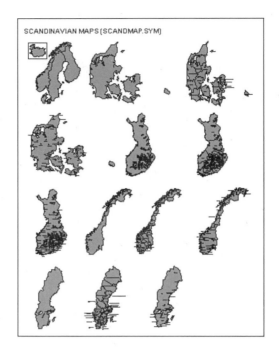

Fig. C.38
Scientific symbols,
Southeastern Asia
maps, and Spanish
symbols contained
in the
SCIENCE.SYM,
SEASIAMAP.SYM,
and SPAIN.SYM
clip art libraries.

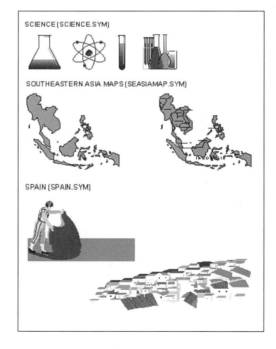

Fig. C.39
Sports symbols contained in the SPORTS.SYM clip art library.

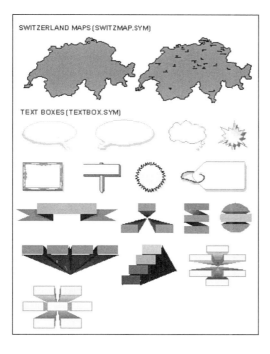

Fig. C.40
Maps of Switzerland and text boxes contained in the SWITZMAP.SYM and TEXTBOX.SYM clip art libraries. You can add your own words to the text boxes.

Fig. C.41
Time, transportation, and British symbols contained in the TIME.SYM, TRANSPOR.SYM, and UK.SYM clip art libraries.

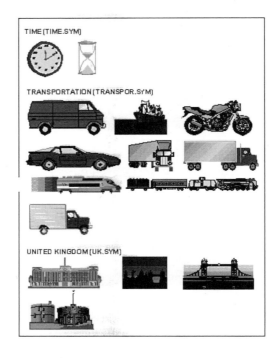

Fig. C.42
United States symbols and maps of the United States contained in the USA.SYM and USAMAP.SYM clip art library.

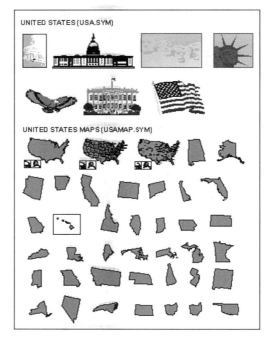

Fig. C.43
Additional maps of the United States, weather symbols, and pictures of women contained in the USAMAP.SYM, WEATHER.SYM, and WOMEN.SYM clip art libraries.

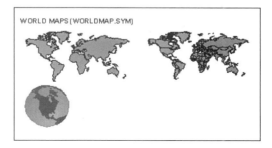

Fig. C.44
Maps of the world contained in the WORLDMAP.SYM clip art library.

Index of Common Problems

Getting Started

Using SmartMaster Sets

Adding Charts to Pages

If you have this problem...	You'll find help here...
You find yourself creating the same chart style over and over again	p. 77
Can't determine whether to use a table or chart in a presentation	p. 85
Charts are cluttered and hard to read	p. 88
Using multiple pie charts, the pie labels run into each other	p. 93
Data in one chart needs to be duplicated exactly in another chart style without reentering all the data	p. 101
Entire lengths of bars in a bar chart don't display	p. 109
Axis titles are taking up too much room on your page	p. 109
A chart would look better if a particular gridline didn't show	p. 118
Rather than explode all slices of a pie chart, you want to move just one away from all the others	p. 121
Previews of charts in dialog boxes take too long to draw	p. 130
An imported chart doesn't appear on-screen with specified legend and labels	p. 131
Two top level positions can't be created in a Freelance organization chart	p. 146
A name in an Org Chart box wraps to the next line	p. 148
When you move one person's box in an Org Chart, the subordinates move, too	p. 151
After ungrouping then grouping an Org Chart, you can't get to the Org Chart InfoBox anymore	p. 152
When you type numbers in a cells of a table, they align to the right, and you want them on the left	p. 167
Text wraps to the next line of a cell in a table	p. 169

If you have this problem...	You'll find help here...
Column width in a table measures in inches, but you need centimeters	p. 170
Changing the background of a table to a darker color makes the numbers hard to read	p. 175

Adding Text and Graphics to Pages

If you have this problem...	You'll find help here...
Text doesn't wrap when you want it to	p. 181
You create a text block, then can't get rid of it	p. 181
Text created with a Click Here block doesn't work with the Curved Text feature	p. 199
Changes to default properties don't work in the next presentation you create	p. 208
After drawing a polyline object, you want to convert it to a polygon	p. 215
When you match text, paragraphs that contain some text with the same style aren't matched	p. 229
Can't ungroup a bitmap image	p. 256
Can't remove an image you added using the Add Logo to Every Page feature	p. 259
Freelance isn't loading a bitmap image referenced within a presentation	p. 263
The Paste Link to Source option is dimmed in the Paste Special dialog box	p. 268
When you go on the road, linked graphics aren't available to your presentation	p. 269
There's a link you no longer need, but Freelance keeps trying to make the link	p. 270
A presentation with many links to graphics takes a long time to load	p. 273

Working with Presentations

If you have this problem...	You'll find help here...
Freelance Spell Check doesn't catch certain spelling errors	p. 282
The Add to Dictionary button is grayed and not available	p. 283
A particular SmartMaster look appears too dark when printed in black and white	p. 286
Someone who doesn't have Freelance on his computer needs to view your presentation	p. 291
Even though User Setup was changed to open in Outline view, a presentation opens in Current Page view	p. 299
Whenever you create a new line of text in Outline view, it appears with a bullet—but you don't want a bullet	p. 303
A document created in a word processor without an outlining feature has to be brought into Outline view in Freelance	p. 307
The presentation requires a unique transition effect between two particular pages	p. 313
You don't want to display certain pages of your presentation—for example, financial data—for a particular audience	p. 315
Sounds associated with objects on a page take several seconds to play	p. 324
A sound clip is perfect for your needs, but too short for the timing of your presentation	p. 330
Objects which seem to fit on a page are halfway off the page in Print Preview	p. 337
When you print handouts in six-page format, text is hard to read	p. 339
The printer you want to print to doesn't appear in the Freelance Print File dialog box	p. 340
A message appears when you try to print that some elements no longer fit on the printable page	p. 341
Colors print much lighter than you expected	p. 344
Colors on slides don't look like those on your computer screen	p. 345

If you have this problem...	You'll find help here...
Freelance charts which filled the page on-screen look smaller when you receive slide output	p. 346
While on the World Wide Web, you can't view hypertext	p. 348
Three-letter filename extensions don't appear when you use Explorer to find a Freelance file	p. 352
Information on a slide in a Freelance presentation doesn't appear	p. 354
A home page HTML file needs to have some text edited	p. 355
While publishing a presentation to the Internet, the Table of Contents option is checked, but the TOC just says Unknown Title	p. 356
A page in a presentation on the Internet just has pictures of Freelance's buttons, but no text	p. 356

Customizing Freelance Graphics

If you have this problem...	You'll find help here...
If you change the first few colors in the color palette, SmartMaster looks have odd colors	p. 382
While viewing a presentation in black and white, you can't edit the colors	p. 383
When trying to print a presentation on a black-and-white printer, colors appear unfocused	p. 385
SmartIcons are taking up too much of the screen, so you can't see all of your presentation clearly	p. 394
SmartIcons you create are all bunched together, and it's hard to find the one you want	p. 397

Index

Complete and Return this Card
for a *FREE* Computer Book Catalog

Thank you for purchasing this book! You have purchased a superior computer book written expressly for your needs. To continue to provide the kind of up-to-date, pertinent coverage you've come to expect from us, we need to hear from you. Please take a minute to complete and return this self-addressed, postage-paid form. In return, we'll send you a free catalog of all our computer books on topics ranging from word processing to programming and the internet.

Mr. ☐   Mrs. ☐   Ms. ☐   Dr. ☐

Name (first) ☐☐☐☐☐☐☐☐☐☐☐☐☐ (M.I.) ☐ (last) ☐☐☐☐☐☐☐☐☐☐☐☐☐

Address ☐☐☐☐☐☐☐☐☐☐☐☐☐☐☐☐☐☐☐☐☐☐☐☐☐☐☐☐☐☐

☐☐☐☐☐☐☐☐☐☐☐☐☐☐☐☐☐☐☐☐☐☐☐☐☐☐☐☐☐☐

City ☐☐☐☐☐☐☐☐☐☐☐☐ State ☐☐ Zip ☐☐☐☐☐ ☐☐☐☐

Phone ☐☐☐ ☐☐☐ ☐☐☐☐ Fax ☐☐☐ ☐☐☐ ☐☐☐☐

Company Name ☐☐☐☐☐☐☐☐☐☐☐☐☐☐☐☐☐☐☐☐☐☐☐☐☐☐☐☐☐☐☐☐

E-mail address ☐☐☐☐☐☐☐☐☐☐☐☐☐☐☐☐☐☐☐☐☐☐☐☐☐☐☐☐☐☐☐☐

1. Please check at least (3) influencing factors for purchasing this book.

Front or back cover information on book .... ☐
Special approach to the content .... ☐
Completeness of content .... ☐
Author's reputation .... ☐
Publisher's reputation .... ☐
Book cover design or layout .... ☐
Index or table of contents of book .... ☐
Price of book .... ☐
Special effects, graphics, illustrations .... ☐
Other (Please specify): _____ ☐

2. How did you first learn about this book?

Saw in Macmillan Computer Publishing catalog .... ☐
Recommended by store personnel .... ☐
Saw the book on bookshelf at store .... ☐
Recommended by a friend .... ☐
Received advertisement in the mail .... ☐
Saw an advertisement in: _____ ☐
Read book review in: _____ ☐
Other (Please specify): _____ ☐

3. How many computer books have you purchased in the last six months?

This book only .... ☐   3 to 5 books .... ☐
2 books .... ☐   More than 5 .... ☐

4. Where did you purchase this book?

Bookstore .... ☐
Computer Store .... ☐
Consumer Electronics Store .... ☐
Department Store .... ☐
Office Club .... ☐
Warehouse Club .... ☐
Mail Order .... ☐
Direct from Publisher .... ☐
Internet site .... ☐
Other (Please specify): _____ ☐

5. How long have you been using a computer?

☐ Less than 6 months   ☐ 6 months to a year
☐ 1 to 3 years   ☐ More than 3 years

6. What is your level of experience with personal computers and with the subject of this book?

	With PCs	With subject of book
New	☐	☐
Casual	☐	☐
Accomplished	☐	☐
Expert	☐	☐

Source Code ISBN: 0-7897-0671-7

7. Which of the following best describes your job title?

- Administrative Assistant ☐
- Coordinator ☐
- Manager/Supervisor ☐
- Director ☐
- Vice President ☐
- President/CEO/COO ☐
- Lawyer/Doctor/Medical Professional ☐
- Teacher/Educator/Trainer ☐
- Engineer/Technician ☐
- Consultant ☐
- Not employed/Student/Retired ☐
- Other (Please specify): _____ ☐

8. Which of the following best describes the area of the company your job title falls under?

- Accounting ☐
- Engineering ☐
- Manufacturing ☐
- Operations ☐
- Marketing ☐
- Sales ☐
- Other (Please specify): _____ ☐

9. What is your age?

- Under 20 ☐
- 21-29 ☐
- 30-39 ☐
- 40-49 ☐
- 50-59 ☐
- 60-over ☐

10. Are you:

- Male ☐
- Female ☐

11. Which computer publications do you read regularly? (Please list)

_____
_____
_____
_____
_____
_____
_____
_____
_____

Comments: _____
_____
_____

Fold here and scotch-tape to mail.